A History of Italian Theatre

With the aim of providing a comprehensive history of Italian drama from its origins to the present day, this book treats theatre in its widest sense, discussing the impact of all the elements and figures integral to the collaborative process of theatre-making. The impact of designers, actors, directors and impresarios, as well as of playwrights, is subjected to critical scrutiny, while individual chapters examine the changes in technology and shifts in the cultural climate which have influenced theatre. No other approach would be acceptable for Italian theatre, where, from the days of *commedia dell'arte*, the central figure has often been the actor rather than the playwright. The important writers, such as Carlo Goldoni and Luigi Pirandello who have become part of the central canon of European playwriting, and those whose impact has been limited to the Italian stage, receive detailed critical treatment, as do the 'great actors' of nineteenth-century theatre or the directors of our own time, but the focus is always on the bigger picture.

Joseph Farrell is Professor of Italian Studies at the University of Strathclyde.

Paolo Puppa is Professor of History of the Italian Theatre at the University of Venice and Chair of the Department of the History of the Arts.

A HISTORY OF
Italian Theatre

Edited by Joseph Farrell and Paolo Puppa

CAMBRIDGE
UNIVERSITY PRESS

CAMBRIDGE UNIVERSITY PRESS
Cambridge, New York, Melbourne, Madrid, Cape Town, Singapore, São Paulo

CAMBRIDGE UNIVERSITY PRESS
The Edinburgh Building, Cambridge CB2 2RU, UK

Published in the United States of America by Cambridge University Press, New York

www.cambridge.org
Information on this title: www.cambridge.org/9780521802659

First published 2006

Printed in the United Kingdom at the University Press, Cambridge

A catalogue record for this publication is available from the British Library

ISBN-13 978-0-521-80265-9 hardback
ISBN-10 0-521-80265-2 hardback

Contents

Illustrations

For permission to reproduce the illustrations used in this volume, we are grateful to the Casa di Goldoni in Venice, the Biblioteca Nazionale in Florence, and the theatre magazine *Sipario*; we are also grateful to the Vittoriale, Lake Garda, for the photographs relating to Gabriele D'Annunzio, and to Francesco Rosi, Luca De Filippo and Carolina Rosi for the photographs of Eduardo De Filippo. Every effort has been made to trace other copyright holders, and any omission will be made good in any subsequent edition of this work.

Contributors

RICHARD ANDREWS is Emeritus Professor of Italian at the University of Leeds. He is the author of *Scripts and Scenarios: the Performance of Comedy in Renaissance Italy* (1993) and has published essays on early modern Italian theatre which deal with the rise of the female performer, with relationships between spoken drama and early opera and with Italian influence on French and English drama. He is currently working on a translation, with analytical commentary, of the *commedia dell'arte* scenarios published by Flaminio Scala in *Il Teatro delle Favole Rappresentative*, 1611.

ALBERTO BENISCELLI is Professor of Italian Literature at the University of Genoa. He is author of *La finzione del fiabesco: Studi sul teatro di Carlo Gozzi* (1986), and editor of Gozzi's *Il ragionamento ingenuo* and of his *Fiabe teatrali* (1994). An expert on eighteenth-century theatre in Italy, he has also written *Le fantasie della ragione: Idee di riforma e suggestioni letterarie del Settecento, Le passioni evidenti: Parola, pittura e scena nella letteratura settecentesca* (1990) and *Felicità sognate: Il teatro di Metastasio* (2000).

PETER BRAND is Professor Emeritus at the University of Edinburgh, Fellow of the British Academy and *Cavaliere* and *Commendatore della Repubblica Italiana*. He is the author of *Italy and the English Romantics* (1957), *Torquato Tasso* (1965) and *Ludovico Ariosto* (1974). Works he has edited include *Modern Language Review, 1970–76*, the *Writers of Italy* series (1974–84) and *The Cambridge History of Italian Literature* (1996).

ROBERTO CUPPONE is director, author and actor, and has some twenty-five theatrical works to his credit. His publications include: *Teatri, città* (1991), *L'invenzione della commedia dell'arte* (1998), *Commedia dell'arte, sogno romantico* (2000) and *Il mito della commedia dell'arte nell'Ottocento francese* (2000). He is editor of Carlo Goldoni's *Cameriera brillante* (2002). He teaches History of Popular Theatre at the University of Venice.

JOSEPH FARRELL is Professor of Italian Studies at the University of Strathclyde. He is the author of *Leonardo Sciascia* (1995) and of *Dario Fo and Franca Rame: Harlequins of the Revolution* (2001). He has edited collections of essays on Goldoni, Fo, the Mafia, Primo Levi and Carlo Levi, as well as editions of plays by Pirandello and Fo. He has translated several Italian dramas and novels, including works by Fo, Goldoni, Sciascia and Vincenzo Consolo.

DONATELLA FISCHER teaches Italian at the University of Strathclyde. She has published widely in Britain, Italy and the USA on modern Italian theatre, with special emphasis on Neapolitan theatre.

RONNIE FERGUSON is Professor of Italian and Head of the School of Modern Languages at the University of St Andrews. His research interests are Renaissance theatre, linguistics and identity studies, with special reference to Venice and the Veneto. He has written or edited six books, including a monograph on Ruzante, *The Theatre of Angelo Beolco: Text, Context and Performance* (2000). He is at present writing a linguistic history of Venice.

ROBERT S. C. GORDON is Senior Lecturer in Italian at Cambridge University. He is author of *Pasolini: Forms of Subjectivity* (1996) and *Primo Levi's Ordinary Virtues* (2001). His recent publications include *Culture, Censorship and the State in 20th-Century Italy* (co-edited with Guido Bonsaver, 2005) and *A Difficult Modernity: An Introduction to 20th-Century Italian Literature* (2005).

CLIVE GRIFFITHS is Senior Lecturer in Italian at the University of Manchester. His research interests include the Renaissance Pastoral and the cultural politics of Fascist Italy. He has published a monograph on the dramatist Giovacchino Forzano.

COSTANTINO MAEDER is director of the Centre for Italian Studies at the Université Catholique de Louvain. He specialises in the history of musical theatre, and is author of *Metastasio, L'Olimpiade e l'opera del Settecento* (1993).

GAETANA MARRONE is Professor of Italian at Princeton University. She specialises in modern Italian literature and post World War II Italian cinema. Her principal publications include *La drammatica di Ugo Betti, New Landscapes in Contemporary Italian Cinema* and *The Gaze and the Labyrinth: The Cinema of Liliana Cavani*.

NERIDA NEWBIGIN is Professor of Italian Studies at the University of Sydney. Her publications in the field of late medieval theatre and spectacle in Florence and Rome include *Nuovo Corpus di sacre rappresentazioni fiorentine* (1983) and *Feste d'Oltrarno: Plays in Churches in Fifteenth-Century Florence* (1996). A joint study with Barbara Wisch, *Acting on Faith: The Confraternity of the Gonfalone in Renaissance Rome*, is in preparation.

GUIDO NICASTRO is Professor of Italian Theatrical Literature at the University of Catania. His works on Sicilian theatre include *Teatro e società in Sicilia* (1978) and *Scene di vita e vita di scene in Sicilia* (1988), while on eighteenth-century theatre he has written *Goldoni riformatore* (1983). Other works include *Il poeta e la scena* (1988) on D'Annunzio, *Letteratura e musica: Libretti d'opera e altro teatro* (1992) and *Scena e scrittura. Momenti del teatro italiano del Novecento* (1996).

GILBERTO PIZZAMIGLIO is Professsor of Italian Literature at the University of Venice. His many writings are mainly concerned with eighteenth- and nineteenth-century literature, with a special focus on the narrative, theatrical and poetic traditions of his native Venice. He is co-editor of the reviews *Lettere Italiane* and *Problemi di critica goldoniana*, as well as of the Esperia collection of classics. He is also editorial director for the Giorgio Cini Foundation in Venice.

PAOLO PUPPA is Professor of History of the Italian Theatre at the University of Venice and Chair of the Department of the History of the Arts. He has written many volumes on theatrical studies, including works on Pirandello, Fo, D'Annunzio, Ibsen, Rosso di San Secondo and two histories of the Italian stage. His plays have been staged both in Italy and abroad.

KENNETH AND LAURA RICHARDS were, respectively, Professors of Drama and of Italian Studies at the Universities of Manchester and Salford. They have worked together on aspects of theatre, and produced the much admired work, *The Commedia dell'Arte: A Documentary History* (1990).

LISA SAMPSON is Lecturer in Italian at the University of Reading. Her publications include a critical edition, with Virginia Cox, of *Maddalena Campiglia's Flori: a Pastoral Drama* (2004). She is the author of the forthcoming book, *Pastoral Drama in Early Modern Italy.*

ANTONIO SCUDERI is Associate Professor of Italian at Truman State University in Missouri. His main interest lies in folklore and popular performance in Italian culture. He is the author of *Dario Fo and Popular Performance* (1998) and editor with Joseph Farrell of *Dario Fo: Stage, Text and Tradition* (2000).

MAURICE SLAWINSKI is Senior Lecturer in Italian Studies at Lancaster University. His publications include *Science, Culture and Popular Belief in Renaissance Europe* (with P. L. Rossi and S. Pumfrey, 1991), critical editions of the *Rime* of Ascanio Pignatelli (1996) and of the *Prose* of Giulio Cortese (2000). He is also the author of essays and articles on late Renaissance and Baroque literature and culture, the modern novel and drama. He was general editor of the comparative literature journal *New Comparisons*, 1992–2003.

FERDINANDO TAVIANI is Professor of History of Theatre at the University of Aquila. His principal publications concern: *commedia dell'arte*, nineteenth-century theatre with special focus on the culture of actors, the theatre of Pirandello, twentieth-century theatre and the relationship between drama and stage practice. He is one of the founders of *Teatro Storia* and of the International School of Theatre Anthropology.

PIERMARIO VESCOVO teaches Italian theatre at the University of Venice. He is Secretary of the editorial committee of the *Edizione nazionale* of the works of Carlo Goldoni. His own main interest is Venetian theatre from the sixteenth to the nineteenth centuries.

SHARON WOOD is Professor of Modern Languages at the University of Leicester. She writes principally on modern and contemporary narrative, and on women's cultural history. Publications include *Italian Women's Writing* (1995), *The Cambridge History of Women's Writing in Italy* (edited with Letizia Panizza, 2000), and *Under Arturo's Star: The Cultural Legacies of Elsa Morante* (edited with Stefania Lucamante, 2005).

JOHN WOODHOUSE is Emeritus Professor of Italian at Oxford. He has written extensively on Renaissance writers, publishing editions of Vincenzio Borghini (1971 and 1974), and critical works on Baldesar Castiglione (1978), Niccolò Strozzi (1982) and courtly literature. He was co-editor of the six volumes of Gabriele Rossetti's *Carteggi (1980–2005)*. His published work on D'Annunzio includes the lyrical anthology

Alcyone (1978), the biography *Gabriele D'Annunzio, Defiant Archangel* (1999), the critical essays *Gabriele D'Annunzio tra Italia e Inghilterra* (2003) and the historical analysis, *Il generale e il comandante: Ceccherini e D'Annunzio a Fiume* (2004).

In search of Italian theatre

JOSEPH FARRELL

The quest for Italian theatre will take the English-language reader into unfamiliar territory, and not only because theatres in New York or London rarely stage Italian plays. The unfamiliarity arises from an anomaly which goes to the very core of theatrical creativity. While the theatrical traditions of other European countries are author-centred, the theatre of Italy has been, through much of its development, actor-centred. Reforms, whether by Carlo Goldoni in the eighteenth century, or by Silvio D'Amico and others in the early twentieth century, have had as one of their central aims the restriction of the power of the actor in the theatrical hierarchy.

It is this dominance of the actor which explains the central paradox of the Italian role in European theatre. If it is beyond discussion that the varied, colourful input of Italian theatre-makers has been profound and indeed decisive in the shaping and development of European theatre, it is equally true that the number of Italian playwrights who could be named by theatregoers of average culture and knowledge would be surprisingly small. Carlo Goldoni and Luigi Pirandello would have unquestioned niches in any pantheon of European drama, but for all the impact of Italian Renaissance theatre, only Machiavelli's *Mandragola* is likely to spring to mind. In contemporary theatre, Dario Fo and Eduardo de Filippo would be guaranteed admission to the modern canon, but it is hard to know whether their places will be enduring.

It is not a matter of foreign ignorance. There is not a repertoire of Italian classics available to Italian directors to compare with the rich legacy of national drama at the disposal of their counterparts in Paris, Madrid, London or Berlin. Italy had no great playwrights' age comparable to the Elizabethan age of Shakespeare and Marlowe in Britain, the *siglo de oro* of Calderon de la Barca and Lope de Vega in Spain, the neo-classical age of Corneille and Racine in France or the Romantic age of Goethe and Schiller in Germany. There were, it is needless to add, such ages in music, architecture, painting, sculpture and poetry, but only at certain select moments could Italian theatre boast of creative writing genius. The drama in which Italy excelled was not prose playwriting, but musical theatre. An opera-lover in any European city would be effortlessly able to reel off the list of composers that the theatregoer would struggle to provide. Aside from internationally renowned figures such as Verdi, Puccini and Donizetti, there were many other craftsmen of music whose works filled theatres, and which satisfied the national appetite for drama. It has been estimated that 80 percent of theatrical productions in the nineteenth century belonged to the category of musical theatre.

In no other theatrical tradition has the space between the stage and the page been so narrow. If Italian theatre has a representative man, in the sense Ralph Waldo Emerson used the term, he has been the actor-author. This central line runs from Ruzante in the early Renaissance years, through the *capocomico*, which translates as lead actor and who was the predominant figure in *commedia dell'arte,* on to De Filippo and Fo in our times. No theatre afforded such control to the actor as did the Italian. The case of *commedia dell'arte* does not require labouring in this context, but it was the seminal theatre which established a tradition. The level of improvisation in the sense of impromptu inventiveness permitted to the individual performer has been no doubt exaggerated. Recent scholarship has uncovered not only the scenarios of *commedia dell'arte,* but also actors' notebooks in which players committed to paper and to memory sections of dialogue which could be used in various situations – in love scenes, in thwarted escapes or in warding off unwanted advances. Originally such comedy was known simply as *commedia all'italiana,* but the later term *commedia dell'arte* went to the heart of the matter with its distinction between the dilettante, aristo-cratic players of early Renaissance drama, and the theatre of the profes-sionals. In the view of the majority of theatre historians, *arte* indicates 'guild', making *commedia dell'arte* the plays produced by the guild of actors. It is interesting that there is no abstract Italian word to translate 'author-ship': the only term that renders the idea is '*paternità*', and the paternity-authorship of the works produced by the members of the actors' guild was claimed by the actors, particularly by the *capocomico*.

These assertions should be taken not to suggest that Italian theatre is unpromising material for a theatrical history, but that a more varied approach is needed than would be appropriate for the history of the drama of other nations. To assess Italian theatre as of only marginal importance is to adopt the viewpoint of an Egyptian tomb-robber breaking into a pyramid in search of gold, and failing to notice the sculpture, paintings, crafts and ceramics all around him. The heritage of Italian theatre is imposing, and its genius multiple. This volume attempts to examine Italian theatre in its rich complexity, and not to focus narrowly on writing alone. It is only in this way that the impact of Italy's theatre in Europe can be fully appreciated. It would be, for instance, hard to underestimate the impact of *commedia dell'arte* on the development of the European stage. France became its second home, with the Comédie Française in Paris feeding off the Comédie Italienne. It was to Italian precedents that Molière looked, as did Marivaux two centuries later when *commedia* was in decline in Italy. *Commedia* troupes dispersed all over Europe, taking up residence in Moscow, Warsaw, Madrid and probably London. The presence of Italian companies in London is subject to controversy, but it is known that Drusiano Martinelli and his troupe visited in 1578. Others followed, so did Italian theatre have an influence on playing and writing at the Globe? This is not the place to examine divided opinions, but the resemblances between Stefano and Trinculo in *The Tempest* and the *zanni* of *commedia* are striking, as is the sheer volume of Shakespeare's plays set in Italy and the number inspired by Italian models. The derivation of *Twelfth Night* from *Gl'ingannati* is example enough.

While *commedia* had the longest-lasting influence, the academies of Renaissance Italy rediscovered, reinterpreted and reinvented classical drama. It was to Italy that all Europe looked for counsel in the arts of stagecraft and playwriting. The distance between the medieval mystery or morality play and the drama of *Cinquecento* Italy, or Elizabethan England, is proof of the profound change in sensibility and culture created by the new learning. Italian academies made available translations of the classical dramatists, firstly Roman and latterly Greek. Terence was published in 1471, Seneca a decade later and Aristophanes in Venice in 1498. The great Athenian tragedians appeared in the first two decades of the following century. The first works to be staged were either productions of the classics or else imitations of them, normally produced in the courts. The works of commanding Renaissance figures like Ariosto, Tasso, Machiavelli all receive sympathetic, insightful treatment in this volume.

The development of Renaissance drama was assisted by the production of commentaries, studies, theories of the nature of tragedy and comedy. Rules began to be codified, and while many may judge this consequence regrettable, these rules determined stagecraft all over Europe. It was at this period too that the thinking which sanctioned the division of drama and the hierarchy of genres which dominated theatrical practice in subsequent centuries was formulated. Tragedy and comedy were part of the inheritance of the classical age, but the pastoral and the wholly new genre of opera appeared. The role of treatise-writers in early centuries, and of critics and reviewers in more recent times, is not overlooked in this volume. It may be fashionable to treat all that smacks of criticism as parasitical, but treatises and reviews have played their part in the creation of theatrical cultures.

Others who made Italian theatre matter in Europe at different times were men like the early Harlequins Tristano Martinelli and Domenico Biancolelli, or later stars like the nineteenth-century 'great actor' Tommaso Salvini. Salvini made a deep impact on Stanislavsky through his meticulous, pre-performance efforts to think himself into a role. The Russian director and theorist recorded with amazed precision the time Salvini took at every stage in his preparation for *Othello,* noting that he was as attentive over states of mind as over details of costume and make-up. Salvini provided Stanislavsky with a model, and through Stanislavsky, the Italian style of performance influenced the modern actor's craft.

A synopsis of this kind risks making sharp distinctions where more gentle variations would be appropriate. Paradoxically, the two best-known names of Italian playwriting – Goldoni and Pirandello – stand outside this tradition, being writers and not performers. There were moments when writers were pre-eminent, including the Venetian eighteenth century, the late nineteenth and early twentieth centuries in Naples and the brief flourishing of 'grotesque theatre'. The Renaissance respected a more conventional division of labour. Conversely, the actor-author has his equivalent in other cultures. Playwrights from Shakespeare and Molière to Harold Pinter, to choose only celebrated examples, were actors, and the comparisons between such Victorian Anglo-American actor-managers as George Alexander in London or John Barrymore in New York and the Italian 'great actors' of the same period discussed in the relevant chapters below is closer than normally admitted. As part of the intention of seeing Italian theatre in an international context, contributors have attempted to give due weight to the impact of foreign writers on the Italian stage, whether Shakespeare in the Romantic age or Ibsen in the early modern period, when their impact on the Italian repertoire was decisive. Shakespeare risked becoming a quarry of grand moments for use by the actor but, as several contributors to this volume underline, it was precisely in this interaction between writer and actor that dramatic creativity in Italy in the age of the 'great actor' was realised.

Tradition is as strong a force as innovation in this seemingly most iconoclastic of genres. Changes may be underway. A new generation of writers is emerging, several of whom now write for the screen as well as for theatre. It may be that the future balance of power will be radically altered.

To do justice to Italian theatre, this volume attempts to discuss theatre in its fullest sense and not merely as dramatic literature, and to include popular as well as high culture. While the efforts of earlier historians like Silvio D'Amico or Mario Apollonio command awed respect, probably no single historian could today attempt to provide a panoramic history of Italian theatre. An international group of scholars has been assembled, each capable of looking outwards at Italian theatre in Europe as well as inwards at the national cultural forces at work. This History offers a perspective founded on the most recent, post-2000 scholarship. The single-volume format imposes limitations, and the project of covering Italian theatre from its origins right up to the present day in one volume is ambitious. The restrictions have been challenging, but gladly accepted. It is for this reason that the apparatus of footnotes and bibliography has been kept to a minimum, but translations have been provided (by the contributors, unless otherwise stated), except where the meaning was obvious.

We mourn the untimely death of Professor Maggie Gunsberg, who was initially invited to contribute to this volume. There are many people who deserve our grateful thanks. Victoria Cooper at Cambridge University Press has provided both gentle encouragement and admirable patience over the years when the volume was in preparation. The main vote of thanks must go to Peter Brand, ex-Professor of Italian at the University of Edinburgh, sharp-minded scholar and generous friend. Peter ought to be listed as third editor, since he took on the work of editing the first part of this book, from the origins to the seventeenth century. In addition to authoring various sections, he also translated the bulk of the Italian contributions. He was continually available for discussion, and it is doubtful if the work would ever have been done without his rigorous but willing assistance.

PART I
The Middle Ages

1 Secular and religious drama in the Middle Ages

NERIDA NEWBIGIN

In the millennium that we call the Middle Ages, between the gradual decline of the Roman Empire and the reawakening of interest in the cultural experiences of antiquity that we call the Renaissance, spectacle flourished in almost every aspect of Italian life: individual rites of passage through life, rituals of propitiation for the next, celebrations in honour of the city's patrons, expression of civic pride and gestures for the pleasure of the city. It was an age without dedicated theatre space, without professional actors, without any desire to distinguish between *festa* and theatre. It did, however, have a vast range of performances: the 'theatre' of preachers and of *giullari*, storytellers, jugglers and tumblers, agonistic entertainments like jousts, horse races, contests of all kinds, ritual processions and propagandistic parades and religious festivals of all sorts. Sundays and holy days gave medieval communities about a hundred days a year to fill with entertainments of various kinds. Before we move on to theatre that is self-consciously theatrical and leaves systematic documentary records of itself through texts, inventories, account-books and official permission to use public spaces, let us look at some of the fleeting images of performance that can be distilled from disparate sources.

Every aspect of theatre in this preliminary chapter is contentious and contested: the supposition of some kind of uniformity throughout the Roman church and across Western Europe; the notion of a popular culture, the supposition that there is any continuity between the popular festivals of the 'Middle Ages' and those that are still alive throughout Italy, replete with lavish costumes, *sbandieratori* and the participation of church, communal officials and the local tourist authority. Nineteenth-century gothic revival, the invention of traditions of the new nation state and their further appropriation by the Fascist regime in the 1920s and 1930s await careful documentation and are not our concern here, but they have coloured scholarship in this field. As we pick our way through evidence in this chapter the reader is invited to regard all assertions with scepticism and to treat every interpretation as suspect.

Plays continued to exist in the Middle Ages. Of Plautus' eighteen plays, only six were known before 1427, and were regarded as less suitable for schoolboys. The more decorous comedies of Terence were read in the schools as examples of everyday conversation, and it was not until the fifteenth-century humanists brought new philological tools that the texts were recognised as verse rather than prose. Like *Hrotswitha* in the tenth century, Petrarch (1304–74) composed in his youth a comedy, *Philologia Philostrati*, probably inspired by the plays of Terence that he had studied. The play is lost and there is no evidence of contemporary performance of it or of his *Triumphs of Love, Chastity, Death, Fame, Time and Eternity* (1351–2), even though they would become a standard part of urban ceremonial from the middle of the fifteenth century.

Secular theatre and spectacle on a large scale died with the Roman Empire: the staging of large spectacles was no longer economically and socially viable, earthquakes made the theatres unsafe, looters stripped anything of value from the sites and new religious mores collided with the way people entertained themselves in groups. There were still courts, and among the members of the courts were professional entertainers. There were also popular entertainers whose activities included dancing, fortune-telling, tightrope-walking, tumbling and walking on stilts. But if we accept a broad definition of theatre as a form of performance to an audience that entails impersonation with word, gesture and appearance, we must exclude these, and our brief examination of the kinds of performance activity that will, with time, become theatre will begin with the texts that are now called *dicerie*.

The *diceria* was a monologue delivered by a performer whose skill in an oral tradition allowed him either to memorise a vast repertoire or else to improvise in prose or verse. A small number of texts of Italian verse monologues appears from the thirteenth century – that is, with the beginning of recreational literature in the vernacular – in which the narrative contains a significant quantity of direct rather than reported speech. The so-called *Ritmo cassinese* and the legend of St Alexis both belong to a thirteenth-century ecclesiastical setting, and were probably delivered by a single performer, but with the *contrasto* of Cielo d'Alcamo, beginning 'Rosa fresca aulentissima' (Sicily, thirteenth century) there is no longer a linking narrative but rather two voices: that of the young woman, the 'sweetest

Figure 1: San Carlo Theatre, Naples. Production of *Napoli milionaria!* by Eduardo De Filippo, directed by Francesco Rosi, 2003 production.

fresh rose' of the first line, surprised in her bedchamber, and that of her suitor, who arrives with a knife (to kill himself if she refuses him) and a book (a bible, he says, on which he swears – probably falsely – to marry her). Worn down, or else convinced, she submits.

'Rosa fresca aulentissima' is just one example of a *contrasto*. Others are debates between Christ and Satan, Carnival and Lent, the Body and the Soul, the Living and the Dead. This last *contrasto* was enormously popular for the next two centuries at least, particularly in the context of Last Judgement pageants.

Masks and masking were also a feature of Carnival, the period between Epiphany on 6 January and the beginning of Lent, when all pleasure of eating and sexual contact ceased. Civic and ecclesiastical injunctions against all forms of misconduct at Carnival mention masks on both men and women as a source of *scandalo*: fighting, harassment of women and lewdness were the inevitable result, but we do not know the purpose. In the late fifteenth century, texts appear showing that young men in groups put on the costumes of a trade or profession and sang songs of extraordinary erotic lewdness: they were perfume-sellers from Valencia, with potions and unguents for every orifice; they were bawdy ladies selling sausages, of every dimension and to please every palate; they could belong to any profession that would lend itself to double entendre. While there is no evidence before Lorenzo de' Medici's time of such performances, it is clear that lewdness and masks were a long-standing feature of Carnival, and it may be that the evidence has simply not survived.

The license of Carnival infiltrated other aspects of later medieval life. In the liturgical drama, that is, the plays in Latin which in some monastic and episcopal churches were incorporated into the liturgy of Easter, Christmas and other feast days, Epiphany was celebrated with particular licence. Italy has no Feast of the Ass such as survives from Rouen, but a thirteenth-century ritual book from Padua prescribes a Play of Herod for the night of Epiphany in which Herod 'out-herods Herod', swinging about an air-filled bladder in his rage as he and his henchmen move about the church striking clergy and laity alike, in memory of the Slaughter of the Innocents. This form of drama in Latin is found throughout the Roman church from its earliest appearance in the tenth century and well into the sixteenth century, and when Hamlet comments on the performance of the leading actor in the *commedia dell'arte* at his mother's court (III.2.13) he is remembering a range of dramatic modes.

While the liturgical drama's Herod is a parody of abuse of power, powerlessness was also the object of satire. From the mid-fifteenth century, we have scenes of rustic yokels interpolated into *sacre rappresentazioni* and on their own. In early sixteenth-century Siena (scarcely medieval but certainly not 'high culture' and Renaissance), secular groups of urban artisans in Florence started putting on sketches in which they satirised peasants from the countryside. Such was their success that they were invited to Rome to perform in the courts of Leo X and the banker Agostino Chigi. This anti-pastoral – again, Shakespeare seems to parody such efforts with the rude mechanicals of *A Midsummer Night's Dream* – may have been an invention of the early sixteenth century, but it seems more likely that parody and satire of rustics were simply part of the vocabulary of the *giullari* and continued until they were re-appropriated in the seventeenth century by the *maggi* and *bruscelli* of the Tuscan countryside, and again by the *teatro popolare* of Monticchiello, Montepulciano and the like.

Popular drama refuses to be defined, and it is foolhardy to suggest that later manifestations had direct medieval antecedents, or to claim direct and unbroken inheritance from the medieval *giullare* to Dario Fo. There is no doubt that oral traditions that survive for centuries in pre-industrial societies can be lost within one or two generations from the moment of re-location in the city, but continuity is hard to prove. Discontinuity is easier. We can say with some certainty that under the influence of charismatic preachers whose preaching led to new kinds of visualisation, some time around the middle of the thirteenth century, groups formed that sought new forms of participation in the stories of the bible. With their meeting rooms as performance space, and with a vernacular whose written conventions were newly established, the confraternities had a milieu in which to begin.

It is traditional to point to a devil pageant on a barge on the Arno in 1304, recorded by Giovanni Villani in his *Cronica* (VIII, 70) for the simple reason that a bridge collapsed under the weight of spectators, as the first manifestation of religious theatre in Florence. No text survives, if indeed there was one, but Dante's tour de force with a dozen devils, all with speaking parts, in Inferno XXI–XXII suggests an easy familiarity with devil pageants; and the names of his devils, Malacoda, Scarmiglione, Alichino and so on, are already, or will become, the standard names of devils in fifteenth-century Florence, and will be reborn in the warty, deformed masks of the *zanni* of the *commedia dell'arte*.

It is not in Florence, however, that 'theatre' re-emerges for the first time since the fall of the Roman Empire, but rather in the lay confraternities of fourteenth-century Umbria. Confraternities were associations of pious laymen whose activities included acts of charity, suffrage masses for the dead and paraliturgical devotions. Typically, their devotion was focused either on the Virgin Mary as intercessor for sinners or on Christ crucified. The latter group practised self-flagellation as a form of penance and as a means of identifying with Christ's suffering. For both groups, the singing of vernacular hymns was an integral part of their devotions, and an extensive repertoire of hymns in the vernacular emerged. Among the known authors of *laudi* is a Franciscan friar from Todi called Jacopone (1230–1306), whose oeuvre contained also *laudi* for two voices, spiritual dialogues between the body and the soul, Christ or the Virgin and the sinner, and his macabre *Contrasto del vivo e del morto,* in which the living man quizzes the skeleton about his missing flesh, eyes, teeth, golden locks and so on, to which the skeleton replies that despite his vanity about them in life, they have all corrupted in the grave. Numerous texts, together with confraternity inventories that regularly mention the *cacciopola* or skeleton that danced from the end of a pole, show the popularity of this theme. No less fortunate was Jacopone's meditation on the representation of the Passion of Christ known by its first line, 'Donna de paradiso', in which eyewitness narrative and direct speech are intermingled; it is this protodrama of thirty-three stanzas plus refrain that marks the beginning of drama in the vernacular.

It is necessary, however, to draw another thread into the story at this stage. From the tenth century, a short but richly textured dramatic element had been added to the Latin liturgy of the highest feast days of Easter Sunday, Christmas and Epiphany. From monasteries and cathedrals throughout Western Europe texts survive with musical notation and stage directions. One of the oldest surviving Italian versions is the eleventh-or twelfth-century text from Montecassino, in which the Angel asks the Maries at the tomb whom they seek: 'Quem queritis?' 'Jesum Nazarenum,' the Maries reply. The Angel points to the empty tomb to show that he is risen: 'Non est hic. Alleluia!' The Passion of Christ became part of the repertoire relatively late. Again, the oldest surviving fragment comes from the Benedictine monastery of Montecassino, and is dated to the twelfth century. The action moves from Judas' contract with Caiaphas through to the Crucifixion, but breaks off as Mary arrives at the foot of the Cross.

From the change in musical notation, it appears that Mary was to deliver her *planctus*, her lament, at the foot of the Cross, in the vernacular rather than in Latin, and similar to the one contained in Jacopone's 'Donna de paradiso' and the dozens of *laudi* that derive from it. The *planctus* had become a major element, and not in just Latin but also in the vernacular; by the beginning of the fourteenth century, it was free-standing. The music of these laments heightens our experience of the Virgin's pain as she gazes on the suffering of her son.

The spiritual *laudi*, in the metres of the popular secular ballads, were organised into *laudari* or anthologies, and in many cases arranged according to the church calendar. The vast majority of these *laudi* are hymns in the modern sense, but in a very small group principally in Umbria we find a significant proportion of dramatic *laudi*, of varying length. Throughout Umbria and the Abruzzi, records survive in the form of dramatic texts and confraternal archives that suggest that the *laudi* were not simply devotional words to assist individual visualisation of and identification with the events of the gospels, but rather they were performed in costume. The *laudario* of the Perugian confraternity of San Fiorenzo, copied from an earlier compilation in the second half of the fourteenth century, contains *laudi drammatiche* for Advent, Christmas, the Annunciation, every day of Lent, Holy Week, the Harrowing of Hell, Easter, Michaelmas, Ascension and Pentecost, St Fiorenzo, St Dominic, the Assumption and a series of *contrasti* under the heading *Laus pro Defunctis*, or devotions for the dead. Some, like the dramatisations of the gospel parables that are the prescribed New Testament reading for each day of Lent, are just three stanzas; others, like the Easter and Christmas plays, are much longer, and may have been performed for a wider audience, as part of the confraternity's contribution to the Easter observances of the church in which they met. Of all the Perugian plays the Easter Saturday play of the Harrowing of Hell is the most attractive to modern readers. As we read it now, it is the imperfect fusion of two earlier *laudi*, one a simple versification of the apocryphal Acts of Pilate, the other, in a different metre, a freer version of the saints' entry into Paradise. The charm of the play, like that of the Acts of Pilate, lies in the simple contrast between the dark, bumbling obtuseness of Infernus, the personification of Hell, and his incompetent prime minister Satan, and the luminous presence of Christ who arrives to free the Old Testament righteous and bind Satan.

Easter plays are probably the most resilient of all the medieval dramatic forms. Dozens of such plays are known, but while they share common sources (the Gospels, the *Meditations on the Life of Christ*, Cicerchia's *Passione* from the late 1300s and Jacopone's *Donna de Paradiso*) there is seldom a direct link from one to the other. With the introduction of printing, however, one text gained enormous circulation: the Passion play performed in the Colosseum at the end of the fifteenth century by the Confraternity of the Gonfalone, which is discussed further below. An eighteenth-century edition of this play is the basis of the play still performed in Biella, most recently for the 2000 Jubilee and in 2005.

The *laudi drammatiche* did not spread to any significant extent outside central Italy, and were barely studied until the 1870s, when the philologists of the newly unified Italy set about defining a 'national literature'. Nonetheless it is in the context of hymn-singing confraternities that plays first appear in Florence, at the end of the fourteenth century, and in the course of the fifteenth century Florentines became pre-eminent in the performance of religious plays, as in all the creative arts. The earliest plays were representations of the Annunciation, Ascension and Pentecost, mounted in the conventual churches of San Felice in Piazza, Santa Maria del Carmine and Santo Spirito. From Heaven constructed high in the church, Angels descended to Earth, mounted on the rood screen or on a platform constructed in the middle of the church and returned again to Heaven, in a blaze of fireworks, lighting effects and singing.

Similarly spectacular were the pageants that formed part of the four-day celebrations for the Feast of St John the Baptist (24 June), and from the middle of the century texts appear that are closely associated with these pageants. The humanist Matteo Palmieri describes the reforms of 1454: a huge procession made up of various confraternities entered the Piazza della Signoria, where each in turn did its *rappresentazione* of a moment in the history of man's salvation from the Creation to the Last Judgement. What had previously been some sort of tableau with limited words and actions and carried in procession becomes a fully acted play, performed with elaborate sets on an *edificio* or portable structure, with the bystanders milling about.

The vogue for this new dramatic form spread rapidly: in the youth confraternities, young men were diverted from the lascivious entertainments of Carnival into the performance of chaste moral plays like Feo Belcari's *Abramo e Isac* ('Abraham and Isaac', a fifteenth-century favourite), and Piero Muzi's *Vitello sagginato* ('Prodigal Son'). Adult groups performed plays concerning the martyrdom of St Bartholomew in Piazza Santa Croce (1453, 1471), and the beheading of St John the Baptist in the field at Porta alla Giustizia (1451), plays with elaborate staging devices that included beheaded dummies and an exploding Herodias.

Until 1478, the year when the attempted assassination of Lorenzo de' Medici brought the golden age of these plays to an end, the *rappresentazioni* dealt principally with biblical stories and major saints. After a hiatus of almost a decade, the plays began to appear again, no longer big public performances, but principally in youth confraternities and convents. In this context Antonia Tanini Pulci composed a small group of saint plays which reflect ascetic concerns of chastity and fidelity. From 1485, the plays began to appear in print, in splendid small pamphlets of twelve to twenty-four pages, illustrated with woodcuts, and in the 1490s a new vogue emerged for plays that dealt with the atrocious martyrdom of virgins: Apollonia, Agata, Barbara, Caterina, Cristina and so on. No contemporary performance records have been found of these plays, so their performance was probably within the walls of the convent or confraternity; they found an avid reading public and were reprinted regularly throughout the sixteenth century, avoiding censorship on account of their size, ephemeral nature and pious content.

The fame of the Florentine *festaiuoli,* the people who performed the *feste,* had spread through Italy. In 1451 Alfonso, King of Naples, sent his court singers to Florence to see how the great *feste* were done; and at the expense of the Signoria, the Sant'Agnese company in Santa Maria del Carmine put on its Ascension play again, out of season, for their benefit. In June 1473, the Roman cardinal Pietro Riario, cardinal nephew of Sixtus IV, who was about to nominate him Archbishop of Florence, summoned a group of *festaiuoli* from Florence to Rome and had them stage half a dozen plays in the *piazza* in front of Santissimi Apostoli as entertainments for Eleonora of Aragon, who was travelling from Naples to Ferrara to marry Ercole d'Este, accompanied by a huge entourage of courtiers and ambassadors from all the Italian states. The Florentines may even have freelanced: a chronicler reports that in Milan, for Easter 1475, some Florentines performed a play on the Resurrection before an audience of 80,000 people. When the inhabitants of Revello, in Piedmont, put together their three-day Passion in 1481, they drew not only on French models but on Florentine printed texts that were already circulating.

Florentines were certainly expected and willing to bring Florentine expertise to play-making in other centres. The designers of court entertainments began experimenting with classical themes in the 1470s. A spectacular banquet in the Roman court of Cardinal Pietro Riario in 1473 saw Mercury, Orpheus, Hercules and other deities as entertainments between the courses; but it was a Florentine, the great humanist poet and scholar Poliziano, who brought together the Florentine *sacra rappresentazione* and the new classicising vogue, and produced for Cardinal Francesco Gonzaga of Mantua the exquisite hybrid, the *Favola di Orfeo*. Eurydice, fleeing from Aristeus, is bitten by a snake and dies. In order to have her back, Orpheus descends to the underworld realm of Pluto and Persephone and charms them with his song. They allow him to take her back to the world of the living on condition that he does not look back. The play embodies the Florentine Neoplatonists' understanding of love's power to restore life and their belief in the power of beautiful words and music. Mercury, messenger of the gods and presiding deity of rhetoric, rather than an Angel, speaks the prologue; the mountain that is a significant scenic element in so many Florentine plays (*Abraham and Isaac, The Ascension*, to name but two) is the scene of Eurydice's death and of Orpheus' song; rather than 'harrowing hell' like Christ, Orpheus uses song to charm the rulers of the underworld, and returns, singing, with his bride. When he loses her, Orpheus renounces female company and to avenge this outrage the Baccantes tear him to pieces. Paola Ventrone has convincingly argued that the play was commissioned in 1473, and was thus the prototype rather than the summation of the other Orpheus plays of the last quarter of the century.[1] Leonardo da Vinci was required to do stage design in the court of Gian Galeazzo Visconti and Isabella of Aragon in Milan, and designed a revolving stage for a play of Orpheus and Eurydice, that apparently transformed the hillside where Eurydice dies into the infernal palace of Pluto and Persephone as Orpheus made his way down.

In Rome, Florence and in Ferrara, from the mid-1480s, humanists were experimenting with performances of Roman comedies in Latin and in Italian but with the expulsion of the Medici in 1494 and their re-grouping in Rome around Cardinal Giovanni de' Medici, the future Pope Leo X, Florence ceded its supremacy in spectacular performance to the courts and did not begin to recover until the 1530s and 1540s. In the archaic mode of the *sacra rappresentazione*, however, Florentines continued to experiment.

Giuliano Dati, a Florentine priest and minor vernacular versifier, brought Florentine form (the *ottava rima*) and technology (winches and frames for lowering Angels to the Cross) to the Roman Gonfalone company's Passion play, and used the printing press to ensure that his text achieved huge circulation. Despite the popularity of Dati's text and its title-page claim to be the play performed every year, the text of the play changed continually in the years between 1490, when performances in the Colosseum began, and 1539, when it was banned by Pope Paul III following an outbreak of violence in the city's Jewish quarter as the players processed back to their oratory.

Dati was the author also of a dozen or so *cantari* or performance poems, which raises the question of another kind of representation. The *ottava rima*, first used by Boccaccio in his *Teseida* in 1341, quickly established itself as the narrative verse form in Italian. Its eleven-syllable lines, rhyming ABABABCC, are simple to construct, easy to memorise and closed by a rhyming couplet to form a self-contained unit. When Italian authors of the fourteenth and fifteenth century started assimilating the chivalric matter of Troy, of France and of King Arthur, they adopted the *ottava rima*. The poems, called *cantari*, were recited by *canterini*, market-place buskers, successors to the *giullari* of the twelfth and thirteenth centuries. The *canterini* had prodigious memories and performance skills, and could recite – possibly even improvise – long narratives, not just the tales of men and arms, ladies and loves, but accounts of recent battles and assassinations, scandal about the farmer's daughter and the priest, miracles of the Virgin, martyrdoms of saints, the life of Christ and the discovery of America. This was the verse form that the Florentines adopted for the *sacra rappresenta-zione*: not a shorter-line ballad metre as in England, but a more literary narrative form, that will be progressively refined at the end of the century by Boiardo, Ariosto and later Tasso, to produce the great chivalric epics that mark the end of medieval romance in Counter-Reformation Italy.

The performance style of the *canterini* is not known. The word (from *cantare*, 'to sing') suggests that they sang or chanted; visual images suggest that they may have accompanied themselves on a one- or two-stringed viol; but there is only the slightest evidence that the *ottava rima* of the *rappresentazioni* was accompanied by music. A note reading 'Cantasi come le stanze d'Abramo' ('to be sung like the stanzas of Abraham') next to an eight-line stanza in a manuscript by Feo Belcari, could refer to the whole play, or to a single speech by the patriarch within the play.

Music was certainly part of the plays. When Herod the Tetrarch orders his birthday feast, he orders musicians as well; when Abraham and Isaac are reunited with Sarah, they sing and dance in a circle, each one accompanied by an angel; when the Apostles return to Jerusalem after the Ascension, they sing a *laude*. The recruitment of musicians was always problematic. The Sant'Agnese company in Santa Maria del Carmine recruited choirboys (*cherichetti*) from the Florentine cathedral, and for Christ and the two boys who were lowered from heaven as angels there was compensation: a cash payment to the tenor who played Christ, and new hose, with leather soles and fancy hooks-and-eyes, for the two Angels. While the actors and crew joined the confraternity in the feast that followed the play, at which large quantities of food and wine were consumed and breakages inevitably resulted, the boys and their chaperone were entertained separately.

The 1495 statutes of the Roman Gonfalone company speak of the responsibility of every individual member to assist in the recruitment of singers and musicians for their Easter plays. From 1501, these plays have an unequivocal musical element in the form of four double choruses that divided the play into a prologue and four parts, and in the 1534 redaction the rubric '*musica*' appears against the parts of the choruses of Prophets and Sibyls, the Patriarchs in Limbo, the Angels, the Pharisees (collectively but not individually), the Woman taken in adultery, the Woman of Cana, the Disciples (collectively but not individually), the Maries. Music comes to play a more significant role in the characterisation of single characters.

All the confraternities responsible for mounting plays acquired sets and costumes. Major sets remained in position throughout the year: Jerusalem and the Mount of Olives were left permanently on the *volte* or masonry rood screen that divided Santa Maria del Carmine in Florence; the machinery of Heaven and Paradise were mounted permanently in the roof. In the Roman Colosseum, the Gonfalone confraternity had a permanent stage that it kept in good repair even in later years when it was unable to perform the play every year; it also acquired a disused chapel in the Colosseum, adjoining its playing space, and stored its props there. In the sixteenth century, when the plays had retreated to the female convents, the sets became less elaborate. A *frottola* or dramatic prologue to an unspecified *sacra rappresentazione* has nuns bustling around gathering costumes and props, but when the play is changed at the last minute from a play of St Alexis (who lived for seventeen years under the stairs), all that is required is the rewriting of the 'polizze sopra gli usci' (signs over the doors). In a later (sixteenth-century) Judith play, the 'places' of the play are marked: 'Castra Assiriorum' (The Assyrian Camp), 'Domus Judith' (The House of Judith), 'Talamus Holofernis' (The Bed of Holophernes), 'Forum' and so on.

Costumes were an essential part of the plays, and like the sets seem to have followed closely the familiar conventions of the visual arts, and possibly even the visual arts of a previous generation. The Virgin wears a blue mantle; Mary Magdalene has a long horsehair wig, coloured (according to the account books) with saffron, and carries her ointment in a precious container; the Angels wear white and have wings. In the records of the Florentine Ascension play, we see the Angels' wings being remade year after year, from whatever materials are available and affordable: peacock feathers hired from the silk merchant; chicken feathers purchased from the poulterer; variously coloured sheets of paper purchased from the stationer. The Apostles have wigs and false beards for realistic effect, but they carry their *segni* ('symbols'), and their robes are not the clothes of humble fishermen but used ecclesiastical vestments. God the Father seldom has a speaking part (the 'Dispute of the Virtues' section of the authentic Feo Belcari Annunciation is a notable exception), but the inventories contain costumes for him, and masks: clearly he was impersonated, but the actor's face was not seen.[2]

Actors did not appear naked. Where the Passion was performed, the inventories contain body-suits in flesh-coloured leather.[3] A *zibaldone* (notebook) of secret devices prescribes sponges impregnated with red dye concealed inside Christ's wig, so that he can sweat blood at the appropriate moment; a tantalising reference in the Gonfalone archives to a costume for Christ being made at the abattoir[4] could suggest that fresh offal – intestines and blood – was used for his costume. From the earliest mention, a flesh-coloured body-suit had been part of his wardrobe.

The martyrdom plays of the 1490s require an extraordinary range of torments with sado-erotic overtones. In the play of St Agatha, her virginal breasts are hacked in an attempt to turn her away from Christ and back to the pagan deities. They are then miraculously healed by St Peter, sent to her by Christ in the guise of a doctor. The authors of the martyrdom plays take one of two lines of approach. If the victim does suffer, then he or she calls for Christ for succour and forbearance; but more usually there is no pain at all. In the play of St Dorothy, the Prefect orders that she be burnt:

Metti a ordine, maestro, una graticola che vi s'arrosta su questa cristicola.	Organise a grill without delay to roast this Christian maiden on today.

Dorothy however feels no pain;

'N un prato iacio di delizie adorno, fra mille fiori e mille dolci unguenti, dove suave- mente intorno intorno spiran grate aure e temperati venti, dove notte non è, ma sempre giorno.	I'm lying in a meadow of delight, amid a thousand flowers and sweet balms, where all around me now there gently breathe most welcome zephyrs and well-tempered breeze; where there is never night, but always day.
EL PREFETTO la dimanda, dicendo: El fuoco non ti cuoce?	THE PREFECT asks her, saying: And does the fire not burn you?
SANTA DOROTEA	
Io non lo sento, tanto è il calor di quel ch'i' ho di drento.	I feel it not, such is the heat of him I have within.[5]

It is a feature of these stories that the torments go on and on: mutila- tion, laceration, boiling pitch and turpentine (in the early years of the sixteenth century the Purification company listed a cauldron among its theatre properties). But always the tormentors are repelled and the victim becomes more eloquent in professing faith in Christ, because simple torture, even the hacking out of her tongue in the case of Santa Cristina, is not enough to silence the saint.

In the final dispatch of the victim, usually by beheading, the audience's sensibilities are carefully respected. St John the Baptist is beheaded, but his soul immediately departs for Limbo, and the audience cannot imagine for a moment that the actor has been harmed. In the play of the Martyrdom of St James the Great, the audience is distracted by action elsewhere so that a dummy can be substituted for the saint.

The devices of these plays never cease to amaze. The illuminations of the Ascension play have been reconstructed through their account books. The heavenly spheres that revolved behind God the Father were represented by wheels on which lanterns were mounted. Some of these shone through a lens constructed from a glass flask, heated and squashed flat, then filled with saffron-tinted water. Mirror fragments were also used to reflect light.

In the days before the performance, barrels of oil (and also a barrel of water, in case of fire) were carried up into the roof-area, and hundreds of tongue-dish lamps were set with wicks and, presumably, some kind of lighting system. For the *Stella Nuova* or almond-shaped frame in which Christ rose up to heaven, Filippo (or Pippo), son of Baldo, a goldsmith of the quarter, devised a copper tube with a pulley mechanism so that when Christ stepped into the *mandorla*, a lighted candle appeared from the tube.[6] It may well be that when the historian and Medici propagandist Giorgio Vasari came to write about the *ingegni* or devices of these plays in the mid-sixteenth century, popular memory had conflated this Filippo with another more famous goldsmith, Filippo di ser Brunellesco Brunelleschi.[7] In his 'Life of Brunelleschi' Vasari describes an umbrella-spoke hemispherical frame that is lowered from Heaven, and from which the *mandorla* then descends for the Annunciation. According to Vasari, live Angels were attached to the spokes. We do not have the inventory of the San Felice company that staged the Annunciation, but numerous other confraternities owned a *Stella*, a huge wooden star construction, decorated with lights and cherubs and angels. In 1422, the painter Masolino painted the moulded leather Angels of the Ascension company's *stella* in the Carmine (Newbigin, *Feste*, vol. I, p. 84 and vol. II, p. 291).

In 1439 a Russian bishop, Abraham of Souzdal, who saw a performance of the Annunciation, was thrilled by fireworks that exploded throughout the church yet burnt nobody.[8] The descent of the Holy Ghost in the Pentecost play was done by sending a plaster dove powered by a rocket along a rope from Heaven to the Upper Room where it ignited the Apostles' gold crowns, packed with fireworks. The Apostles in the Upper Room were not live actors but life-sized wooden dummies in costume, the same wooden dummies that were displayed around the table of the Last Supper on Maundy Thursday. After the display of fireworks, the door below, representing the gates of Jerusalem, opened to allow actors playing the parts of the Apostles to come out and preach. Fire, however, has always been the enemy of theatres, and in 1471, unextinguished embers from the play caused old Santo Spirito to burn down (even as the new one was being built, to Brunelleschi's design), God's retribution, according to the chronicler, for staging the play out of season, in Lent (Newbigin, *Feste*, vol. II, pp. 746–52).

In the last quarter of the fifteenth century, other forms of theatre were being explored in other contexts, but principally in the Carnival season.

In the all-male atmosphere of Pavia, a university town south of Milan, students experimented in the dramatisation of misogynistic and misanthropic comedy in Latin; in the schools and courts, young men performed the comedies of Plautus and Terence, the tragedies of Seneca, and on one celebrated occasion Alessandra Scala, daughter of the Florentine Chancellor, recited a speech from Sophocles' *Electra*, to great acclaim. (Ventrone, *Gli araldi*, 1993, p. 28). Performing in plays had entered the humanistic curriculum; memorising, acting a role and speaking and moving in public were all part of a young man's education for public life.

Carnival was traditionally the time for masking and misbehaviour. It is Florence, again, that provides us with most evidence of performance in Carnival, and principally through the songs that appeared in the last decades of the fifteenth century. The polyphonic music for some of these *canti carnascialeschi* survives in sixteenth-century collections of *laudi spirituali*, although it is still unclear whether the lewd or the spiritual version came first.

The progressive aristocratisation of Italian society between the end of the fifteenth century and the beginning of the sixteenth century shifted the festive resources of Italian society from the hands of the lay confraternities into the princely courts, and princes had different priorities and different tastes. Lorenzo de' Medici may have written a *sacra rappresentazione* for his son's confraternity, but for public consumption in the St John the Baptist procession of 1491, he commissioned a series of triumphs on neo-classical themes. The inspiration for these performances came not from the performers themselves, but from the prince who commissioned and controlled new kinds of artistic endeavour to the glory of himself rather than of God and the city. And it is in this new court-centred culture that new models of theatre will be pioneered in the coming centuries.

Notes

1 Ventrone, '"Philosophia'", pp. 137–80. Ventrone has recently argued that the *Annunciation* of 1439 was performed in San Marco ('"Una Visione"', 2001, pp. 39–51).

2 Newbigin, *Feste*, vol. II, pp. 536 and 537.

3 The Gonfalone inventory for 1492 includes: 'a garment for Christ, flesh-coloured damask, new, lined with leather. Item, a pair of drawers for Christ', *Archivio Segreto Vaticano, Arciconfr. Gonf.* 1218, fo. 13v.

4 'I paid master Evangelista the tailor at the abattoirs 20 *bolognini* to sew Christ's clothes, and also Ciaffoni to take the meat to the vineyard at [their church of] the Santi Quaranta', *ibid.*, 133, fo. 21r (21 April 1517).

5 *Rappresentazione di Santa Dorotea vergine e martire*, Florence, Francesco di Giovanni Benvenuto, 31 March 1516, lines 193–4, 204–10.

6 The *Stella Nuova* was commissioned in 1447 (see Newbigin, *Feste*, vol. I, pp. 122–6), and is described in detail in the 1467 inventory (text, *ibid.* vol. II, pp. 535–6, and translation, vol. I, pp. 74–5), by which time it is called the *Sole*.

7 Brunelleschi's *ingegni* are not mentioned in the first edition of the *Vite*, and are added tentatively ('Dicesi ancora che. . .') in the second edition of 1568.

8 Newbigin, *Feste*, vol. I, pp. 3–7 for his description of the Annunciation, and pp. 60–3 for his description of the Ascension.

Bibliography
Scripts

La Passione di Revello, ed. A. Cornagliotti, Turin, 1976.

Laude drammatiche e rappresentazioni sacre, ed. V. De Bartholomaeis, 3 vols., Florence, 1943.

Nuovo Corpus di sacre rappresentazioni fiorentine del Quattrocento, ed. N. Newbigin, Bologna, 1983.

Sacre rappresentazioni dei secoli , XIV e XVI, ed. A. D'Ancona, 3 vols., Florence, 1872.

Trionfi e canti carnascialeschi toscani del Rinascimento, ed. R. Bruscagli, 2 vols., Rome, 1986.

Uffici drammatici padovani, ed. by G. Vecchi, Florence, 1954.

Criticism

Barr, C. 'Music and spectacle in the confraternity drama of fifteenth-century Florence: the reconstruction of a theatrical event', in T. Verdon and J. Henderson (ed.), *Christianity and the Renaissance: Image and Religious Imagination in the Quattrocento*, New York, 1984, pp. 176–204.

'A Renaissance artist in the service of a singing confraternity', in M. Tetel, R. G. Witt and R. Goffen (ed.), *Life and Death in Fifteenth-Century Florence*, Durham, 1989, pp. 105–19 and 216.

Ciappelli, G. *Carnevale e Quaresima: comportamenti sociali e culturali a Firenze nel Rinascimento*, Rome, 1997.

Cioni, A. *Bibliografia delle sacre rappresentazioni*, Florence, 1961.

Cruciani, F. *Teatro nel Rinascimento: Roma 1450–1550*, Rome, 1983.

D'Ancona, A. *Origini del teatro italiano*, 2 vols., 2nd edition 1891; reprint Rome, 1966.

De Bartholomaeis, V., *Le origini della poesia drammatica italiana*, 2nd edn, Turin, 1952.

Delcorno Branca, D., 'Un camaldolese alla festa di San Giovanni. La processione del Battista descritta da Agostino di Porto', *Lettere italiane*, **55** (2003), 1–25.

Eisenbichler, K. *The Boys of the Archangel Raphael: A Youth Confraternity in Florence, 1411–1785*, Toronto and Buffalo, 1998.

Esposito, A. 'Le "Confraternite" del Gonfalone (secoli XIV–XVI)', in L. Fiorani (ed.), *Le confraternite romane: esperienza religiosa, società, committenza artistica*, Rome, 1984, pp. 91–136.

Hatfield, R. 'The Compagnia de' Magi', *Journal of the Warburg and Courtauld Institutes*, **33** (1970), 107–61.

Lasansky, D.M. 'Tableau and memory: the Fascist revival of the medieval/renaissance festival in Italy', *The European Legacy*, **4** (1999), 26–53.

Machette, A. 'The Compagnia della Purificazione e di San Zanobi in Florence: a reconstruction of its residence at San Marco, 1440–1506', in Wisch and Ahl, *Confraternities*, pp. 74–101.

Il movimento dei Disciplinati nel settimo centenario dal suo inizio (Perugia – 1260): Convegno internazionale, Perugia, 25–28 settembre 1960, Perugia, 1962.

Nerbano, M. 'Cultura materiale nel teatro delle confraternite umbre', *Teatro e storia*, Annali 4, **12** (1997), 293–346.

'Play and Record: Ser Tommaso di Silvestro and the Theatre of Medieval and Early Modern Orvieto', *European Medieval Theatre*, **8** (2004), 127–71.

Newbigin, N. 'Il testo e il contesto dell'Abramo e Isac di Feo Belcari', *Studi e problemi di critica testuale*, **23** (1981), 13–37.

'La Rappresentazione di Sa' Iacopo Maggiore', *Studi e problemi di critica testuale*, **46** (1993), 43–67.

'Piety and politics in the *feste* of Lorenzo's Florence', in G. C. Garfagnini (ed.), *Lorenzo il Magnifico e il suo mondo*, Florence, 1994, 17–41.

Feste d'Oltrarno: Plays in Churches in Fifteenth-Century Florence, 2 vols., Florence, 1996.

'Agata, Apollonia and other martyred virgins: did Florentines really see these plays performed?', *European Medieval Drama*, **1** (1997), 77–100.

'The Decorum of the Passion: the plays of the Confraternity of the Gonfalone in the Roman Colosseum, 1490–1539', in Wisch and Ahl, *Confraternities*, pp. 173–202.

Pulci, A. *Florentine Drama for Convent and Festival: Seven Sacred Plays*, trans. J. W. Cook, Chicago, 1996.

Risultati e prospettive della ricerca sul movimento dei Disciplinati: Convegno internazionale di studio, Perugia, 5–7 dicembre 1969, Perugia, 1972.

Steinitz, K. T. 'A reconstruction of Leonardo's revolving stage', *Art Quarterly*, 140 (1949), 325–38.

Tissoni Benvenuti, A. and Mussini Sacchi, M. P. *Le corti padane*, Turin, 1983.

Trexler, R.C. 'Ritual in Florence: adolescence and salvation in the Renaissance', in C. Trinkaus and H. Oberman (eds.), *The Pursuit of Holiness in Late Medieval and Renaissance Religion*, Leiden, 1974, pp. 200–64.

Public Life in Renaissance Florence, New York, 1980.

Ventrone, P. (ed.). *Le Tems revient/'L tempo si rinuova: Feste e spettacoli nella Firenze di Lorenzo il Magnifico*, Milan, 1992.

Gli araldi della commedia: teatro a Firenze nel Rinascimento, Pisa, 1993.

'"Philosophia, Involucra Fabularum": La fabula di Orpheo di Angelo Poliziano', *Comunicazioni sociali*, **19** (1997), 137–80.

'"Una visione miracolosa e indicibile": Nuove considerazioni sulle feste di quartiere', in *Teatro e spettacolo nella Firenze dei Medici: Modelli dei luoghi teatrali*, Florence, 2001, pp. 39–51.

Vitale-Brovarone, A. *Il quaderno di segreti d'un regista provenzale del Medioevo: Note per la messa in scena d'una Passione*, Alessandria, 1984.

Weaver, E. *Convent Theatre in Early Modern Italy: Spiritual Fun and Learning for Women*, Cambridge, 2002.

Wisch, B. 'The Passion of Christ in the art, theater, and penitential rituals of the Roman Confraternity of the Gonfalone', in K. Eisenbichler (ed.), *Crossing the Boundaries: Christian Piety and the Arts in Medieval and Renaissance Confraternities*, Kalamazoo, MI 1991, pp. 237–62.

Wisch, B. and D. Cole Ahl (eds.). *Confraternities and the Visual Arts in Renaissance Italy: Ritual, Spectacle, Image*, Cambridge and New York, 2000.

Young, K. *The Drama of the Medieval Church*, 2 vols., Oxford, 1933.

PART II

The Renaissance

2 The Renaissance stage

RICHARD ANDREWS

Although the influence of Italian Renaissance models on theatre in the rest of Europe is frequently acknowledged in detail, it is still not always fully recognised how Italy, in the sixteenth century, was the source of radical innovations which have had a fundamental effect on performed art in what we now think of as 'Western' culture and civilisation. This remains true even though Italy has left us very few individual play scripts now perceived as possessing lasting quality. It was Italian Humanists who set in motion a series of major transformations in terms of how theatre was conceived and managed. These affected on the one hand the structure and content of plays, and on the other hand the social, physical and economic organisation of theatres and theatre performances. The scholarly dramatists who pioneered this revolution, before and after the year 1500, could not have envisaged some of the developments which would eventually arise from it. The invention just before 1600 of opera, a genre now central to Western performance culture, was initially stimulated by a determination to recapture all the elements of Greek tragedy. Humanists of a century earlier would fully have understood this motivation, even if the results went beyond anything they could have imagined. By contrast, they would neither have understood nor approved the professional troupes who turned theatre into a commercial activity from around 1550 onwards (and who are to be dealt with in a separate chapter of this volume). Nevertheless, it can be argued that *commedia dell'arte* was a logical development of a new attitude to drama which the Humanists had helped to create. Certainly the content of *arte* scenarios was dependent sometimes to a slavish degree on the formulaic characters and plots first established by *commedia erudita*, the genre through which Humanist theatre first established itself.

It was also in Italy, at this time, that there occurred the most unexpected and shocking revolution of all – the appearance of professional female performers in drama both spoken and sung. There was no Humanist or neo-classical logic behind this introduction of actresses and *prime donne* into high cultural life. It occurred in a professional context, at a date still impossible to determine precisely but probably in the 1540s; and it was accepted cautiously but permanently by European society, in the face of formidable prejudices, for reasons which even now are hard to analyse. No other major theatrical culture in the world – Chinese, Indian, Japanese – ever spontaneously chose to tread this particular road. But Western theatre, opera, cinema and television have made the female star or *diva* a central part of the experience which they have to offer; and we must accept as a fact, even if we cannot entirely explain it, that this phenomenon began in sixteenth-century Italy.

Italian Humanists insisted dogmatically that, in the new cultural world which they were creating for society's élite, ancient Greek and Roman models should be followed and medieval ones obliterated. All the drama of the recent past was seen as totally lacking in cultural and (just as importantly) social prestige. This attitude had a radical effect on the composition of plays and on the attitudes expected from audiences. On the one hand, it transformed the techniques and practice of dramaturgy. It became obligatory to divide plays into five acts, a structure which did not exist formally in the Greek and Roman plays regarded as canonical models, but which had been imposed on them retrospectively by scholars in late antiquity. More authentically, the Humanists insisted on sharply distinguishing separate genres of comedy and tragedy, with pastoral as a later and more innovative addition. Eventually, from the 1560s onwards, Italian scholars inflicted dramatic theory and practice with the constraints of the 'three unities' – time, place and action – allegedly derived from Aristotle. (These rules were then adopted rigorously by 'classical' dramatists in France; but they were taken with much greater pinches of salt in England and Spain, where there was more continuity with the imaginative and poetic insights of pre-Renaissance drama.)

Equally important was the promotion of playwriting from an ephemeral and occasional activity to the rank of high artistic creation, worthy of being preserved and studied on the same level as epic and lyric poetry, like the masterpieces of Greece and Rome. With the rise of new technology, this also meant that plays, like those other compositions, were worthy of being preserved in print. This attitude was established with very little fuss in Italy, as much as a century before Ben Jonson was derided in England for publishing his dramatic *Workes* in 1616. Such a rise in status also aided the progressive transformation of play performance into an autonomous cultural activity, in contrast with the strictly occasional character of medieval religious and courtly drama. The Humanists, wedded as they were to gentlemanly amateurism, probably never intended the inevitable corollary, that theatre should become a commercial enterprise. In fact the whole history of the dramatic art in sixteenth-century Italy can be seen as a struggle between scholarly intentions and practical demands – both sides of the conflict being firmly rooted in real passions and real social pressures which were characteristic of the period and the place. Before investigating the outcome as regards play texts themselves, we must summarise the history of 'theatres' as concrete venues for performance during the Renaissance, Mannerist and Baroque periods in Italy.

The physical context of performance

The desire to resurrect ancient modes of dramaturgy was naturally associated with attempts to understand and re-create ancient theatre architecture. At this time, the notion of a whole building dedicated to performance and to nothing else would be an innovation; but it was also a logical, even unavoidable product of the passion for imitating the classical world. Intense study was devoted by some to such archaeological evidence as was available, in particular to Vitruvius' *De architectura* of the first century AD. In the meantime, however, makeshift venues were needed quickly, and ideas on scenography were developing independently out of Renaissance achievements in perspective painting. Real theatre spaces thus developed in a pragmatic, piecemeal (and cheaper) way, and the archaeologists were overtaken by events. The first separate dedicated theatre building actually constructed in Italy, the Teatro Olimpico at Vicenza, was not opened (with a production of Sophocles in translation) until 1585. It is ironical, considering that Italy had launched the attitudes which led to such a project, that this is actually nine years later than the opening of Burbage's 'Theatre' in London.

The earliest productions of *commedia erudita*, and later of classical five-act tragedy and pastoral, were determinedly amateur, and sponsored by princely courts or by gentlemanly clubs – they took place in existing indoor locations adapted for performance. These were either public rooms in rulers' palaces, or spaces in private houses or the premises of Academies. Eventually some rooms were refurbished into permanent performance spaces. An early such attempt in the Ferrara ducal palace, supervised by

Figure 2: Illustration of an Italian Renaissance stage.

Ariosto in 1531, was destroyed by fire almost immediately. Half a century later, the Medici theatre inside the Uffizi palace in Florence (by Bernardo Buontalenti, 1585–6) became an example of what rulers thought was appropriate and affordable. Seating plans varied; but they always involved segregation of the sexes. Frequently the area designated for the princely patron, or for the guest of honour, was raised or highlighted so as to have the status almost of a second stage. The performing area itself was a raised platform at one end of the room, which might sometimes be closed by curtains but was not initially framed by a proscenium arch. The 'picture-frame' effect was none the less implicit, because the 'unity of place' which was first copied and then theorised from classical models suggested a static rather than changeable scenography. From the very earliest productions (probably from Ariosto's *Cassaria* of 1508 in Ferrara), professional artists were drafted in to produce an illusionistic perspective backcloth depicting a townscape or other suitable panorama. The stage thus depicted an autonomous fictional territory, which operated by coherent and familiar rules of time and space. It mirrored the world inhabited by the audience, but was self-contained and separate from that world. To use the terminology eventually adopted by theorists, the space thus created was both 'rational' and 'verisimilar'. The use of perspective painting to support this illusion was a satisfactory marriage between classical dramaturgical practice and the most up-to-date resources which were currently being applied to the visual arts: it must have helped to convince an audience that these ancient formats of staged fiction could be adapted to provide an art form for their own times.

Such scenographic practices developed and became canonical, in most Italian centres, over the first forty years of the sixteenth century: they were retrospectively codified by Sebastiano Serlio in his *Secondo libro dell'architettura* of 1545, which offered descriptions and illustrations of standard sets for comedy, tragedy and pastoral (or 'satyric'). (In fact it is striking to find the last of these mentioned so early, granted that pastoral was not at that date fully established as a 'regular' five-act genre.) Whether or not these structures and designs really had anything to do with what could be deduced about Greek or Roman theatre became increasingly irrelevant, though claims for their authenticity continued to be made. By the time the Teatro Olimpico did open, its curved auditorium and its elaborate architectural *frons scenae* were at least partly authentic, in terms of copying ancient Roman models, but no longer reflected the most common performing or scenographic practices. The next attempt was the smaller theatre designed in Sabbioneta in 1588, for the Gonzaga rulers of Mantua; followed in 1618 by the much larger Teatro Farnese in Parma. This last, with its huge but flexible stage space, proscenium arch, stalls and rising tiers of seats in an elongated horseshoe, clearly points to what became standard for European theatres and opera houses – it only needs the addition of the hierarchically vertical tiers of *palchi*, or boxes, which emerged in early Venetian theatres also in the early seventeenth century. All Italian purpose-built theatres had roofs: drama was seen as a winter activity to be pursued indoors.

Meanwhile, an increasing demand for pure visual spectacle contrasted with the static constraints of neo-classical drama: this trend produced new kinds of dramaturgy, but also innovations in scenography. For pageants and interludes, and then later for the operas which developed out of them, stage engineers began to create elaborate movable and moving scenery, able to produce miraculous effects and transformations: they were in fact building on experience gained in the fifteenth century, in religious dramas mounted in churches. The Florentine interludes at the Uffizi, for a grand-ducal wedding in 1589, were an internationally famous event, establishing for all Europe that Italians were the leaders in this development, and leading thereafter to bids from other countries to hire their technical expertise. Once again, it was the Teatro Farnese in Parma which incorporated both the space and the machinery for producing such effects as part of the basic structure of a permanent theatre building.

Along with physical changes in performance spaces came social and economic changes, in terms of why, when and for whom theatre was performed: the eventual outcome was that audiences were asked to pay for their entertainment. Commercial theatre developed first of all in Venice: as early as 1517 there are records of tickets being sold for shows in private houses. Full public theatres developed in the same city in the 1580s, as money-making enterprises conceived by noble merchant families: rooms in their palaces, and then whole buildings, were redesigned for permanent performance use. As the seventeenth century progressed, it was Venice which led the way for the rest of the Italian peninsula in developing venues, and promoting commercial theatre and opera, in ways which might still be recognised in the twenty-first century.

Renaissance Bibliography
Scripts

Accademia degli Ingannati. *Il sacrificio degli Intronati: Gli ingannati* (anastatic reprint), ed. Nerida Newbigin, Bologna, 1984.
Aretino, P. *Tutte le opere: Teatro*, ed. G. Petrocchi, Milan, 1971.

Bargagli, G. *La pellegrina*, ed. Florindo Cerreta, Florence, 1971.
'Bibbiena' (Bernardo Dovizi). *La Calandra*, ed. G. Padoan, Padua, 1985.
Commedie del Cinquecento, ed. N. Borsellino, 2 vols., Milan, 1962–7.
Giraldi Cinzio, E. B.: see the editions of *Selene, Epizia, Eufimia, Gli Eudemoni* and
    Gli Antivalomeni, Lampeter, 1990–, with Introductions and notes by
    P. Horne.
Il teatro italiano: Vol. II, *La commedia del Cinquecento*, ed. G. Davico Bonino; *La
    tragedia del Cinquecento*, ed. M. Ariani, Turin, 1977–8.
Piccolomini, A. *L'amor costante* (anastatic reprint), ed. N. Newbigin, Bologna, 1990.
Teatro del Cinquecento: I, La tragedia, ed. R. Cremante, Milan, 1988.

Criticism

Andrews, R. 'Printed texts and performance texts of Italian Renaissance comedy',
    in Dashwood and Everson, *Writers and Performers*, pp. 75–94.
    Scripts and Scenarios: The Performance of Comedy in Renaissance Italy, Cambridge,
    1993.
    'Shakespeare and Italian comedy', in A. Hadfield and P. Hammond (ed.),
    Shakespeare and Renaissance Europe, London, 2004, pp. 123–49.
Attolini, G. *Teatro e spettacolo nel Rinascimento*, Bari, 1997.
Baratto, M. *La commedia nel Cinquecento: Aspetti e problemi*, Vicenza, 1975.
Beacham, R. C. *The Roman Theatre and its Audience*, London, 1991.
Borsellino, N. *Rozzi e Intronati: Esperienze e forme di teatro dal 'Decameron' al
    'Candelaio'*, Rome, 1974.
Clubb, L. G. *Italian Drama in Shakespeare's Time*, New Haven and London, 1989.
Clubb, L. G. and Black, R. *Romance and Aretine Humanism in Sienese Comedy*,
    Florence, 1993.
Cruciani, F. *Il teatro italiano del Rinascimento*, Bologna, 1987.
Dashwood J. R. and Everson, J. E. (eds.). *Writers and Performers in Italian Drama from
    the time of Dante to Pirandello: Essays in Honour of G. H. McWilliam*,
    Lampeter, 1991.
Ferroni, G. *Le voci dell'istrione: Pietro Aretino e la dissoluzione del teatro*, Naples,
    1977.
    Il testo e la scena: Saggi sul teatro del Cinquecento, Rome, 1980.
Folena, G. (ed.), *Lingua e struttura del teatro italiano del Rinascimento*, Padua, 1970.
Greco, A. *L'istituzione del teatro comico nel Rinascimento*, Naples, 1976.
Guidotti, A. *Il modello e la trasgressione: Commedie del primo Cinquecento*, Rome, 1983.
Herrick, M. T. *Comic Theory in the Sixteenth Century*, Urbana, IL, 1950.
    Italian Comedy in the Renaissance, Urbana, IL, 1960.
Horne, P. R. *The Tragedies of G. B.Cinthio Giraldi*, Oxford, 1962.
Howarth, W. D. *Comic Drama: the European Heritage*, London, 1978.
Kenyon, N. and Keyte, H. *Una stravaganza dei Medici: The Florentine Intermedi of
    1589*, London, 1990.

Osborne, P. G. B. *Giraldi's Altile: The Birth of a New Dramatic Genre in Renaissance Ferrara*, Lampeter, 1992.

Pieri, M. *La nascita del teatro moderno in Italia tra XV e XVI secolo*, Turin, 1989.

Povoledo, E. 'Origins and aspects of Italian scenography', in N. Pirrotta (ed.), *Music and Theatre from Poliziano to Monteverdi*, trans. K. Eales, Cambridge, 1982, pp. 281–373.

Salingar, L. *Shakespeare and the Traditions of Comedy*, Cambridge, 1974.

Sanesi, I. *La commedia*, 2 vols., Milan, 1911.

Seragnoli, D. *Il teatro a Siena nel Cinquecento*, Roma, 1980.

Stäuble, A. *La commedia umanistica del Quattrocento*, Florence, 1968.

Weinberg, B. *Trattati di poetica e retorica nel Cinquecento*, 2 vols., Bari, 1970–4.

Zorzi, L. *Il teatro e la città: Saggi sulla scena italiana*, Turin, 1977.

3 Erudite comedy

RICHARD ANDREWS

In the development of an Italian drama based on the imitation of ancient models, comedy takes clear chronological precedence: in performance terms, neither tragedy nor 'regular' pastoral were attempted earlier than the 1540s. It is not difficult to understand why the more light-hearted genre came first. Of the genres of ancient theatre which were available for Humanist study, it was the Roman comedy of Plautus and Terence which was most approachable. Far fewer people got to grips with the ancient Greek language, for all its prestige, than with Latin. Moreover, to understand Greek tragedy required an enormous leap of the social and religious imagination, while the comedy of Aristophanes employed a subversive mockery of living individuals and institutions with which Italian Renaissance society was explicitly unwilling to cope. By contrast, even before the year 1500, Roman comedies were well known in the schoolroom, and therefore familiar at least to an upper-class male audience. Terence had long been studied just for his moral aphorisms, and knowledge of Plautus had been boosted by the rediscovery of twelve new comedies in 1429. Plautus and Terence were first performed experimentally in Latin in universities and academies. From the late fifteenth century in princely courts, especially those of the Este rulers of Ferrara, they were given in long-winded verse translations. Then, in the early sixteenth century, new plays were composed in the same style, but with a crucial (and previously unheard-of) tendency to use prose more often than verse.

Plautine and Terentian comedy was known to have been adapted from the Attic 'New Comedy' of Menander and others, of which the Renaissance had no examples available. But the fact that the Romans had copied and adapted the Greeks encouraged Italians to do the same in turn with the Romans: it legitimised the procedure known in rhetorical theory as *contaminatio*, whereby 'theatergrams' of character, plot and scene structure could be borrowed, reworked and permuted from earlier sources. In its content Roman comedy was an essentially playful genre, which mocked social stereotypes in a generalised and harmless way, allowed controlled anarchy and mayhem to dominate the stage for a while, but restored some kind of order in its dénouements. (And in this respect it conformed easily to the long-standing institution of Carnival, the season when the earliest 'erudite' comedies were often first staged.) Most of all, the kind of society with which it played its games was surprisingly similar to the one in which Italian Renaissance aristocrats and merchants still lived. The world of Roman comedy was obstinately urban rather than rural in its power structure, its economics and its prejudices, as Italian society, based on city-states, had continued to be. (There was in Italy none of the fascinated agonising, which pervades English Jacobean comedy, about the emergence of the city as a new factor to contend with in a society still ideologically dominated by the great country houses of the gentry.) The fundamental hierarchical tensions about which most of the taboo-challenging jokes were made – conflicts between fathers and sons, and between masters and servants – were still entirely recognisable. The one area where fashions and tastes had moved on was in the type of sexual intrigue preferred as the basis of the story: young men pursuing prostitute slave girls, with whom they were temporarily infatuated, had to be replaced by a different sort of youthful infatuation which could lead to marriage. This, as we shall see, was rapidly achieved by the blending of narrative material derived from medieval romance and *novella* into the intrigue structures of the Roman sources. Most other Roman plot conventions were inherited without difficulty, including the very limited range of characters which this brand of comedy normally contained: wimpish young male lovers; irascible, miserly, sometimes lustful fathers; astute irrepressible servants or slaves; braggart soldiers; parasites; entertainingly unscrupulous villains, often in the role of pimps.

The striking under-development of female roles in Roman comedy was also copied, to begin with, in these new Italian models. This is a fact that needs to be recognised if we are to construct an accurate overview of European theatre history. We tend to see early modern comedy as a genre which creates sympathetic female characters and then affords them considerable initiative in the plot. Although the first moves in this direction were in fact made in Italy (more specifically in Siena, as will be detailed below) – and even though it was the Italian professionals who first set female performers to play female roles – the attractively subversive, truly comic feminism which we might now associate with the genre was really developed much more in England and France than in Italy. Such evidence as we can decipher suggests that roles for Italian star actresses in both scripts and scenarios, in the later sixteenth century, placed their emphasis on stylised sentimentalism and rhetorical heroics, rather than on warm-hearted female common sense. They therefore overlapped more, in this initial Italian phase, with characteristics also developed in tragedy and pastoral.

As well as actually copying Roman plots, *commedia erudita* distinguished itself firmly from medieval theatre in a number of ways. It practised a genre distinction which was also a social segregation: its characters were taken exclusively from a middle and lower range of urban society. (The ruling class was to be depicted in tragedy; and the countryside was dealt with in a range of other ephemeral genres, which eventually transformed themselves into 'regular' pastoral drama.) It restricted itself in practice – and then later also in published theory – to a single immovable street setting, and to an action lasting not more than one day. (The resulting impossibility of staging domestic scenes indoors was a severe limitation, which one day would have to be removed. The breakthrough was achieved in France rather than Italy, most of all in the comedies of Molière.) The new comedy tried to offer a self-contained drama, with little or no acknowledgement of the spectators who were watching it: this was a convention difficult to maintain in comic monologues, but it was a principle which nevertheless underpinned all Italian drama which imitated the classics. The dramatic language used was mimetic, rather than poetic or allusive: instead of exploring inner psychology or wider implications, it offered an exterior imitation of how characters might behave and sound to an observer, granted their personalities and their predicaments. And this last trend was accentuated by the new unprecedented tendency to write comic texts for performance in prose rather than verse – a practice which may have arisen by accident rather than by design, but which was clearly preferred by audiences since it rapidly became the norm. (Verse comedies, amounting to less than one fifth of sixteenth-century production, include the later plays of Ariosto and a relatively high proportion of those written in Florence.) This is another relatively neglected Italian influence on the rest of Europe: the first ever English play text in prose was George Gascoigne's 1566 translation of Ariosto's *I suppositi*.

It was in fact Ludovico Ariosto who effectively launched the new genre of originally composed 'regular' comedy: at the Este court in Ferrara, with

La Cassaria (1508, 'The Play of the Strong Box') and *I suppositi* (1509, 'The Substitutes'). (In 1503 there had been a shorter five-act play called *Formicone*, composed in Mantua for schoolboy performance before Isabella d'Este.) From then on, *commedia erudita* developed – slowly at first – in various other Italian cities. The performance context varied with the political and social structure of the state concerned. The patronage of an absolute ruler and his court, as in Ferrara and Urbino, was not available in republics like Siena and Venice: here other arrangements had to be made which were dependent on individual enterprise, on nascent Academies, or on clubs and confraternities working more loosely within a state context. Florence was a republic, at least in name, until 1530, and then it became a Medici principality; so there a courtly structure imposed itself relatively late on a previously more fluid type of organisation. It was in the courts of Ferrara and Florence, more centralised and more determined to spend money on display, that the classical-style texts always risked being swamped by elaborately staged interludes mounted between the acts, involving professional singers, dancers, musicians and designers.

In this context, rivalry between the different states did produce attempts to establish identifiable local styles: none the less, Humanist theatre was such a minority activity that everyone learned from reading everyone else's texts, especially in the earliest years of the genre. Other contributors to this volume will show how *commedia erudita*, and some associated forms of theatre, evolved separately in Ferrara, Florence and the Venetian Republic. We begin, however, with one play from one of the minor courts which had a seminal influence on the development of classical comedy in Italy as a whole.

Bibbiena's *La Calandra*

The most reprinted *commedia erudita* of the century, and one of the most frequently performed, was *La Calandra* ('Calandro's play'), composed by Bernardo Dovizi da Bibbiena, a political adviser to the Medici family who ended his career as a Cardinal. It was mounted in Urbino in 1513, as part of an elaborate festivity to celebrate a treaty, and was directed by Count Baldassare Castiglione, who will later include Bibbiena in *Il cortegiano* ('The Courtier') as one of the circle of friends at the Urbino court discussing the behaviour of the perfect courtier: Bibbiena is given the task of talking about jokes and the causes of laughter. With this comedy Bibbiena becomes the second identifiable author, after Ariosto, to experiment with the new genre in performance: *La Calandra* would prove immensely influential. While Bibbiena's play has clear echoes of Ariosto's early comedies, the Ferrarese seems to return the favour with the reminiscences of *La Calandra* in his later plays. The first of the twenty-two Renaissance editions of Bibbiena's comedy appeared in 1521.

The plot deals with the misunderstandings revolving around a pair of identical twins, and thus alludes to Plautus' *Menaechmi*, which was well known from performances in translation. But a scurrilous, titillating twist is provided by the fact that the twins are of different sexes, and both addicted to cross-dressing to conceal their true identities. The resulting hilarious confusions of gender roles are developed in the context of an adulterous affair, in which an impossibly gullible husband is roundly humiliated. The husband is named Calandro, after Boccaccio's well-known fictional idiot Calandrino, and so the title and the general spirit of the play allude at least as much to the most bawdy stories in the *Decameron* as to Plautus, although Bibbiena defers minimally to the conventional moral code by marrying the twins off swiftly at the end to spouses whom the audience do not meet.

In some of the longer speeches, Bibbiena unblushingly recycles passages of Boccaccio's prose, following the views of another member of the *Cortegiano* circle, Pietro Bembo, whose advice to writers of the day was that they should imitate Boccaccio for prose and Petrarch for verse, and a profusion of popular Tuscan expressions gives a liveliness to Bibbiena's dialogue, encouraging Machiavelli along a similar path in the *Mandragola* soon after. Bibbiena's dependence on Boccaccio will have reassured an audience unaccustomed to the new form of drama that this is a world of comic fiction with which they are already familiar. The exploitation of *novella* material, to complement Plautus, was an important step for Humanist comedy, taken significantly early. At the same time, many of the scenes in which Calandro is mocked by his servant Fessenio are played directly at the audience and have the self-contained feel of vaudeville sketches. Already one detects a tendency for simple performance values to compete with, and even to suppress, the more 'literary' desire to construct an autonomous coherent fiction bound by rules of verisimilitude. The aesthetic criteria of scholarly dramatists and the audience's desire for sheer entertainment are pulling potentially in different directions: the latter preference would later be exploited by the more performance-oriented *commedia dell'arte*.

Note

For publications relevant to this chapter see the Renaissance bibliography, pp. 36–8.

4 Ariosto and Ferrara

PETER BRAND

The prominence of Ferrara in the early history of the Italian theatre is perhaps surprising: comedy, pastoral and tragedy were all crucially influenced by writers active at the Ferrarese court where the Este family had control from early in the fourteenth century until late in the sixteenth. The Estense leaders were quick to realise the importance of public ceremony and spectacle in reinforcing their despotic but broadly popular rule, and throughout the *Quattrocento* a succession of jousts, parades, ceremonial entries, religious processions, musical performances, Carnival festivities and other street entertainments helped to impress on the Ferrarese of all classes the wealth and power of their rulers and the advantages of a dutiful submission. The chroniclers of such events admiringly liken the centre of the city to a theatre, an impression that persists with visitors throughout this period. A bedazzled Tasso in 1565 declared that the whole city seemed to him 'like a wonderful, extraordinary stage-set'.[1]

In addition to the public ceremonies and festivities more formal dramatic entertainments both religious and secular began to emerge early in the *Quattrocento*. As elsewhere in Italy the church sponsored religious performances (*sacre rappresentazioni*) which continued throughout the century: the pious Ercole d'Este (1471–1505) was a keen promoter of Passion plays and others on the lives of the saints which were performed in the churches or in the piazza, where much of the city's public ceremonial was enacted: on one occasion Ercole is reported to have washed the feet of 143 poor persons on a platform specially erected in the square, taking care to ensure that the stage properties were kept for subsequent comedies. There was also a current of amateur dramatic activity in the university where the students put on readings of Roman plays and their own irreverent farces in Latin. But a new, more ambitious secular drama in the vernacular was beginning to emerge, inspired variously by classical models, Italian narrative sources and native chronicle. This was sporadic and experimental, mostly hybrid in nature and slow to develop into any recognisable genre, although the labels of *comedia* and *tragedia* were sometimes claimed. Francesco Ariosto drew on Ovid for a *'comedia', Iside*, performed before Leonello d'Este in 1445, and a *Comedia d'Hippolito et Leonora*, based on Florentine chronicle, was acted by members of the Este family in 1492.

Various mythological and pastoral entertainments in the form of 'eclogues' were also frequently given, anticipating the emergence of the pastoral play in the late fifteenth century. Niccolò da Correggio's *Cefalo*, a five-act mythological play based on Ovid was given a splendid presentation at court in 1487. He called this a *'fabula'*, not sure whether it was a tragedy or a comedy. Antonio Tebaldeo called his version of Poliziano's *Orfeo*, recast in five acts with a tragic chorus, a *'tragoedia'*, as did Antonio Cammelli his *Filostrato e Pamphila* (1499), a five-act dramatisation of Boccaccio's story of Guiscardo and Ghismonda. Perhaps the best of these early Ferrarese plays was Matteo Maria Boiardo's *Timone*, a dramatised version of a dialogue by Lucian which he turned into an allegorical *'comedia'* at some point in the 1480s. We do not know whether this was actually performed – both texts and information about performance are scarce for the fifteenth century.

It was not Lucian, however, but the Roman comic dramatists, Plautus and Terence, who would determine the future of comedy in Italy, and here Ferrara was strongly placed thanks to its university and strong Humanist tradition. The appointment of the distinguished scholar Guarino da Verona as tutor to the young Leonello d'Este in 1429 would prove a key factor in the acclimatisation of Roman comedy in Italy. Guarino persuaded Leonello to use his influence to obtain the recently discovered codex of twelve previously lost comedies of Plautus which Guarino then copied; and it was another tutor to the Este family, Giovanni Aurispa, who in 1433 found the manuscript of the fourth century Donatus' commentary on Terence. Both these discoveries generated great excitement in the scholarly community and initiated a succession of editions, translations and then performances of the Latin comedies, the first of which, Plautus' *Menaechmi*, was given in Ferrara in 1486. Thereafter Italian versions of Roman comedies were performed regularly in Ferrara as standard entertainment for favoured visitors or during Carnival.

The key figure in this process was a poet in Cardinal Ippolito d'Este's service at the beginning of the sixteenth century, Ludovico Ariosto, future author of the *Orlando furioso*, the most successful of a long line of chivalrous romances with which *cantastorie* (minstrels) had been entertaining Italian and particularly Ferrarese audiences for the past two hundred years. These oral recitations were themselves mini dramatic performances in which the narrator mounted a bench and chanted his tale, acting out his material with the aid of a tattered script and to the accompaniment of a drum or stringed instrument, urged on by a lively audience, whether in the ducal palace or in the square outside. Ariosto's familiarity with these scenes led him naturally into other forms of entertainment. In 1493 he accompanied a group of twenty Ferrarese actors to Pavia to perform a series of Roman comedies for the Sforza family, and soon after this he was translating various Roman comedies for the Estensi in Ferrara. Then he produced an original play of his own in the vernacular.

This was *La cassaria*, a five-act comedy in prose, performed with *intermezzi* of music and dance in a hall in the palace during the Carnival celebrations in Ferrara in March 1508. A second performance was given in 1529, and several others, in a revised version, in 1531–2, all in Ferrara. If not strictly the first vernacular comedy on the Roman model to have been composed in Italy, *La cassaria* was the first to make its mark in performance and to receive wide publicity, and it provided the model for the comic dramatists who followed. A second comedy, *I suppositi*, also in prose, was written for Carnival the following year and was performed in the palace, with *intermezzi* and a pantomime at the end, in February 1509. A further performance was given in the Vatican in March 1519 at the request of the Pope, who was said to have been heartily amused by the ribald humour that scandalised some other members of his party. Ariosto revised this play and recast it in verse some time between 1528 and 1531, but we have no evidence that this version was ever performed.

Ferrara's involvement in the war between France and Spain inter-rupted theatrical entertainment in the city after the 1509 performance of *I suppositi*, and Ariosto's third comedy, *Il negromante* ('The Necromancer'), which he had begun that year, was not completed until 1520, following a request from Leo X for a play for the Carnival in Rome. It was not, however, performed until the Ferrarese Carnival of 1528, in a revised version. Meantime comedy had moved on elsewhere in the peninsula with performances of Bibbiena's *Calandra*, Machiavelli's *Mandragola* and Ruzante's *Pastoral*, among others – so it is no surprise that Ariosto's last comedy, *La Lena*, performed for Carnival in Ferrara in 1528, proved to be his most ambitious and sophisticated play. Another comedy, *I studenti*, which Ariosto had begun in this later phase of his career, remained unfinished and was completed after his death in separate versions by his son Virginio and his brother Gabriele.

Ariosto's comedies were all written for performance during Carnival and were put on at court at the expense of the Este family and under the direction of the author, who on various occasions recited the Prologue himself. The actors were assembled from the gentlemen of the court, reinforced by semi-professionals – minstrels, jesters, *cantastorie* and others, sometimes borrowed from nearby Mantua or Padua. The *sala grande*, suitably furnished for each occasion, was large, said to hold several thousand people, sometimes crammed so tightly that they could not raise their arms to blow their noses. All classes were admitted: gentry, court servants and Ferrarese citizens alike, subject to the discretion of the door-keepers and the availability of space, and audiences could be quite rowdy. They had come to expect an impressive spectacle (which the religious performances already provided): in 1486 for a staging of the *Menaechmi* expensive machinery was installed to move a boat with oars, sails and ten persons across the stage. Showy costumes added to the expense: for the wedding of Alfonso and Lucrezia Borgia in 1502, when several Roman comedies were staged, a parade of 110 costumes was arranged beforehand to show that they had all been specially made for the occasion and that none was to be used twice.

All four of Ariosto's comedies are explicit imitations of plays by Plautus or Terence: they all centre on family problems, and particularly on the efforts of young men abetted by their servants to obtain girls denied them by their elders: deception and disguise are their prime tools, making for scenes of outrageous and boisterous humour whether they succeed or, as is often the case, fail – leaving it to the late revelation of a long-lost identity to remove the obstacles to marriage and a happy ending. Women's roles are restricted and acted by boys. The classical 'unities' are observed with a single action presented on an unchanged street-scene within a limited time-space. Monologues and asides, eavesdropping and overhearing, mistaken identities, addresses to the audience, humour from double entendre, horse-play and other staple devices of Roman comedy are the norm. As with other genres at this time the imitation of classical sources is explicitly acknowledged: in the Prologue to *I suppositi* the author justifies his dependence on Plautus and Terence on the grounds that they, in their time, had imitated Menander and Apollonius, and there is in fact a strong likeness between the three comic theatres, New Greek, Roman and the Italian of Ariosto.

At the same time the Roman sources are localised and modernised: the settings, after the Greek Mytilene of *La Cassaria*, are explicitly Italian: Ferrara or Cremona. There are frequent allusions to local places, customs, even contemporary personalities: well-known Ferrarese drunks (Cucchiulino, Moschino), a surveyor (Torbido), the court dwarf (Santino) etc. Messengers are sent off along recognisable routes and there are jibes at local officials and sharp practices – nothing so drastic as to reflect discredit on the Este family but enough to win approval from the locals. And in the later plays two contemporary types join the cast of stock Roman characters – the Necromancer or quack astrologer, who exposes the credulity of Italians of all classes, and the pimp Lena, drawn straight from the streets of Ferrara.

This last play, *La Lena*, shows us Ariosto branching out boldly with a secondary action that comes to outshine the primary one in an approach to a more realistic comedy of manners. Lena is here made the mistress of the girl's father and has a complaisant husband who takes advantage of his wife's liaison to live rent-free in her lover's house. This lifelike trio rumble along discontentedly behind the cardboard lovers for most of the play but are given the stage to themselves in the final scenes of the revised version, half reconciled but still complaining, as if underlining the continuum of real life in contrast with the artificial ending of Plautine comedy. And for this clever cameo of contemporary Ferrarese society the contrived disguises and concealed identities of Roman comedy are omitted.

The context of course is radically different from that of the Roman plays, with the courtly occasion markedly influencing the performance – above all in the accompaniment of elaborate *intermezzi* between the now obligatory five acts. Plautus' comedies were performed without a break to avoid the audiences drifting away to rival attractions nearby, but the Roman theorists, with Greek New Comedy in mind, insisted on a five-act structure, and the editors of late antiquity felt obliged to insert act-divisions in their texts of Roman comedy. Ariosto's adoption of the five-act structure served therefore both to underline his classical credentials and to allow time for the interludes of spectacle and music customary at court performances. These would in due course prove a more dependable audience attraction than the comedies themselves.

A more demanding challenge for the Ferrarese playwright, however, was that of finding a language that could match the sparkle of Plautus or the elegance of Terence. For comedy a language reflecting everyday usage was clearly desirable, but most of Ariosto's audience spoke a dialect unintelligible outside Ferrara and the domestic vernacular which Ariosto produced with a wider audience in view didn't somehow ring true – Machiavelli jibed that Ariosto had to leave out jokes altogether because he couldn't use the obscure Ferrarese witticisms and he didn't know any more accessible ones. The result was a rather flat and wooden dialogue compared with that of *La mandragola*.

The problem was compounded by the choice of medium – prose or verse? Ariosto originally composed *La cassaria* and *I suppositi* in prose but later recast them in verse, which he then used for the later *Negromante* and *Lena* from the start. Verse enhanced the prestige of his theatre in that it followed classical precedent but the choice of a suitable Italian metre was a difficult one. The sacred theatre and the translations of Plautus and Terence employed octaves or tercets, which imposed an artificial structure on dialogue, and most of the successful dramatists who followed Ariosto used prose. Ariosto's choice fell on the unrhymed *sdrucciolo*: as, for example, 'Vorrebbe il dolce senza amaritu-dine' ('He wants the sweet without the bitter'; *Lena*, II. 2). He may have felt that this came closest to the *iambic senarius* of Roman comedy and to everyday speech, but whatever the reason for his choice it found few admirers.

Nevertheless, Ariosto's comedies were enthusiastically applauded in Ferrara and he was unable to stop the rash of pirated editions that followed. These and Ferrara's political and cultural links with other Italian courts (Mantua and Padua particularly, but also Rome, Urbino, Venice, Pavia and Milan) ensured that his success did not remain purely local; already in Urbino in 1513 Bibbiena's *Calandra*, for example, shows clear echoes of *I suppositi*. And all over Italy, where comedy became the dominant dramatic genre, it was Ariosto's model that prevailed – even to the extent of curbing innovation: the most lively and original comic dramatists who followed – Machiavelli, Aretino, Ruzante – all tended to fall back in their later years on the erudite prototype, which was seen as seminal, so that the classical stimulus brought something of a national dimension to comedy, in place of the provincial farces and pantomimes of the past. Other European dramatists took note, even if branching out in their own fashion, as did Lope de Vega and Shakespeare. But even in England George Gascoigne's translation of *I suppositi* (*The Supposes*, 1566) was hailed as the first prose comedy in English literature and Edmund Spenser composed five comedies (now lost) on the 'classic' model of Ariosto.

Note

1 See T. Tasso, *Dialoghi*, ed. E. Raimondi, 3 vols., Florence, 1958, vol. II, ii, p. 675.

Bibliography

Scripts

Ariosto, Ludovico, ed. C. Segre, *Tutte le opere*. Vol. IV, ed. A. Casella, *Commedie*, Milan, 1974.
    The Comedies of Ariosto, trans. Edmond M.Beame and Leonard G. Sbrocchi, Chicago, 1975.

Criticism

Brand, P. *Ludovico Ariosto,* Edinburgh, 1974.
Catalano, M. *Vita di L. Ariosto*, 2 vols., Geneva, 1930.
De Luca, A. *Il teatro di L. Ariosto*, Rome, 1981.
Scoglio, E. *Il teatro alla Corte Estense,* Lodi, 1965.
Segre, C. (ed.) *L. Ariosto: lingua, stile e tradizione,* Milan, 1976.
See also in the Renaissance bibliography, pp. 36–8 above, the entries under Cruciani, Ferroni, Folena, Greco, Guidotti and Zorzi.

5 Machiavelli and Florence

PETER BRAND

Republican Florence, as compared with Ferrara, was slow to develop any formal secular theatre in the fifteeenth century. Much of the public entertainment continued to take place in the streets, during Carnival or on special occasions when the guilds mounted elaborate displays of spectacle, music and dance, and the *cantastorie* set up their platforms in the *piazze* to attract audiences with the traditional tales of chivalry and romance. By the late fifteenth century, some of this popular culture was beginning to translate into more permanent form in the colourful *canti carnascialeschi* of Lorenzo de' Medici and the *Morgante* of Luigi Pulci. But it was the religious confraternities which dominated much of the festivities with their devotional processions and performances, in the churches or in the *piazze* outside, of *sacre rappresentazioni*, presentations of Christ's Passion or the lives of the saints, in which Florence led the way for the rest of the peninsula – the surviving scripts of these plays come predominantly from Florence.

This being so, the Humanists' attempts to put on rival presentations of Roman comedy faced frequent objections from the church authorities, who protested against the 'shameless' actors of secular plays. Nevertheless, teachers and students in the schools and the university did succeed in mounting performances of the Roman plays, in Latin and in translation, although such presentations occurred less frequently than in Ferrara, Venice or Rome. The students who acted Terence's *Andria* at the school of Giorgio Antonio Vespucci in 1476 were encouraged to put on further performances at the home of members of the Medici family and then in the Palazzo della Signoria. However a performance of Plautus' *Menaechmi* in 1488 by pupils of Paolo Comparini was preceded by a prologue lamenting the hostility of 'sanctimonious spoilsports'.

The key figure in the Florentine contribution to the new vernacular theatre was Niccolò Machiavelli, whose *Mandragola* dates from 1518, but there were other Florentine playwrights in the early years of the sixteenth century who were experimenting with vernacular comedy. Lorenzo di

Filippo Strozzi composed a five-act *Commedia in versi* about 1506, and another comedy, *La Pisana*, somewhat later, but there is little extant information. Another Florentine, Jacopo Nardi, is reported to have got his *Commedia dell'amicizia* performed before the Signoria during the Gonfalo-niership of Piero Soderini (between 1502 and 1512). He confessed he was not sure to which genre his play belonged: it was in five acts, in a variety of metres, and had a cast of characters and final recognition scene reminiscent of Roman comedy, but it was based on a novella from the *Decameron* (x. 8), a morally uplifting one, as was his second comedy, *I due felici rivali* ('The Two Happy Rivals', 1513, based on *Decameron*, v. 5). It is interesting to find this frank mixture of Roman and medieval elements at this early stage in the evolution of Italian comedy, and particularly to note the prominence of Boccaccio, whose tale of rival lovers probably derives in its turn from a Roman comedy, Plautus' *Epidicus*, which thus regains its original dramatic form in a new life.

Machiavelli claims in his Prologue to the *Mandragola* that he has written it in order to

> . . .fare el suo tristo tempo più suave,
> perch' altrove non have
> dove voltare el viso.

(Teatro, p. 68, lines 51–2)

(make his unhappy life more agreeable, because he has nowhere else to turn his face)

since he had been deprived of office on the re-entry of the Medici to the city in 1512. *La mandragola*, probably written in 1518 and performed in a private house in Florence the same year, was an immediate success. Further performances followed in Rome and Venice, and in the Romagna shortly after, and there were numerous printed editions throughout the sixteenth century. It has retained its popularity to the present day and is generally reckoned the best Italian comedy of the Renaissance. It was not in fact Machiavelli's first or only play – he had earlier written a comedy, *Le maschere* ('The Masks'), said to be in the style of Aristophanes, and now lost. He made several translations of Roman comedies, one of which, a mostly literal version of Terence's *Andria*, survives, as well as a free adaptation of Plautus' *Casina*, which we will consider shortly.

La mandragola takes its title from the mandrake root, said in Machiavelli's day to act as a fertility drug, but also to poison the first person to touch it after it was dug up, so that this task was normally entrusted to a dog. Machiavelli constructs an elaborate practical joke on the basis of this belief. Callimaco, having fallen in love with the beautiful wife of the elderly Florentine lawyer, Messer Nicia, enlists the services of a wily go-between, Ligurio, who devises an outrageous plan: Callimaco is disguised as a doctor so that he can persuade Nicia, who is desperate for an heir, to administer a mandrake potion to his wife Lucrezia, and to avoid the unfortunate fate of dying suffered by the first man to lie with her thereafter, by bundling some young stranger from off the streets into bed with her. After this Nicia will be free to enjoy his normal relations with his wife, since the conspirators intend to pass off Callimaco in disguise as the poor stranger. Nicia agrees but foresees trouble in persuading Lucrezia. Ligurio's solution is to enlist the services of the lady's confessor, Frate Timoteo, and her mother, to persuade her to abandon her scruples – which they do with some extraordinary, Jesuitical, one might say Machiavellian, arguments. The *beffa* is totally successful: Callimaco is actually pushed into bed with Lucrezia by her unsuspecting husband, who is so delighted at the prospect of an heir that he gives Callimaco the key to his house, and Lucrezia agrees to become his mistress.

In its day the *Mandragola* was praised as a model comedy and it does conform to the Roman norm in its five-act structure and its adherence to the unities of time, place and action. But modern scholars almost unanimously class it as exceptional – not least because of its condoning of adultery at the end; and the action itself is unusually simple and straightforward, a *beffa* which succeeds in its every particular without any of the conventional obstacles that beset the standard Roman intrigue and so not needing any final recognition scene to solve the problems that have arisen. We recognise it immediately not as a Roman comedy but a Boccaccesque novella, with a narrative rather than a dramatic *raison d'être*. The plot is in fact close to Boccaccio's story of Ricciardo Minutolo (*Decameron*, III. 6) and there are unmistakable reminiscences of other *novelle*: for example, Nicia comes close to Boccaccio's simpleton, Calandrino, at times. Machiavelli seems to have difficulty in stretching his successful *beffa* over five acts and intersperses a good deal of Carnivalesque farce: Callimaco's impersonation of a doctor and his examination of the urine sample that Nicia extorts from Lucrezia for example, and the elaborate disguise of the conspirators as revellers, with a mock-deafness scene and a good deal of horseplay. The bedding of Lucrezia is narrative rather than dramatic material, of course, and the final act comes as something of an anti-climax where we can't really share the hilarity of those who have taken part in the joke.

In his recourse to the *Decameron* Machiavelli follows the contemporary Florentine dramatists, Strozzi and Nardi, mentioned above, but he was probably most influenced by Bibbiena's practice in *La Calandra*, anticipating a development which will become increasingly prominent in the sixteenth century and challenge the model of Roman comedy which Ariosto's comedies had offered. Machiavelli's use of prose also distinguishes his comic practice from that of Ariosto who had turned to verse for his first draft of *Il negromante* ('The Necromancer') by this time (after the prose of his first two comedies). Subsequent Florentine comic playwrights regularly followed Machiavelli's example. The latter went so far as to deny Ariosto's comedies any real comic flair on account of his poor dialogue, which he attributed to Ariosto's Ferrarese background and language. Comedy was to make people laugh, for which Machiavelli considered witty language and local, topical jests indispensable: and the *Mandragola* is full of colourful, idiomatic expressions grounded in everyday, Florentine usage. Messer Nicia is the prime exponent of this with his crude, popular and slangy speech: 'Cacasangue!' ('bloody shit!') is a typical interjection, 'Cacastecchi' ('stick-shitters') a characteristic term of abuse; Ligurio mocks Nicia's boasted travels (as far as Pisa!): 'avendo voi pisciato in tante neve' ('you who have peed in so many snows', 1.2). Some of Machiavelli's popular expressions seem to have defeated even the Florentines. When his compatriot Guicciardini planned a performance of the play in the Romagna he had to ask for the meaning of one passage:

LIGURIO: Noi torniamo ora!
NICIA: Come disse la botta all'erpice! (*Teatro*, p. 102)
(LIGURIO: Back soon!
NICIA: As the toad said to the harrow! [which kept returning and scraping its back])

The anchoring of this outrageous fantasy in the everyday life of contemporary Florence is no less appealing to a modern than it must have been to a contemporary audience. Machiavelli follows Ariosto and Bibbiena in setting his play in modern Italy and making the recent wars the background of his action. But more than this he seems to write with his contemporary analysis of history and politics still echoing in his mind, as

we see from his prologue to *Clizia*, where he insists: 'Se nel mondo tor-
nassino i medesimi omini, come tornano i medesimi casi, non passer-
ebbono mai cento anni che noi non ci trovassimo un' altra volta insieme
a fare le medesime cose che ora' (Teatro, p. 23); ('if the same people came
back into the world it wouldn't take a hundred years for us to find
ourselves doing exactly the same things again that we have just been
doing') – the basis of his belief that we can learn from history and that
political science is indeed possible. And the almost clockwork success of
the scheming on the stage seems to underline this. It seems like another
challenge to Ariosto, whose comic actions are explicitly attributed to
Fortune. Machiavelli's characters mouth the same adages that we find in
the *Principe*: 'Io ho sempre sentito dire che gli è ufizio d'un prudente
pigliare de' cattivi partiti el migliore' (*Teatro*, p. 94); (I've always heard
it said that a wise person, faced with various bad options, should take the
best', *Mandragola*, III. 1) The seduction of Lucrezia is carried on in the
language of a military campaign, and her acceptance of Callimaco is
presented like that of a besieged city welcoming its conqueror: 'io ti
prendo per signore, patrone, guida: tu mio padre, tu mio difensore' (v. 4);
('I take you as my lord, my patron, my guide: you are my father, my
defender') – which has encouraged some rather extravagant readings of
the play as political allegory, equating Lucrezia with Florence, Callimaco
with Lorenzo de' Medici and Nicia with Piero Soderini. But the current of
political allusion and innuendo cannot disguise the essence of Carnival
extravaganza in this outrageous farce, which was intended above all to
make people laugh, even if its stark picture of self-interest ruling supreme
leaves a bitter taste. Could Machiavelli's Florence really have been as
cynical as this – the priests as corrupt, the lawyers as petty, the mothers
as indifferent, the lovers as calculating? Some critics indeed have seen *La
mandragola* not as the quintessential Italian Renaissance comedy but as its
most compelling tragedy.

If the bitterness of the *Mandragola* seems to reflect something of
Machiavelli's continued resentment at his exclusion from political office,
it is tempting to associate the comparative geniality of *Clizia* with the
upturn in his personal fortunes some five or six years later. *Clizia* is a free
adaptation of Plautus' *Casina*, written in January 1525 and performed in a
private house the same month. Plautus' play is a light-hearted farce based
on the obsession of an elderly lawyer Lysidamus with his young ward
Casina, a girl of unknown parentage who has grown up in his house and

also attracted the affection of his son. The old man's scheme in the *Casina* is to make her his mistress by marrying her to a compliant servant, but his wife proposes a rival candidate. They resort to the drawing of lots, which favours Lysidamus, but he is thwarted in his scheme to take the bride-groom's place in bed by his wife's counter-plan of substituting a boy, dressed as Casina, who beats up the old man and humiliates him. A couple of lines in Plautus' Epilogue tell us that Casina will be revealed to be of good family and can therefore marry the son.

Machiavelli's treatment of the Roman comedy provides a good illustration of Italian 'imitation' of ancient sources generally. While preserving the outline of Plautus' action, he recasts the structure and refashions the characters – only the central portion of *Clizia* follows Plautus at all closely (from III. 3 to V. 8) the rest being Machiavelli's own invention. Significantly, he introduces the son, Cleandro, who does not appear in *Casina* but occupies centre-stage for all of Machiavelli's first act, thus providing us with a rather more serious, typically Terentian contest between father and son in place of Plautus' music-hall battle between husband and wife. Machiavelli also stages the final recognition scene where Cleandro is enabled to marry Clizia, thus restoring the love-interest of the Greek source, which Plautus had decided to skate over. Also revealing is Machiavelli's refashioning of the relationship between the old lawyer and his wife, who is pained rather than infuriated by her husband's senile infatuation, contrasting his orderly, responsible way of life in the past with his present loss of sense and dignity. The balance of power between the two is delicately distributed: he is half afraid of his wife but she is wary of opposing him too openly.

This comparatively realistic treatment of the main characters is matched by that of the action, which is deliberately brought as close as possible to the modern audience. Machiavelli, like Bibbiena, adopts a local setting and claims to have staged a contemporary event identical to the ancient one, and he adopts a modern colloquial language with a good deal of local idiom and slang, as he had done in the *Mandragola*. But the *Clizia* is a very different play from the earlier one, with a moral lesson clearly expounded, and underlined in the prologue: the errant Nicomaco promises to return meekly at the end to his former responsible habits. The sharp, aggressive tone of the *Mandragola* disappears, the author having decided not to speak ill this time ('essendosi rimasto di dir male' – prologue). Critics have generally found *Clizia* a calmer play, reflective of a less aggrieved

Machiavelli at this later stage of his life – but it is also indicative of the pull of the conventional 'erudite' comedy model, which provided playwrights with the framework for a workaday play, one which they could turn to if their originality and invention ran out – as Ruzante and Aretino later would find. And Florentine comedy in the mid-sixteenth century would follow Machiavelli's example, combining the erudite model with the wealth of material drawn from the Italian *novella*.

Bibliography
Texts

Machiavelli, N. *Tutte le opere*, ed. M. Martelli, Florence, 1971.
  Teatro: Andria, Mandragola, Clizia, ed. G. Davico Bonino, Turin, 1979.
  The Literary Works of Machiavelli, trans. J. R. Hale, Oxford, 1961.

Critical studies

Aquilecchia, G. 'La favola Mandragola si chiama', in G. Aquilecchia (ed.), *Collected Essays in Italian Language and Literature Presented to K. Speight*, Manchester, 1971, pp. 73–100.
Dionisotti, C. *Machiavellerie*, Turin, 1980, pp. 267–364.
Parronchi, A. 'La prima rappresentazione della *Mandragola*', *Bibliofilia*, 64 (1962), 37–86.
Ridolfi, R. R. *Studi sulle commedie del Machiavelli*, Pisa, 1968.
Sumberg, T. A. '*La Mandragola*: an interpretation', *Journal of Politics*, 23 (1961), 320–40.
See also, in the Renaissance bibliography, pp. 36–8 above, the entries for Andrews, Borsellino, D'Ancona, Ferroni, Folena, Sanesi, Stauble.

6 The Intronati and Sienese comedy

RICHARD ANDREWS

In Siena one of Italy's first Academies, the Intronati ('Deaf and Daft'), established a unique club atmosphere, which eventually provided models, social even more than theatrical, for the rest of the peninsula. They regarded this as a collective enterprise, and their half-dozen published comic dramas are now recognised as having all been written by a collaborative team, whether or not they were then attributed in print to a named author. Their most famous and influential comedy, *Gli ingannati* ('The Deceived', 1532) was presented and printed (in 1537) simply as the work of the Academy. Its central amorous confusions are repeated in Shakespeare's *Twelfth Night*, of which it has long been recognised as an indirect source; so, like *La Calandra* ('Calandro's Play'), it involves a male and a female twin, and cross-dressing. However, it combines some of Bibbiena's cheerful scurrility with a number of other tones, most of which are not attributable to imitation of Plautus and only indirectly to imitation of Boccaccio. The female twin Lelia is partly a trickster, but also partly an unjustly suffering heroine determined to recapture her man; and the dénouement of the play (unlike that of *La Calandra*, but like that of *Twelfth Night*) is a restoration of orthodox social order. Lelia's predicament is expressed in lamenting speeches which are not entirely comic, and which for the first time make some attempt to give an inner life and psychological consistency to a female character. Meanwhile, the raucous female servants systematically defeat and humiliate the male characters around them. This cautious but unmistakable feminism (at least relative to what was being expressed elsewhere) can be traced back to formats of pre-Humanist drama associated particularly with Siena. In particular, enterprising but virtuous and sympathetic heroines had been welcomed on to the stages of this city before, so the Academy was satisfying some expectations already existing in its small community. Those theatergrams draw in their turn on the more sentimental and picaresque features of medieval *novella* and romance.

At the same time, the distribution of stock characters within the narrative of *Gli ingannati* foreshadows the standard roles of a typical *commedia dell'arte* company of a few decades later: we find unmistakable antecedents here of the old fathers, the lovers, the subversive servants, the braggart Captain and the pedant/Dottore, mostly relating to each other in ways that would then be repeated in *arte* scenarios.

The collective task of composing (and perhaps also of staging) *Gli ingannati* for the Intronati Academy had been masterminded by Alessandro Piccolomini (1508–79), a Humanist scholar who eventually became a bishop. The next two plays produced by the Intronati were attributed in print to him as author, but were still in practice the result of extensive collaboration. In terms of originality and of subsequent influence, the small Sienese team continued to punch above its weight: those next two comedies were reprinted, like *Gli ingannati*, significantly often during the rest of the century. *L'amor costante* ('Constant Love', composed for 1536, first printed 1540) again attempted to combine 'erudite' comedy formats with the celebration of a romantic heroine, this time a character whose female obstinacy was less associated with trickery and mischief. Conceived to be played before the Emperor Charles V, the play also contained performance elements which we would now associate with court masque. *Alessandro* (1543–4, first printed 1545) has some episodes of cross-dressing and sexual ambivalence even more daring than those of *Gli ingannati*; and it adopts the clear *commedia dell'arte* strategy of running a romantic or emotional plot in parallel with separate stories in which more ridiculous cartoon-like characters are roundly humiliated.

Meanwhile, Alessandro Piccolomini was exploring a methodology of his own whereby stock speeches and repertoire scenes from comedy would be collected in what we would now call a database, for reuse and adaptation by other dramatists. We learn of this project in a letter published in 1561, though none of the material which it produced has survived. This apparently eccentric enterprise is instructive about attitudes to theatre which were widespread at the time, and pursued by more than just one individual. The 'modular' approach to dramaturgy, whereby existing units of psychology, plot and scene structure can be recycled with modifications in innumerable different plays, can be seen as typical of Italian Renaissance theatre: it lies behind the techniques of *commedia dell'arte* improvisation as well as explaining some of the more repetitive elements of scripted comedies before and after 1600.

A comedy composed by the Intronati team in the 1560s, and attributed formally to an academician named Girolamo Bargagli (1537–86), was left in a Medici drawer for two decades, and then staged in 1589 with some cuts and alterations as part of the Grandducal wedding celebrations in Florence. Siena had by this time been absorbed into the Grand Duchy of Tuscany. *La pellegrina* ('The Pilgrim-Woman') gained extra prominence from its association with this hugely publicised event, but its workmanlike structure and well-judged sentimental appeal would probably have been influential anyway. One of its two central female characters is another obstinately faithful heroine: she disguises herself as a pilgrim in order to recapture a husband who has abandoned her because he thinks she is dead. Her role is built around extensive speeches calculated to wring a tear from the spectator's eye, and seems in retrospect to be tailor-made for the new breed of professional rhetorically trained actresses; though it is unlikely, in an amateur academic context, that Bargagli or Piccolomini would actually have thought in those terms twenty years before. Whether they did or not, this was yet another comedy which concentrated on female emotion and female fidelity in a manner which was becoming typical of the tragic and pastoral genres. Once again, perhaps for the last time, Sienese dramatists were setting a trend.

Such 'promotion' of female characters was not always accepted by *commedia erudita* dramatists in other Italian centres. It did not in itself lead to the introduction of female performers: back in 1532, Lelia and her twin brother were certainly intended to be played by a single boy actor. However, in the context of comedy in Europe as a whole, over the next two and a half centuries, the plays composed in Siena by the Intronati are significant landmarks.

7 Ruzante and the Veneto

RONNIE FERGUSON

On the European level, Venetian stage practice in the late Renaissance was seminal although, paradoxically, Venice had been marginal to the paradigm shift which, around 1500, had reintroduced scripted comedy on the Graeco-Roman model to Italy. In fact, the theatrical trajectory of the Venetian state in the sixteenth century is curiously similar to the development of its painting and architecture in this period: from periphery to centrality as a result of its cultural receptivity and a creative conflation of native and imported traditions. Venice's pre-eminence in the later sixteenth century as a thriving centre of commercial theatre and as an exporter of stage models, types and language was therefore surprising to the extent that she had not participated in the theatrical revolution maturing in courts and urban centres in the north and centre of the peninsula in the opening decades of the century. However, by 1550 Veneto theatre, having absorbed the hegemonic conventions of the five-act *commedia* model elaborated in Ferrara, Mantua, Florence, Urbino and Rome and having grafted them on to the rootstock of its own theatrical practices, was shifting the centre of gravity of Italian comedy: from script to scenario, from monolingualism to multilingualism, from amateur to professional. The key mediator in this pivotal evolution from page to stage was the Paduan playwright, actor and director Angelo Beolco, known as Ruzante (born c.1496–1502, died 1542), the most complex theatrical practitioner of the Renaissance and, with Goldoni, one of the comic geniuses of Italian theatre.

A summary chronology of Ruzante's career pattern makes manifest his eclectic receptivity to all theatrical cultures, home-grown and imported, of the time. It suggests a restless experimenter, creatively transgressing formal boundaries in his attempt to express his evolving vision and, in the process, reshaping contemporary expectations and taste. It allows us, before proceeding to a fuller appraisal of his achievement, to consider his influence and legacy in and beyond the Veneto.

Beolco's activity and output spanned twenty years (*c.*1517–*c.*1537) in the crucial period of development of Renaissance comedy. In the decade preceding his debut Venetian audiences were accustomed, at state and private festivities and functions, to the following types of stage show: lavish masked pantomimic entertainments called *momarie* or *demonstrationi*; buffoon *intermezzi*; modest, home-grown farce in the local dialect(s); pastoral eclogues; and, on more formal occasions, Roman comedy revivals in Latin or in translation. When he first took to the stage in the *Serenissima*, the city was only beginning to be exposed, fully ten years after Ariosto had revived European scripted comedy on the Plautine and Terentian model, to cutting-edge examples of the new *commedia regolare* in Tuscan, such as Machiavelli's *La mandragola* (first performed in Venice in 1522).Within little over a decade Beolco had explored the local and external manifestations of this lively but largely undistinguished theatrical scene in novel ways, infusing them with an unprecedented quality of content and an entirely new human dimension.

In *La pastoral* (*c.*1517–21, 'The Pastoral Play'), *La Betia* (*c.*1524–7), *Prima oratione* (1521, 'First Oration'), *Lettera giocosa* (*c.*1522, 'The Joyful Letter'), *Dialogo facetissimo* (1528–29, 'Witty Dialogue'), *Seconda oratione* (1528, 'Second Oration'), *La moscheta* (*c.*1528–32, 'Posh Talk'), *Parlamento de Ruzante* (*c.*1529, 'The Veteran'), *Bilora* (*c.*1530, 'Weasel'), *La Fiorina* (*c.*1532, 'Flora's Play'), *L'Anconitana* (*c.*1534–5, 'The Woman from Ancona') and *Lettera all'Alvarotto* (*c.*1536–7, 'Letter to Alvaratto') he synthesised and expanded to breaking point the possibilities of all the native Veneto comic genres in dialect, endowing his stage persona, the peasant-clown 'Ruzante', and the other peasant figures who animated his creations, with a vitality and a social, psychological and linguistic realism unknown in Veneto or other Italian farce. By the early 1530s he was experimenting with such renewed farcical traditions within the disciplines of the five-act format, in *La moscheta* and *La Fiorina*. Simultaneously, having collaborated with Ariosto in Ferrara, he was adapting Plautus, Terence and the lessons of Ariosto and Bibbiena to create dialect and multilingual regular comedies of refreshing originality in *La Piovana* (*c.*1532, 'The Girl From Piove') and *La vaccaria* (1532–3, 'The Cow Comedy'). In his last surviving stage comedy, *L'Anconitana*, he stretched the formal unities of time, place and action, combining conventional love-intrigue plot with expert stage-business, with modular gags and with the singing and dancing which had been a regular feature of his work. Such ground-breaking juxtaposition of elite plot structure and popular clowning within a multimedia and multilingual entertainment was prophetic of the direction taken in the second half of the century and beyond by Veneto and Italian theatre. In *L'Anconitana* Beolco almost certainly played alongside the writer and professional actor Andrea Calmo (1510–71), whose theatre points even more strongly in the direction of the *commedia dell'arte*. It is also significant in this regard that Beolco obsessively reworked his own scripts and was, unlike his great contemporaries Ariosto, Bibbiena, Machiavelli and Aretino, reluctant to fix the evanescent moment of performance in print. None of his plays was published in his lifetime. Indeed, three (*La pastoral, La Betia* and *Lettera giocosa*) only survived in manuscript form and remained unpublished until the twentieth century. Some of his plays, including the (semi) comic monologues *Prima oratione* and *Seconda oratione* were clearly one-offs. It can hardly be a coincidence that within three years of his death the first known professional touring troupe was signing a legal contract in Padua itself.

After Ruzante's death his influence on Veneto theatre was pervasive. The comic stage-style which flourished in Venice in the mid and later sixteenth century is known as *commedia plurilinguistica*, that is polyglot or multilingual theatre. This was a strongly performance-oriented genre, characterised by verbal pyrotechnics and slapstick, and unmistakably pre-figuring the *commedia dell'arte*. The conventional love intrigue of literary comedy became the pretext for farcical action and the pell-mell alignment of languages, dialects and accents (including Venetian, Tuscan, Paduan, Bergamask, pidgin Greek and Spanish), in large-scale productions played, one may surmise, to an increasingly eclectic public.[1] Formative influences on it were undoubtedly the pioneering verbal and staging experiments of Ruzante (although Beolco's expressionistic deployment of languages was markedly closer to reality), as well as the routines of popular Venetian *buffoni* (clowns), and the taste for wordplay and mimicry which was a characteristic of the multinational emporium that was Renaissance Venice. Its outstanding exponents were Ruzante's collaborator Andrea Calmo, Gigi Artemio Giancarli (died before 1552) – author of *La capraria* (1544, 'The Goat Play') and *La zingana* (1545, 'The Gypsy Play') – as well as Marin Negro, writer of *La pace* (performed in the open air on Campo dei Frari in Venice c.1553, published 1561). Andrea Calmo's theatre, in particular, awaits reappraisal and recognition. Calmo was a Venetian actor, playwright and poet, whose farcical, hectic comedies feature an entertaining

Figure 3: Elsa Vazzoler and Cesco Baseggio as Gnua and Ruzante in *Parlamento de Ruzante*. Produced in Venice, 1954.

babel, and he neglects coherent story-line and character in favour of subplots, types, gags and verbal expressionism. *Las Spagnolas* (1549, 'The Spanish Play'), *Saltuzza* (1551), *La potione* (1552, 'The Potion'), *La Rhodiana* (1553, 'The Rhodes Play'), *La Fiorina* (1553, 'Flora's Play') and *Il Travaglia* (1556, 'Travaglia's Play') demand to be seen rather than read. Ruzante's direct influence on *arte* theatre is harder to gauge but there is evidence that his work may have been exploited, like some of Calmo's writings, as a repository of types and situations for improvised comedy.

What relationship there is, if any, between Ruzante's theatre and the elusive trend in Venetian Renaissance drama known as *commedia cittadina* is unclear. Surviving examples are too few to allow safe conclusions, but it appears to be a comic type native to Venice and remarkable both for its urban domestic realism and for its unselfconscious use of dialect and language for realistic rather than expressionistic effect: features which, intriguingly, apply, in part, to Beolco's own theatre of his central period (1528–32). Characteristic is the charming, anonymous *Dialogo di Lucrezia* (*c.*1530–40, 'Lucretia's Dialogue') a sequence of eight brief domestic scenes in naturalistic Venetian, set in a middle-class home and featuring an overbearing mother, an impatiently confined daughter and a sympathetic-ally complicitous servant. The outstanding surviving example of the genre is the anonymous, powerfully erotic *La Veniexiana* (*c.*1535–7, 'The Venetian Woman'), one of the most original plays of the Renaissance, but which, to protect the privacy of the real Venetian aristocrats almost certainly alluded to through its protagonists, may have remained unperformed in the sixteenth century. The plot concerns Giulio, a Lombard passing through Venice, who woos Valiera, a young married noblewoman. She consents to a rendezvous. A widow, Anzola, also a patrician, is likewise attracted to Giulio, and tricks him into going to her palace for a night of love. Furious, Valiera nonetheless gives herself to Giulio. *La Veniexiana* is unusual in its non-caricatured employment of Tuscan (Giulio), Venetian (the noblewomen and their serving girls) and Bergamask (the porter, Bernardo), and its mainly indoor action. In a climate where Neoplatonic and Petrarchan treatments of love were the rule, the play is remarkable, also, for its uninhibited exploration of the power of lust over its aristocratic women protagonists. The two central females are not courtesans, they are respectable; they are the subjects not the objects of desire; and their self-centred, at times manipulative, passion is examined without a trace of idealism.

Angelo Beolco was the bastard son of a rich Paduan mercantile family, of noble origins, which had developed strong connections with Padua University, one of Renaissance Europe's great centres of learning. His father rose to become Dean of the Faculty of Medicine and Arts there and eventually took a doctorate in medicine. Angelo had an upbringing in the city, where the family's comfortable residence and associated cloth outlets were situated, but also in the countryside round Padua (the 'Pavan') where his family owned houses and property. Upon his father's death in 1524 Angelo inherited a modest amount of money: certainly not enough to keep him in the manner to which he had been accustomed. He was to remain on good terms with his family, though, and would later act financially on behalf of his three half-brothers. He married before 1527, but appears not to have lived with his wife. In the early 1520s he befriended, and subsequently obtained employment as agent of, the wealthy Venetian polymath Alvise Cornaro (c.1475–1566), in whose Paduan palace he resided for most of the remainder of his life.

Several factors in his upbringing and adulthood appear to have been particularly significant for his artistic development. A close reading of the Ruzante corpus and of the reaction of his contemporaries to it suggests an intelligent, probing artist acutely aware of the partial immunity afforded him by his clown status and popularity, expertly treading a fine line between entertaining and provoking his elite audiences, but sometimes overstepping the mark into controversy, in terms of obscenity but also of socio-political topicality. It is arguable that this restless provocativeness may, in part, be associated with his ambivalent status as the illegitimate son in a rich family. Angelo's upbringing in both city and country seems more clearly significant. His remarkable linguistic expertise in *pavan* (the rustic dialect of his beloved Paduan countryside), which he transformed by artistic mimesis and with which, welding it inextricably to gesture, he energised the wordiness of Renaissance theatre, derived initially from his childhood contact with the peasant world of the Veneto. The unprecedented understanding of the peasant mentality and empathy for peasant concerns which demarcates Beolco's depiction from the stereotypical portrayal, in medieval and Renaissance Italian literature, of the yokel as figure of fun or idealised Arcadian, is also attributable to the playwright's early rural experiences. The trademark ideological leitmotif of *la snaturalitè* (the natural), in language, manners and morals, which sustains his entire output, undoubtedly evolved, too, from his early absorption of down-to-earth country values.

Beolco's family business background and his own later entrepreneurial activities, on his own behalf and for Cornaro, also contributed to imprinting on his mind the lesson of the primacy of *la roba* (possessions), giving a hard, materialistic edge to his depiction of human motivation, particularly in *Seconda oratione, Parlamento, Bilora* and *La moscheta*. This sometimes brutal Ruzantian materialism is altogether more profound than the cruelty of the *beffa* tradition, derived from the Boccaccian novella, which dominated *commedia regolare*. His dual urban–rural upbringing runs through the anti-urban, anti-intellectual polemic of his early works (*La pastoral, Lettera giocosa* and, especially, *Prima oratione* and *La Betia*) and is pointedly apparent in the realistic dramas of his central period (the one-act *Parlamento* and *Bilora* and the five-act *La moscheta*). In these plays, the actions of *deraciné* peasants are explored in the alienating and exploitative world of the city. Their city–country antagonism is a grating and, for Beolco's Venetian audiences, uncomfortable undercurrent.

That Beolco was educated as a gentleman is patent from the reading revealed by his plays. He knew the canonical writers of Italian literature: Dante, Petrarch and, especially, the great source of Renaissance theatrical situations, Boccaccio. He made use of the language and conceits, often with parodic or satirical intent, of key Renaissance cultural figures such as Bembo, Sannazaro and Colonna. The contemporary theatrical classics of Ariosto, Bibbiena and probably Machiavelli, influenced him. He used the theatre of Plautus and Terence both in translation and in Latin. A frequenter of Cornaro's learned 'court', and of intellectuals of the stature of Sperone Speroni (1500–58), his outlook reveals the influence of the Aristotelianism which typified Renaissance Padua. It was also deeply affected in the middle and late period (*Seconda oratione, La Piovana, La vaccaria, L'Anconitana* and *Lettera all'Alvarotto*) by the philosophical currents of Epicureanism and Stoicism which lent, in the twilight of his career, a new spirituality to his trademark materialism and vitalism. To the end he maintained, in the name of the natural, a polemical hostility to the classicising tendencies of Italian High Renaissance culture. He had heard and read academic rhetoricians and could reproduce, for his own comic and subversive ends, their techniques, in bravura-monologue encomia of the city (prologue of *La Betia*) and of person and country (*Prima oratione*). He knew of, and deplored, humanist-inspired antiquarian tendencies such as the commemorative medal and collections of statues (*Prima oratione*). He understood, but disapproved of, the Platonist-inspired idealism originating in Medicean Florence with Marsilio Ficino (1433–99), which had become fashionable in the Veneto. He implicitly exposed impractical highmindedness to ridicule (*La pastoral*) and explicitly condemned the cardinal humanist value, *fama* (fame, in *Prima oratione*). Above all, the Neoplatonic and

Petrarchan idea of love, written about and discussed endlessly in the sixteenth century, was anathema to him. He burlesqued it in a mock love letter delivered as a monologue (*Lettera giocosa*), through the crude pragmatism of the Bergamask doctor Mastro Francesco (*La pastoral*) and, above all, with brutal audacity, in *La Betia*, where he conducted a point-by-point demolition of its iconic imagery based on accurate and unmistakable references to a seminal text, Bembo's *Gli Asolani* (1505, 'The Asolo Dialogues'). His polemic against the academy is less apparent in his later works, but a deliberate anti-bookishness persisted and it is, significantly, sound natural inclinations, not books, which lead 'Ruzante' towards happiness in the dream scene of his final work, the *Lettera all'Alvarotto*.

The most important personal relationship for Beolco's artistic development was that with Alvise Cornaro: agricultural improver, expert on architecture and hydraulics, indefatigable self-aggrandiser and health fanatic, whose *Trattato della vita sobria* (1566, 'Treatise on the Sober Life') became an international best-seller. With the remarkable Venetian businessman and Maecenas who was in self-imposed 'exile' in Padua in pique at his inability to convince the Venetian government to recognise his patrician status, he shared friendship and three passions: music, hunting and theatre. In the grounds of his Paduan residence, Cornaro had constructed in 1524 his splendid *all'antica* stone loggia in the form of a five-arcade *frons scenae*: probably, in effect, the first modern permanent theatre.[2] In front of this structure Beolco certainly performed his comedies for the entertainment of his own and Cornaro's friends and for distinguished guests, contributing at times to exalting Cornaro's self-image as a *uomo da ben* (socially responsible gentleman), and on occasion dovetailing his own humane interest in the peasantry with a subtle form of propaganda for his friend's aims of awakening Venice to the role of the *terraferma* (mainland), where its economic future was to be, and of winning recognition for Cornaro's spearheading role in enlightened agricultural practices and land reclamation. The troupe which Cornaro sponsored and of which Beolco was the playwright, director and star actor, was composed of affluent young Paduans, including Beolco's best friend and principal acting partner, the young patrician Marco Aurelio Alvarotto (died 1568). Based on a nucleus of 'permanent' players from the Cornaro circle, the troupe, which in all likelihood employed women for the female roles,[3] was amateur or at most semi-professional in status, but professional to all intents and purposes. In this company Beolco evolved his 'Ruzante' persona, with that linguistic virtuosity, stage presence and timing which, according to his first (and eye-witness) biographer B. Scardeone (1478–1572), enthralled audiences. With its flexible number of players Beolco went on to perform before an aristocratic public in Padua but also at the most varied venues in Venice and elsewhere in the Veneto as well as at the Este court in Ferrara, becoming, in the words of the title pages of his printed works, confirmed by the surviving records of contemporary reaction to his performances, *famosissimo* and *nominatissimo* (very famous and celebrated). The weight of family commitments and his own activities as a businessman, allied to his exhaustion of the possibilies of comic theatre available to him, appear to have occasioned his retirement from the stage in the mid-1530s. He died in 1542, on the eve of producing and acting in one of the first Italian tragedies, Sperone Speroni's *La Canace* ('Canace's Play'), for an entirely new type of sponsor, the Accademia degli Infiammati in Padua.

Beolco's fruitful association with an exceptional patron was the key practical factor in the fulfilment of his theatrical talent. Not only did Cornaro provide him with a measure of leisure and security, and a home-based theatrical environment, but his patronage also enabled Beolco to go far beyond the university fringe theatre where he certainly made his debut with *La pastoral*, exposing him to a stimulating range of venues, genres and performers in Venice and beyond, and thereby fuelling his formal and thematic development. In the early 1520s Cornaro gained access for Ruzante to the Compagnie della Calza, the clubs of young aristocrats who in the early and mid sixteenth centuries had official responsibilty for organising entertainments in Venice, and who took part personally in masked pageants, choreographed allegories and the more respectable forms of comedy. For seven successive years (1520–6) Beolco and acting partners did the rounds of the Venetian theatre season, mainly, but not exclusively, confined to Carnival. He acted side by side with the Compagnie and their professional collaborators in the grandest palaces in Venice: Ca' Foscari at San Simeon Piccolo, Ca' Arian al Anzolo Rafael, Ca' Contarini at Santa Giustina, Ca' Pesaro at San Beneto, Ca' Trevisan on the Giudecca, probably Ca' Priuli at San Severo, and even in the Doge's Palace. He sang and paraded, alongside popular entertainers and tumblers, in their street pageants, and also acted, apparently on a freelance basis, before a socially mixed public at the crowded auditorium at the Crosichieri monastery near San Zanipolo: one of the first known entrance-by-payment theatres in Italy.

The chronicler Marin Sanudo (1466–1536) recorded in his diaries nine or ten performances in Venice involving Ruzante. His terse accounts are indispensable but limited in information about staging and fail to link performances to named Ruzante plays. Nonetheless it is safe to conclude that Ruzante, with his companions, played indoors in the *palazzi* of Venice to a maximum audience of some 350 patrician spectators, including women, in the richly decorated and tapestried *portego*. This was the great rectangular *salone* running the length of the first floor, or *piano nobile*, and ending in the *loggia* overlooking the canal at one end and the courtyard at the other. If the play followed a banquet, as in Ruzante's appearances at Ca' Foscari, Ca' Pesaro and Ca' Trevisan, then the stage would have been set up at one end of the *portego*, with spectators remaining at their tables, which ran the length of the walls. On pre- or post-prandial occasions, raised, raked seating was the norm, with men and women segregated and the stage in its end location. This was also the arrangement for the performance of *La vaccaria* at Cornaro's Paduan residence, recorded by Sanudo in 1533. Beolco's monologues, *Prima oratione* and *Seconda oratione*, performed at the former residence of Caterina Cornaro in Asolo before the wealthy prelates Marco and Francesco Cornaro, were undoubtedly after-dinner entertainments involving minimal sets. In his Ferrarese performances in 1529, 1530 and 1532 Beolco either entertained with banquet *intermezzi* or performed before painted perspective sets, notably in Ariosto's famous *Teatrino*. He certainly brought back from Ferrara the classic regular comedy formula of urban backcloth flanked by a *praticabile* (three-dimensional) house to his subsequent performances in Padua. Internal and external evidence suggests that Beolco experimented with stage space in Venice in unconventional ways, dictated less by precedent and practice than by the functional demands of each play and performance. The unique stage sketch surviving in a manuscript of *La Betia* is symptomatic of his eclectic originality. It shows a rear-stage alignment of three buildings, recalling the *luoghi deputati* of the *sacra rappresentazione*. Spaces between them suggest free-standing structures, and this is confirmed by the text. Two at least of the buildings were practicable. Separating them was a fence over which stage business and dialogue were conducted. Access to the stage was by a lateral *via pubblica*, apparently perpendicular to it, and markedly unlike the central entrance of the canonical *scena comica*.

Beolco initially made his name as the outstanding performer of *vilanesca* or country-style farce in that *pavan* dialect which would become synonymous with rurality in the Veneto and which figures in each of Beolco's fourteen surviving works. He did so at a time when for complex socio-cultural reasons there was a vogue for all things rural in Venice. *Vilanesca*, the native Paduan tradition of comic theatre, had its roots in the folklore of the region but was re-elaborated and performed by intellectuals. Its most typical form was the *mariazo* or wedding play in the *frottola* metre of which a handful of examples from the late fifteenth and early sixteenth centuries survive. These were lively farces, laced with sexual innuendo, in which two country lads contended for the hand of an earthy, sharp-tongued peasant girl. Once she had made her choice (the better provider of sex and/or money) there ensued a picturesque wedding ceremony, with enumeration of dowry items. This tradition formed the backbone of Beolco's comedy in terms of peasant protagonists, conflict situations, female characterisation, truculent materialism and language. His vast verse comedy, *La Betia*, dilated all the strands of the *mariazo* and was the apotheosis of the genre. Beolco rapidly drew from his Venetian experiences, enriching his repertoire from the two farcical genres native to Renaissance Venice: *buffonesca* and *bulesca*. From the great *buffoni*, like Zuan Polo (d.1540) whom he worked alongside, he absorbed quick-change routines, knockabout stage business, patter monologues and linguistic virtuosity (adding their favourites, Bergamask and Venetian, to his *pavan*). From *bulesca*, an offshoot of *buffonesca* which gave the well-heeled public a vicarious thrill with its low-life characters, and whose best example is the anonymous *La bulesca* (c.1514, 'The Bully Boy Play'), he derived the seedy urban setting and the demobbed soldier and prostitute figures of his central period dramas. In *Parlamento*, *Bilora* and *La moscheta*, Beolco fused the lessons of all three strands. In the late 1520s, at a time of war, famine and peasant emigration to the metropolis, he elaborated a series of dark comedies whose peasants came close to three-dimensionality and tragedy. Fuelled by his own humanity and personal experience of the predicament of Venice's loyal rural subjects, and with the probable sponsorship of two Compagnie della Calza, the Zardinieri and the Ortolani, whose leaders opposed the policies of the controversial Doge Andrea Gritti (reigned 1523–38), Beolco incorporated implicit and explicit political barbs against Venice. With these terse, sombre and controversial masterpieces, offering up to his privileged spectators an unflattering image of their city and a chilling picture of the period's underprivileged victims, Angelo Beolco broke new ground in Renaissance theatre.

Notes

1 Although the Prologue of Negro's *La pace* and the various redactions of the *Proemio* of Calmo's *Il Travaglia* by the learned churchman Sisto Medici continue to hint at an essentially aristocratic public. See S. Nunziale, *Marin Negro, La pace*, Padua, 1987, pp. 24–33; Ferguson, 'Staging scripted comedy', pp. 51–2 and Vescovo, *Da Ruzante a Calmo*, pp. 315–21.

2 The recently restored *loggia*, built by Giovan Maria Falconetto, is now the centrepiece of the Casa Cornaro complex in Padua, off Via Cesarotti. It is illustrated and analysed in Calendoli and Berti, *Ruzante:Tempi di Casa Cornaro*.

3 On the controversial question of whether women or men played the female roles in Beolco's theatre see Ferguson, *Theatre of Beolco*, pp. 181–3. My assumption that real women were involved was also shared by Giorgio Padoan, in his edition of *La pastoral*, 1978, pp. 178–9. See also Messisbugo in the edition by F. Bandini of *Libro novo*, p. 39.

Bibliography

Scripts

Anon., *La Veniexiana, Commedia di Anonimo Veneziano del Cinquecento*, ed. G. Padoan, Padua, 1974.

Beolco, A. ('Ruzante'), *Teatro*, ed. L. Zorzi, Turin, 1976.

    La Pastoral, La Prima Oratione, Una Lettera Giocosa, ed. G. Padoan, Padua, 1978.

    I Dialoghi, La Seconda Oratione, I Prologhi alla Moscheta, ed. G. Padoan, Padua, 1982.

    The Veteran ('Parlamento de Ruzante'), and Weasel ('Bilora'): Two One-Act Renaissance Plays, trans. with Introduction, Notes and Bibliography by R. Ferguson, New York, 1995.

Calmo, A. *Rodiana*, ed. P. Vescovo, Padua, 1985.

    Il Travaglia, ed. P. Vescovo, Padua, 1985.

Giancarli, Gigio Artemio, *La Capraria, La Zingana*, ed. L. Lazzerini, Padua, 1991.

Messisbugo, Christoforo da, *Libro novo nel qual s'insegna a far d'ogni sorte di vivande*, Ferrara, 1549, ed. F. Bandini, Venice, 1960.

Sanuto, M. *I Diarii*, ed. R. Fulin *et al.*, 58 vols., Venice, 1879–1902.

Scardeone, B., *De antiquitate urbis Patavii et claris civibus Patavinis*, Basel, 1560.

Criticism

Ancilotto, P. 'Un buffone a Venezia nella prima metà del Cinquecento', *Quaderni di Teatro*, 8 (1986), 85–122.

Calendoli, G. and Berti, M. *Ruzante: Tempi di Casa Cornaro*, Padua, 1995.

Cocco, E. 'Una compagnia comica nella prima metà del secolo XVI', *Giornale Storico della Letteratura Italiana*, 65 (1915), 55–70.

Ferguson, R. 'The influence of Venetian popular theatre on Ruzante's *Parlamento* and *Bilora*', *Italian Studies*, 51 (1996), 113–33.

    The Theatre of Angelo Beolco: Text, Context and Performance, Ravenna, 2000.

'Staging scripted comedy in Renaissance Venice (1500–1560): a survey of the evidence', in B. Richardson *et al.* (ed.), *Theatre, Opera and Performance in Italy from the 15th Century to the Present. Essays in Honour of Richard Andrews*, Leeds, 2004, pp. 39–54.

Fido, F. 'Il teatro di Andrea Calmo fra cultura, "natura" e mestiere', in M. De Panizza Lorch (ed.), *Il teatro italiano del Rinascimento,* Milan, 1980.

Padoan, G. *La Commedia Rinascimentale Veneta,* Vicenza, 1982.

Vescovo, P. *Da Ruzante a Calmo,* Padua, 1996.

8 Aretino and later comic playwrights
PETER BRAND

Aretino

Pietro Aretino's five highly original comedies span the years 1525–45, bridging the gap between the early theatrical experiments of Ariosto and Machiavelli and a new wave of comic production in the middle of the century; they also reflect the diverse range of theatrical contexts which he experienced successively in Rome, Mantua and, finally, Venice in the course of his remarkable career. Aretino, 'the man from Arezzo', was of humble origins and little formal education but he succeeded, without money or Latin, in battling his way to a life of fame and luxury thanks to the eloquence of his tongue and of his pen, alternately flattering and intimidating his wealthy patrons. His shameless self-promotion colours all his comedies as well as the other genres he practised – lyric, epic, dialogue, letters, tragedy – all of which he bends to the demands of his overweening personality, so memorably captured by his friend Titian's portrait.

The earliest of Aretino's comedies, *La cortigiana* (1525, 'The Courtesan'), presents a scathing portrait of the court of Rome where he served his apprenticeship – we are promptly plunged on to the streets of the city with fishermen, pedlars, bakers, pimps and prostitutes, all jostling each other in a helter-skelter of over a hundred scenes loosely strung together. The action is split between the adventures of two visitors to the city who are mercilessly gulled by the locals: the Sienese Maco, who is so desperate to become a courtier that he submits to being 'formed' in a steam-press; and Parabolano, a Neapolitan who is fobbed off with a slovenly baker's wife in place of the fine lady he pines for. This is Rome seen from the under-side, not the refined halls of Castiglione's *The Courtier*, manuscript copies of which were circulating at this time, but the *tinello*, the servants' eating quarters, where the walls are filthy with the grease wiped off messy hands and the bawd Aluigia laments that her mistress is to be burnt just because she has drowned an unwanted baby, 'come s'usa' ('as we all do' – II. vii; v. xv).

It is not just the courtly code of *The Courtier* that is subverted but the dramatic model of erudite comedy itself. Indeed Aretino's play has been called a *controcommedia*, a deliberate challenge to the classical conventions: his *Argomento* (Prelude) begs for patience if anyone spoke out of turn because they lived differently there from how they did in Athens. There is no traditional family dispute, no long-lost relative to provide a final recognition scene and happy ending; no real development in terms of character or situation. It is more of a revue than a comedy, with much of the laughter coming from the stock devices of the Neapolitan farces and the pre-Rozzi Sienese sketches which Aretino had seen performed in Rome before Leo X – chases and beatings, absurd disguises, quick-fire repartee and back-chat – even at the expense of his own play: when a cheated fisherman turns up at the end demanding justice he is told to clear off and 'non uccider la nostra comedia' ('don't wreck our comedy!' v, xxii).

Aretino does moderate his stance a little when he comes to revise his early draft, made in 1525 (and not published until recent times).[1] The text printed in his day is a rewrite of 1534, when he had moved to Venice and had different things to say about Rome and his erstwhile friends and foes – and he seems now to be trying to give a little more dignity and respectability to his play. So he reduces the disorder, links the scenes and the two separate actions rather better, and he revises the language, which had much preoccupied him in the early draft – so that one of the actors in the Prologue complained that he worried too much about how the characters talked. But Aretino had good reason to establish his linguistic credentials at a time when the *questione della lingua* was being fiercely debated. He is aggressively critical of what he considers pedantic, literary Italian: the 'insalatuccie fiorentine' (Florentine garnish) of the Petrarchists, and he wants to demonstrate the real spoken language of Rome, which was earthy and plurilingual; but he also champions the Tuscan he has learned from his mother in Arezzo – and his revised text is more in line with the literary norm championed by Bembo. He was faced with the eternal problem of the Italian theatre of finding a spoken language that could be understood across the different regions of the country, but his ambiguous stance failed to resolve the problem – the standard modern edition of his theatre is equipped with a glossary of over 2,000 terms for the benefit of the Italian reader.

Aretino's second comedy, *Il marescalco* ('The Blacksmith'), was written in 1527 for performance in Mantua before the Marquis, whose protection he had sought on leaving Rome that year, and it is closely connected with his new situation. *Il marescalco* dramatises a practical joke which the Marquis is imagined to have played on his stable master, a well-known homosexual, who is frightened into believing that his master has a wife for him, not knowing that a boy is to be substituted for the bride on the wedding-night, as in Machiavelli's recent version of Plautus' *Casina*. The action on the stage can be seen as Aretino's oblique commentary on his own ambiguous situation at court, implicitly targeting the bullying Marquis, whose fawning courtiers are obliged to play along with his whim without being let into the secret, although we, the spectators, know what is happening and can enjoy the fun. The joke is really *novella* material as the courtiers realise: 'Che cento novelle!' they laugh at the end, and the joke wears thin when stretched over the obligatory five acts. Aretino sticks closer here to the classical model, as befitted a tribute to the Marquis, with a single action ending in a traditional recognition scene and a happy ending – like Machiavelli's *Casina*.

Aretino returned to the theatre after a gap of nearly eight years during which he had taken up residence in Venice, where he wrote *Talanta* in 1542 at the request of a company of Venetian gentlemen calling themselves the Sempiterni. It was then given a splendid performance with an elaborate perspective set by Giorgio Vasari featuring some of the most famous monuments of Rome. The action revolves around the suitors of the courtesan Talanta and their long-lost, cross-dressed children. Talanta explicitly echoes Terence's Thais in his *Eunuch* – Aretino's closest approach to Roman comedy up to that time. This is, however, a typical mid-century version of the ancient model with a much complicated intrigue involving three suitors, two cross-dressings, two recognitions and various sentimental and Romantic scenes. And in the Counter-Reformation atmosphere, with Aretino on the look-out for ecclesiastical preferment, a markedly moral tone is adopted, with the courtesan decorously married off at the end and the happy outcome attributed not to Chance but Divine Providence (v,1). A good deal of the old Aretino survives, however, especially in the comic action, with the self-contained *lazzi* which anticipate *commedia dell'arte*: quick-fire disguises, duping of simpletons, even a failed attempt to mount a mule. The actors in fact seem to have gone too far down-market for the liking of the author in dressing his dialogue in a *lingua da plebe* (proletarian language) to which he objected.[2]

We have no evidence of any performance of either of Aretino's last comedies, *Lo ipocrito* ('The Hypocrite'), published in 1542 and *Il filosofo* (1545, 'The Philosopher'). The former draws heavily on literary sources (Plautus, Boccaccio, Boiardo) and has a new target, a religious hypocrite on whom the action is focused, and a Mannerist slant similar to that of *Talanta*: this time there are five married or eligible daughters with their attendant problems and suitably moral solutions (even a puff for breast-feeding!); and there is an element of pathos with attempts at suicide, and a curious mixture of realism and fantasy (one lover turns up with a Phoenix feather he has been sent away to collect). But the dominant refrain is the hypocrite's unctuous preaching of charity and his advice to the harassed father to make a joke of his problems because, at the end of the day, *'todos es nada'* (it's all an illusion) which Aretino seems to apply in Erasmian fashion to the theatre itself.

Il filosofo resembles *Lo ipocrito* in combining a practical joke from the *Decameron* with another target for abuse – this time the *filosofastro* Platar-istotele, who is eventually persuaded to abandon his senseless philosophis-ing and return to his neglected wife. The treatment is similar to that of *Lo ipocrito* with the overblown music-hall language pushed to new extremes of inflation: 'donne astute talmente che distrigano intrighi che non gli distrigarebbe il distriga i distrigamenti' ('women who are so cunning as to unravel ravels which no unraveller would ever unravel', IV.3). *Il filosofo* may have been performed soon after 1545 in Pesaro and again later in Vicenza. We have little information about the performance of any of Aretino's comedies, other than *Talanta*, but we know that he left his mark on the theatre with the printed editions of his plays, which were widely read, despite the church's prohibition, soon after his death in 1556, and were reissued in different guises early in the seventeenth century.

Later *Cinquecento* comic playwrights

Regular or 'erudite' comedy on the Roman model, which had been the dominant form of theatre in the first half of the *Cinquecento*, by the middle of the century was widely felt to be in decline. The Florentine playwright Anton Francesco Grazzini ('il Lasca') lamented in the Prologue to his *Gelosia* (1551, 'Jealousy') that recent comedies were unbearably repetitive and tedious, and the same complaints were being voiced a generation later by the poet and critic Battista Guarini: without the *intermezzi*, he wrote, nobody could stand comedy any longer.[3] There was no one of the stature of the great playwrights of earlier times, no Ariosto, Machiavelli or Aretino to come to the rescue, and the attempts to strengthen comedy's appeal with ever stronger measures of the same ingredients failed to work: plots became ever more complicated, disguises and recognitions increasingly bizarre, the language acquires more baroque extravagance and genre distinctions become more blurred – tragedy, comedy and pastoral overlap with each other and improvised comedy surges ahead.

The decline of regular comedy coincides to some extent with the outbreak of literary theorising that followed the publication in 1548 of Francesco Robortello's commentary on Aristotle's *Poetics* – which was largely concerned with tragedy and epic, and tended to treat comedy as an inferior genre. But comic playwrights were led to defend their territory so that treatises on comedy began to appear and writers to attach theorising Prologues to their plays. Their predecessors were not ignorant of the comments on comedy in Horace, Donatus, Cicero and other classical writers who had bequeathed them a widely accepted set of comic conventions which the new theorising age tended to rigidify, attempting to impose rules for the so-called unities of action, time and place, the number of characters permitted on the stage or of entrances allowed for a single character, the types and nature of the characters etc. And, as the religious and moralising pressures of the Counter-Reformation grew, the loose moral ways and anti-clerical satire of comedy came under attack, and a new, more serious comedy emerged.

In Florence, one of the more active centres, erudite comedy on the Machiavellian model persisted into the mid-century, as for example in Grazzini's three-act farce *Il frate* (1540, 'The Friar') where the Friar uses the same Jesuitical reasoning as Frate Timoteo had done in the *Mandragola*, but here exploits it to get into bed himself with the wife he has tricked, and is welcomed as family friend and confessor henceforth. Grazzini wrote several comedies on the erudite model liberally dotted with the disguises and recognitions which he himself criticised. Giovan Maria Cecchi also admitted in the prologue to his *Assiuolo* (1549, 'The Owl') that he had tried to do without these devices, but had failed. His play is based on another of the *beffe* from the *Decameron,* which were elaborated and complicated as the years passed until they became barely comprehensible – not only does the wife in *L'assiuolo,* disguised to trap her errant husband, get bedded by the young lover, but the latter's rival finds he has mistakenly made love to a woman who thought she was in bed with her brother-in-law, who mistakenly believed. . . Cecchi was a prolific dramatist who wrote both bawdy comedies and 'spiritual' plays where the traditional *sacre rappresentazioni* appeared in new 'erudite' guises.

A new type of serious comedy, more in keeping with the spirit of the times, was Girolamo Bargagli's *La pellegrina* (mid 1560s, 'The Pilgrim') for Cardinal Ferdinando de' Medici and performed at his wedding in 1589 (see above, p. 34). The *pellegrina* (Drusilla) is a young woman of exemplary virtue and intelligence who dons a pilgrim's garb to track down her long-lost lover and, when she finds him, does not spare him a sermon on the duties of a 'cuore generoso' ('generous heart') and trust in God's guiding hand. Drusilla is a prime example of a much favoured character in latter *Cinquecento* comedy, aptly dubbed by Louise Clubb as a 'woman of wonder':[4] the woman who takes her destiny into her own hands, often in male disguise – after the fashion of Lelia in *Gl'ingannati*, staged a generation earlier by the same company of *Intronati* of Siena, of which Bargagli became a member.

In Rome Aretino's *Cortigiana* was echoed some ten years later by Annibale Caro's *Gli straccioni* ('The Ragged Rascals') written for the court of Paul III in 1544. The *Straccioni* are two colourful Aretinesque figures roaming the streets of the city, and Caro's play was so peppered with local, contemporary allusions as to deter him from accepting invitations to put it on in Pesaro and Bologna in the 1560s. *Gli straccioni* was based on an episode from Achilles Tatius' *Leucippe and Clitophon*, which became a favourite source for comic playwrights at this time, providing a stronger dose of pathetic and romantic adventures than the over-exploited Plautus and Terence. Caro uses his preface to justify his choice of a multiple plot, with its almost incredible mixture of different vicissitudes, but his pathetic tale never tips into tragedy thanks to the interspersion of farcical scenes and reminiscences of the *Decameron*.

Bernardo Pino firmly excluded comic material that could be considered morally questionable from his *Ingiusti sdegni* ('Unjustified Rages' – performed in Rome in 1553, and reprinted many times in the following decades), claiming that he had included only respectable characters – a policy he advocated later in his treatise on *Il componimento della commedia de' nostri tempi* (1578, 'The Composition of Comedy in our Time'), where adultery, rape and other vicious conduct is debarred from the stage and only correct social behaviour is to be represented. The same message is conveyed in the Perugian Sforza Oddi's *Prigion d'amore* (1589, 'Prison of Love'), which he defined as a *commedia grave:* tragedy was required to liberate republics of tyrants, comedy of Spartacuses and Catilines (i.e. to teach social and political conformity). Oddi, like Caro, turns to Achilles Tatius for the pathetic adventures of his *Morti vivi* (1576, 'Living Dead') which, like his *Erofilomachia* (1572, 'The Struggle of Love and Friendship'), centres on conflicts of sexual love with friendship, honour and loyalty, and celebrates the submission of personal feelings to social and political duty. There is little that is comic in any of Oddi's later plays.

In the Veneto Andrea Calmo and Gigio Giancarli were producing their multilingual farces and farcical comedies in the middle decades of the *Cinquecento* and the busy Venetian presses turned out a succession of mediocre plays from such writers as Ercole Bentivoglio, Girolamo Parabosco and Ludovico Dolce, who appended his views on comedy to his translation of Horace in 1559. Here he insists, like most of his contemporaries, on the moral function of the genre; and his *Il Marito* (1560, 'The Husband'), an adaptation of Plautus' *Amphitruo*, despite its Boccaccesque and Machiavellian reminiscences, does contrive a sort of moral conclusion. Luigi Groto, the blind Veneto poet, was equally at home with tragedy and comedy: his *Emilia*, composed in 1579 to inaugurate a new theatre in his native Adria, combines stock comic intrigue with stirring patriotic tributes to *La Serenissima*.

The South of Italy made relatively little contribution to the comic theatre in these years but later in the century a dramatist of real talent emerges in Naples: the philosopher Giambattista Della Porta wrote some twenty-nine much applauded comedies, fourteen of which survive in editions published originally between 1589 and 1616. Various of these were performed at the viceregal court, some in lavish productions. Della Porta was an expert in stagecraft and mastered the art of the mixed comic/serious play, contributing little that was truly original in plot or dramaturgy but exploiting the heritage of the erudite theatre with great effect. His comedies often have serious or tragic plots in which characters facing threats of death or danger meet them with honourable, even heroic conduct and are rewarded with happy outcomes. The serious action may be interspersed with scenes of straight comedy, even farce and buffoonery. *La fantesca* ('The Maidservant'), for example, has two outrageous Spanish Captains squaring up to each other, grotesque disguises, a mock deafness episode and abundant sexual allusions and innuendo. Della Porta tended to use such scenes to season his serious messages about the nature of women, of honour and good government or philosophical issues such as the interaction of appearance and reality. The fame of this Neapolitan dramatist spread as far as France and England: there were adaptations of his comedies in Cambridge and on the London stage in the early seventeenth century.

The last truly memorable comedy of the *Cinquecento* also comes from the pen of a Southerner and was set in Naples. Giordano Bruno, the philosopher burnt for heresy in 1600, wrote a long five-act comedy in 1582 entitled *Il candelaio* ('The Candlestick'), which probably was never performed. The title alludes to an elderly homosexual turned woman-chaser who becomes the victim of some merciless gulling together with two other favourite comic targets, an alchemist and a pedant. If we wonder how the most profound and committed thinker of late sixteenth-century Italy came to write a farcical comedy we are informed in a Dedicatory Letter that this play really reveals the author's true disposition – presumably his ability to laugh at the world that would eventually condemn him to the stake. The interweaving of separate actions concerning the three victims in some seventy-five anarchical scenes is strongly reminiscent of Aretino's *Cortigiana,* as are the local, contemporary allusions, the numerous secondary characters and the exuberant, earthy language; both plays are over-brimming with tricks of every sort, disguises, cuckoldings, thefts, physical and verbal abuse – the *lazzi* which at this time were equally a resource of the scripted as of the unscripted stage. But Bruno's play takes Aretino's satire a stage further, becoming a serious attack on what he saw as the ills besetting a decadent Italy: linguistic corruption, pseudo-science and pedantry.

Few of the late *Cinquecento* comedies that we have mentioned are read today, let alone performed, but they are far from negligible nonetheless. Some of them made their way to France, even England, where the Italian experiments with mixed genres did not go unnoticed. Dolce's *Il ragazzo* (1541, 'The Boy') was copied by Larivey; Grazzini's *Spiritata* (1560, Enchanted) was adapted for the English stage as *The Bugbears* a few years later and Della Porta's *Duoi fratelli rivali* (1590– 'Two Rival Brothers') was a source for Rotrou's *Célie.* But the future in Italy was with other genres: as we have seen, comedy through much of the sixteenth century was often overshadowed by the colourful *intermezzi* that accompanied it, with their attractive music and dance; and comedy now had new, powerful rivals in the pastoral, the improvised theatre and of course the musical drama.

Notes

1 For the revision of the 1525 text of *La cortigiana* see Ferroni, *Le voci dell'istrione,* ch. 3, and for Aretino's language generally, see Mario Tonello 'Lingua e polemica teatrale nella *Cortigiana*' in G. Folena (ed.) *Lingua e struttura,* pp. 203–89.

2 For the language of the *Talanta* see Ferroni, *Le voci dell'istrione*, pp.248–50; and for an interesting discussion of the Erasmian features of the comedy see Cairns, *Pietro Aretino,* ch. 7.

3 See Battista Guarini, *Compendio della poesia tragicomica,* ed. G.Brognoligo, Bari, 1914, p. 268.

4 See Louise Clubb's invaluable books *Giambattista Della Porta* and *Italian Drama in Shakespeare's Time,* where she has aptly coined the phrase 'woman of wonder' for this character, and 'theatergram' for the stock theatrical situations recurrent in the comedy of this period.

Aretino Bibliography
Scripts

Aretino, P. *Tutte le opere: Teatro,* ed. G. Petrocchi, Milan, 1971.
Cairns, C. (ed.), *Three Renaissance Comedies: Ariosto's* Lena, *Ruzante's* Posh Talk, *Aretino's* Talanta, Lampeter, 1991.

Criticism

Baratto, M. *Tre studi sul teatro: Ruzante, Aretino, Goldoni,* Venice, 1964.
Cairns, C. *Pietro Aretino and the Republic of Venice,* Florence, 1985.
Innamorati, G. *Tradizione e invenzione in Pietro Aretino,* Messina, 1959.
Petrocchi, G. *P. Aretino tra rinascimento e controriforma,* Milan, 1948.
See also the Renaissance bibliography, pp. 36–8 above, entries for Clubb, Ferroni and Folena.

Later sixteenth-century comedy
Scripts

N. Borsellino (ed.), *Commedie del Cinquecento,* 2 vols., Milan 1962.
G. Bruno, *Il candelaio,* ed. G. Barberi Squarotti, Turin, 1964.

Criticism

Baldi, G. 'Le commedie di Sforza Oddi e l'ideologia della Controriforma', *Lettere italiane,* 23 (1971), 43–62.

Bonora, E. *Retorica e invenzione,* Milan, 1970.

Clubb, L. G. *Giambattista Della Porta,* Princeton, 1963
   Italian Drama in Shakespeare's Time, Yale, 1989.

See also the Renaissance bibliography, pp. 36–8 above, entries for Andrews, Clubb, Ferroni, Herrick, Sanesi, Weinberg.

9 Tragedy

RICHARD ANDREWS

Commedia erudita offered undemanding entertainment; pastoral (which is treated separately below) was more complex, but still capable of being heartwarming. Italian Renaissance audiences were less certain that they wanted to have their emotions stretched by tragedy, but the prestige attached to the genre in antiquity made it more or less mandatory on Humanist dramatists to attempt it sooner or later. Ancient models loomed large, but were also intimidating. The Greek masterpieces had a huge reputation, but were linguistically less accessible and culturally extremely remote. The Roman Seneca, on the other hand, was better known and highly revered, and it was his monotonously bloodthirsty models which defined 'tragedy' for most Renaissance readers and imitators. It is ironic that many scholars now believe that Seneca's tragedies were written for recitation and private reading rather than performance (though this view is not unanimous). It is possible, however, that the same is true for many of the eighty or more tragedies which were composed and printed in sixteenth-century Italy. In fact, the first Italian original tragedy, Gian Giorgio Trissino's *Sofonisba*, was composed in 1515, first performed in French in 1556 and first performed in Italian in 1562.

It is also noteworthy that the vast majority of published Italian tragedies received only one printing. The small number of authors and titles which attracted significantly more attention than that are largely covered below in this brief overview.

The fact that printed texts existed before any performance was mounted stresses the initially academic nature of the exercise, and makes it more predictable that practice in stage tragedy was accompanied from the start by copious theorising and debate. Such theory is associated in turn, inevitably, with the rediscovery of Aristotle's *Poetics*, the work which became so central to all Renaissance arguments about artistic creation. (The text became fully available to scholarly readers in 1536, in an edition with a facing-page Latin translation.) Many of its concepts were applicable also to literary compositions other than stage tragedy. Major debates revolved round the central tenet that 'art is imitation'. In relation to tragic drama, but also to non-theatrical genres such as epic poetry, the nature of 'imitation' was questioned and minutely analysed. How should fictional 'imitation' relate to 'verisimilitude', that is to the plausibility which fictional stories needed to possess? Was it permissible to 'imitate' stories taken from history, from legend or mythology, or invented purely by the author's imagination? Contrasting views, meticulous and dogmatic, were propounded on all these questions. The need for plausibility was attached (again, for all genres of writing) to the need for a moral message which would persuade a reader or spectator: we are more likely to be convinced, it was argued, if we find characters and events humanly believable in the first place. In relation to tragedy in particular, the moral of a play was defined with reference to the recommended Aristotelian effect of *katharsis*, a term which produces notorious difficulties of interpretation even today.

Arguments raged equally vigorously over matters more specific to the composition and staging of a dramatic text. Inevitably, although Aristotle writes most explicitly about tragedy, non-tragic genres were drawn into the debate. We have already referred in a previous section to the 'three unities', and to the prohibition of direct address to the audience (except in Prologues, which were a separately sanctioned exercise). In tragedy, however, critics who preferred Greek models to Latin ones banned the use of Prologues themselves, and also rejected the five-act structure, which did not seem to correspond to the practice of Sophocles. Differences between Greek and Latin sources also gave rise to uncertainty about the function of the Chorus. Some models used it as a participant in the action, engaging in dialogue with other characters: but it clearly also had a function of independent commentary. This, in a different way, provoked more questions about messages being addressed directly to the spectators. Scholars also realised, in a tentative way, that Greek choruses were likely to have been sung rather than merely spoken. There were already discussions about the use or otherwise of music in drama, especially in the more lyrical genre of pastoral. Several decades before the creation of opera (whose beginnings are usually dated by historians to the late 1590s, with *Dafne* by Corsi and Peri), one can see some of the ideas and arguments which eventually produced the new genre.

On a simpler technical level, the types of verse used in composing tragic plays were subject to contrasting prescriptions. A statistical majority, perhaps, of Italian Renaissance tragedies were composed on what was claimed to be a Latin model: this involved a separate Prologue; five acts, each ending in a reflective chorus; a Chorus which commented separately on the action, rather than engaging in direct dialogue; and a form of blank verse (*endecasillabi sciolti*) for most of the text, with more varied lyrical metres for the choruses. But to every one of these tendencies there were frequent exceptions.

Trissino's *Sofonisba* had pioneered, even invented, the blank verse; but from other points of view its author explicitly chose to look to Greek models. His story was a simple one, of a Numidian princess choosing suicide rather than the humiliation of captivity by her Roman enemies. Although the play was not performed until much later, Trissino managed immediately to set a number of patterns which were followed by others – not least a tendency to give female characters as high a profile as was given to male ones, and to invest them with heroic aristocratic virtues. (This, after all, is also true of Greek and Roman tragedy, for reasons which are still the subject of debate.) Sofonisba is also presented as being in love with a general fighting on the Roman side: this clash between love and political allegiance was also to have a long history in tragic and operatic theatre.

Sofonisba was printed twenty-three times between 1524 and 1620 – by far the largest number of reissues achieved by any Italian tragedy. Another early experiment which was probably never performed was written by Giovanni Rucellai in friendly rivalry with Trissino: it is entitled *Rosmunda*, and deals with a story of bloody revenge on the part of a princess of the Gepids against her Lombard conqueror, in a semi-legendary sixth century AD. This work also attracted the interest and approval of scholars, and was printed six times between 1525 and 1593.

However, the first actual performance of an original tragedy was organised in 1541 by a Ferrarese scholar and author, Giambattista Giraldi Cinzio. The event was mounted in his own house but under Este ducal patronage. The play, *Orbecche*, followed the 'Latin' pattern outlined above, and was impeccably Senecan in its lurid tone. The plot, though, is based on a story by Boccaccio (*Decameron* IV, I: this story of Tancredi and Ghismonda was dramatised more openly by later tragedians, with fewer alterations in names and settings). The tale of a daughter marrying against her father's wishes, and of his tyrannical punishment resulting in her killing him in retaliation, is highly melodramatic. Nevertheless, it does relate to real Renaissance dilemmas: the contrasting demands of romantic love and family duty, and the question as to when royal or princely power becomes tyrannical and therefore illegitimate. Similar questions – and particularly the conflict between the private inclinations and the public duty of a member of the ruling class – became standard in tragedy. However, Giraldi, responding very probably to the preferences of his audience, was uneasy about developing a genre which led a virtuous hero or heroine to a painful death. When he theorised about tragedy, in his *Discorsi intorno al comporre dei romanzi, delle comedie e delle tragedie* (1553, 'Discourse on the Composition of Romances, Comedies and Tragedies') he showed a preference for what he called 'tragedie a lieto fine' (tragedies with a happy ending), in which, after various moments of terror and suspense, the villain would be punished and the hero or heroine saved. This was a specialised interpretation of *katharsis*, twisted to satisfy Christian morality. The *Discorsi* sparked off a heated debate with Sperone Speroni, who had published a more eccentric tragedy, *Canace*, in 1542. The quarrel provided publicity for both writers, and helped to promote increased interest in tragedy as such.

Giraldi's eight other tragedies were only printed once, in a posthumous anthology, whereas *Orbecche* received eleven separate editions. Most of them are documented as having been performed or at least publicly read. Unlike *Orbecche*, they followed the principles which he had declared in the *Discorsi*, with the dénouements imposing poetic justice. His practice paved the way for a development which other writers could call *'tragi-comedia'* (a word taken from the Prologue of Plautus' *Amphytruo*), though that term was developed, as will be explained below, particularly in relation to more serious manifestations of the pastoral genre. Not all tragic dramatists were as squeamish, however, and many Italian Renaissance tragedies used the death of an admirable protagonist to exalt virtues of constancy and fortitude in the face of earthly destiny. A heavenly reward was often implicitly or explicitly suggested, in line with increasing Counter-Reformation anxieties about the moral function of art.

Aretino's *Orazia* (1546) features military and patriotic heroism triumphing inhumanly over family affections, in a story which was to be taken up later by Corneille. It is a difficult play to decipher for the modern reader, especially in terms of its likely staging; but it has been taken seriously by modern commentators, and was reprinted under a false title and attribution in 1604 in order to evade the church's blanket ban on all works written by its author.

Lodovico Dolce produced a series of workmanlike tragedies for the Venetian market, and possibly for Venetian audiences, though it is frustratingly difficult to reconstruct where and to whom they were offered. Many of them are effectively rewritings in Italian of Sophocles, Euripides or Seneca, but with enough intervention to allow the plays to be seen as Dolce's own work. He distinguished these compositions from his separate anthology of avowed translations from Seneca, a volume published simultaneously with his 1560 anthology of more original versions. (He thus ended up having produced two separate versions of Seneca's *Thyestes*.) Later he wrote and had performed the less classically based *Marianna* (1565), which is a straightforward piece of pathos about the unmerited sufferings of the Jewish queen at the hand of Herod, the tyrant himself being more plausibly characterised than most similar figures. (This play must have become known in England, as it is a likely inspiration for *The Tragedy of Mariam* by Elizabeth Cary, published in 1613 – the first known neo-classical dramatic composition in English by a woman.)

Torquato Tasso, in *Torrismondo* (composed in the 1570s, printed 1587), rewrote the story and dramatic structure of Sophocles' *Oedipus Tyrannos* into the setting of an exotic Scandinavian kingdom. Luigi Groto's *Adriana* (or *La Hadriana*, published in 1578 with ten further reprintings) is recognisably a version of what we now know as the Romeo and Juliet story, set in antique times in the poet's native Adria. It boasts a speech 349 lines long (II. 2) in which the hero justifies himself to the heroine for having unwittingly killed her brother.

This last characteristic is not as freakish as it may appear. Italian Renaissance tragedies were built largely round declamation, and in this indeed they can be said to follow their Senecan model with some accuracy. Messenger roles, which narrated horrific offstage events at great rhetorical length, were often the parts reserved for the best actors. Audiences were expected to surrender themselves to the power of oratory rather than the interplay of dialogue. When professional *arte* companies took on the performance of tragic scripts, as well as comic scenarios, such eloquence was established even more firmly as being permitted to heroines as well as to heroes; and the more serious material helped to establish the reputation and status of actresses such as Isabella Andreini. It is not at all fanciful to see big emotional speeches as having the function of operatic arias without the music. In 1608, Arianna's *Lamento* in the opera by Monteverdi was premiered with resounding success by a singer who was also a *commedia dell'arte* actress – Virginia Andreini Ramponi, Isabella's daughter-in-law.

The most direct influence on the new genre of opera comes from the equally new pastoral drama of the Renaissance. However, Humanist tragedy also played its part. It shared with pastoral its tendency towards set-piece declamation. Its mandatory classical use of a chorus must have been easier to stage, and perhaps also had a better theatrical rationale, when the words were sung rather than recited. In addition, tragedy offered moments of suitably excruciating emotional suspense; and a range of exotic palatial locations on which scenographers could exercise their imagination, in an age which was increasingly demanding the highest possible level of visual spectacle. Italian classical tragedy therefore did help to launch the music drama which Western culture sees rightly as one of its most important inheritances from Italy.

By contrast, on the face of it, the genre may seem to have left nothing to our surviving repertoire of spoken drama: modern theatre practitioners, even in Italy itself, are practically never tempted to revive an Italian tragedy from the sixteenth century. However, the simple fact of recreating and staging a genre which called itself 'tragedy' set off trains of thought which were fruitful in European drama generally. Direct detailed influences on Shakespeare, or on other writers of serious drama in England and Spain, may be hard to trace, since in both those theatrical traditions there flourished a creative independence, in relation to strict classical precept, which seems to rise above and obliterate any principle of imitation. On the other hand, however, it is impossible not to trace the seventeenth-century French classical masterpieces of Corneille and Racine straight back to their generic Italian sources, however much difference of quality and profundity one may then choose to detect.

Meanwhile, in Italy itself, we may speculate that unadulterated tragedy never gained the kind of allegiance from audiences which they were ready to grant to less gloomy forms of theatre. The evidence for this lies in the very desire to create 'tragicomedy' in the first place; in the regular mingling of the serious elements of tragic drama with structures and moods taken from other genres; and in the tendency to surround potentially austere stories with the extra excitement provided by scenic spectacle, or by musical delivery, or by both. The commitment of Italian aristocratic culture to the Greek and Roman ancients was strong and binding, and tragedy therefore had to be granted the kind of formal prestige which had been inherited from those revered models. Nevertheless, the pursuit of theatre as a leisure activity for the upper classes – in the face of serious unease from the church about its acceptability – was ultimately also motivated by hedonism; and pure tragedy was perhaps difficult to reconcile with a desire for relaxation or entertainment.

Note

For publications relevant to this chapter see the bibliography appended to chapter 2 (pp. 36–8).

10 Pastoral drama

LISA SAMPSON

Around the mid sixteenth century, with the *commedia erudita* and neo-classical tragedy well established, Humanist dramatists began to experiment with a third 'regular' genre: the pastoral play. Known variously as *favola* or *tragicommedia boschereccia/pastorale*, it evolved at a time when theatre was undergoing significant transformations with the rise of the *commedia dell'arte* and later of opera. The *pastorale* rapidly became one of the most characteristic dramatic forms of its time, gaining enormous popularity especially through such high-profile plays as Torquato Tasso's *Aminta* (first performed 1573?) and Giambattista Guarini's *Il pastor fido* ('The Faithful Shepherd', printed 1589/90). Although few other examples are well known today, some 200 were published during the sixteenth and seventeenth centuries, and they were frequently performed especially in private courtly and literary circles. The genre also influenced writers beyond national borders, particularly in France from the late 1580s, culminating in the plays of Racan and Mairet in the 1620s, and to a lesser extent, given the different socio-political conditions, in Spain and England.

Experimentation to create a 'regular' pastoral genre, in five acts and observing the neo-classical unities, was initiated by the pioneering dramatist and theorist Giambattista Giraldi Cinzio, who sought to revive the ancient 'third' genre of satyr drama (burlesque plays featuring satyrs and gods performed at Greek festivals after a trilogy of tragedies). This occurred as comedy was losing favour with elites because of its increasingly formulaic qualities and less exclusive status, while tragedy held only limited appeal. Yet, in reality, pastoral drama emerges from a long and heterogeneous tradition stretching back to classical antiquity. This ranges from learned and popular works for the stage (including courtly eclogues, pastoral dialogues, rustic farces and mythological *intermezzi* set to music) to less obviously performance-orientated forms, such as lyric verse, elegies and romances like those of Boccaccio and Jacopo Sannazaro (1458–1530). Given this enormous diversity, some selection is necessary in the present discussion. Only works specifically intended for performance will be considered, and analysis will begin with late fifteenth-century works, leaving aside important medieval examples like the *pastourelle* and religious drama, and end with the transformation and decline of the genre around 1700.

First, it will be helpful to trace some of the frequently recurring themes and concerns of pastoral drama. Set in an idealised, green landscape often identified as Arcadia, this features a 'noble' cast of shepherds and nymphs who indulge in courtly pastimes such as hunting, singing and, particularly, amorous pursuits. A contrasting earthy dimension is provided by a lustful satyr or rustic goatherd, while the (mostly implicit) presence of pastoral deities like Diana, goddess of chastity, the woodland god Pan and the god of Love confers a pseudo-religious dimension to the action. With its mythological setting and characters, the pastoral play lacks the kind of verisimilitude found in comedy and tragedy. Indeed, there is little sense of any 'real' countryside in pastoral at all. The landscape self-consciously alludes, rather, to literary precedents going back to Theocritus' *Idylls*, Virgil's *Bucolics* and Ovid's *Metamorphoses*, as well as Petrarch's lyric verse, Boccaccio's romances, Sannazaro's *Arcadia* and episodes from Ariosto's *Orlando furioso*.

Pastoral drama is predominantly concerned with different aspects of the love experience, as explored through staged discussions and scenes of lovers' persuasion and dejection. Eventually, mismatched couples are happily united, sometimes through divine intervention or, in less regular examples, magic (as in Shakespeare's *Midsummer Night's Dream*). This frequently entails the change of heart of a nymph who at first fiercely defends her chastity, but is later persuaded to marry, mirroring idealised social practices. Female characters therefore play a significant part in pastoral drama, which generally shows a 'feminine' preoccupation with the inner life of the emotions, as opposed to external reality. Such concerns could be heightened by representing states of madness, dreams and magical or divine occurrences, which were given some credibility by the green setting and proved effective dramatically. Sensual episodes were inevitably suggested, long equated with the pleasures of nature, as in the topos of the *locus amoenus*. Even so, any risqué quality could be mitigated by the supposedly remote setting of Arcadia, and by associating unbridled eros with the baser characters. In the Counter-Reformation age where questions of decorum, both literary and moral, were increasingly of concern to writers and audiences, pastoral drama could therefore still be considered suitable for polite society.

The popularity of pastoral drama lay not only in its subject matter but also in its versatility in terms of performance. The classical association of Arcadian herdsmen with musicians and poets meant that musical, sung and danced episodes could realistically be integrated within the plot. It could be staged indoors and, more cheaply but still elegantly, outdoors in private gardens and aristocratic villas. Furthermore, the fact that the pastoral set only required generic properties like trees, huts and sometimes a temple, meant that scenographic innovations (including machines and elaborate stage architecture) and *arte* techniques could easily be incorporated. From what can be deduced from surviving texts, plays often seem to have included some comic stage-play, such as a satyr being outwitted by a nymph, or goatherds coming to blows. Otherwise, they consisted mainly of lengthy Petrarchan laments and persuasions to love by the 'nobler' characters. The artificial lyric quality was reinforced by the fact that plays were usually composed in verse. Typically, regular pastorals appeared in unrhymed mixed *endecasillabi* and *settenari*, though other metres and rhymes were occasionally included to indicate moments of emotional intensity, or used in inter-act choruses and spectacles (*intermedi*) when added. 'Irregular' plays explored greater metrical variety and even began to be composed in prose from the early seventeenth century.

While popular in practice, the 'third' genre occupied an ambiguous status in theoretical terms. Unlike the canonical tragedy and comedy, the pastoral drama had evolved independently of classical precedents and, until the late sixteenth century, it lacked the kind of neo-Aristotelian codification increasingly demanded by serious dramatists since the 1540s. The situation changed when the Paduan-based critic, Giason Denores, in 1586 indirectly attacked Guarini's still unpublished *Il pastor fido*. Guarini's response (*Verrato*, 1588) stimulated a wider debate on pastoral and tragicomedy which lasted well into the following century, producing numerous critical writings. These explored many of the same theoretical issues raised in earlier debates on tragedy, particularly concerning the verisimilitude, decorum and proper function of the genre. The 'modern' pastoral drama was criticised in particular for inappropriately mingling discrete comic and tragic conventions, as well as for its unduly serious and lengthy neo-classical form, given that its simple subject matter had until recently been loosely structured in one or three acts, or as short dialogues modelled on

Virgil's *Eclogues*. Guarini drew on Aristotle to defend his pastoral play as a modern outgrowth of the classical eclogue, and developed a definition of tragicomedy as a distinct 'third' genre, combining only select, tempered elements from tragedy and comedy. Crucially, he also argued that the form's main function was not to provide moral instruction, but entertainment. This view marks an important shift in attitudes to drama at the turn of the century, gradually moving away from a moralising Horatian and Counter-Reformation position towards a more hedonistic view, pointing forward to baroque aesthetics.

Nonetheless, regular pastoral drama in practice continued to serve predominantly as a convenient form of courtly entertainment. As in Virgil's *Eclogues*, the fictional veil of pastoral could be used to allude flatteringly and indirectly to the real world of the audience, as well as for covert moral and political satire. Ovid's *topos* of a primitive, innocent and happy Golden Age allowed pastoral to criticise contemporary civilisation (especially as epitomised by the court) and to explore the individual's conflict between social responsibilities and natural desires. The association of pastoral with a prelapsarian existence and its apparent humility and simplicity in style and content had also long made it a means of conveying religious themes, as in Petrarch's allegorical eclogues and nativity scenes in *sacre rappresentazioni*. In the hands of late fifteenth-century Humanists like Sannazaro, Arcadia returned to being a largely pagan mythological world marked by its own religious rituals, though with a strong Neoplatonic dimension. This ostensibly pagan portrayal persists in most regular pastoral drama produced during and after the Council of Trent (1545–63), though disguised Christian elements occasionally surface (notably in Guarini's *Pastor fido*). The pastoral drama's oblique and supposedly fictional status therefore made it an ideal imaginative and dramatic medium for its time.

Having outlined some features of pastoral drama, let us now explore general developments within the genre. From the late fifteenth century, a diverse range of 'irregular' forms of pastoral drama was performed in major urban cultural centres and especially in courts. Many works (some of which were in Latin) are now lost, suggesting their occasional and ephemeral nature. Existing examples include *drammi mescidati* (mixed drama with pastoral, tragic and comic scenes) by the court Humanists Poliziano (1454–94; *Orfeo*, performed Mantua 1471/80) and Niccolò da Correggio (1450–1508; *Cefalo e Procri*, performed Ferrara 1487), who use Ovid as a key source for themes of love, loss and transformation in a mythological setting. Dramatic eclogues were also composed to allude playfully to the patron and the performance context in pastoral guise, as in the elegant *Tirsi* (performed in Urbino, 1506) by Baldassarre Castiglione and Cesare Gonzaga.

By comparison, the eclogues of 'L'Epicuro Napolitano' (identified as Antonio Marsi, *c.*1475–1555) – *Cecaria* or *Dialogo di tre ciechi* ('Dialogue of Three Blind Men', performed 1523) and particularly *Mirzia* (composed *c.*1523–8) – offer greater dramatic potential. Luigi Tansillo (1510–68), also Neapolitan, substantially borrows from these plays in his *I due pellegrini* ('The Two Pilgrims', composed *c.*1527). Like *Cecaria*, this represents rather stylised characters protesting their amorous despair to each other, culminating in their attempted suicide. They are dissuaded by the voice of a beloved dead nymph coming from within the very tree from which they were about to hang themselves. A livelier counter-tradition was provided in the form of rustic dramatic works performed by itinerant (semi-) professionals from the Veneto and Tuscany, including Ruzante and pre-Rozzi Sienese dramatists like Niccolò Campani ('Lo Strascino'). Their representations of 'realistic' peasants, often speaking in dialect and making satirical and even obscene allusions, were popular with elite audiences, though less decorous elements were later toned down when incorporated in regular pastoral drama.

This 'irregular' tradition was gradually unified according to classical conventions by humanist experimenters mainly from Ferrara, a centre famous for its theatrical achievements. Arguably, the first step was taken by Giambattista Giraldi Cinzio, who with his *Egle* (1545) aimed to create the first modern example of the ancient satyr-play and stimulate its revival, as noted in his (unpublished) treatise, *Lettera . . . sovra il comporre le satire* (*c.*1554, 'Letter on Composing Satyr-drama'). The play is set in a primitive Arcadia and features a simple *inganno* (deception) plot devised by the fallen nymph, Egle, whereby the chaste nymphs of Diana are to be led into the clutches of a Dionysian cast of lascivious satyrs and fauns. Giraldi's expertise as a practical dramatist ensured the inclusion of various effective scenes, drawing on earlier eclogues and much reused later, such as the meeting of a reluctant nymph and her suitor, and a choral dance. But the satyrs' surprise attack on the dancing nymphs, and the latter's chaotic flight (followed by their offstage Ovidian-style transformation into natural phenomena), would have been more problematic to stage. The semi-divine cast without shepherds, the moralising message and tragic ending, ultimately explain the limited success of *Egle*, now considered something of an anomaly in terms of the genre's overall development.

Agostino Beccari's *Il sacrificio* ('The Sacrifice') is generally regarded as the first 'regular' pastoral play. Its action largely follows the complex structure of *commedia erudita*, interweaving the trials of Callinome (a chaste nymph of Diana), Melidia, who is secretly engaged to Carpalio, and the fickle nymph Stellinia. The varied dramatic episodes would have entertained the Ferrarese ducal family for whom it was first performed (like Giraldi's *Egle*) in 1554 (printed 1555; revised in 1587). These include a prayer sung by a priest of Pan and a shepherd chorus (III. 3), comic tricks involving the satyr, as well as offstage romance elements (a man's transformation into a wolf, Callinome's fight with a boar, a magic potion). Beccari's triple plot structure was adopted in Agostino Argenti's more static *Lo Sfortunato* ('The Unfortunate Man', first printed and performed in Ferrara in 1567) and in the director-dramatist Leone de' Sommi's *Irifile* (performed around that time in Mantua), which uses magic to more spectacular effect. Alberto Lollio, however, chose a single plot for his *Aretusa* (Ferrara, 1564), resolved by the thereafter often repeated device of recognition of lost children. These plays show the variety of the few known experiments with 'regular' pastoral drama produced before the early 1570s, mainly by Ferrarese writers connected to the court and literary coteries. Around the same time, other plays less preoccupied with classical ideals of unity and verisimilitude were staged, including the Venetian Alvise Pasqualigo's *Gli Intricati* ('People in a Predicament', performed 1569?); and *Calisto* (first performed *c*.1561) by the actor-dramatist Luigi Groto of Adria. Groto's popular *Pentimento amoroso* ('Love's Regret', performed 1565/1572?), however, shows greater regularity and decorum.

The status of pastoral drama was considerably raised with the composition, and especially the publication in 1580/1, of *Aminta* by Torquato Tasso (1544–95). Unusually, this play adopts a linear single plot without magical or farcical episodes, more reminiscent of tragedy than of comedy. It portrays the travails of the eponymous young shepherd as he tries to woo the chaste nymph, Silvia, and the process of her emotional maturation and gradual conversion to love. The play was apparently first performed in 1573 by the *Gelosi* acting troupe in the exclusive gardens of a Ferrarese pleasure palace, and it quickly became a favourite with professionals as well as erudite amateurs. This may seem surprising, since the play contains almost none of the standard spectacular elements of pastoral drama.

Virtually all the dramatic events (Aminta's two suicide attempts, Silvia's near-rape by a satyr and her supposed death in the jaws of a wolf) take place offstage, so feelings of horror or erotic suggestions are conveyed through narrated accounts. Furthermore, the lovers never actually appear together, and there is no dancing, or singing except perhaps in the choruses. These and the messenger's reports (both characteristic of tragedy) would have provided much of the play's appeal on stage, but most valued of all was its exquisite lyric style.

Given Tasso's status as the leading poet of his day, it is not surprising that *Aminta* enjoyed huge success in print: by 1600 it had appeared in twenty-seven editions and was translated into French (1584), and reworked in English (1591). However, it seems to have been composed originally to entertain the dramatist's patron, Duke Alfonso II of Ferrara. The play alludes to the court in pastoral guise, but it also evokes characters and places that are difficult to identify with this setting. A somewhat ambiguous attitude towards the court emerges from the Prologue where the god of love describes his escape from this environment to the freer and less affected pastoral world. This perspective is further explored in the famous chorus to Act 1, which rejects the archetypal courtly value of 'honour' in favour of hedonistic enjoyment of sensual love unfettered by guilt, as in the Golden Age. A more explicitly satirical passage (1. 2. 215–311) was apparently added after publication.

As the first authoritative model of pastoral drama, *Aminta* was rapidly seized upon for scenarios, episodes and characterisation by a wide range of writers from all over the peninsula. Yet most dramatists tended to avoid its more transgressive aspects, and continued to adopt complex plot structures like Beccari's with staged action. (Ongaro's *Alceo*, 1582, is exceptional in closely following *Aminta*'s plot, though transposed to a 'piscatorial' or marine setting.) For instance, the Venetian director-critic Angelo Ingegneri's *Danza di Venere* (1584, 'Dance of Venus') includes a choral dance as well as scenes of madness popular with professional actors. Intriguingly, Ingegneri's play was first performed by a group of young ladies under female patronage at the small court of Soragna, near Parma (1583), a context with which two of the first known female writers of pastoral plays (and indeed of secular drama) were connected: Barbara Torelli Benedetti (*Partenia*, MS, c.1587) and Maddalena Campiglia (*Flori*, 1588). For these elite women pastoral drama would have seemed suitably decorous because of its apparent modesty and 'private' subject matter, especially when given a tragic bias like *Aminta* and an added spiritual dimension. But where Torelli's nymphs predominantly conform to feminine ideals, Campiglia presents a singular pro-feminist challenge through her protagonist, Flori. Mad at first with amorous grief for a dead nymph, she is cured, through a sacrifice, of this 'impossible' passion only to fall in love with a foreign shepherd. Polemically, she later rejects marriage and chooses instead a chaste, spiritual union with him, which will better enable her to fulfil her literary ambitions.

By comparison, *Mirtilla* (also printed 1588) by the *commedia dell'arte* diva Isabella Andreini appears more light-hearted with its conventional promotion of earthly, marital love. It gained immediate success, probably largely due to Andreini's professional renown, appearing by 1620 in ten editions and a French translation (1602). The *Mirtilla* favours a more comic, lively model of pastoral drama, with tricks played on the satyr (III.2) and a singing competition between two rival nymphs (III.5). However, the author's cultural discernment and moral respectability is also clearly displayed to offset negative ideas about actresses. Besides the fairly superficial debt to Tasso's *Aminta*, there are copious allusions to classical mythology. Notably, Ovid's tale of Narcissus is reworked dramatically in a key scene where the haughty nymph Ardelia falls in love with her own reflection (IV.4).

Tasso's most ambitious and contentious imitator was his Ferrarese rival, Giambattista Guarini (1538–1612), whose immensely popular *Pastor fido* (begun c.1580; published 1589/90) was instrumental in consolidating the fortunes of the genre in theory (as noted) and practice, especially with reading audiences. In keeping with the author's monumentalising aims, the *Pastor fido* is roughly three times the length of *Aminta*, and introduces an explicitly tragic dimension, especially indebted to Sophocles' *Oedipus Rex*. This is evident in the main plot, which concerns the tragic conflict of the heroine-nymph (Amarilli), torn between her unspoken feelings for Mirtillo (the 'faithful shepherd') who she knows loves her, and her duty, as divined through an oracle, to marry the son of Arcadia's priestly ruler and save her country from a divine curse. The tension peaks when she is falsely accused of adultery and Mirtillo offers to die in her place, culminating in a spectacular sacrifice scene (v.3–4). However, in accordance with tragicomic decorum, death is averted when, after various complex twists in the plot, Mirtillo's real identity is discovered and the oracle's riddle solved. The couple are finally free to marry and Arcadia is saved. More properly pastoral ingredients like hunting episodes, an echo scene and sensual innuendos are mostly confined to the lighter secondary plot, while comic elements are provided by the lascivious nymph Corisca and a satyr.

The *Pastor fido* includes many pleasing spectacular features, including an elaborately choreographed dance, a slapstick tussle over a hair-piece and various lyric passages which were later set to music separately as madrigals. Yet, overall, it promotes a moralised form of pastoral, in line with Counter-Reformation sensibilities, where religious and secular authorities feature conspicuously. Famously, Guarini polemically revises the hedonistic dictum of Tasso's Golden Age chorus ('S'ei piace, ei lice' – 'if it is pleasing, it is permitted') in his own version, which proposes the conflation of sensual love with legitimate marriage ('piaccia se lice' – 'let it please if it is permitted'). Finally, the Providential design of the play, in which the Arcadians are brought blindly through a tortuous series of events to a happy ending, suggests a strong Christian dimension, as does the underlying allegory of the faithful shepherd's self-sacrifice to redeem Arcadia.

Guarini's *Pastor fido* proved demanding to stage, but was performed lavishly in 1598 to mark a dynastic wedding in Mantua. Many plays, however, continued to be designed for small-scale and, increasingly, academic audiences. The most successful pastoral play after the *Pastor fido*, Guidubaldo Bonarelli's *Filli di Sciro* ('Filli of Skyros', published 1607) was in fact composed for the Ferrarese *Accademia degli Intrepidi* ('The Intrepid Ones'). The play has a tragic bias, being set on a Greek island under Thracian tyranny; and it dramatises a bizarre academic debating point in the secondary plot, in which one of the nymphs is equally and simultaneously in love with two shepherds. *Filli* reveals a taste for pathos, horror and the marvellous that became characteristic of 'literary' pastoral plays (as well as of pastoral verse) from the early seventeenth century. Romance elements like accounts of exotic travels were often added as well, indicating the general tendency for such plays to become longer and more serious, as 'closet drama' intended for reading rather than performance.

At the same time, a number of plays retained a comic bias and were sometimes influenced by *commedia dell'arte* practices. Professional troupes frequently performed both regular scripted pastoral plays and improvised scenarios, and actors and directors themselves turned their hand to such works. For instance, Francesco Andreini (husband of Isabella) published two *favole boschereccie* (woodland fables) in 1611, while their son, Giovanni Battista Andreini (1576–1654), the most famous actor of his age, includes amongst his diverse dramatic compositions two pastoral tragicomedies, *Lelio bandito* (1620, 'Lelio banished') and *La Rosella* (1634), as well as pastoral comedies and mixed plays. The first printed collection of scenarios by Flaminio Scala (*Teatro delle favole rappresentative*, 1611) also contains one labelled 'pastorale' besides others with pastoral elements. By this time, pastoral drama was increasingly merging with various literary, spectacular and dramatic forms. Its integration of danced episodes resulted in three (lost) pastoral ballets by Laura Giudiccioni Lucchesini, set to music by Emilio de' Cavalieri (performed at the Florentine court in the 1590s). More importantly, pastoral drama contributed to the development of *melodramma* in Florence. The earliest known operas (*Dafne*, 1594, lost; *Euridice*, 1600) are based on short mythological pastorals by Ottavio Rinuccini without act divisions, set to music by Jacopo Peri (the second, also by Giulio Caccini), which exploit the pastoral's lyric qualities.

Arguably, the last noteworthy Italian pastoral drama was *Endimione* (1692) by Alessandro Guidi, a member of the newly founded Roman Academy of Arcadia, which claimed the pastoral idiom as a means of restoring classical ideals of poetic purity and simplicity in opposition to baroque 'excess'. The taste for this kind of drama ended in Europe with the decline of the court system and the academies that had patronised it, though other non-dramatic pastoral forms remained popular. While it might be concluded that Italian pastoral drama represents a relatively limited theatrical genre per se it should however be recognised as enabling creative experimentation with traditional genre boundaries and conventions. Through its gradual undermining of the neo-classical canon, this essentially hybrid genre may be seen to prepare the way for 'modern' forms like opera that could respond to popular demand for new kinds of theatre.

Bibliography

Andrews, R. 'Pastoral drama', in P. Brand and L. Pertile (eds.), *The Cambridge History of Italian Literature*, Cambridge, 1996, pp. 292–8.

Bruscagli, R. ' L'*Aminta* del Tasso e le pastorali ferraresi del '500', in AA. VV., *Studi di Filologia e Critica offerti dagli allievi a Lanfranco Caretti*, 2 vols., Rome, 1985, vol. 1, pp. 279–318.

Carrara, E. *La Poesia pastorale. Storia dei generi letterari italiani*, Milan, 1909.

Chiodo, D. 'Tra l'"Aminta" e il "Pastor fido"', *Italianistica*, 24, 2–3 (1995), 559–75.

Clubb, L. G. *Italian Drama in Shakespeare's Time*, New Haven and London, 1989.

Cox, V. 'Fiction, 1560–1650', in L. Panizza and S. Wood (eds.), *A History of Women's Writing in Italy'*, Cambridge, 2000, pp. 54–7.

Godard, A. 'La Première Représentation de l'*Aminta*: La court de Ferrare et son double', in A. Rochon (ed.), *Ville et campagne dans la littérature italienne de la Renaissance*, Paris, 1977, vol. II: *Le Courtisan Travesti*, pp. 187–301.

Henke, R. *Pastoral Transformations: Italian Tragicomedy and Shakespeare's Late Plays.* London, 1991.

Herrick, M. T. *Tragicomedy: Its Origins and Development in Italy, France and England*, Urbana, IL, 1962.

Pieri, M. *La scena boschereccia nel rinascimento italiano*, Padua, 1983.

Sampson, L. 'The Mantuan performance of Guarini's *Pastor fido* and representations of courtly identity', *Modern Language Review*, 98, 1 (2003), 34–52.

Weinberg, B. *A History of Literary Criticism in the Italian Renaissance*, 2 vols., Chicago, 1961.

11 *Commedia dell'arte*

KENNETH AND LAURA RICHARDS

The sixteenth-century Italian drama discussed in the preceding chapters – comedy, tragedy, pastoral and the various hybrids that emerged from them – were all invariably played in socially exclusive performance places, like large rooms or halls in courts, learned academies and patrician houses, and usually acted by males: scholars, students, courtiers or young gentlemen. This was essentially an amateur stage, and it has generally been thought convenient to distinguish it from the theatre of the professional players, usually known today as the *commedia dell'arte*. That Italian professional theatre has customarily been considered distinctive in the history of post-medieval European theatre in that it was itinerant, performed in a range of performance-places, more particularly *al fresco*, was of the popular meridian, employed actresses and mingled masked and unmasked performers in the acting of plays which were not scripted, but improvised on the basis of short scenarios, or *canovacci* (plot and action outlines). However, that customary understanding of the *commedia dell'arte* requires some modification.[1]

The term *commedia dell'arte* appears to derive from eighteenth-century usage, its meaning later further conditioned by nineteenth-century assumptions about theatre. In the sixteenth and seventeenth centuries, descriptive terms for the improvised drama of the Italian professional theatre were different, and included the *commedia Italiana*, or *degli zanni*, or *a soggetto*, or *mercenaria*. In modern usage, when referring to the theatre of the past the term *commedia dell'arte* tends to provide loose umbrella coverage for many different kinds of Italian professional theatre; for in the sixteenth and seventeenth centuries throughout the peninsula, and indeed beyond it, troupes of all levels and qualities made some use of masks and improvisation. These troupes ranged from the highly sophisticated court-patronised or court-oriented companies, through touring troupes of more modest status and accomplishments, to itinerant bands of trestle-stage entertainers and players supporting the activities of mountebanks. Although there was much mobility, there were also significant divides between the troupes. Certainly, not all professional performance can be considered 'popular': first, a number of contemporary commentators, and indeed some leading players themselves, distinguish firmly between the high status, court-oriented companies and lesser travelling troupes, many religious and secular moralists reserving their ire for the latter; second, the main companies seem not to have been in evidence at those major attractions for popular entertainers, the great Continental fairs; third, contemporary English commentators on Italian improvising players describe, invariably in disparaging tones, what they consider to be a mode of below-stairs mountebank street theatre apparently a world away from the performances given at Continental courts by companies like the Gelosi, the Confidenti and the Fedeli.[2]

Furthermore, quite what was meant at the time by 'improvised' is less than wholly clear, and the extent of its practice may have been greater abroad than in Italy. The first historian of the Italian professional stage, Luigi Riccoboni (1676–1753, stage-name Lelio), has some instructive things to say about performance, including the following:

> The Italian players don't always use to play their parts extempore; they have, as I shall shew by and by, sometimes learned it by heart, according to the different ages in which they lived. But in those courts in Europe who are not so well acquainted with the Italian language, and where the Italian players are sought after and encouraged, they have gone entirely to the extempore manner, and it is under this character that they are known over all Germany, and particularly in France.[3]

As Riccoboni indicates, the reputations Italian players enjoyed for performing only by improvisation was largely based on an assumption about their mode of performance in countries beyond Italy, where for obvious reasons Italian scripted drama was of little appeal to audiences ignorant of the Italian language. Nor was improvised performance unpremeditated: the writings of Domenico Bruni (1580 to early seventeenth century, stage-name Fulvio), Flaminio Scala (fl. late sixteenth to early seventeenth century, stage-name Silvio) and Pier Maria Cecchini (1575–1645, stage-name Fritellino) in their different ways indicate that parts were very carefully prepared. In the early modern Italian theatre improvisation on the basis of a scenario was highly collaborative and essentially a way of 'making' the commercial product, a play; in short, actors and actresses, first working at preparation stage with a *corago* (often the *capo comico*), then in actual performance, themselves fulfilled the function of the dramatist. Further, certainly in the major companies, the players sometimes acted fully scripted plays, many of them in their textual form of great technical elaboration and literary merit: one celebrated instance is the involvement of the Gelosi company in the first performance of Torquato Tasso's highly formal poetic pastoral drama, the *Aminta* in 1573; another is the production by the Uniti troupe of Gian Battista Guarini's no less verbally elaborate pastoral play, *Il pastor fido* ('The Faithful Shepherd'), in Bologna on 17 December 1623. Again, quite a number of professional players, including major figures like Scala, Silvio Fiorillo (fl. late sixteenth to early seventeenth centuries), Cecchini and Niccolo Barbieri (1576–1641, stage name Beltrame), wrote plays.[4] Some of these may strike us as mere literary exercises, far too interminable and verbose to have actually been performed, but in fact many are no more so than other plays of this period which were certainly acted; then, just as now, what appeared on the stage was not necessarily all of, or only, what appeared in print. Of course, that must also apply to the plays companies are known to have acted, like those remarked above. It is also relevant to note that *dilettanti* wrote plays employing the type-characters and motives of the professional improvised drama, and that from the later decades of the sixteenth century improvisation was popular among amateurs.[5] Finally, some of the more marked emphases in what are often considered the defining characteristics of *commedia dell'arte* – off-the-cuff improvisation, marked emphasis on physicality and buffoonery, a pronounced farcical dimension, colourful masked figures and the use of a polyglot dialogue – may have been largely developed for, or during, foreign touring and residence.

What ultimately distinguished full-time professionals, whatever their status, was that for varying periods, often for much or all of their lifetimes, they were committed to the theatre as a way of earning a living for themselves and their families. That applied as much to the highly talented *comici* who operated under noble patronage, like those attached to, or under the aegis of, courts like those at Mantua, Modena and Florence, as it did to the lesser troupes. For the Italians, just as for the Elizabethan acting companies, economics and patronage were great determinants, shaping what could and could not be done. Audience likes and dislikes were crucial. Municipal tolerance of playing was important. Patrician patronage could exercise great influence not only on the careers of players, but on the content of the pieces performed; nor could such high-level patronage always be relied on, even when a player was in royal employ. A member of the Duke of Modena's troupe, while in London in 1678, heard that his wife and children had been reduced to indigence in his absence, and had to plead with the Duke to relieve them. Then, even more than now, acting was a precarious craft to take up, and many who did so lived much more than now on the margin of society, welcomed by some, treated as highly suspect by others, anathema to a few. Nor were charges of unreliability, deviousness, promiscuity and criminality wholly unwarranted; social marginality and financial indigence encouraged such vices, as did itinerancy and the need to please. Significant is the fact that in the late sixteenth century and early decades of the seventeenth century, many of the leading players strove, through their example, published writings and pursuit of academic and royal honours, to exculpate the majority of their profession from charges of immorality and social deviancy.

The first sure record we have of the existence of a fully fledged and legally constituted professional acting company is that of a troupe formed in Padua in 1545. The articles of agreement signed between the members of this troupe – all of them male – and renewed a year later, suggest it was essentially a small co-operative, working on an equal-share basis, and anxious from the outset to include provision in the contract for all likely situations and eventualities. As such it is an invaluable document, touching on matters of troupe-leadership, travel, discipline, division of earnings, provision for sickness and even support services, including the purchase of a horse to transport effects from town to town:

> Item, that a horse shall be bought from the communal fund of the company, that shall carry the belongings of the brothers from place to place.

> Item, that when the company reaches Padua, which should be in the month of June, then the money in the box shall be divided equally.

> Item, that at the beginning of the month of September next the said company, subject to the afore-mentioned penalties, being all in agreement, shall go each his own way.

> Item, that the said companions together shall not play cards with each other nor do anything else but take meals.[6]

Many troupes in the sixteenth century and later were almost certainly of modest means – as probably was this company – eking out a living as best they could, and disbanding when convenience or necessity obliged. However, by the end of the century some had acquired great reputations not only within, but far beyond the Italian peninsula.

The introduction of actresses in the 1560s almost certainly marked a new phase in the development of the companies: their appearance helped to balance the comedy by giving more realism to the romantic plot lines, and was probably a calculated bid for greater commercial appeal. Their arrival also seems to coincide with, or to be quite rapidly followed by, the presence in the troupes of actors better educated and more socially sophisticated than was common among the popular street and Carnival entertainers. It is from the 1560s onwards, too, that we find some companies increasingly looking to indoor performance places for their regular public and commercial, as well as more exclusive court activities. Inevitably, it is about the major companies, usually performing to socially more select audiences, that we know most, for more traces of their activities have survived in court and municipal account books, and private journals, letters and similar literary records maintained by the educated elite. Of the poorer troupes, although many may have been celebrated by word of mouth, we know little. Indeed, the hard fact is that even for the major companies, from the sixteenth century through to the eighteenth, extant records are decidedly patchy.

Probably before the end of the 1560s the characteristic composition of the majority of the major companies had been established, and it was to remain virtually the same for nearly two hundred years, notwithstanding that much in performance styles, materials and techniques changed. In response to the needs of improvised drama, troupe complement was schematised according to a balance of masked and unmasked character types (*tipi fissi*), familiar from the extant *scenari* and the rich surviving iconography: two *vecchi*, or old men – Pantalone (also known as Magnifico), Gratiano etc.; two *zanni*, or comic servants, Arlecchino, Brighella etc.; two pairs of lovers; a *servetta*, or servant maid, a Capitano, or Captain, and assorted walk-ons. It has been argued that the very origin of the improvised drama is to be found in Magnifico-Zanni sketches. These masks and type-figures all carry rich social relevances, pointed up in dress, language, gesture and manner: thus Pantalone is a kind of Venetian merchant; the Dottore has hints of the Bolognese academic about him; Zanni is a kind of Bergamasque *facchino*, and the Capitano, often complicator of amorous imbroglios, sometimes a kind of airy or blustering Spanish *hidalgo*. This social rooting has led some commentators to see the *commedia all'improvviso* as often markedly satirical.

Of the foremost sixteenth-century acting companies, perhaps the most celebrated was the Gelosi. At various times its complement included a number of the leading performers of the day, among them Francesco Andreini (1548–1624) and his wife Isabella (née Canali, 1562–1604), the former for a time the troupe's *capo comico*, the latter the most celebrated actress of the age and a noted poetess. Others of note in the troupe at the end of the sixteenth century (although the dates of all are uncertain), were Vittoria Piissimi (*prima donna*) and Aurelia Romana (*prima donna*), Giulio Pasquati (Pantalone), Silvia Roncagli (Franceschina) and Simone da Bologna (Zanni). The Gelosi, like other troupes, formed, broke and re-formed; there are then, in a sense, several companies of the Gelosi, and their personnel similarly changed from time to time. Other major sixteenth-century troupes included the Confidenti, the Accesi, the Uniti and the Desiosi, most continuing into the seventeenth century, when they were joined by companies like the Affezionati, sometimes travelling under the name of the Confederati – suggesting a troupe amalgamation – and the Fedeli, a company about which perhaps more information has come down than about any other, in part because it was formed and led by Giovan Battista Andreini (*c.*1576–1654, stage-name Lelio), son of Francesco and Isabella, the most important Italian actor-dramatist of the seventeenth century, and in part because it quite frequently performed in Paris and at the French court and drew the comment of contemporaries. The corpus of G. B. Andreini's dramatic work is only now beginning to attract the attention it merits, more perhaps for its theatrical qualities – its use of spectacle, music and dance – and its position between the scripted, improvised and *melodramma* stages, than for its literary quality *per se*; it is clear that Andreini was an important and probably influential *homme du théâtre*, and the activities of this company made a considerable impact. Probably surviving into the 1640s, the Fedeli included in its complement at various times such distinguished performers as Andreini's first wife, Virginia Ramponi (*c.*1583–*c.*1628, stage-name Florinda), a capable singer as well

Figure 4: Pantalone 1550 – Masques et bouffons.

Figure 5: Harlequin 1570 – Masques et bouffons.

as actress, and the great Arlecchino, Tristano Martinelli (1556–c.1630), younger brother of the Drusiano mentioned below as being in England in the 1570s.[7]

In many instances players were known as much by their stage as by their given names, and in *commedia a soggetto* some acted throughout their lives the role with which they started in the profession; yet others changed role when age seemed to make that advisable, or when they conceived of a new type they were keen to introduce: thus Francesco Andreini apparently began as a lover, before switching to Capitano del Val Inferno, and Silvio Fiorillo developed the Pulcinella mask after acting Captain Matamoros. Capitano, the *zanni*, Pantalone, Dottore, the lovers and the other types, were all open to change over time and to innumerable interpretations according to the age, appearance, personality, and physical and histrionic gifts, tricks and mannerisms of the individual performer. Further, different *canovacci* called for the same type to be performed in different ways, and with the passage of time styles and fashions in dress, deportment and speech changed and were reflected in the way the types were presented. However, as we have noted Luigi Riccoboni to remark above, many Italian actors and actresses were well capable of discarding the masks and roles of the improvised drama altogether and of assuming parts in scripted plays. If the comments of Francesco Gabrielli (1588–1636, stage-name Scappino) are to be taken as accurate and representative, clearly some were and some were not possessed of this admired and professionally useful versatility. Writing in a letter of 6 January 1627 to the Secretary to the Duke of Mantua he observes of certain fellow players, the first an actress from a rival troupe, the other two actresses he is keen to promote:

> Lavinia is not much good in improvised pieces, so the company could not use her in other than scripted plays . . . Celia is the leading *prima donna* of the stage both in scripted and improvised plays, for if the company or others bring out devised pieces of new comedies she will perform them immediately, which Lavinia and other actresses would not until they had thought through the content of the *soggetto* for a month beforehand. I will say nothing about Flavia, for she is the best *seconda donna* now acting, whether in scripted or improvised plays.[8]

The history of the professional theatre at this time is very much the history of actors, but unfortunately we still know comparatively little about the lives and work of even the major players. For example, much has been written about Isabella Andreini, including at least one biography, but our knowledge of her personality and private life is slight, and that of her theatrical activities, while more considerable than for most actresses of her generation, is nonetheless limited; the lengthier accounts of her career thus tend to lean heavily on discussion of her poems and letters. Much the same goes for the career of her husband, Francesco, although about him there are a few intriguing details: before becoming an actor, he was a soldier and a prisoner of the Turks for eight years; before leading the Gelosi he was with the Uniti, and was possibly its *capo comico*; there are extant portraits of him, and we can also glean a little additional information, such as the role he played and the way he played it, from his writings. But useful as these details are, they are scanty, and with respect to the careers, styles and personalities of most of the other leading *comici dell'arte* of the seventeenth century we are similarly ill informed.

A glance at a scenario from the collection published by Flaminio Scala in 1611, *Il teatro delle favole rappresentative, ovvero la Ricreazione comica, boscareccia e tragica,* will give some idea of the sort of dramatic materials which were employed in improvised drama and suggest ways performers may have sought to bring the skeletal plot lines alive in performance. Some 750 *canovacci* have survived in seventeenth- and eighteenth-century collections, but it is often difficult to determine if these were prepared for professional or amateur performance. The Scala collection is therefore convenient to use for illustrative purposes, for not only is it early, but it seems pretty certainly to be of professional provenance, even if possibly polished by Scala for publication and addressed to an amateur readership. Taken together with Andreini's collection of Capitano–Zanni dialogues, the *Bravure del Capitan Spavento* ('The Ploys of Captain Spavento') and some other extant dialogues and outlines of *lazzi* – short passages of physical and verbal business – it provides some indication of the materials employed by the professionals. On reading the Scala scenarios it is evident the *comici* drew for their plots on ancient drama, erudite comedy, popular literature and, probably, the oral tradition; the influence of Plautus' plays and Renaissance Plautine imitations in particular seems to have been strong. But scenarios cannot be read like play texts, nor are they performance texts; their function was probably to serve as mnemonics to the players, perhaps before and during performance, and while they are helpful in indicating kinds of plot and setting, specifying exits and entrances, and pointing up props, costumes, *lazzi* and occasional business, it is hazardous to attempt to extrapolate too much from them. Again, they were almost certainly changed over time and accommodated to the actors' varying needs.

Il capitano ('The Captain'), is a short Scala scenario with a very complicated, but fairly characteristic plot of love entanglements, flight, pursuit, comic complications and happy resolutions. We encounter the quite customary grouping of the characters by family: Pantalone, his son Oratio, and his servant Pedrolino; Dottor Grattiano, his supposed daughter Flaminia, and his house servant Arlecchino; Cassandro, his son Cinthio, and daughter Isabella. In addition, there is a Capitano (actually Cinthio), who gives his name to the piece; a kind of *servetta* (Franceschina); a nurse supposed to look after Isabella; and a call for soldiers, footmen and musicians. As so often in the scenarios, at least until the mid seventeenth century, properties are of the simplest: a table and chairs, sweets, wooden chests, a jewel box and weapons. However, unusually as far as setting is concerned, here there is specific call for a garden to be arranged at one side of the stage. The action is set throughout in Milan, but the characters have arrived from a variety of cities including Siena, Rome, Naples and Bologna, this multiplicity of place-reference perhaps calculated to appeal to the geographically diverse audiences encountered by a travelling company. The picaresque nature of the piece is conveyed not by movement of scenes from one locale to another, but by reference to the characters' origins and what has happened to them before the start of the action. From the Argument we learn that Cassandro, and his son and daughter, are from Siena. A Captain, passing through Siena on the way to Naples with his soldiers, encountered Cinthio, who decided to enrol as a soldier with him, and Cassandro, seeking to restrain his son, followed the two of them to Rome, where he saw them embark for Naples. Attempting to pursue them, Cassandro had to be rescued at sea from marauding Turks by a galley of the Grand Duke of Tuscany. Meanwhile Franceschina and Cassandro's daughter, Isabella, left behind in Siena, had set off for Bologna, where Isabella was handed over to the care of a gentlewoman, while Franceschina headed on to Milan in pursuit of a lover. At the same time, Dottor Grattiano has come to Milan with his supposed daughter, Flaminia (really the long-lost daughter of Pantalone, stolen as a child by gypsies); his dearest wish is to marry her to Pantalone's son, Oratio, actually, of course, her brother. In the scenario. after innumerable twists and turns of fate, all confusions in the tale are resolved, lost children are restored and marriages arranged.

It is scarcely necessary to emphasise that as a story the piece is manifestly a contrived and extravagant fiction, rooted in consciously complicated plot lines, confusions and disguises. Pantalone unquestioningly hands over ransom money to Pedrolino on being told his son Oratio has been captured by bandits; Isabella dresses up as a soldier to general bewilderment; Cassandro appears not to recognise his daughter when he meets her, and instantly agrees to become a soldier himself; Oratio and Pedrolino appear to have obtained money by signing up to be soldiers, but exactly when, why and how much they have been paid is less than clear. On hearing that the Captain loves Isabella, Flaminia immediately agrees to marry Oratio, and it is only at the beginning of Act III that we learn Pedrolino is the husband of Franceschina. This is comedy that delights in its own artificiality: the incredible is made acceptable and engaging by the sheer *brio* with which incident is piled on incident, mistake on mistake, confusion on confusion. The complexity of the story-line gives some indication of how much had to be carefully explained in the dialogue and, further, how that dialogue must have entailed very sophisticated working out by the actors, with character relationships and plot throughlines carefully pointed, if the story was not to be incomprehensible to the spectators. Little here in performance could have been wholly unpremeditated.

Whether the scenario had actually at some time been prepared for a company in which Francesco Andreini took the *Capitano* role is unclear: but it is interesting that it bears the name of his mask, and reference to Cassandro's capture by the Turks seems to glance at Andreini's imprisonment and service with the army of the Duke of Tuscany. Like Elizabethan plays, scenarios would certainly have been adapted according to the needs of acting companies and the skills, personalities and experience of particular players. But exactly how the *comici dell'arte* worked on a piece like *Il capitano* – how they actually put such a play together – is a matter that remains rather elusive. Niccolo Barbieri, whose long career spanned mountebank and court companies, wrote in 1643 that 'the players study and stock their memories with a great load of things, like wise sayings, conceits, love discourses, imprecations and outbursts of desperation or despair, in order to have them ready when needed, and their studies are in tune with the lineaments of the figures they perform', an account confirmed by Cecchini's comments on improvisation. The kinds of material to which the *comici* turned are amusingly illustrated in one of the prologues written by the actor Domenico Bruni, in which a servant bewails the running about she is put to in order to supply the players with the books they need to prepare their roles:

> Oh Lord! Just listen to it. In the morning the signora calls me: 'Hey, Ricciolina, bring me the material I need to study for the lover's role of Fiammetta.' Pantalone insists I get the letters of Calmo. The Capitano wants the *Bravure* of Capitan Spavento. Zanni asks for the witty pieces of Bertoldo, the *Fugilozio* and the *Hours of Recreation*. Graziano needs the *Sentenze dell'Erborente* and the *Novissima Polianta*, while Franceschina wants *La Celestina* to learn vulgarity. The *innamorato* asks for the works of Plato. . .[9]

Typical other reading might include Petrarchan sonnets, soliloquies and heroic speeches from scripted plays, wise sayings and apothegms, fine Platonic arguments on love, life, beauty and virtue, and pungent macaronic verses on senile lasciviousness or female frailty. By memorising particularly choice passages, lines or turns of phrase, the players would build up a stock of materials – *contrasti, dialoghi, soliloqui* – which they could use as occasion permitted. In improvisation, then, part of the art with respect to the spoken elements lay in the skill with which 'borrowed' materials and actor-interpolations, including wholly spontaneous ones, were woven seamlessly into dialogue appropriate to the performance abilities and the stage personality of the particular actor and the nature of the role performed.[10] Thus when taken seriously, preparation required dedicated study, entailing as it did selection, premeditation and calcula-tion of what might be used when and where, while performance itself involved delivery of what had been prepared, together with quick re-sponses to opportunities provided by the dialogue and the actions of stage colleagues, and to the changing moods and reactions of the audience.

Nearly all the extant *scenari* have marked contemporary emphases, including wide-ranging reference to people and matters of general interest to spectators of the time: to plague, piracy, robbers, money-bags, mounte-banks, street barbers and dentists, ghosts, devils, soldiers, policemen, foreigners, particularly Turks, and so on. They tend to be rather less specific about place, and while the action of a scenario may be described as taking place in Florence or Bologna, compared to the *commedia erudita* there is rather less reference to particular squares, streets and buildings. *Scenari* were not only comic. Although comedy dominated, there are extant scenarios in several genres, including tragicomedy, tragedy, pastoral and, by the turn of the century, semi-operatic pieces. One inescapable fact about many of the *canovacci*, although some commentators have tended to play it down, is the extent to which they exploit sexual reference and the erotic appeal of actresses: thus in the Scala collection we may briefly note how in *Il finto negromante* ('The Fake Magician') Oratio has made Pantalone's daughter, Flaminia, pregnant, Isabella is pregnant by Flavio and Gratiano jokes about getting women with child; in *La gelosa Isabella* ('The Jealous Isabella') Burattino invites Pantalone and Gratiano to enjoy the company of courtesans at his inn, Oratio asks Franceschina to sleep with him and Franceschina, after engaging in 'much lewd banter', even after the entry of her mistress Flaminia, continues to behave 'in a lascivious manner' with him. Cross-dressing, undressing on stage and night scenes with actresses appearing dishevelled in scanty attire are fairly stock features of the scenarios, as too are opportunities for sexually suggestive business, vulgar jokes and double entendres. In this respect, the scenarios reflect the unabashed directness of the age and the earthy bluntness characteristic of both popular and elite comedy. The varied social rootings of the stage figures, as well as the sex and age conflicts, the cross-dressings and the disguisings and masquerades, all suggest engagement with class and gender issues, but the elusiveness of the skeletal scenarios as performance texts inhibits interpretation.

For major touring companies, the main working areas in the Italian peninsula for much of the period considered here were probably much like those a company manager in 1640 told Ottonelli made up his troupe's annual tour:

> 'From Bologna to Milan, from Milan to Genoa, from Genoa to Florence, from Florence to Venice, where the company concluded at Carnival time.'[11]

But companies also toured further south, in and about Rome and Naples and into Sicily. By the 1570s at the latest the *commedia dell'arte* companies had also taken to foreign travel, the leading troupes either making their own *grandes tournées* or being sent for a short period by a noble patron as a goodwill gift to a foreign court. While there were occasional conflicts between the French players and the Italian, the former seeing their livelihoods challenged, the popularity of the Italians among spectators was considerable:

> On Sunday 19 May [1577] the Italian actors called the Gelosi began to perform their plays in the hall of the Hotel de Bourbon in Paris, requiring four *sols* a head from each French spectator wanting to see them act, and such a throng assembled that the four best preachers in Paris would not draw so great a crowd to their preaching . . .[12]

What attracted large audiences to the entertainment offered by the players was doubtless much the same in Paris as it was in Italy and elsewhere; it was comprehensively described by Niccolo Barbieri in his defence of the players' craft:

> If I am not wrong, the reasons people attend plays are the following: many are curious to see how good the actors are, and many are inclined to any new attractions: this one goes out of boredom, because he does not know what to do with himself: many go to hear original turns of phrase and fine discourses, and others to hear the comic roles: an individual thinking of becoming a player himself may go to learn, someone else for the conversation of his friends: another in the hope of cadging from an acquaintance: yet another to avoid an hour gambling, another to banish dull spirits, another to observe behaviour, or not to seem miserly or ignorant, another out of habit, and another because he sees that others go.[13]

Abroad, as in Italy, audiences seem to have been socially diverse; in early modern Europe social orders from the highest to the lowest enjoyed many of the same styles and kinds of entertainment, it often being special occasions or particular performance places which occasioned exclusion. In the late sixteenth century in Florence a passage-way linked the ducal palace to the Teatrino di Baldracca: the passage led to a screened and grilled balcony where the duke and his guests could watch unobserved by public audiences performances by the *comici mercenari*.

Paris and the other seats of the French court were particular magnets for the troupes: early visits included the company of Zan Ganassa (Alberto Naseli, fl. late sixteenth to early seventeenth century) in Paris in 1570–1, and the first visits of the Gelosi to the French court occurred in 1571 and

1577. But touring was widespread, to the German states, Spain, France, the Low Countries and beyond to Scandinavia, while in the eighteenth century it extended as far as Russia. At various times throughout the period major towns like Vienna, Dresden, Warsaw, Stockholm and St Petersburg were particular draws thanks to the patrician patronage they provided and a general public eager for theatrical fare. In several countries, notably Spain and Russia, the activities of the Italian *comici dell'arte* contributed significantly to the development of native theatre. Touring abroad was in most instances quite profitable, otherwise it would not have been undertaken, for it could be costly, exhausting and occasionally dangerous. Not only major companies toured. There is ample evidence that quite modest charlatan-led troupes were regular performers beyond the peninsula. The Swiss traveller Thomas Platter is witness to one such company:

> The show began after dinner with a very amusing comedy, which lasted for a good hour or two, and before a throng of spectators. Following this, Zani, the head of the troupe, having opened up a large chest which they had brought with them, was asked by his companion, dressed as a doctor, what the chest contained. Zani promptly replied in a high-sounding way that he had brought it from Turkey, where he had bought marvellous prescriptions and acquired many occult recipes.[14]

It was probably more from the *comici dell'arte* he encountered during his apprentice years in the provinces than from the great actor Tiberio Fiorilli (?1608–94, stage-name Scaramuccia/Scaramouche) that Molière learned and borrowed much, and the materials and techniques of the Italians later exerted considerable influence on French dramatists like Fatouville and Regnard. There are few traces of them or their influence in England, however: one of the earliest troupes to visit was a company led by Drusiano Martinelli that came over from the Low Countries in 1577; after that the only Italian troupe known to have visited England through to the closing of the theatres was one led by a certain Curtesse in 1602. That England was no draw is understandable: it was expensive and time-consuming to reach, a Protestant country not always welcoming of Catholics, actresses were not tolerated and the English professional theatre was sophisticated in its organisation and not conspicuously sympathetic to foreign competition. In countries where they were well received, the Italian players made a point of accommodating their performances to local needs. That was most conspicuous in France, where professional jealousy was eclipsed by royal enthusiasm. They quickly adjusted to French tastes, habits and language, and increasingly exploited scenic effects in order to attract French audiences and to compete with native French comedy, intrapolating French into their Italian speech and fashioning a kind of polyglot stage dialogue, eventually even turning to the use of texts prepared by French dramatists. Where at the turn of the sixteenth century Italian had been perhaps the leading modern European language, known by many at the courts and encouraged by Italian princesses resident abroad, like Maria de Medici, by the mid seventeenth century it had begun to lose that prominence. The outcome in the theatre was the eventual emergence of what was in effect a distinct theatrical kind that blended elements of the Italian and French languages and their dramatic and theatrical cultures.

Foreign touring could be profitable, a way of expanding markets and useful in times of serious local trouble at home, like political and social disturbance, war and plague. The timing of visits abroad, and the sorts of places visited, had to be chosen with some care: religious and political hostility, and even the opposition of theatrical rivals, could play havoc with profits. Long-distance travel could be precarious, too, with respect to health and family relationships, for periods spent abroad were often lengthy and travel difficult. It also required careful arrangement, that included obtaining a passport, getting permission to leave, acquiring letters of recommendation and protection, sometimes bidding departure from wife and family and then, at the end of a visit, eliciting from the foreign patron permission and passport to leave, and so on. Nor could a trouble-free time, nor a welcome at the end of the journey, nor a happy and profitable sojourn, nor an easy departure, be casually anticipated. For the major companies, the records suggest that touring in France was a fairly regular activity in the early decades of the seventeenth century, and in the late 1650s and early 1660s a permanent company came gradually to be established there under the patronage of Louis XIV. From the time of the establishment of this Italian company, the Comédie Italienne, the most distinguished Italian players of the second half of the seventeenth century were resident either semi-permanently or for lengthy periods in Paris, achieving their great reputations more there than in Italy itself: Tiberio Fiorilli, Domenico Biancolelli (?1636–88, stage-name Dominique), Evaristo Gherardi (1663–1700, a celebrated Arlecchino) among them.

Success on Italian stages may have come to be seen as a stepping stone to the richer pickings to be had in Paris, or to hopefully profitable invitations to other courts: like the sojourns of the eighteenth-century players Gaetano Sacchi in Moscow, Andrea Bertoldi (Pantalone) and Cesare D'Arbes (Pantalone, *c.* 1708–78) in Dresden, and Antonio Sacchi (1708–88, stage-name Truffaldino) in Lisbon. In turn, French staging practices were almost certainly fed back into the Italian theatre in the mid and late seventeenth century, possibly encouraging more emphasis to be put upon physical and farcical business and greater recourse to the use of scenic decoration and effects. With respect to the last point, it is difficult to separate French influence from that of a new Italian theatrical kind becoming increasingly popular, first in the courts, then from 1637 in the public theatres, at Venice and soon elsewhere, and a central ingredient of which was rich stage-spectacle, namely *dramma per musica*, or opera – with the emergence and establishment of which the *comici dell'arte* were certainly involved.

The later seventeenth-century activities of the *comici* are not well documented, but a number of fine actor-managers were active on the touring circuits, among them Francesco Gabrielli, Giovanni Andrea Zanotti (1622–95, stage-name Ottavio), Marcantonio Carpiani and Bernardino Coris (about both of whom little is known). Doubtless, too, much fine theatre was performed of which no report has come down. Theatre is a highly social art, and dependent on favourable social conditions. The seventeenth century saw adverse political and economic changes in the Italian peninsula which worked to the detriment of theatre patronage. Further, first at patrician levels, then with a broad public, *melodramma* became fashionable, offering serious competition to the work of the regular theatre players. To retain their appeal some players, *zanni* in particular, seem to have had recourse to ever more crude and crowd-catching business, issuing in what came to be seen as the decadence of the improvised drama. Perhaps the most important, and certainly a most versatile, *capocomico* at the end of the century, was Luigi Riccoboni, of particular importance because he sought to effect reform of a decaying skill. Actor, manager, scenario-writer and, as noted above, historian of the Italian stage, Riccoboni tried to restore a degree of traditional expertise and professional seriousness of purpose to the theatre of his day, advancing new scripted work and disciplining the excesses of the improvised re-pertory, while at the same time accommodating presentation to the most

advanced theatrical means: the scenarios he himself devised for performance manifestly call for the sophisticated scenery and machines of the
baroque stage, and dance is a prominent feature of the dramaturgy. But
in Italy Riccoboni's endeavours met with only partial success.

Unfortunately, in Paris in 1697, over-confidence and satirical *brio* led
to the performance of a piece, *La Fausse Prude*, interpreted by the French
court as a slight on the King's mistress, Madame De Maintenon. The details
of the ensuing scandal, revealing of the rivalries and hostilities which
possessed the Franco-Italian stage at the end of the century, have proved
of recurring fascination to theatre historians; at the centre of them seems
to have been the aforementioned Angelo Costantini. Louis XIV took
action directed at the collective: he expelled the Italians from Paris, an
exodus that excited poetic lamentations and at least one fine painting
depicting their woebegone departure. Some may have crossed the Channel
and, by performing in the English fairs, possibly helped to generate the
English pantomime. The Italians returned to Paris only in 1716, after the
death of Louis XIV, when Riccoboni brought a troupe under the patronage
of the Duke of Orleans. But much was not changed. After initial success,
Riccoboni's repertoire palled with the Parisian public and he turned
increasingly to pieces written in French, encouraging the work, among
others, of Marivaux. In England the harlequinade flourished for more
than a century, as did what some have thought to be a remote *commedia
dell'arte* offshoot, the Punch and Judy show.

Although a detailed history of the actors and companies in the eighteenth-
century Italian states remains to be written, we are at least fortunate in
having several important sources of information, notably the memoirs
of the Venetian dramatists Carlo Goldoni and Carlo Gozzi, and the
confessions of that other Venetian, Giacomo Casanova. All have much
to say about actors, actresses and theatres, as well as the stages of the
opera seria and *buffa*, particularly those of Venice, the centre of much of
the most vital Italian drama and theatre of the middle decades of the
eighteenth century. Here we need only remark the importance of Goldoni in
developing Italian scripted comedy by disciplining and then discarding the
masked figures, but retaining much of the rapid accumulation of incidents
and the balletic dramaturgy which characterised the improvised comedy.
His reforms did not in themselves kill that comedy, even if they helped
gradually to transform it. Indeed, Goldoni himself at times worked closely
with important later *capocomici* including Girolamo Medebach (1706–90)

and Antonio Sacchi (1708–88, stage-name Truffaldino). But by the time Goldoni entered the theatre, in the 1740s, a casualness and easy lassitude in attitudes to performance seem to have been widespread, and the theatre seemingly had ceased to attract many players of intellectual distinction. Carlo Gozzi suggests as much in his memoirs:

> I have been acquainted with both actors and actresses who have not even had [the ability to read and write] and yet they carried on their business without flinching. They got their lines read out to them by some friend or some associate, whenever a new part had to be impressed in outline on their memory. Keeping their ears open to the prompter, they entered boldly on the stage, and played a hero or a heroine without a touch of truth. The presentation of such characters by actors of the sort I have described abounds in blunders, stops and stays, and harkings back upon the leading motive, which would put to shame the player in his common walk of life.[15]

Although the death of Sacchi is often taken to mark the passing of the improvised drama, it persisted in various guises and changed modes through the late eighteenth century and well into the nineteenth in Naples and elsewhere in southern Italy, in the performances of players like Pasquale Altavilla (1806–72) and Antonio Petito (1822–76). It entered, too, into the spirit of the English harlequinade and pantomime and the Romantic mime of French boulevard entertainers like Jean-Baptiste Debureau. In one way or another *commedia all'improvviso*, or a conception of what it had once been, has impressed itself firmly on much later Italian dramatists as different as Luigi Pirandello, Eduardo De Filippo and Dario Fo, who have been greatly in its debt. Indeed, many would argue that its impact has been and continues to be international – in the twentieth-century theatre, opera, the visual and plastic arts, circus, silent comic film and television 'sit-com', all drawing inspiration from it.

Notes

1 Recent Italian scholarship has encouraged rethinking: see particularly Tessari, *'Industria' e 'Arte giocosa'* and *'La Maschera'*; Taviani and Schino, *Il Segreto*; Zorzi, *L'attore.*, Ferrone, *Comici.*

2 Richards and Richards, *The Commedia dell'Arte*; Katritzky, 'Was commedia dell'arte performed by mountebanks'.

3 Cited in Richards and Richards, *The Commedia dell'Arte*, p. 122 (English translation of 1744).

4 For example Scala, *Il finto marito* (1619); Fiorillo, *I Tre capitani vanagloriosi* (1621); G. B.Andreini, *Le due comedie in comedia* (1623); Barbieri, *L'inavertito* (1629). For a modern edition of key play texts and discussion see Ferrone, *Comici.*

5 Richards and Richards, *The Commedia dell'Arte*, pp. 48ff.

6 For the whole see *ibid.*, pp. 44–6.

7 When a scheduled singer fell ill, Virginia Ramponi famously took over at the last moment the lead role in Monteverdi's *dramma per musica, Arianna* (1608).

8 Cited in Richards and Richards, *The Commedia dell'Arte*, pp. 124–5.

9 Cited in *ibid.*, p. 149.

10 What Leone de'Sommi has to say about staging and acting in his *Quattro dialoghi* is relevant, notwithstanding that his work refers mainly to staging the *commedia erudita.*

11 See G. D. Ottonelli, *Della Christiana Moderatione del Teatro*, Florence, 1652, p. 128.

12 Cited in Richards and Richards, *The Commedia dell'Arte*, p. 269.

13 Cited in *ibid.*, pp. 99–100.

14 Cited in *ibid.*, pp. 270–1.

15 Cited in *ibid.*, p. 294.

Bibliography

Apollonio, M. 'Il duetto di Magnifico e Zanni alle origini dell'Arte', in M. T. Muraro (ed.), *Studi sul Teatro Veneto tra Umanesimo e Rinascimento*, Florence, 1971.

Artoni, A. *Il teatro degli Zanni: Rapsodie dell'Arte e dintorni,* Ancona and Milan, 1996.

Bourqui, C. *La Commedia dell'Arte. Introduction au théâtre professionnel italien entre le* XVIe *et le* XVIIIe *siècles,* Paris, 1999.

Ferrone, S. 'Attori, professionisti e dilettanti', in L. Zorzi, G. Innamorati and S. Ferrone (eds.), *Il Teatro del Cinquecento,* Florence, 1982.

Ferrone, S. *et al.* (eds.), *Comici dell'Arte. Corrispondenze: G. B. Andreini, N. Barbieri, M. Cecchini, S. Fiorillo, T. Martinelli, F. Scala,* 2 vols., Florence, 1993.

Giardi, O. *I comici dell'Arte perduta. Le compagnie comiche italiane alla fine del secolo* XVIII, Rome, 1991.

Heck, T. H. *Commedia dell'Arte. A Guide to the Primary and Secondary Literature,* New York and London, 1988

Henke, R. *Performance and Literature in the Commedia dell'Arte,* Cambridge, 2002.

Jolibert, B. *La commedia dell'arte et son influence en France du* XVIe *au* XVIIIe *siècle,* Paris and Montreal, 1999.

Katritzky, M. A. 'Was *commedia dell'arte* performed by mountebanks? *Album amicorum* illustrations and Thomas Platter's description of 1598', *Theatre Research International*, 23 (1998), 104–26.

Lea, K. M. *Italian Popular Comedy: A Study in the Commedia Dell'Arte*, 2 vols., Oxford, 1934.

Mosele, E. (ed.), *La Commedia dell'Arte tra Cinque e Seicento in Francia e in Europa*, Fasano, 1997.

Rasi, L. *I comici: Italiani: biografia, bibliografia, iconografia*, 3 vols., Florence, 1897–1905.

Richards, K. and R. *The Commedia dell'Arte: A Documentary History*, Oxford, 1990.

Salerno, H. F. (ed. and trans.), *Scenarios of the Commedia dell'Arte. Flaminio Scala's Il teatro delle favole rappresentative*, New York, 1967.

Scott, V. *The Commedia dell'Arte in Paris 1644–97*, Charlotteville, VA, 1990.

Sica, A. *Eros dell'Arte. Lo spettacolo delle Maschere*, Palermo, 1999.

Sommi, Leone de. *Quattro dialoghi in materia di rappresentazioni sceniche*, ed. F. Marotti, Archivio del Teatro Italiano, no. 1, Milan, 1968.

Taviani, F. and Schino, M. *Il segreto della commedia dell'arte*, Florence, 1982.

Tessari, R. *La Commedia dell'Arte nel Seicento. 'Industria' e 'Arte giocosa' della civiltà barocca*, Florence, 1969.

La Commedia dell'Arte: La Maschera e L'Ombra, Milan, 1981.

Théâtre Forain, *La Commedia dell'Arte, Le Théâtre Forain et les Spectacles de Plein Air en Europe XVIe – XVIIIe siècles*, Paris, 1998.

Zorzi, L. *L'attore, la commedia, il drammaturgo*, Turin, 1990.

PART III

The Seventeenth Century

12 The seventeenth-century stage

MAURICE SLAWINSKI

Spectacle was central to seventeenth-century life. Choreographed performances ranging from the solemn christening of princely offsprings to
the equally solemn dissection of criminals' cadavers by eminent physicians
sought to entertain, educate, persuade, stigmatise deviance, promote loyalty and community. Above all, in this 'dramatised' culture spectacle
became an important tool of absolutist government, with its emphasis on
propaganda, containment, control, the shaping of collective identities and
individual subjectivity in what, it has been argued, was the first 'mass'
society.

Emblematic of the effort to regulate spectacle so that what could be
seen coincided with what the state wished to display was the development
of scenic perspective. The stage was no longer to be simply a 'realistic'
mirror of its audience's world (as in the painted urban backdrops of the
previous century), but an ideal image of harmony which emanated and
could only be fully appreciated from the position of the prince. The result
was the establishment in 1586 of the first permanent, proscenium-arch
court theatre in the Uffizi of Florence, soon imitated in other major centres.
Although by the mid seventeenth century this had produced entrepreneurial adaptations, for the next two hundred years the *teatro all'italiana*,
adopted throughout Europe, would retain the imprint of its courtly origin,
particularly as regards the structural imperative of establishing a unique
panoptical point from which the whole spectacle – stage *and* audience –
could be perfectly viewed. It was the all-encompassing perspective given
by the princely seats facing the stage that guaranteed and authorised the
imperfect views which by (social as much as visual) degrees were afforded
to other spectators.

The development of theatrical space, its technologies (movable sets,
lighting, sound effects) and the 'language' of spectacle and performance
evolving out of them were almost entirely Italian achievements of the
late sixteenth and seventeenth centuries, exhaustively codified in treatises

like Nicola Sabbatini's *Pratica di fabricar scene e macchine ne' teatri* (1637–8, 'Art of Constructing Scenery and Machines for the Theatre') and exported with little or no further development throughout Europe. But when we turn our attention to what was performed on the Italian stage at this time, the picture that emerges is contradictory and in many respects disappointing. Permanent theatres open in every major city and even towns of a few thousand inhabitants; Italian princes continue to commission spectacles of great complexity and magnificence, assiduously imitated by provincial elites; companies of Italian players criss-cross the peninsula and tour the rest of Europe; opera houses are active for ever-longer seasons; publishers issue an endless stream of dramatic literature. Yet this intense, richly documented activity appears neither to have produced a significant canon of dramatic works nor (if we exclude *dramma per musica*, as the earliest form of opera was usually called) a distinctive tradition to compare to those of England, France or Spain.

The locations of theatre

Theatrical activity in the seventeenth century developed in three distinct locations. First, emerging out of earlier court entertainments, came princely *gran teatro*, in which the dramatic text soon ceased to play a central part, submerged by increasingly elaborate scenic effects, music and dance. As the staging of a five-act play interspersed with *intermezzi* gave way to a single integrated performance, the play became little more than the pretext for a series of spectacular set pieces in which each visual *coup de théâtre* introduced songs and dances so complex as to demand professional performers. The prototype of such spectacles was Gabriello Chiabrera's mythological-piscatorial *Il rapimento di Cefalo* ('The Rape of Cephalus'), performed in Florence in 1600 for the wedding of Maria de'Medici. *Gran teatro* led directly to the evolution of commercial opera, but though it came to rely on the same pool of professional performers it remained quite separate, by virtue of dynastic content, more lavish spectacle and the fact that the texts recited or sung were generally written by courtiers rather than theatre professionals.

As for the latter, they included both the *comici dell'arte* and the impresari, librettists and performers of commercial opera. Early in the century the two entertainments alternated in the same theatres, and even shared some performers, but as tastes changed and musical theatre grew more complex, both their personnel and audiences became differentiated. Opera was established as the favoured entertainment of nobility and wealthy middle class, performed in increasingly elaborate spaces. Conversely, the *comici* now addressed predominantly popular audiences, and were relegated to more makeshift playhouses. Though they occasionally revived classics such as Guarini's *Pastor fido*, most of what they performed, scripted or *all'improvvisa*, originated within the troupe. In this respect, practices were not dissimilar from those of the opera houses, except that while the latter produced a whole new category of stage authors, only one playwright of real significance emerged from the ranks of the *comici*.

The third kind of *Seicento* theatre was characterised by being non-commercial and the importance it attached to the play text, which may help explain why it accounts for the vast majority of published plays. As the linear descendant of the humanist-inspired drama of the sixteenth century, it might be termed 'literary' theatre, but is perhaps better described as 'academic', since its 'natural' location was the academy, that peculiarly Italian literary and social club which brought together the lay and ecclesiastical magnates of the locality, the lesser nobility and their client intellectuals (lawyers, doctors, teachers, priests). Sacred dramas performed in churches or religious colleges also essentially belonged to this category (the clerics involved often formally constituted themselves into academies for the purpose). But while this theatre was non-professional, it was not amateur in the modern sense. The part it played in a dramatised society was far more significant, not just a pastime for its producers and an entertainment for its consumers, but a means of negotiating status, social relations and collective identities. For its authors in particular, the *letterati* who by the early seventeenth century were emerging as distinct social subjects, writing, performance and publication were becoming crucial self-defining activities.

Courtly, commercial and academic theatre might periodically come into contact at the margins, and exchange characteristics. Stage machines devised for the court were quickly adopted by the commercial theatre, while the convoluted plots of the latter influenced court tastes. Professional actors sought to raise their social standing by writing to the parameters of academic theatre. Academic theatre sometimes emulated the professional stage – notably in Florence, where in the 1620s the Accademia degli Incostanti ('Academy of the Inconstant'), noble youths directed by the notary-turned-playwright Iacopo Cicognini (1577–1633), competed for audiences and Medici patronage with the Comici Confidenti. Nevertheless, the three locations remained largely separate. While in contemporary England and France we find a continuum of theatrical activity, where different kinds of theatre exist in close interrelation, with no clear boundaries between them, and princely patronage of key professional companies set the tone for the country as a whole, in Italy this was not the case.

One reason was the absence of a single unifying power. Another was the limited nature of Italian absolutism, founded on compromises with provincial elites jealous of their traditions and autonomy. The resulting institutional and geographic fragmentation was compounded by the ambivalence of the one authority extending throughout Italy, the Counter-Reformation church, acutely aware of how spectacle could promote its objectives, and equally aware of potential dangers. Secular theatre generally was open to misuse, hence controlled, restricted and subjected to the competition of lavish *sacre rappresentazioni*. But most threatening was commercial theatre, with all the excesses to which the profit motive might lead, and the suspicion of immorality surrounding its (mixed-sex) troupes. In Rome itself the ban on actresses meant the virtual exclusion of the *comici dell'arte* as well as the late establishment (1671) and temporary closure (1697) of commercial opera houses. Elsewhere the church could only exhort, but there too its suspicions contributed to the gradual marginalisation of the *comici* and the affirmation of opera, more acceptable because more exclusive.

Plays and playwrights

There exists, to date, no comprehensive study of *Seicento* dramatic literature, and it is therefore necessary to preface what follows with the caveat that it is based on partial knowledge. Tragedy has been studied more extensively than comedy, and while what was produced in a few major, mainly northern cities has been described in some detail, what went on elsewhere remains largely unexplored. Given that some of the most interesting dramas of the period were the work of isolated figures writing in relative obscurity, it is perfectly possible that others no less significant remain yet to be discovered.

In the absence of a better guide, a rapid survey of the *Catalogue of Seventeenth-Century Italian Books* in the British Library (BL) may give some idea of the extent and nature of the phenomenon. It lists some 700 editions of theatrical works, by almost 300 authors from every part of the peninsula,

distributed fairly evenly throughout the century. BL collections are estimated to include between a quarter and a sixth of all Italian books of
the period, suggesting that in excess of 3,000 dramatic texts were published in the course of the century. The real figure, however, may well
be much higher (provincial imprints are under-represented in the BL,
which, for example, holds just 30 of the 456 opera *libretti* known to have
been published in Bologna). To this must be added a sizable number of
extant manuscript plays, and references to many more lost altogether: a
vast mass of texts, few of which have been read, let alone performed, for
three hundred years. (By comparison, we have records of 2,000 plays
and masques of the Tudor and Stuart periods, of which just 500 survive.)

More than a quarter of the BL collection consists of *libretti*, unadorned
booklets intended for sale to prospective theatregoers. This contrasts with
play texts, whose larger formats and often considerable length betray
their primarily literary interest. Of these approximately 150 are comedies,
perhaps surprisingly in view of the limited attention devoted to the genre.
Most date from the first half of the century, though there are hints of
modest revival after 1680. A number originate from the professional
companies, and many more are written in their imitation, but even in this
most 'lowbrow' genre the majority belong to the academic stage. Next,
pastorals account for 103 editions, concentrated in the first third of the
century. A substantial number of reprints testify to their popularity. Against
these we find just 81 tragedies, somewhat more evenly spread through
the century, whose formats suggest that vanity played a significant part in
publication: the commercial risk of issuing costly quartos meant that
printers were unlikely to do so unless subsidised by author or patron. As
many texts again are religious dramas, often luxury publications associated
with the institution or individual promoting the spectacle. Finally, we have
19 'tragicomedies', spread quite evenly throughout the century, and it is
with this apparently least practised of dramatic genres that one might
begin some observations concerning the content of seventeenth-century
dramaturgy.

Tragicomedy originates in pastoral. It combines tragic pathos with
decorous comedy, leading to a positive resolution of the *peripeteia*, and
finds justification in late Renaissance theories of genre extrapolated from
Aristotle. But from the turn of the century we find, alongside *tragicommedie
pastorali* other texts simply designated *tragicommedie,* whose setting is

courtly (e.g. Federico Della Valle's *Adelonda di Frigia*, first staged in 1595, and Giovan Battista Leoni's *Antiloco*, published in 1597). Both kinds address a relatively sophisticated, mixed audience (as against the overwhelmingly male academic audience of 'regular', Aristotelian-inspired tragedy) whose principal interest lies in the portrayal of intense, often contradictory emotional states (*affetti*) felicitously resolved. And alongside them we find another sub-genre, the *tragedia a lieto fine* (tragedy with a happy ending), differing by virtue of the absence of comic elements, examples of which appear throughout the century, beginning with Giulio Strozzi's *Erotilla* (1615).

What these new types of drama also have in common is their combination of familiarity and novelty, often achieved by remarkable instances of hybridity: grafting on to the dramatic plot devices derived from romance, mixing the historical, mythological and wholly fictional; now ostentatiously adhering to Aristotelian rules, then no less ostentatiously breaking them. Giuseppe Artale's *Guerra tra vivi e morti* (1679, 'War Between the Living and the Dead') is an extreme example, both in content and chronology, hence a kind of concentrate of seventeenth-century dramaturgy, starting with the biography of its author (1628–79), whose rootlessness, precarious social identity and lack of lasting institutional recognition are typical of *letterati*, and may help explain two key characteristics of academic dramaturgy, its excess and apparent lack of engagement with the contemporary world. Divided, unusually, into three acts, its prose oscillates between the lapidary and merely stentorious, while its bizarre plot superimposes the Oedipus story on to a romanticised version of that of Semiramis, dispatching the tragic agnition of the former in the second act, while the love contests of the latter are resolved by further agnitions in the third (when the now blind Oedipus returns to act as marriage broker). Never staged, virtually unstageable, wholly lacking in characterisation or dramatic tension, the *Guerra* is an elaborate exercise in antithesis. This insistence on a single rhetorical figure as thematic key to the whole; its wilfully undialogic language; the combination of austerely classical with oriental elements; the multiple agnitions borrowed from the *commedia erudita* of the later sixteenth century, all bespeak that pursuit of *meraviglia* (astonishment) which the greatest theorist of Baroque 'wit', Emanuele Tesauro, justified as a response to the *svogliatura del secolo*, the combination of over-sophistication and *ennui* which distinguished the seventeenth century.

The tragic stage

The desire to astonish reaches its apogee in the improbably complex plots of commercial opera, where happy endings also predominate, but is no less evident in straight tragedy. It animates, not surprisingly, the Spanish-inspired dramas of Iacopo Cicognini's son Giacinto Andrea (1606–c.51), the century's most prolific stage author, to whom are attributed some fifty plays, best known of which is *Il tradimento per l'onore* ('Betrayal for Honour's Sake'), published 1664. This intricate prose tragedy, recounting the revenge of one Duke Federico on his wife Armidea and her lover Alfonso, revolves around the oxymoron of honourable treachery, the constant subject of Federico's soliloquies. But more important than this contrived inner conflict are the opportunities for melodrama, including the onstage banquet in which Alfonso is dispatched, and a pathetic climax when Armidea is murdered after a scene in which the reading of *Il Pastor fido* serves a function similar to the 'Willow Song' in *Othello*.

It is symptomatic of our imperfect knowledge of *Seicento* theatre that we do not know exactly who performed Cicognini's plays, or even which (including *Il tradimento*) really are his, although residence in Venice and his authorship of *libretti* suggest that he wrote for the professional stage. While most academic dramatists paid formal homage to Aristotle, they too were strongly inclined to satisfy their contemporaries' *svogliatura*. Thus we find a similar mixture in the work of Prospero Bonarelli (1580–1659), whose verse tragedy *Solimano* (first performed in 1618 by the 'academicians' of his native Ancona, published 1620), dealing with ostensibly historical events in the recent Ottoman past, self-consciously advertises the implausible compression within the statutory twenty-four hours of a complex mixture of epic and romance elements, political machinations and high pathos. This, and its oriental setting, proved sufficiently popular (on the written page at least) to warrant six reprints, the last in 1658, a clear pointer to continuity of tastes through the century.

Nor was religious tragedy immune from temptation. The tone is set by the Jesuit Bernardino Stefonio (1560–1620), whose Latin verse tragedy *Flavia*, a story of Christian martyrdom under the Emperor Domitian, was performed at the Collegio Romano in 1600. Its derivation is Senecan, but to the bloody dénouements (the heads of the protagonist's sons are paraded before him at what should have been a resolutory reunion) are added demonic apparitions conjured up by a necromancer who is repeatedly foiled by the equally spectacular interventions of St John the Apostle. By mid-century the more gratuitous pretexts for eye-catching stage effects have been curbed, but we still find strong elements of sensationalism, even in socially integrated authors committed to the rigorous classicism promoted by Pope Urban VIII and his Barberini nephews, like Giulio Rospigliosi (1600–69), the future Clement IX, and another Jesuit, Sforza Pallavicino (1607–77), a cardinal from 1659. Rospigliosi's *libretto* for a trend-setting *tragedia sacra per musica, Il Sant'Alessio*, lavishly staged in 1632 to inaugurate the Barberini theatre, consists of episodic encounters providing opportunities for pathos, moralising, some decorous comedy and supernatural apparitions, right through to a martyrdom which effectively turns the formal tragic conclusion into a happy ending. Twelve years later Pallavicino engaged in a similar operation in *Il martire Ermenegildo* ('The Martyr Ermenegildo'). The eponymous hero is converted to Christianity by his wife Ingonda, and put to death by his pagan father King Leovigoldo, after refusing to abjure his new faith. Within this minimal plot, devices borrowed from romance (Ingonda, disguised, attempts to free Ermenegildo, but fails when he does not recognise her; Leovigoldo's repentance comes too late to stop the execution) postpone the inevitable conclusion, introducing a modicum of action and pathos in a supposedly regular tragedy otherwise wholly lacking in dramatic interest.

Rospigliosi was sufficiently uneasy about the licence he had taken with Aristotle to preface the 1634 edition of his *libretto* with a letter defending his work's unity and the propriety of a tragic hero distinguished not by hubris but 'outstanding goodness and sanctity'. Pallavicino, whose *Trattato dello stile* (1646, 'Treatise on Style') would become a quasi-official manifesto of classicism, also appealed to Aristotle's authority for a view of the genre which in reality was very different, confusing catharsis with rhetorical persuasion. Similar views would be expressed in a *Dialogo sopra le tragedie* ('Dialogue Concerning Tragedies'), by another future cardinal, Giovanni Delfino (1617–99), who argued that tragedy should portray 'the misery and retribution that come of evil-doing'. The *Dialogo* was written in the 1660s alongside three political tragedies, *Cleopatra, Lucrezia* and *Creso*, which may adhere to this dictum but which are more notable for lengthy philosophical-scientific disquisitions, and are as attention-seeking in their bookish way as the plot twists of his contemporaries. Never performed, they were only published in 1733. Nor was the assertion that the function of tragedy was moral persuasion restricted to clerics associated with the Counter-Reformation. Similar views are expressed by secular theorists, including Bonarelli in his *Lettere in vari generi* (1632, 'Letters in Various Genres') and the Rovigo lawyer Baldassare Bonifacio (1584–1659), who defended his tragedy *Amata* in a series of *Lettere poetiche* (both 1622). These combine the conventional 'rhetorical' interpretation of catharsis with a self-serving reading of classical practice which borders on the arbitrary (as when Bonarelli justifies his omission of choruses by arguing that these were reserved for the expression of joyful states of mind, which would have been inappropriate in *Il Solimano*; or when Bonifacio defends the presence of amorous subplots in a 'political' drama).

But a clearer understanding of the spirit of Aristotelian poetics did not necessarily produce more successful dramas, or help avoid the pitfalls of *svogliatura*. The most notable attempt at 'pure' Aristotelian tragedy was perhaps that of the Paduan nobleman Carlo de'Dottori (1618–80), who may also have been influenced by Corneille, to whom, virtually alone among seventeenth-century dramatists, he alludes. His *Aristodemo*, privately performed in 1654, is a verse tragedy which, save for having no chorus, follows Aristotle's precepts closely. Set in a quasi-historic ancient Greece, it ostensibly concerns the conflict between 'reason of state' and affective bonds. Aristodemo, claimant to the Crown of Messene, is ordered by the Oracle to sacrifice his daughter Merope to ensure victory over Sparta. But in reality there is little tension between or within the central characters (father and daughter both seek 'glory', which for him means kingship and for her the renown of martyrdom). Instead, we have several twists of the plot: Merope is only designated for sacrifice after the original choice, Arena, flees; to prevent Merope's death, her betrothed Policare claims she is pregnant with his child, not a virgin fit for sacrifice, provoking Aristodemo into killing her with his own hands; discovering too late that she was unblemished, he claims that the sacrifice has been performed, but the Oracle denies its validity; Arena is found and duly sacrificed, only for Aristodemo to discover she too was his daughter; finally accepting the consequences of his ambition, he commits suicide. All this is punctuated by lengthy monologues full of rhetorical questions, appeals to the gods and apostrophes to personified abstractions which strive for pathos and metaphysical resonance, but never quite go beyond the assumption of a series of dramatic postures.

The one notable exception to such excesses is Federico Della Valle (1560–1628). Though chronologically situated at the turn of the century, his cultural isolation and singularly pure classicism make it easier to discuss him at the end. Della Valle held minor court offices in Turin and Milan, and it was on a Turin court occasion that his tragicomedy *Adelonda di Frigia* was staged. The regular tragedies, *La reina di Scotia* ('The Queen of Scotland'), *Esther* and *Judit* (published 1626–7), were only ever given private readings, and attach more importance to poetic than theatrical values. This is particularly true of *La reina*, representing Mary Stuart's final hours in terms of Catholic martyrdom, one of the few Italian plays of the period based on contemporary events, and arguably the finest of his works, despite being almost devoid of incident. In fact, Della Valle's tragedies are not so much dramas as elegies for disembodied voices (characterisation is minimal; the preferred verse line is the lyrical *settenario*). Meditations on the illusory nature of earthly power and status, the vicissitudes of fate, death, the mystery of the Divine Will and man's inability to understand His design are rooted in a particularly sombre version of Counter-Reformation Catholicism. They may also reflect more personal disappointments (there is a strong undercurrent of anti-court polemic). The effect is not conventionally dramatic, but they achieve genuine tragic pathos, all the more powerful because Della Valle's characters, unlike those of the other dramas we have discussed, seem conscious that the postures and roles they have assumed are not of their own choosing.

The comic stage

While tragic drama was overwhelmingly learned, the development of comedy was strongly influenced by the 'improvised' plays of the *comici*. Setting aside the survival of *commedia erudita* early in the century, it is these that set the tone for two of the three kinds of scripted comedies original to the century: those produced by or in emulation of the *comici dell'arte* (as in the case of Jacopo Cicognini), and the variant genre of the *comedia ridicolosa*, popular in Rome in mid-century.

A number of plays have survived, written by professional actors and closely related to the larger number of surviving *canovacci*. No doubt several more have been lost. In one sense, this authorial activity was an extension of the *comici*'s practice of combining improvisation with memorised set speeches on 'stock' arguments, but it was also, like their other published writings, an attempt to elevate their status, and that of their profession, by placing their work in the realm of 'literature', competing on equal footing with academic authors.

The most notable such player-author, and the only one to leave behind a substantial corpus of texts, was Giovan Battista Andreini (1576–1654), who has been described as Italy's most important seventeenth-century playwright. This valuation is probably true with regard to stageworthiness, perhaps less so of content, despite recent attempts to read deeper significance into his work. Given the *comici*'s concern to 'dignify' their profession, it is hardly surprising that Andreini's first published work should have been a tragedy. It is, however, for thirteen comedies published between 1613 and 1639, plus a manuscript version of the Don Juan story, *Il convitato di pietra* ('The Guest of Stone') that Andreini is now better known. In many respects these plays are typical products of the *commedia dell'arte*: plots are derived from the same Plautine and *novella* sources as the *commedia erudita*, but with greater space given to comic servants and elders and to verbal humour; characterisation is generic, psychological insights minimal; there is no attempt to situate the action in any precise social context.

However, the opportunity for slapstick afforded by the *canovacci* is curtailed, while Andreini's plots are much more intricate (more competing lovers; more twins and disguises; more agnitions). And as in tragic theatre, alongside this complication there is a tendency to emphasise the sentimental and sensational, notably with narratives of barely avoided incest and homosexual temptation which have provoked a recent revival of interest. Unfortunately, this seems partly founded on misreading, as will be shown by a rapid consideration of his most explicitly 'deviant' storyline, the 'lesbian' love between man-hating Florinda and man-scorned Lidia of *Amor nello specchio* (1622, 'Love in the Mirror'). The two heroines may indeed find consolation in sharing a bed, but what takes place during the night is left to the 'morning after' imagination of the comic servant Bernetta, who evokes a night of 'touching breasts . . . giving kisses, gossiping', only to compare such sapphic pleasures unfavourably with the delights to be had when the feminine 'lyre' is played by a masculine 'bow'; after which, the sudden appearance of Lidia's identical twin brother Eugenio provides Florinda with the requisite 'bow' and leads Lidia to a reconciliation with her erstwhile lover Silvio. What may or may not have happened before this 'proper' fulfilment of feminine desire is 'something worthy rather to be left unspoken, than told', as the play's epilogue puts it. To deny or occult something belies one's preoccupations, but while there is no doubt that here as in any number of seventeenth-century texts of all kinds deviant desires are never far from the surface, that is not quite the same as saying that they are 'explored', or even that their resolution in favour of heterosexual love is intentionally questioning and ironic. Rather, having applied a novel twist to the feminised eroticism made fashionable by *Aminta* and *Il pastor fido*, Andreini resolves it in a traditional, if contrived, masculine way, confirming the impossibility of 'love in the mirror' (i.e. of the same sex), and sweeping any homoerotic resonances under the carpet. His greater interest, here as in all his dramatic output, lies in role-playing (Florinda and Lidia, no less than Aristodemo or Merope, are striking poses, experimenting not with sex but with different ways of representing their femininity), and with the nature and function of theatricality.

This metadiscourse is made explicit in Andreini's *Le due comedie in comedia* (1623, 'Two Plays Within a Play'), with its Chinese-boxes structure of incomplete, interrupted play-performances by competing academic and professional troupes called to the household of theatre-loving merchant Rovenio. But clever as this theatre-machine is, complete with reflections on whether its truth lies in the fact that 'making plays, we will discover that this whole world is nothing but a play', neither here nor elsewhere does Andreini sound the psychological or metaphysical depths associated with contemporary Spanish and English meditations on theatrical illusion. He remains, more modestly, a consummate theatre professional who delights in displaying, and making his audience aware of, his mastery of stage conventions.

It was in all probability the fact that professional players were least welcome in the Papal States (and banned outright from the Holy City for lengthy periods) that determined the development of the other major kind of popular comedy, the *comedia ridicolosa*, predominantly associated with Rome, where its chief exponents, the lawyer Virgilio Verucci (c. 1585–c. 1663) and the painter Giovanni Briccio (1581–1646) operated. Again, it combined plot lines derived from *commedia erudita* with the comic stage business and linguistic inventiveness of improvised plays: in particular, it added to stock characters and *lazzi* a third comic ingredient which also has precedents in the *commedia dell'arte*, the use of a variety of languages and dialects, or parodies thereof (with mutual incomprehension and misunderstandings a major source of amusement). Taken individually, the interest of these plays is modest, but collectively they are worthy of attention on at least two levels. In the first place, they are more place-specific than any of the other dramatic texts we have encountered, rooted in the peculiarities of what was still at the time Italy's one truly European capital, hence a certain measure of social realism. Secondly, the fact that much of their humour comes from the co-presence of different languages – the literary Italian of noble and middle-class characters, the various dialects of their servants, the mix of Italian and native language spoken by foreigners – is itself a direct reflection of the Roman situation and the city's cosmopolitanism compared to Italy's other political and cultural centres. It was precisely because Rome still drew and mixed together men from all over Italy and beyond that this kind of comedy could prove effective. The corollary was that it did not travel. Its cosmopolitanism was the very reason for its limited appeal, reminding us of a further factor behind the anomalous development of commercial theatre in seventeenth-century Italy compared to the rest of Western Europe: the fact that without a political centre there could be no linguistic centre. The polyglot *comedia ridicolosa* was arguably as far along the road to forging a single dramatic language as Italy could go. An academic theatre in the (written) literary language of the Italian elites was possible, as were two kinds of commercial theatre in which non-verbal communication was dominant (music; and the mimicry and *lazzi* of the *comici*). What was not possible, it seems, was a popular theatre, accessible to socially mixed audiences throughout Italy, which combined dramatic action with the evocative powers of the word.

As for the third kind of comedy new to the century, the fact that this was also characterised by linguistic variety, and depicted something like the daily life of the lower classes, might suggest that it too addressed the popular end of theatrical audiences, but this was not the case. The play which might be seen as its prototype, *La Tancia*, by Michelangelo Buonarroti the Younger (1568–1646), was first performed at the Medici court in 1611. Tancia and her peasant suitors may be rather more concerned with everyday needs than Guarini's shepherds, while their language approximates to the vernacular of the Tuscan countryside, where the traditional *maggi* and *bruscelli* celebrating the *calendimaggio* (May Day) were still popular. Far from depicting the realities of peasant life, however, the play is a condescendingly sentimental recreation, related both to pastoral escapism and to earlier town-set representations of the prince's 'gift' of peace and harmony to his subjects. The play's only genuinely popular aspect is its author's fascination with the varieties of Tuscan. Buonarroti was in fact involved in the production of its first dictionary, and his other major dramatic work, the vast five-play cycle *La fiera* ('The Fair'), was once thought to have been written for no better reason than to give literary dignity to Tuscan words not previously attested by written sources. We now know that the work, running to well over 30,000 lines, originated as a single play of more manageable proportions, performed at the Medici court in 1619. But whether in its original or expanded version, this tableau of Florentine life, mixing realistic comic characters with allegorical ones representing various aspects of contemporary society, belongs more to the realms of literature than drama.

La Tancia, on the other hand, is eminently stageworthy, lively and charming, though both theatrically and ideologically conservative, as are similar comedies written for aristocratic and academic audiences through-out the century in a combination of Italian and a variety of local dialects. Despite these similarities, one should beware of treating them as a distinct, consciously developed sub-genre; each belongs to a particular milieu, and the influence of Buonarroti is probable, but by no means certain. The best known of these, from the opposite end of the century (the dates are uncertain, but most likely the 1690s), are *I consigli di Meneghino* ('Meneghino's Advice'), by the Milanese gentleman Carlo Maria Maggi (1630–99) and *El Cont' Piolet* ('Count Piolet'), by Marquis Carlo Giambat-tista Tana of Turin (1649–1713), singled out for supposedly pointing the way forward to Goldoni and his Enlightenment 'reform' of the stage. But here too what we have is an essentially condescending look at stock types from the lower orders, remote from Goldoni's carefully individualised characterisation, or his disenchanted, subtly subversive portrayal of inter-class relations. They differ from the rest of seventeenth-century dramaturgy because they accept, and even seek to make a virtue of, their localism but, rather like contemporary 'genre' paintings of beggars, they too are above all a further instance of the pursuit of ingenious novelties.

Drama in a dramatised society

The seventeenth century's efforts to chart new territories thus bespeak not a concern to produce a drama more attuned to the realities of the age, so much as uncertainty as to the role of the dramatic arts, dramatic authors and perhaps even the audience itself in a 'dramatised society'. If there is a core of real feeling and originality (as opposed to mere novelty) in the century's theatre it lies in the preoccupation, across the whole range of theatrical genres and production contexts, with the closely interrelated issues of reason of state, dissimulation and role-playing, demonstrating with various degrees of self-consciousness how, far from exercising choice, individuals bend themselves to or are bent by their imposed roles. From these issues dramatists occasionally go on to touch on the illusory nature of any socially constructed reality and the consequent precariousness of self-representation, making theatre itself a metaphor for that precariousness. Perhaps more than in any play, this fascination with theatre which is also a form of alienation from society finds expression in the extraordinary stage devices of the greatest theatre 'amateur' of the age, Gian Lorenzo Bernini (1598–1680).

Bernini is best known as an architect and sculptor, whose major contribution to the fabric of baroque Rome has often been read in terms of its theatricality. Like other architects of the period he frequently designed sets and stage effects for court spectacles, but he also wrote plays, of which only one survives, an untitled manuscript dubbed *L'impresario* by its modern editors, which belongs both to the genre of *comedia ridicolosa* and to meta-theatre (its plot concerns the staging of a play). The most remarkable relics of his theatrical interests, however, are contemporary accounts of the concluding *coup de théâtre* of three of the spectacles he produced in mid-century. In one, the audience was apparently treated to a stage recreation of a recent flood of the Tiber which was so realistic that they fled to avoid the rush of water (contained at the last by some consummate engineering). In another, the curtain opened to reveal a second crowded auditorium identical to the real one, after which it closed again, and a *zanni* appeared in front of it to perform a comic routine, but periodically, sounds of laughter could be heard, as if something much more amusing was being performed in the 'other' theatre. In the third, the audience about to leave the auditorium was treated to the spectacle of its own departure, as the curtain went up for a final time to reveal a replica of the square facing the theatre, full of the bustle of carriages which gradually disappeared, leaving the space empty and dark. No better metaphors could be found for the fear that what took place on stage, for all its contrivance, might overwhelm real life, the anxiety as to where a truly effective drama might be found and the suspicion that the audience itself could be the real spectacle, unwitting performers in a play not of their making, and destined to fade into nothing.

Bibliography

Scripts

Andreini, G. B. *Amor nello specchio*, Rome, 1997.

Artale, G. *Guerra tra vivi, e morti*, Parma, 1990.

Bernini, G. L. *L'Impresario*, Rome, 1992.

Buonarroti, M. Jr, *La Fiera* (definitive version of five, five-act plays), ed. A. M. Salvini, Florence, 1860.

  La Fiera (five-act version, c.1619), ed. U. Limentani, Florence, 1984.

Cicognini G. A. *Il tradimento per l'onore*, Rome, 2002.

La commedia italiana da Cielo d'Alcamo a Goldoni, ed. M. Apollonio, Milan, 1947 (contains plays by Federico Della Valle), Turin, 1995.

Teatro del Seicento, ed. Luigi Fassò (includes plays by Buonarroti, Dottori, Maggi, Tana), Milan, 1956.

La tragedia classica dalle origini al Maffei, ed. G. Gasparini, (includes dramas by P. Bonarelli and G. Delfino), Turin, 1976.

Criticism

Angelini, F. *Il teatro barocco*, Rome and Bari, 1975.

Carandini, S. *Teatro e spettacolo nel Seicento*, Rome and Bari, 1990.

Fabbri, Paolo, *Il secolo cantante. Per una storia del libretto d'opera nel Seicento*, Bologna, 1990.

Molinari, C. *Le nozze degli dei. Saggio sul grande spettacolo italiano nel Seicento*, Roma, 1968.

Rebaudengo, M., *Giovan Battista Andreini tra poetica e drammaturgia*, Turin, 1994.

PART IV

The Enlightenment

13 Arrivals and departures

JOSEPH FARRELL

When Luigi Riccoboni, actor, playwright and author of theatrical tracts, took his company from Venice to Paris in 1716 to reconstitute itself as the Comédie Italienne, he had the front curtain of his new venue, the Hôtel de Bourgogne, embellished with a phoenix and the swaggering words, 'Je renais.' The original Italian troupe in Paris had been disbanded in 1697 on the orders of Louis XIV, so the slogan had a local reference, but it could be applied to much of the theatre of the eighteenth century, and not only in Italy.

Riccoboni (1676–1753) is himself an emblematic figure of his time and of theatre in an age of reform. His father, Antonio, was a famous Pantalone, and Luigi devised the character of Lelio as his own contribution to the *commedia dell'arte* stable. He was the creative actor-author of the Italian tradition, and in Paris the company often staged scripts written by him, but he was, as were many in the century, infected by the yen to implement reform. He had not been notably successful in introducing reforms in the San Luca theatre in Venice, which was one of the reasons he moved to Paris, but he was convinced that even if traditional comedy filled the stalls, there was a need to raise the moral and literary tone of the drama offered on stage. In particular, he came to believe that tragedy should have a higher place, and he commissioned translations of Racine and introduced audiences to the tragic works of his contemporary, Scipione Maffei. He was also author of *Dell'arte rappresentativa* (1728, 'On the Dramatic Art'), a work in verse which was an invaluable record of the theatre of his time as well as a call for reform and improvement.

In some countries, the Enlightenment is known as the Age of Improvement, and the tag would be suitable for Italian theatre in this century. The contemporary repertoire in Italian theatre was rich and varied, and audiences were plainly catholic in their acceptance of all forms of theatre – *commedia dell'arte,* comedy, tragedy, *melodramma,* opera: it is tempting to add to that list the more ephemeral vogue for the *comédie larmoyante* or for *chinoiserie,* and even more tempting to create a special category for Venetian theatre itself, granted the sheer wealth of talent which the city in its decline produced. Venice, which in the eighteenth century had more theatres than Paris or London, was a microcosm of the disputes and debates over theatre, and not only the theatre of that century. The Goldoni–Gozzi fracas was not merely a quarrel over reform versus reaction, but also one which pitted two antagonists of genius against each other in a deeper, more intriguing and enduring debate over observation and imagination, realism and fantasy as the very origins of theatrical inspiration. Goldoni, a realist ante litteram, claimed the twin sources of his inspiration were Theatre and the World and, as was already clear from his introduction to his early *Don Giovanni Tenorio,* he had scant sympathy for fantasy. His Harlequin, however often and in how many guises he appears in his plays, is not the shamanic, pre-rational force the character had been on his introduction to the popular stage: he is the prankster, the trickster, the rascal who is master of his own destiny and who will knowingly deceive two masters to fill his own, permanently empty, belly. Goldoni's Pantalone is no longer an ageing lecher, but 'the respectable merchant of my nation', as he put it in his *Memorie italiane,*[1] the sort of man who could be met on the streets of Venice and whom Goldoni celebrated in such plays as *La bottega del caffè* ('The Coffee House'). Goldoni's inspiration was taken not just from the twin sources he indicates but also, and mainly, from the reality he inhabited and the society in transition he observed, where the old order was under threat and no new order had definitively emerged. On the other hand, Gozzi spurns all forms of creativity based on observation and relies instead not merely on exoticism and unfamiliar locations but on untrammelled fantasy. His are fables which may be occasionally meant as a commentary on morals and mores he despised, but which are set in a dimension which can be visited only in the imagination.

If in retrospect this appears an age singularly endowed with theatrical talent, it did not seem so to the practitioners of the time. There may have been disagreement over the nature of the malaise, but there was widespread agreement that theatre was in a condition of decadence and in need of reform. It was not only practitioners who entered the debate over such matters as Aristotle and his rules: pamphlets and treatises abounded, and the gazettes, a feature of eighteenth-century intellectual life, provided a home for men who can be regarded as the first critics and reviewers. German theatre is said to begin with reasoned criticism above all from

Ephraim Lessing, who only later developed into a playwright. In Italy, Giuseppe Baretti and Gasparo Gozzi in Milan, like Addison and Steele in London or Diderot in Paris, participated in debates over the direction of drama. More lengthy and pondered tracts included *Della ragion poetica* (1704, 'On Poetic Reason') by Gian Vincenzo Gravina, *Della perfetta poesia italiana* (1706, 'On Perfect Italian Poetry') by Ludovico Antonio Muratori, *La bellezza della volgar poesia* (1730, 'The Beauty of Vernacular Poetry') by Giovanni Maria Crescimbeni, as well as theoretical works by Metastasio, Riccoboni and Gozzi. Perhaps the most significant was the satirical treatise, *Il teatro alla moda* (1720, 'Fashionable Theatre'), by the composer Benedetto Marcello. Marcello was scathing on the inadequacies of the theatre of his time. His tract was illustrated by two cartoonists and caricaturists of unusual talent, Anton Maria Zanetti and Mario Ricci, whose artwork flayed the poseurs and dandies who populated theatre at that time. One of Zanetti's targets was the castrato known as Caffariello, depicted walking off with the theatre on his back, to denote the fact that theatres emptied when his arias were completed. This is the Caffariello lampooned by Goldoni in his *Mémoires* as the effete *habitué* of the Milan salons, and the man who ridiculed Goldoni after his reading of his first work, *Amalasunta*. It was clear, said Caffariello, that Goldoni had read Aristotle, but he was unaware that musical theatre had its own distinct rules. Stung by the criticism, Goldoni threw his script away, but if he never learned to respect the rules, the episode did teach him the need to write not in the abstract but for a troupe composed of a specific number of performers of each sex, each expecting parts requiring their specific skills.

When Goldoni had established himself, he became the greatest reformer of them all. Riccoboni was out to reform *commedia dell'arte,* and Goldoni may have set off with the same aim, outlined in the manifesto-play *Il teatro comico* (1750), but his disgust with the current state of the genre was more profound. His removal of the masks, his insistence on the priority of the script over improvisation, his moves to dethrone the performer in favour of the writer led de facto to the ending of the long, glorious *commedia dell'arte* tradition. His reform programme was paralleled by the efforts of Apostolo Zeno and Metastasio in the *melodramma,* or musical theatre. Zeno advocated the use of subjects not just from ancient Greece but from modern history, and even managed to produce a work based on Don Quixote. Carlo Gozzi has the reputation, rightly, of being a reactionary, but in theatre at least, he too ended up, objectively, on the side of the reformers. He began his literary career as a root-and-branch opponent of Goldoni, and never wavered in his hostility to Enlightenment thought. He never did mitigate his criticisms of Goldoni's sympathetic depiction of the new Venetian bourgeoisie or his satire on the aristocracy, but even if Gozzi believed he was reinstating the *commedia dell'arte,* in the end he accepted in practice Goldoni's reforms. Only in his first work, *L'amore delle tre melarance* ('The Love of the Three Oranges'), did he produce an outline script which looked for the collaboration of the improvisational skills of actors, but thereafter he produced fully written scripts. In Gozzi, the character of Pantalone, through whose transformation Goldoni's whole reform process could be judged, is given the same dignity, the same psychological characteristics, the same moral gravitas, the same role as spokesman for civility and cultured behaviour as he had in Goldoni.

Eighteenth-century tragedy was a more paradoxical case. In tragedy, the reign of Aristotle, or at least of the rules which it was believed Aristotle had prescribed in his *Poetics,* was undisputed all over Europe. Addison in England, Home in Scotland, Voltaire in France and Alfieri in Italy all applied the three unities that were considered to be as intrinsic to the essence of tragedy as was the fourteen-line structure to the sonnet. The case of Voltaire is particularly curious. In every other field, he was impatient with dogmas and absolutism, yet in tragedy, which he expected to be the foundation of his enduring reputation, he embraced the Aristotelian faith and even, famously, dismissed Shakespeare as a 'barbarian not devoid of genius' for ignoring the unities. Alfieri adhered to the unities, but for him too the initial spur was a belief, expressed in his autobiography, that Italian theatre was in an infirm state, that the native tragedy lacked rigour, robustness and some connection with the national feeling. Although his context was different, Alfieri too advocated reform.

Italian theatre in the eighteenth century has, for once, much in common with theatre elsewhere in Europe. The Enlightenment was a movement in which the whole continent, excepting Spain but including the normally insular Britain, participated. The Italian contribution to Enlightenment thought may have been of lesser importance than that of France, Germany or Britain, but in theatre the Italians were still the leading spirits. A caricature by Zanetti in the series to accompany Marcello's work shows another castrato, Antonio Bernacchi, a coloratura singer known for his agile improvisational skills, with notes emerging from his mouth and floating over Saint Mark's Square. If he was mocked gently at home, Bernacchi was much admired abroad, and had appreciative audiences in London and Munich. Handel wrote arias specifically for him. Italian theatre was part of the culture in countries other than Italy. The diaspora of talent meant that there was a well-trodden path between Venice, Paris and Vienna. Apostolo Zeno and Metastasio were given the position of court, or 'Caesarean', poet in the Imperial court in Vienna, and it was in Vienna that Antonio Salieri (1750–1825) and Lorenzo da Ponte (1749–1838), the first now remembered (unjustly) for his rivalry with Mozart and the second as Mozart's greatest librettist, established themselves, although da Ponte later moved to New York to establish the first American opera house. Italian writers drew on the work of other nations as subjects for their work, but their work was performed as Italian in many capital cities.

If Vienna offered royal patronage, the theatres of Paris and, more especially, Venice relied on a new figure, the commercial impresario, and played to a new, bourgeois audience and responded to their demands. Even the National Hoftheater of Vienna was given over to a lessee by Maria Teresa in 1740. One of the most symbolic of incidents was related by Alfieri in his autobiography, where he gives vent to his contempt for Metastasio when he sees the court poet, gartered and gaitered, genuflecting before the Empress Maria Teresa. Neither Alfieri nor Metastasio were exactly representative of universal trends, but two worlds collided in that scene. Metastasio was no robotic slave but he was the last representative of an older view of the creative artist as dependent on grace and favour. Alfieri would not bow to any representative of any court, and in his treatise *Del principe e delle lettere* ('On the Prince and Letters') he called for the complete autonomy of the author.

The aristocratic Alfieri was a special case, for a significant characteristic of eighteenth-century drama is the high level of professionalism of its practitioners, in the literal sense of the term. These were artists who, working in commercial theatre, had to be sensitive to audience demands, but who had to comply firstly with the requirements of company leaders and theatre managers. In London Dr Johnson expressed the matter neatly in a verse manifesto he wrote for the opening of Drury Lane: 'We who live to please must please to live.' The first consequence is that the playwrights of this age can be differentiated from the playwrights of the Baroque age who preceded them and from the Romantics who succeeded them. The court playwrights, like Metastasio, had to appeal only to a select audience, and were free of the demands of the accountant or impresario, unlike a Goldoni. It was an age of transition, and Gozzi was contemptuous of Goldoni for being a paid employee, but neither man could permit himself the lofty, dismissive hauteur of later Romantic writers towards audiences or readers. Goldoni sold his labour, and satisfied the requirements of a contract signed with impresarios like Girolamo Medebach or Giuseppe Imer.

What finally makes the Italian eighteenth century unique is the dominance of the playwright in the theatrical process. As has been pointed out elsewhere in this volume, the defining characteristic of Italian theatre consists in the centrality afforded to performer rather than, as elsewhere in Europe, to the writer. The result of the eighteenth-century reforms was the self-affirmation of the dramatist. Goldoni, Gozzi, Alfieri, Metastasio, and Apostolo Zeno were the dominant creative spirits of the time, and it is in their work that the struggle between conservatism and reform was fought out, and it is for their work that this century's theatre is memorable. For a time, Italian theatre came into line with theatre elsewhere, even if it was only a passing phase. In the next century, the 'great actor' would reassert the primacy of the performer.

Italy's theatre, like its counterparts elsewhere in Europe, demonstrates the innovative brio, the inventive comic genius, the arm's length fascination with the revolutionary thought of the Enlightenment, the ambivalent relations with the new bourgeoisie who demanded to see themselves and their new society on stage, the uneasy attitude towards the rules – Aristotelian and otherwise – which still held sway in many sectors of theatrical life and which often conflicted with the desire for change, or rebirth. Eighteenth-century Italian dramatists may not have shown the psychological subtlety of Marivaux (who learned his trade by watching the Italian players in Paris) or the subtle plotting of Beaumarchais, the passion for toleration in society of Lessing or the political enthusiasms of Schiller, but by their sustained creativity and in their innovative zeal, they left a theatrical legacy which is part of today's international repertoire.

Note

1 Carlo Goldoni, *Memorie italiane,* ed. Guido Davico Bonino, Milan, 1983, p. 189.

14 The Venetian stage

GUIDO NICASTRO

Throughout the eighteenth century, Venice, with numerous theatres scattered throughout her territory and with her long and distinguished tradition, could claim undisputed primacy in the dramatic arts. Even in this period of comparative decadence following the splendours of the Baroque age, at least eight theatres were regularly and continuously open in the city, quite apart from the numerous public and private little theatres which further enriched the scene. Responsibility for their management and therefore for Venetian theatrical policy rested mainly with the aristocratic families who owned them, such as the Tron family, proprietors of the San Cassiano, which staged the first public lyric season in 1637, or the Grimani with the San Samuele and San Giovanni Grisostomo theatres, or the Vendramin, owners of the San Luca. In other cases, management was entrusted to impresarios, as was the case with the Sant'Angelo, which counted among its patrons Antonio Vivaldi, Gasparo Gozzi and his wife Luisa Bergalli, as well as the actor-manager Gerolamo Medebach, with whom Carlo Goldoni collaborated. A broad public flocked to these theatres, consisting not just of aristocrats but also of the middle and lower classes, attracted especially by the operas and comedies staged in the autumn or Carnival seasons, but also at the Feast of the Ascension and sometimes even in summer.

The genres which attracted most attention at the beginning of the century were *melodramma* and *commedia dell'arte*, which had been the dominant forms in the seventeenth century. This had important consequences, notably the unquestioned pre-eminence of music and scenery in *melodramma*, and of the actors in comedy. In both cases this was a theatre which gave priority to art forms which were distinct from literature, or 'poetry', as it was then called. By the eighteenth century, however, these genres seemed repetitive and played out. In the economic crisis in Venice in the early days of the century, the magnificent stage-spectacles of baroque *melodramma* had become a pale and distant memory, although this is not the only explanation for the crisis facing opera. The best evidence comes from the Venetian writer and composer Benedetto Marcello (1686–1739) in his *Teatro alla moda* ('Fashionable Theatre') published in 1720, a witty and mordant pamphlet offering back-handed advice to all those involved in the musical theatre (poets, composers, impresarios, singers, designers, dancers etc.) and providing keen insight into the state of opera, then at the mercy of those *prime donne* whose every whim had to be indulged by all, poets, composers and impresarios alike.

The picture that emerges is one of widespread and extreme decadence, as is clear from the onslaught launched on poets in the first chapter:

> First of all the modern Poet need not have read, or ever read, the ancient Latin or Greek writers. After all, the ancient Greek and Roman writers never read the moderns. Nor need he acquire any knowledge of Italian verse or metre, except for some superficial idea that if the Verse is made up of 7 or 11 syllables, he is at liberty to compose, as he wishes, lines of 3, 5, 9, 13 or even 15 syllables.

If poets were ignorant, so too were composers and musicians, bereft of the basics of their trade:

> The modern composer of music need not have any knowledge at all of the Rules of composition, apart from a few universal practical principles . . . the modern *Virtuoso* need not have sung scales, nor ever do so, thus avoiding the risk of straining his voice, or striking the right note, or singing in time, these things being quite out of keeping with modern fashion.[1]

All the characters appearing in this brief work, especially the *virtuose* (leading ladies), who along with their mothers engage in lively exchanges in Bolognese dialect, show us the depths to which *melodramma* had sunk at this time, but Benedetto Marcello does not propose a reform of opera by eliminating the negative aspects of the Baroque. He prefers to stress how incongruous and absurd the whole scene was, but since he revels in hyperbole the negative picture he presents is often remote from reality: for example, he lists Antonio Vivaldi among the ignorant composers, and the frontispiece of the first edition seems to refer to him. However, there can be no denying that the musical and theatrical world of the time gives evidence of the excesses which Marcello's satire flays so mercilessly. It is no accident that his satire was so influential, or that throughout the century the leading authors of the day drew attention to the vices and weaknesses of contemporary theatre, both in witty, caustic comedies and comic interludes and in the more serious, measured form of the essay. Francesco Algarotti's *Sopra l'Opera in Musica* (1755, 'Essay on the Opera') championed the primacy of poetry over music and the other components of *melodramma*. A common theme links *Il teatro alla moda* to works such as Pietro Metastasio's *L'impresario delle Canarie* (1724, 'The Impresario From the Canaries'), Carlo Goldoni's *Teatro comico* (1750) and *L'impresario delle Smirne* (1759), Ranieri de' Calzabigi's *Opera seria* (1769) and Giambattista Casti's *Prima la musica e poi le parole* (1786, 'First Music, Then Words'). These are not merely noteworthy examples of theoretical debate; they are also involving and involved representations of the world of theatre on the Venice–Vienna axis, written in the margins of the new writing which was itself concerned with the reform of stage practice and the elimination of the most obvious incongruities.

The situation in prose drama was not much different from that in musical theatre, particularly as regards comedy, which at the beginning of the century was still dominated by a *commedia dell'arte* now incapable of producing original situations, dialogue or gags. A fresh approach, new forms and materials that could give fresh impetus to the theatre were needed, and it was in Venice that the initiative was taken for the renovation of the structure of comedy – although the reform process affected theatre as a whole – and where the most innovative aspects of the culture of the movement known as 'Arcadia' and later of the Enlightenment received encouragement.

In Venice the actor Pietro Cotta 'conscious of the exhaustion of improvised comedy, attempted to relaunch a refined pastoral and tragic repertoire in the style of Tasso, Guarino, Trissino and the great French dramatists (Corneille and Racine), and to support the first experiments in contemporary tragedy, such as Dottori's *Aristodemo*, performed in 1699'.[2] Still in Venice, the Modenese actor Luigi Riccoboni (1686–1753) attempted to make his mark with a serious repertoire favouring both classic works from the past and such new plays as Scipione Maffei's *Merope*, which was strikingly successful in Venice in 1714 after its premiere in Modena the previous year. However, Riccoboni's production of Gabriele Ariosto's *La scolastica* ('The Scholastics') was a complete failure, as a result of which he left for Paris.

Riccoboni's initiative, like others of the time, was prompted by a theoretical assessment of the defects of contemporary theatre, but there was no repertoire of dramatic works which put the reform principles into practice. That required an author who could bring to life on stage, and not just in the study, productions equal to the aspirations of the new age. There was of course such an author, Carlo Goldoni, and it was thanks to him that Venice's comic theatre, musical and otherwise, struck out on a new path, and that comedy became pre-eminent in the theatre, even overtaking serious opera, which, after the glories of the Baroque period, had been reformed at the beginning of the century by Apostolo Zeno (1668–1750).

Apostolo Zeno was a Venetian writer who went to Vienna in 1718 as court poet, having previously made a name for himself in his own city as creator of reformed *melodramma*. Respect for the unities of time, place and action, moral treatment of amorous material, limitation of the role of the chorus and exclusion of comic characters were the principles of a severe and grandiloquent style of drama which drew its subjects from ancient Greece and Rome. The new *melodramma* dates from 1695 with *Gli inganni felici* ('Happy Deceit', published in 1774 by Gasparo Gozzi in a volume entitled *Poesie drammatiche*). The decisive proof of Venice's importance as venue for serious opera was Pietro Metastasio's choice of the city for the opening performance of his *Siroe* in 1726.

Nevertheless, *melodramma* in the eighteenth century lost its supremacy to comedy, which now had three theatres devoted to it: the Sant'Angelo, the San Samuele and the San Luca, where Goldoni's comedies were staged and where he implemented his reforms, causing Venetian theatre to make a quantum leap. It was not just a question of considering the days of *commedia dell'arte* over and the time ripe for a new scripted comedy, without masks: Goldoni's originality lay principally in the links he forged between his works and the life surrounding him, which he called the 'World'. There had been some moves in that direction by certain late seventeenth-century comic writers: Giovanni Bonicelli, author of *Pantalon spetier* (1703, 'Pantalone the Apothecary'), and Tommaso Mondini, who wrote *Pantalon mercante fallito* (1608, 'Pantalone the Bankrupt'), both plays notable for 'the inclusion of real-life events which could easily be identified and for their everyday language'.[3] These were, however, simply brief interludes in the traditional structures of 'ridiculous comedy'.

Goldoni's work is of a different order. His comedies are not the sterile fancies of some remote man of letters, but works which owe their existence to the author's active involvement in a vibrant theatrical world, and which take as material for his drama the everyday life of Venetians and Italians. Goldoni forged a realistic theatre. There can be arguments over the direction and depth of this realism but there can be no disputing the originality of his approach or the close and continuous observation of the people and the life of the city he sets at the centre of his theatre.

A theatrical revolution takes place in Venice in the middle decades of the century, between 1748 and 1762, the years of Goldoni's reform and of his heated debates with his contemporaries, Pietro Chiari and Carlo Gozzi. Gozzi's *Fiabe* (1761–5, 'Fables') enjoyed immediate, enormous success, and were to become for the Romantics and for the twentieth-century Futurist avant-garde the very emblem of a visual, anti-realist theatre. Pietro Chiari (1712–85) never experienced the same success, and for good reason. A priest from Brescia who came to Venice in 1747 and remained until 1762, he produced an extensive range of comedies from 1749 when he was taken on by the nobleman Michele Grimani to write for the San Samuele theatre, where the company directed by Giuseppe Imer was in residence. His *La scuola delle vedove* ('The School for Widows') was written in response to Goldoni's *Vedova scaltra* ('The Clever Widow'), which had proved a great success at the Sant'Angelo. Bitter polemics between the two writers ensued.

Chiari's comic production continued uninterruptedly thereafter. He was initially highly successful with his prose comedies, with masks, written between 1749 and 1752 for the San Samuele and San Giovanni Grisostomo theatres, and then with his verse comedies produced between 1753 and 1762 at the Sant'Angelo (which Goldoni had abandoned for the San Luca), and later still for the San Giovanni Grisostomo. In 1756 he published his *Commedie in versi* ('Verse Comedies'), prefaced by a *Dissertazione storica e critica sopra il teatro antico e moderno* ('Historical and Critical Dissertation on Ancient and Modern Theatre'), where he set out his dramatic theory.

At the beginning, he did no more than partially draft his plays, sketching out the parts of the stock characters. His preference was for subjects from the mainstream European narrative tradition, for example the trilogy based on Fielding: *L'orfano perseguitato* ('The Persecuted Orphan'), *L'orfano ramingo* ('The Stray Orphan'), and *L'orfano riconosciuto* ('The Orphan Recognised'). Similarly, *Marianna o sia l'orfana* ('Marianne, or the Orphan Girl') and *Marianna o sia l'orfana riconosciuta* ('Marianne, or the Orphan Girl Recognised') were taken from Marivaux's *Vie de Marianne*.

Often his subjects were inspired by Goldoni: *Molière, marito geloso* ('Molière, the Jealous Husband') is based on Goldoni's *Molière*. Goldoni's comedies on classical subjects gave rise to Chiari's *Marco Accio Plauto* (1755), *Diogene nella botta* ('Diogenes in the Barrel'), *Socrate filosofo sapientissimo* ('Socrates the Sage Philosopher'), and to the more ambitious plan for a two-part tetralogy in blank verse (1759–61) on the Trojan War. Chiari also produced comedies with bourgeois settings, such as *Il buon padre di famiglia* ('The Good Family Man') and *La buona madrigna* ('The Good Stepmother').

Imitation of both classical and contemporary models is explicitly part of Chiari's dramatic theory and allows him to extend his sources of inspiration:

> I have heard it said many times that the comic writer has two masters, the world and the theatre, but there should be no separation between the present world and the living theatre, and those of the past: that is, there should be no separation between observations of everyday life and material obtained by study, which is incomparably more extensive.[4]

So what lay at the root of the rivalry between the two dramatists, apart from the obvious commercial competition? In *La scuola delle vedove*, written in response to *La vedova scaltra*, Chiari attacked one of the key components of Goldoni's reform with the proposal that the comic characters in that play, each from different regions, should each speak in their own language, as had happened in *commedia dell'arte*. Goldoni replied in a *Prologo apologetico*: 'It is not language that makes comedy, but characters.' Chiari adhered to a traditional view of comedy and Goldoni charged him with lack of truth-to-life and immorality. The quarrel raged on until 1756–7, when the nobleman Carlo Gozzi attacked them both as bourgeois writers who had to work for a living and who looked to make a profit from it.

Similarities between the two cannot hide the deep divisions underlying their disagreement. Chiari rejects Goldoni's realism and opts for adventure and romance. Changes in eighteenth-century society and culture mean for him that the character, left at the mercy of strange and contradictory events, has to shape his own destiny. In spite of all his theories in support of verisimilitude and naturalness on stage, Chiari gives his versions of his rival's scripts an anti-realist twist. Moreover, while a moral renovation of everyday Venetian life was intrinsic to Goldoni's programme, Chiari's plays seem to lack a moral and philosophical core, notwithstanding his adoption of some Enlightenment principles: the defence of nature and the rights of women, for example, or his declarations against social injustice. Chiari has little interest in reforming the structure of drama, and his style often seems 'agitated, bombastic, inflated, full of aphorisms, metaphors, similes', as Goldoni described it in *I malcontenti*. Carlo Gozzi was of the same view, as he explains in his *Memorie Inutili* ('Useless Memoirs'):

> As for Father Chiari, he had an excited, disordered, impetuous and pedantic mind; obscure plots worthy of astrology; seven-league leaps; isolated scenes, quite disconnected from the action and weighed down with sententious, philosophical, garrulous preaching; some good theatrical twists; some wickedly accurate descriptions; pernicious morals; the most turgid and bombastic writer to receive the adoration of this century.[5]

Yet for all his defects Pietro Chiari was an important figure in the history of eighteenth-century Venetian theatre, almost the alter ego of Goldoni, who was tempted to follow his rival's lead on more than one occasion. It was no accident that when the one left Venice the other did so too, but perhaps there were no room for either when public favour turned to the fables and spectacles provided by Carlo Gozzi.

In the twenty years they had been working in Venice, there were many changes in the theatre, in both comedy and opera. There had been no comic opera in Venice in the first two decades of the century, so that even Goldoni had to make his mark with intermezzos between acts of *opera seria,* but the influence of Neapolitan opera led to the appearance of the so-called *dramma giocoso.* From *La contessina* ('The Countess') in 1743 onwards, Goldoni established himself in the new genre, producing more than fifty works in a distinctive style of his own. From that point, Venetian comic opera was distinguished by the emphasis given to the orchestrated finales of each act, the presence of pathetic characters and situations and the careful division of characters into comic, serious and semi-serious. It is in this form that it reaches Lorenzo Da Ponte (1749–1838), who succeeded in breaking out of these rigid partitions with the trilogy of operas he wrote in Vienna for Mozart (*Le nozze di Figaro, Don Giovanni, Cosí fan tutte).*

With the departure of Chiari and Goldoni and the closure of the brief interlude of Gozzi's *Fables,* Venice lost the central role it had enjoyed in the history of Italian and European theatre, even if there were authors and works who brightened its fading image at the end of the century. The spread of the new *larmoyant* (tearful) theatre, based largely on translations made by Elisabetta Caminer Turra, should not be overlooked, nor should the presence in Venice of such comic playwrights as Francesco Albergati Capacelli (1728–1804), a follower of Goldoni but also influenced by Gozzi, notably in *Il sofà* (1770). Camillo Federici (1749–1802) was Piedmontese but lived mainly in Padua and Venice and confined himself to the new *larmoyant* genre. S. A. Sogràfi (1759–1819), a prolific author of the so-called Jacobin theatre, enjoyed success with his *Il matrimonio democratico ossia il flagello dei feudatori* ('Democratic Marriage or The Scourge of the Land-lords') in 1797 at the ex-San Giovanni Grisostomo theatre, renamed Teatro Civico. Sogràfi's most memorable play was his one-act *Convenienze teatrali* (1794, 'Theatrical Conveniences'), an amusing satire of the world of opera, which was followed by *Le inconvenienze teatrali* ('Theatrical Inconveniences', 1800).

These writers, however, are insufficient to challenge the picture of relentless decline. Many writers and artists from Venice and elsewhere now made their home in Paris and Vienna, where Italian theatre, especially musical theatre, enjoyed a better fate, but the crisis confronting Venice at the end of the century was not limited to theatre and the arts. The days of the Republic were numbered, and after the loss of political independence in 1797, it would no longer be possible to speak of a specifically Venetian theatre, except as a marginal component, in one region, of the theatre of Italy.

Notes

1 B. Marcello, *Il teatro alla moda*, pp. 21, 30 and 39.
2 L. Zorzi, *Il teatro e la città*, p. 263.
3 C. Alberti, *La scena veneziana*, p. 63.
4 P. Chiari, *Commedie in versi dell'abate Pietro Chiari*, vol. x, p. 234.
5 C. Gozzi, *Memorie inutili*, pp. 206–7.

Bibliography

Editions

Chiari, Pietro, *Commedie dell'abate Pietro Chiari*, 10 vols., Venice, 1756–62.
Gozzi, Carlo, *Memorie inutili*, ed. G. Prezzolini, Bari and Rome, 1910.
Marcello, Benedetto, *Il teatro alla moda*, ed. A. Marianni, Milan, 1959.
Zeno, Apostolo, *Drammi scelti*, ed. Max Fehr, Bari and Rome, 1929.

Critical works

Alberti, C. *La scena veneziana nell'età di Goldoni,* Rome, 1990.

Alberti, C. (ed.), *Pietro Chiari e il teatro europeo del Settecento,* Vicenza, 1986.

Algarotti, F. 'Saggio sopra l'opera in musica', in G. Da Pozzo (ed.), *Saggi,* Bari and Rome, 1963.

Madricardo, C. and Rossi, F. (eds.), *Benedetto Marcello: la sua opera e il suo tempo,* Florence, 1988.

Mangini, N. *I teatri di Venezia,* Milan, 1974.

Turchi, R. *La commedia italiana del Settecento,* Florence, 1985.

Zorzi, L. *Il teatro e la città: saggi sulla scena italiana,* Turin, 1977.

15 Carlo Goldoni, playwright and reformer

PIERMARIO VESCOVO

The most significant figure in Venetian, indeed Italian, theatrical history made his mark, neither suddenly nor rapidly, in a Venice where fashionable, civil society was unusually attentive to theatre. The city was well endowed with theatres of various sorts, each offering different styles of drama and different repertoires, so there was keen competition for aristocratic capital investment, for audiences, for *capocomici* and theatre companies. Elsewhere a similar talent, even if gifted with exceptional insight, would probably have treated the stage as an ephemeral literary enterprise, capable at best of attracting audiences of aristocrats and cultured dilettantes.

Goldoni's Venetian career spans a relatively brief space of time, covering periods at the San Samuele (1734–44), the Sant'Angelo (1748–53) and the San Luca (1753–62) theatres. As 'theatre poet', he moved from half-service to full-time work, switching from one theatre to another, making his debut in a relatively peripheral area of the city and ending up in the centre of its social and commercial life. His rivals, Pietro Chiari and Carlo Gozzi, followed the same path.

The Goldoni who emigrated to Paris (in 1762, until his death) did not enjoy the success the Venetian Goldoni had known, mainly because of the comparative lack of competition in the French theatre, with its rigid separation of venues and genres as compared with the free movement between repertoires in Venice. In France the different genres were performed in specific venues, rather than in response to the tastes and inclinations of audiences. The established itinerary in Paris could at best involve a move from one to the other pole, from the improvisational traditions of the *teatro all'italiana* (which required only scenarios) or of musical theatre (requiring *libretti* alone) to the sphere of the recognised 'national' genres – which, for an Italian, with performance at the Comédie Française and entry into the ranks of the court, unquestionably constituted 'success'.

His elaborate autobiographical project covers a period of more than thirty years and takes in the so-called *Memorie italiane,* that is, the prefaces

Figure 6: Portrait of Carlo Goldoni.

to the various volumes of the Pasquali edition (Venice, 1761–4, ceasing with the seventeenth volume of the forty planned, the last two volumes printed 1777–8) and the later French *Mémoires,* and focuses entirely on Goldoni's theatrical output, following a plan he had outlined long before on stage and in print. The French autobiography can be considered not so much an attempt to provide a truthful reconstruction of the past as a contribution to the story of a life and theatrical oeuvre, as the subtitle indicates, or an attempt to reconsider his life in relation to his writing.

The education of the young Goldoni was Italian in the fullest sense, and in no way restricted to his place of birth. The variety and breadth, geographically, of his experience in his formative years are evident from his attendance at a Jesuit school in Perugia, a Dominican school in Rimini, his subsequent entry, after receiving the tonsure, into the Ghisleri College in Pavia and then the resumption of his legal studies in Padua (all the while following the career-moves of his father, an unlicensed medical practitioner). Still in his youth, Goldoni gained a view of the world outside Venice, and so returned with a more mature insight and, one may infer, an ability to judge his mother tongue from the outside and to use it to fulfil his own needs. Without this vast and not solely bookish culture, he might perhaps never have become an exceptional Venetian, and Venetian dialect, writer, but with the wide experience of life he had acquired he was able to provide Italian and European literature with one of the most conspicuous examples of the elevation of dialect writing to a level where it could convey a vast range of socio-cultural nuances from different environments. When, after his thirty-fifth birthday, he spent a long period in Tuscany he was able to resist the process of 'Florentinisation' which affected so many non-Tuscan writers before and after him.

San Samuele

Having spent a couple of years without finding an 'honourable' profession, and not feeling any vocation for law, Goldoni signed a contract in 1734 with the aristocrat Grimani, proprietor of the theatres of San Giovanni Grisostomo and San Samuele, of which he became director in 1737. His first productions for the 'spoken' theatre (which in that venue played a subordinate role to musical theatre) are tragedies and tragicomedies (*Belisario*, 1735; *Don Giovanni Tenorio*, 1736; *Rinaldo di Montalbano*, 1737), after which he moved to comedy. All discussions of Goldoni's theatre identify *Momolo cortesan* (1738–9, 'Momolo the Gentleman') as the beginning of his 'reform'. In the author's own words, this was the first experiment with the protagonist's part fully scripted but the play otherwise left to improvisation. Only with *La donna di garbo* ('The Polite Lady') in 1793 did Goldoni provide a fully written play. The role of Momolo, played without a mask by Francesco Golinetti (the Pantalone of the Giuseppe Imer company), recurs in two further plays in the following seasons: *Momolo sulla Brenta* (1739–40, 'Momolo on the Brenta') and *Momolo mercante fallito* (1740–1, 'Momolo the Bankrupt'). These youthful experiments made use of a character, Momolo, already familiar to Venetian theatre and a speciality of Golinetti, and took their inspiration from some very successful *commedia dell'arte* scripts which in their turn derived from various fully scripted comedies of the late seventeenth century, such as *Pantalone bullo* ('Pantalone the Lout') by Giovanni Bonicelli (subsequently, as *Momolo bullo,* part of the *commedia dell'arte* repertoire) and Tomaso Mondini's very popular *Pantalone mercante fallito*.

The (relatively) youthful Goldoni's comic talent at the San Samuele theatre can be judged by his *intermezzi per musica*, which reveal a mature writer confident of his standing in this field. His choice of the comic genre as testing ground will be emphasised in his *Mémoires*, while he will say little on his later, extraordinarily prolific activities as producer of libretti for musical theatre. He prefers to portray this youthful period almost exclusively as one where he sowed the seeds that would eventually produce 'ripe and succulent fruit' in his comedies. From a long list of titles (particularly concentrated in the 1734–7 seasons), it is worth noting *La birba* ('The Scamp') and *Monsieur Petiton* (both plurilinguistic, the former providing some exquisite caricatures of street idlers and scroungers, the latter a deft sketch of a fashionable gentleman speaking a tortured French) and, more particularly *La bottega da caffè* ('The Coffee-House') and *L'amante cabala* ('The Intriguing Lover'), both rich in their portrayal of Venetian ambience, almost prototypes for the better plays that lay in the future (but free of all trace of moralising).

Sant'Angelo

Mounting debts forced Goldoni to leave Venice for Tuscany, where he worked as a lawyer in Pisa for three years, from 1745 to 1748, after which he abandoned law. The first part of his autobiography ends with an account of the forty-year-old lawyer agreeing with Cesare D'Arbes, the Medebach company Pantalone, to leave the legal profession and take on an engagement as a 'company-poet'. The contract he signed with Girolamo Medebach brought him into contact with a less prestigious company, consisting of itinerant or street actors and ex-acrobats turned performers, although there were also some more serious figures, like D'Arbes. The company hired the Sant'Angelo theatre and, not having an established tradition to break, regular public to disappoint, nor aristocratic impresario to oblige (problems that became more pressing when Goldoni moved to the larger Teatro San Luca), showed itself willing to take the risk of backing Goldoni's project. The Medebach couple and their troupe were thus able to support him in the bold undertakings that followed, such as the 1750 production of *Pamela*, based on Richardson's novel, Goldoni's first comedy without masks and first adaptation from a novel.

If the exploitation for the theatre of his experience as a lawyer was at first quite mechanical and predictable – the Doctor's maid Corallina in the *Donna di garbo* becomes a lawyer in skirts because of her position as the

Doctor's housemaid – the same cannot be said of the dramatisation of the disturbing, disconcerting, dramatically colourful and socially significant trial at the heart of *L'uomo prudente* ('The Prudent Man'). Some have seen *L'avvocato veneziano* ('The Venetian Advocate') as a 'political comedy', but the description could equally apply to such other works of this period as *La putta onorata* ('The Respectable Girl'), *La buona moglie* ('The Good Wife'), *Il cavaliere e la dama* ('The Gentleman and the Lady'), *La figlia obbediente* ('The Obedient Daughter'), *La moglie saggia* ('The Wise Wife') and *Il feudatario* ('Lord and Master'). The centrality and extraordinary novelty of this theme in the Sant'Angelo period are undeniable, although other topics are not excluded. It could be added that the comic model adopted here, with its strong emphasis on 'political' morality but with a high dose of tension arising from an existential and dramatic ambiguity, represented clearly what contemporary Venetian society, at a time of civil improvement or self-justification, fragmented and riven as it was between inbred conservatism and demands for change, was looking for. The audiences found themselves participating in a complex dramatic debate rather than being confronted with a prejudged ideology.

Further characteristics, evident particularly in the 'poetics in action' of Goldoni's play *Teatro comico* ('The Dramatic Theatre') and in the preface written at the same time for the Bettinelli edition (1750), include the equation between the term 'reform' and the demand for a more prestigious role for the theatre-poet, and the contraposition of written script not only to improvisation but, more generally, to the low quality of drama produced by actors. The writer is the figure who attempts to assert his authority over the tradition and repertoire of *commedia dell'arte*, partly through setting out a systematic programme but also by the sheer volume of his output in the 1750–1 season, an output known as the 'sixteen new comedies'.

The maturity of Goldoni's theatre in this season is probably most evident in *La bottega del caffè* ('The Coffee House'), the epitome of his new dramatic method. In the first printed edition, the masks initially used in performance are suppressed, and the virtuous Brighella, a figure from the *commedia* tradition, is transformed into the character Rodolfo. His opposite number, the villainous Pandolfo, runs the gambling-house, where money and reputation can be lost (as opposed to the coffee-house, which is not only an honest business but a decent place where good is done to others). For the crowd of miscreants (from the hardened gambler to the bogus count) and the women involved with them (from the neglected wife to the 'pilgrim' and the ballerina), the malicious Don Marzio is not just a mischief-maker but also a sort of scapegoat to facilitate their return to the 'respectable' life. With an 'infallible' watch that tells the wrong time, and with the help of his short sight and lorgnette (which presumably is equally fallible), Don Marzio's 'poor vision' manages after all to grasp the truth, or at least to create the conditions for doing so; he becomes the dynamo of the plot, the heart of the intrigue, the link between actions destined to follow separate routes, as well as the incarnation of the ambiguity of theatre. He even ends up as a not totally unsympathetic character, fulfilling a clearly central role on the stage. The final rejection of Marzio is a mechanical but necessary outcome of the 'moral' premises of the system, of the world reinterpreted from the point of view of the honourable owner of the *caffè*: it outlines, or inaugurates, a significant statement of Goldoni's system of values.

La locandiera (1753, 'The Innkeeper') is a further but more fruitfully ambiguous step along this road. Written with the intention of 'promoting' Maddalena Marliani, the company serving-maid, to a leading role, it became a masterpiece which combined satire against a passive or newly acquired nobility with a 'women's revenge' devised, inside the dramatic fiction, by the protagonist against a worthy but misogynist aristocrat. From this perspective, on the level of the victims in the fiction, the Cavaliere di Ripafratta becomes the most serious and emblematic character of Goldoni's whole production. The two actresses, Ortensia and Dejanira, attempt to pass themselves off as noblewomen, but their efforts can delude only the most naïve of the other characters. Nevertheless, these efforts are an allusion to the theatre in its most literal sense. The connection, or rather the opposition, between the deception practised by the actresses and that practised by Mirandolina on the Cavaliere is conscious and significant, in that the character who defends himself against the 'falsehood' of a trad-itional theatrical fiction (the actresses in disguise) proves incapable of penetrating the falsehood practised by the innkeeper (her feigned affection for him). The 'women's revenge' coincides with the 'theatre's revenge': Mirandolina's game, in this reformed theatre, exposes the very instruments of theatre's fascination: she personifies the seductive duplicity not just of a woman but of a stage which mirrors life. Goldoni's comedy shows (perhaps more clearly than the author intended) that lessons provided *a posteriori* cannot withstand that fascination, any more than theatricality can be condensed to a rational theory of principles.

San Luca

Goldoni's move from Sant'Angelo to San Luca, from a smaller to a larger theatre more closely bound to traditional repertoires, reveals in the early stages an author unsure of himself in the face of the different conditions and work-practices of his new venue. His first comedies here look designed to unsettle both old and new viewpoints, and represent a signal retreat from his recent practice as he attempts to adjust to a company specialising in *commedia dell'arte*. The dimensions of the new stage seem to nullify the familiar, conversational atmosphere of Goldonian comedy.

The author was thus obliged to present the situation as the relaunch of an unproductive enterprise: 'the store that had closed opens another branch with new products'. Apart from practical consequences and implications, the competition provided by Pietro Chiari, who took over the vacant writer's post at the Sant'Angelo, had the undeniable merit of forcing Goldoni away from the tried and tested repertoire, down new paths and out of the impasse he had arrived at with his early plays. The 'new products' are mainly imported, borrowed from other areas and genres, with the attractive addition of verse, the Martellian couplet, which Goldoni had experimented with in his *Molière* and which Chiari now adopted.

Commercial considerations apart, the options chosen by Goldoni at this stage can in fact be seen as logical developments of his recent practice: in particular the change from prose to Martellian verse (invented by Pier Jacopo Martello in imitation of the French alexandrine) is not simply a response to new competitive pressures. Goldoni's choice of verse, far from contradicting the preference for prose expressed in the *Teatro comico*, is actually a justifiable alternative, a widening of his horizons, a time when masks are definitively superseded and the sets and range of genres much expanded. The first season contained two innovations that are particularly significant for different reasons: the relaunch of tragicomedy in exotic settings with the highly successful, and wholly admirable, *Sposa persiana* (autumn 1753, 'Persian Spouse'), as well as the first example of a 'European' comedy, the *Filosofo inglese* (Carnival 1754, 'The English Philosopher'). These two different levels of exoticism, remote and near, clearly illustrate an unexpected widening of vision as against traditional comedy and its *milieux*.

The actual genesis of the *Sposa persiana*, the production that inaugurated the highly successful run of exotic tragicomedies (originally called 'comedies of an oriental character'), was connected to the craze for geographical exploration. The staging of novelties of this kind showed itself to be, once suitably disguised and reimagined for more sophisticated tastes and cultures, capable of giving new life to familiar genres and attitudes, and of embellishing traditional middle-of-the-road comedy. The inspiration for the *Filosofo inglese* was the popularity in contemporary society of English culture, imported into Venice mainly by the British Consul, John Smith, to whom the play is dedicated. The case of the *Sposa persiana* is particularly instructive in regard to the crucial importance of onstage performance and the actual reception of a play as opposed to the author's own initial intentions. As had already happened during the final seasons at the Sant'Angelo, where, with the character of the maid, Maddalena Marliani had overshadowed that of the *prima donna,* here too a play based on the supremely moral wife, Fatima, played by the *prima donna* Teresa Gandini, sees its basic premise overturned when the dominant character on stage turns out to be the initially negative Ircana, 'a haughty and overbearing woman' who used her charms to win the heart of Tamas, Fatima's husband. In view of the play's enormous success with the public, the company's second actress, Caterina Bresciani, coaxed or coerced the author to invent two further episodes of the Persian tragi-comedy. Hand in hand with the promotion of this actress, for whom Goldoni would create the finest roles of his finest period, such as the restive Giacinta in the *Trilogia della villeggiatura* ('The Holiday Trilogy'), went the revival of the transvestite role played first by Pietro Gandini and then by Giuseppe Lapy, which opened up a new and fruitful vein of bawdry promptly included in the Venetian comedies themselves. The licence of Carnival and especially the freedom allowed by verse provided cover for some dubious allusions and doubles entendres.

Confronted with Chiari's successes with the historical play, Goldoni on his travels around Italy prepared the ground for his return to Venice and for his most ambitious season to date, a summa of all the various theatrical genres, to be performed using 'various metres and subjects'. There were to be nine texts dedicated to the nine Muses, who provided the title for his project and the 'theme' for the 1759–60 season. His programme was undoubtedly influenced by Martello's example in differentiating the genres metrically, but the importance of his exposure to broader neo-classical influences during his stay in Rome remains to be studied properly (in 1759 Winckelman was at the Villa Albani, where Mengs was painting *Il Parnaso*).

Goldoni experimented boldly, unquestionably influenced by commercial competition but also by more serious ambitions, testing the limits of his abilities and his language, of his poetic world one might say, taking his project as far as it could go. The failure of these productions, at least in comparison to such masterpieces as *I rusteghi* ('The Boors'), cannot be blamed on his meekly returning to his normal repertoire after this challenge to Apollo. It marks an extreme point in the eighteenth-century experimentation with genre. The theatrical history of the verse plays and the protracted competition between Chiari and Goldoni ends on this high note, but now there appeared on the Venetian scene, to have his say or give the last unexpected twist to the process of experimentation, a new writer, Carlo Gozzi, his fables filled in equal measure with tragic horror and the comic gags of stock characters, with blank verse and improvised escapades.

This demanding season, which had its impact on the techniques of theatre practice and resulted in a series of plays planned organically and not just as a result of an individual play's success, produced other startling innovations, as for example *La guerra* ('The War') and the *Trilogia della villeggiatura*.

Venice on stage

Goldoni cannot be said to have invented a new genre, since popular, female, ensemble comedy existed before him, but the move from the ephemerality of the stage – with its annual, familiar ritual of Carnival performance accompanied by dances, acrobatic displays and displays of skill – to the printed page brought with it a new seriousness and sense of literary responsibility. That is the gist of the comments provided in the printed prefaces to his individual plays, each showing a growing awareness of status and dignity. His concern over the inadequate knowledge of Venetian dialect outside Venice, first voiced in the preface to *La putta onorata* ('A Girl of Honour') and subsequently repeated in prefaces to other comedies, is given definitive, objective statement in the prologue to *Le baruffe chiozzotte* ('The Chioggia Squabbles'), where he designates comedy as the point of arrival after his struggles with popular pieces: 'I have written my *Tabernarie* [tavern plays], my *Poissardes* [fish-market sketches], as well as my *Pamela, Terence, Tasso,* and *Persiane,* and so many more that should satisfy the most serious and fastidious critic.'[1]

With *La putta onorata* Goldoni makes his 'discovery of morality', perhaps the key to his first reform, in that most popular and most commonly

Figure 7: Scene from *The Family of the Antiquarian* by Carlo Goldoni.

Figure 8: Scene from *The Liar* by Carlo Goldoni.

performed genre, Venetian drawing-room comedy. The sequel, *La buona moglie* ('The Good Wife'), is followed on the Sant'Angelo stage by a compact sequence of predominantly ensemble plays with women in the leading roles. These embrace a broad range of social levels from *I pettegolezzi delle donne* (Carnival 1751, 'Women's Gossip'), a bright but still conventional play, to *Le donne gelose* (Carnival 1752, 'Jealous Women'), undoubtedly the masterpiece of Goldoni's first manner, which shows a perfect, unrivalled fusion of traditional features and the author's own individual input. The horizon narrows with *Le donne gelose*, where all characters are members of a single social and linguistic class with the sole exception of a colourful Arlecchino, free of the conventional rigidity of the stock character and more in keeping with the porters and pimps of local tradition. At the heart of this comedy is the character of Siora Lugrezia, played by Maddalena Marliani, an easy-going, self-confident woman who loves the theatre and earns her living by small-time wheeling and dealing and ventures at the gambling table.

The use of verse provided Venetian comedy at San Luca both with an instrument capable of giving poetic expression to a real world too banal and particular to be represented in prose and with a vehicle for softening its cruder tones. In *Massere* (1755, 'Housewives'), Goldoni introduced in the figure of Anzoletto, 'a young businessman', a character whose function is to act as the amused spectator of superior social standing but involved in popular intrigues, who very clearly represents inside the action the point of view of the author and of the upper classes, and who articulates the reasons for the amusement and delight aroused by this kind of play: 'Some work all night, some play; I like to be with the girls', and further on, 'Everybody has fun in their own way. I have fun with the girls. Why worry? I enjoy myself and it doesn't cost much' (I. 8). It is no longer the lower classes who go to see themselves represented on stage in characters like Catte or Lugrezia, but people of a higher social class mixing with the people to enjoy a theatre that reflects reality. That is equally the function of the Cavaliere in *Il campiello* ('The City Square'), and of the philosopher Isidoro in *Le baruffe chiozzotte* (which also has some autobiographical elements) – characters with one foot inside and one outside the fiction.

Il campiello (1756) is a reconstruction of a particular locality, with a set looking out on to the street from the interior and comprising situations presented 'vertically' as well as 'horizontally'. For the author this implies, as is clear from the stage directions, a more complex combination of dialogue and instructions for the actors' movements, resulting in a work which at key points resembles a musical score. The idea of 'orchestration', in the musical and proto-directorial sense appropriate to theatrical performance, is perhaps the best key to understanding the precise nature of an operation which opens the stage up increasingly to ensemble playing and movement, and demands a richer modulation of the various means of expression. Goldoni's technique in *Il campiello* is to blend a multiplicity of elements of a very precise nature in such a way as to achieve an authentic 'atmospheric realism'. Verse predictably acts as a filter for this demand for 'plebeian' mimesis, not only giving the shouting and brawling a respectable form but also lessening the crudity of some of the more pointed situations.

After other Venetian plays in verse, Goldoni returned to prose, aiming at a broader tonal register and downplaying the picturesque. He devotes more attention to character, situation and language, as in his admirable *I rusteghi* (1760), a comedy set in the confined domestic circle of the lower bourgeoisie, with their antiquated customs and exaggerated exclusiveness. These are no longer stagnating Venetian merchants, but newcomers from the mainland not noted for 'refinement' (and once again hostile to Carnival and theatre). This line of development leads to the extraordinary, perhaps caricatured, figure of *Sior Todero brontolon* ('Todero the Grumbler'). Alongside these comedies targeting the meanness of the tight-lipped, unsociable former peasants can be set the plays portraying the extravagance and ostentatious luxury of a bourgeoisie who ape the behaviour of the aristocrats, as in *La casa nova* (1761, 'The New House'). Rejecting the restrictions of the traditional genre, these plays bring Venetian comedy into the broader domain of the Italian comic theatre, with which it shares most of its subjects and motifs. Venetian comedy thus abandons its cosy, restricted ambience to acquire a precise, realistic mode, only differentiated from Italian comedy by its closer attachment to a local reality.

Goldoni made what appeared to be, and indeed transpired to be in the light of his departure for Paris, a final venture into the popular tradition with *Le baruffe chiozzotte* (1762), a summa of the genre. In parallel, in bourgeois drama, he employed Carnival to provide a memorable background for the highly successful *Una delle ultime sere di carnevale* ('One of the Last Evenings of Carnival'). With *Le baruffe* Goldoni continued, or rather concluded, his experiments with popular characters, moving away from the working people of Venice to those of the lagoon. Now at the peak of

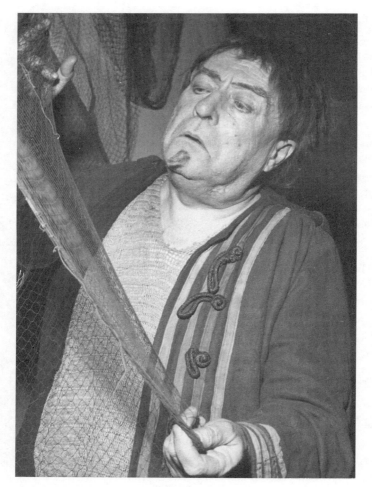

Figure 9: Cesco Baseggio in *The Chioggia Squabbles* by Carlo Goldoni.

his powers of composition and orchestration, he decided to revert to prose. Of all his plays, this is the most deeply rooted in the theatrical tradition, and his departure from Venice has given added poignancy to the autobiographical, emblematic aspects of the character of Isidoro, transforming certain aspects into a comedy about the author, and making allusions which are clearly reflections on his own career. The departure of the lawyer for other horizons – in other words, his return to the city – seems to denote a definitive break with the world of the people, whose vitality is captured here for the last time. Even more revealing is the equally fine *Una delle ultime sere di carnevale,* a carefully composed farewell to the bourgeois, family stage. The supper-scene recapitulates the main phases of the author's theatrical career, each phase represented by a different character who seems to take on double roles: the offhand Momolo being the writer as young man, and Anzoletto representing the author-role; the former destined to survive and 'become an adult', get married and acquire a recognised professional status, but the latter destined to depart. The broader 'allegory', as that term was understood in the eighteenth century, uses a group of workmen in a textile factory and a metaphorical commercial organisation to allude to the San Luca company, from the impresario Zamaria to the workmen-actors.

This comedy represents and exemplifies the minimal distance between theatre and real life, between the 'allegory' of the author's experience and the apparently casual re-creation of the everyday world from an accumulation of trivial circumstances. What makes this a masterpiece is the correspondence between the plane of referential fiction, a group of workmen who happen to eat together one evening during Carnival, and the allegory that is superimposed upon it, transforming the individuals who have gathered there into spokesmen for the 'destiny' of the author.

The Paris period

Even before his departure from Venice, there were clear signs, particularly the deadlock following the 'Nine Muses' project, of the exhaustion which made Goldoni's final seasons more difficult. Anxious and restless as he was, Goldoni was apparently keen to try his luck elsewhere, to take on new audiences and conditions.

His first play in Paris, *L'Amour paternel,* is another experiment with allegory, this time with a lighter, more ironical, typically eighteenth-century allusiveness. A hard-up Pantalone sets off to join his brother Stefanel in Paris, intending to share his brother's fortune. In Lyons he learns that the brother has died suddenly, and when he arrives in the capital he discovers that French law prevents him from inheriting any of his brother's property, and that it is his task to support his young nieces, Clarice and Angelica. When Goldoni himself arrived in Paris, like Pantalone in Lyons, he received the unwelcome news that the Comédie Italienne and the Opéra Comique had merged, dealing a devastating blow to the status of comedy in the capital.

The Comédie Italienne staged Goldoni's best-known repertoire, which meant his successful scenarios, in a hybrid idiom which is not quite that set out in *Una delle ultime sere* (something 'equally pleasing to both nations'), but one which has Harlequin and Scapin speak French and which aims at making the comic action intelligible to an audience unfamiliar with Italian. The challenge facing Goldoni was to find a new dramaturgy, different from his practice in Italy and appropriate to an 'orchestrated' theatre, even if that meant sacrificing the primacy of the script. His 1763 scenarios, perhaps his most original, comprise a highly successful trilogy – *Les Amours d'Arlequin et de Camille, La Jalousie d'Arlequin* and *Les Inquiétudes de Camille* – with the leading roles taken by the characters of Camilla (the actress Camilla Veronese) and Arlecchino (Carlin Bertinazzi). A bolder experiment was the dual language *L'Eventail/Il ventaglio* ('The Fan'), which, in spite of its deftly designed structure, failed to produce that appeal to the two cultures that Goldoni achieved in the trilogy. It was conceived both for full performance on the French stage ('where the actors have to perform more with actions than with words') and as an outline script with stage directions and unchanging scenery. In the case of *L'Eventail*, the attempt to rise above 'farce' (in its literal meaning of a mixture of genres) and low-level, stock-character theatre resulted in total failure, but can be seen as a bold attempt to create from the improvised theatre a stage comedy in a recognised style. The relative success of the performance in Venice, where this approach was no novelty, marks the end of Goldoni's operations as 'scripter of *canovacci* [outline plots]' and of attempts to capture the vivacity of real life on the stage. 'The taste for good comedy has vanished in this country', he wrote in June 1763, deploring the low expectations of the audiences at the Italian Theatre in Paris, where the 'maximum success' was achieved by the most trite means and stereotyped formulae, paralleling what happened on the French stage with its *couplets, tirades* and *fautes de détail.*

Goldoni's activities as 'designer of outline plots', sending his 'designs' to Venice, gradually petered out. For the French court, he wrote *Le Bourru bienfaisant*, which was performed on the occasion of the marriage of Marie Antoinette and the Dauphin. It was a triumph at the Comédie Française on 4 November 1771, and raised Goldoni from the depths of 'farce' to the heaven of royal comedy.

Theatre historians used to say, and some still do, that after this, or after the following, unsuccessful play, *L'Avare fastueux*, Goldoni laid down his arms and retired to dedicate his remaining years contentedly to his *Mémoires*, or alternatively to end them miserably, far away from the court. General and exaggerated conclusions of this nature, while making colourful and romantic reading, do not fit the facts. Goldoni's undeniable withdrawal from both the writing and directing of new plays (except for the three new musical *libretti* written between 1777 and 1779, and not without interest) did not result in a complete cessation of all theatrical activity on his part. In the 1780s and 1790s, he undertook some occasional rewriting of earlier works, and set about preparing his definitive image for posterity. What has been called his 'reinvention' or 'idealisation' at this time was not so much a case of setting the record straight as, principally, an attempt to explain his intentions as distinct from actual achievements.

Works for music

Alongside Goldoni's vast production for the 'spoken' theatre can be set the scripts he wrote to accompany musical scores. This was a substantial output of more than seventy titles, from *I sdegni amorosi tra Bettina putta de campielo e Buleghin barcariol* (1733, 'The Amorous Tiffs Between Bettina the Street-girl and Buleghin the Boatman') to *Il talismano* and *Vittorina* (1779), his last original piece of work in any genre. There were some highly successful phases, including his collaboration with Baldassare Galuppi and his Europe-wide success with *Buona figliola* ('Good Daughter'), set to music by Niccolò Piccinni. It is difficult to avoid the temptation to treat this vast production as though it were only a 'parallel' to his real work, and there is a logic to the recent tendency to evaluate the different phases and types of his writing for music as though it were a process of action and reaction, or even of opposition, to his 'principal' works, the comedies. His experimentation with new themes and broader cultural interests, especially in the 1750s, resulted in a wide range of settings from the fantastic to the *conte philosophique* (*Bertoldo, Bertoldino e Cacasenno*) – which would play a prominent part in the 'querelle des bouffons' – to more contemporary subjects, closer to comedy in their satire of customs or caricature. *L'Arcadia in Brenta*, one of Goldoni's most attractive works either as playwright or librettist, exemplifies this trend. This is a Goldoni of considerable interest, far removed from the standard image, revelling in the freedom afforded him from canons of verisimilitude and 'good taste', deft in his employment of magic and other distancing devices, skilled in the use of Arcadian landscapes and fanciful scenery, released from the *politesse* of comedy, at home with doubles entendres, and thus able to give voice to the equivocal worlds of fishwives and bird-hunters. Freed from the bourgeois world of comedy, Goldoni produces a sequence of highly significant scripts embracing a broad spectrum of country settings, of peasants and workmen (as in the superb *Amor contadino* ('Country Love') and *Amore cortigiano* ('Courtly Love'), and also of the provincial nobility. The world of opera as seen through the disenchanted gaze of the poet Lorano Glodici (a transparent anagram) is memorably recorded in *Bella verità* ('Beautiful Truth'), which occupies a symbolic position parallel to *Una delle ultime sere,* perhaps suggesting that Goldoni's creation was less random than he made out.

The list of titles could be extended further to illustrate the great variety of Goldoni's subjects and settings. The brilliance and abundance of his production and his genius for experimentation of genre and form make Goldoni the greatest comic librettist in eighteenth-century Europe.

Note
1 Carlo Goldoni, 'L'autore a chi legge', in *Le baruffe chiozzotte*, Venice, 1993, p. 77.

Bibliography
Editions

Edizione Nazionale Goldoniana, ed. S. Romagnoli, Venice, 1993 – some forty volumes have appeared to date.

Critical works

Cozzi, G. 'Note su Carlo Goldoni, la società veneziana e il suo diritto', in *La società veneta e il suo diritto,* Venice, 1997.
Fido, F. *Guida a Goldoni: Teatro e società nel Settecento,* Turin, 1977.
Folena, G. 'Goldoni librettista comico', in *L'italiano in Europa: Esperienze linguistiche del Settecento,* Turin, 1993, pp. 307–24.
Padoan, G. *Putte, zanni, rusteghi: Scena e testo nella commedia goldoniana,* Ravenna, 2001.

16 Carlo Gozzi

ALBERTO BENISCELLI

When in the late 1750s Carlo Gozzi (1720–1803) made the acquaintance of Antonio Sacchi, the celebrated *capocomico* (actor-manager) who had been co-author and lead actor in Goldoni's *Servant of Two Masters* and who had recently returned to Venice after a lengthy tour which had ended in Portugal, Gozzi was ready to turn his back on the disputations in the Academies which had characterised the initial phase of his literary production, and to take that decisive step which would win him a place among the most important theatrical writers of eighteenth-century Italy and Europe.

The Gozzi family had moved to the Veneto in the sixteenth century, taking possession of lands in Friuli which gave them a meagre income and a noble title. Carlo was born on 13 December 1720 to Jacopo Antonio and Angela Tiepolo. His hostility towards the dominant Enlightenment thought was apparent from the outset when he made the choice to look backwards, imitating or championing Tuscan fourteenth- to sixteenth-century authors (the short-story writers, Sacchetti and Fiorenzuola, the neglected Pulci, Burchiello and Berni), and to set himself up as leader of the most reactionary wing of the Venetian Accademia dei Granelleschi, noted for its hostility to all ideological or formal innovation. Inside the Academy, he saw off the more moderate tendency, led by his elder brother Gasparo, which was open to dialogue with contemporary society.

The Sacchi troupe was one of the most famous and important of the age, but their inability to adapt to scripts which were daily becoming less and less suitable for improvisation, or even to act without masks, as Carlo Goldoni's reform programme required, had relegated them to the margins of Venice's intense theatrical life. Gozzi's encounter with Sacchi caused him to start scribbling prologues, lines of dialogue and plots, anything which would help the company win back public trust and an audience. Previously in pamphlets or tracts issued as member of the Granelleschi, such as the anti-Goldonian *Tartana degli influssi per l'anno bisestile* (1756,

Figure 10: Portrait of Carlo Gozzi.

'Disquistion on Influences for the Leap Year'), which sets out the issues in his quarrels with Goldoni and Pietro Chiari, the other fashionable writer of the age, or in *Il teatro comico all'osteria del Pellegrino* ('The Comic Theatre at the Pilgrim's Inn')[1] a powerful exercise in dramatic criticism and lucid dismemberment of Goldoni's plays, *La putta onorata* ('The Honourable Young Woman') and *La buona moglie* ('The Good Wife'), or the mock-heroic epic *Marfisa bizzarra* (begun in 1761 but completed in 1768), Gozzi had given proof of a singular ability to swim against the tide in the turbulent waters of Venetian theatre. None of these prepared critics or audiences for the evening of 21 January 1761, when *L'amore delle tre melarance* ('The Love of the Three Oranges') was premiered.

The play dramatises the story of a melancholic prince, who has been cursed by an evil fairy and whose subsequent happiness and very life depend on finding the enchanted fruit. Under the inadequate protection of an incompetent magician, the prince and his faithful companion set off on the perilous quest. The tale has roots in folklore, and one precise predecessor in literature, *Le tre cetra* ('The Three Citron Trees') from the *Cunto de li cunti* ('Tale of Tales') by the seventeenth-century Neapolitan writer, Giovambattista Basile. It is worth underlining the allegorical and parodic aims, the mixture of folklore and literature which are present in Gozzi's script, the more so since Gozzi himself attested to these intentions when, ten years later, he bowed to the insistent pressure of the publisher Colombani and decided to issue the tale in the unusual format of a 'reflective analysis'. The prologue alone was in print at the first performance, while the plot development was barely sketched out and only a few passages had been fully written. In 1772, while engaged on fleshing out that early outline, Gozzi added an apparatus of stage directions, as well as notes on the scenic and technical devices, the polemical objectives of the work and the audience response. He also took the opportunity to explain fully the metatheatrical significance of his deliberately provocative work. Not only do the doltish magician and the wicked fairy represent Carlo Goldoni and Pietro Chiari, engaged in warfare against each other to conquer the Venetian stage, but all the fantasy scenes are part of a debate on the styles and genres of contemporary drama, whether Goldoni's low-life 'tavern pieces' or the long-winded, lachrymose 'tragedies' written in bombastic alexandrines by Chiari. The happy ending which allows the prince to find happiness and love is due to the random but decisive intervention of his idiot companion, Truffaldino, that is, to the theatrically triumphant lesson of *commedia dell'arte*.

Having carefully analysed the reaction of an amused but largely convinced audience, Gozzi understood that the magical fable had a theatrical potential which was not to be undervalued. Instead of insisting on the mask-parody aspects, the writer set more store on the theatrical impact itself, on how fable and fantasy can be staged, on the charm of their performance. It was not that Gozzi abandoned his plan to produce anti-Goldonian works but, to accomplish this end, he now chose a different approach. Instead of the direct polemic or the derisory jeer, he placed his trust in the power of individual genres of theatre and of differing language registers, each carefully studied and devised to suit different tales. This decisive change of direction lies behind the meticulous, complex phases of drafting and redrafting of *Il corvo* ('The Crow') and *Il re cervo* ('The Stag King'), premiered in October 1761 and January 1762.

The use of adapted texts – once again Basile's *Cunto de li cunti,* and two stories from *Le cabinet des Fées,* the French eighteenth-century, forty-one volume anthology of 'oriental' tales – aided the dramatist in crafting or reconstructing specific stories: one concerns Millo, who becomes the melancholic King of Frattombrosa by magic, and Armilla, the young daughter of a wizard who alone can save his life; another features King Deramo and his wife Angela, whose happiness, destroyed by magic secrets and treacherous courtiers, can be restored through labour and dedication. The use of these texts also permitted him to cluster around the inner core of those tales the entire performative range previously exhibited in *Three Oranges* and which he intended to extend with the introduction of the *zanni* and the *magnifico,* stock characters from *commedia dell'arte.* Their tasks and functions, however, were made more specific, and their roles and language patterns set in a hierarchical arrangement with pride of place given to the upper-class characters.

Before the memory of the enormous success with Venetian audiences of *The Stag King* had faded, Gozzi turned his attention in January 1762 to *Turandot,* whose success persuaded Sacchi to move his company to the larger Sant'Angelo theatre. *Turandot* too, like its successors, was inspired by the repertory of Franco-oriental tales, and with it Gozzi threw down the gauntlet to his detractors. He eliminated the magical effects or transformations which might have won facile public approval, to focus on the much debated, serious themes present in the source material. Gozzi picked out episodes of courage and passion involving the beautiful but cruel princess of China, who spurns the proposal of marriage made by the bold, unknown Tartar prince at the risk of his own life, and focused his plot on encounters between the protagonists, on the repeated grand gestures of the prince and the ever more tormented resistance of the princess, all in a melodramatic crescendo of variations on the themes of generosity, pride, honour and ultimately love. With *Turandot,* in other words, the dramatic-pathetic nucleus which underwrites the whole exotic fable stands out in its own right. In Gozzi's view, the power and dramatic force of the lovers' 'heroism' is in no way undermined, but rather reinforced, by the use of the 'marvellous' with which he had been experimenting since *The Stag King*.

From the same inexhaustible 'Oriental' reservoir, Gozzi next drew a second story of 'mad' love, which was also a splendid tale of magic. The plight of a fairy-princess who falls in love with a mortal man in defiance of the decrees which rule her world, and who was required to commit such acts as would make her intended spouse curse her, thereby putting him under an obligation to submit to punishing trials if he were to win her back, gave him the plot for *La donna serpente* ('The Serpent Woman'), premiered in October 1762. The effect of the choice of the world of fable with accompanying, heightened spectacle is to deepen further the gulf which separates planes of reality – deranged for the *zanni*, rational for the *magnifico* – from the dimension of dream, which emerges victorious. The final arrival, brought about by the power of magic, in remote realms of gold, the quintessentially eighteenth-century (and Voltairean) symbol of happiness, endows the journey of the two lovers with a paradigmatic value which far surpasses any melodramatic clash between reason and madness, and has a resonance for the innermost function of theatre as a radical alternative to the 'world'.

The impact achieved by *The Serpent Woman* was decisive and rich in metatheatrical implications. The succeeding theatrical fables (*Zobeide,* autumn 1763, *I pitocchi fortunati* ('The Fortunate Beggars') and *Il mostro turchino* ('The Turquoise Monster', both November–December, 1764) are no more than repetitions of a formula which was now familiar and played out, and which Gozzi was unable to revive by further innovations. If anything, the drama was weighed down by the welter of stage directions and, in the case of *Zobeide,* with excessive 'tragic' sentiments. Gozzi seemed even to react to his own awareness of the exhaustion of his creativity. Being the persistent experimenter he always was, he decided to overturn everything once more, to find new ways of reintroducing his own, still unchanged ideas on theatre, to return to eighteenth-century atmospheres and themes with fresh touches and a fresh montage. To achieve this, he went back to the sources of his theatrical inspiration, and in January 1765, wrote *L'augellin belverde* ('The Beautiful Green Bird'), the ideal sequel to *Love of the Three Oranges*. The tenth fable, *Zeim, re dei geni* ('Zeim, King of the Genies'), staged in November of the same year, did nothing to lessen the approval which had greeted *Green Bird,* Gozzi's triumphant finale.

In the kingdom of Monterotondo, the 'melancholic' prince has in the meantime been widowed as a result of the intrigues of his terrible mother, who had ordered the burial alive of his young wife and the murder of his twin children. The twins had, it transpires, been saved by adoptive parents of humble birth, but had been corrupted by exposure to the Enlightenment outlook. They will pay for their youthful arrogance by a fabulous process of initiation, based in part on a tale from a seventeenth-century collection, the *Posilicheata* by Pompeo Sarnelli, before the inevitable happy ending. The play marks the final, important turning point in Gozzi's theatre. The work does not have the parodic aims of *Three Oranges*, nor does it exalt some alternative, exclusive primacy of grand gestures and feelings, as had been the case with the 'tragicomedies' of his middle period. It is instead 'philosophical', that is, concerned with setting out an educational itinerary. The fantastic and theatrical elements are present, not any longer to show their remoteness from reality, or to establish alternative, self-contained worlds beyond the reach of the *hoi polloi*, but to be part of that reality, to alter it and thus indicate new convictions and new styles of behaviour. The narrative flow and the succession of dramatic twists are swift, the rhythm thus attained lightens the ideological presuppositions and the play brings protagonists, supporting characters and even spectators to a collective and 'open' final conversion. This remains the most brilliant, and certainly the best known, dénouement to any of Gozzi's works.

In reality, Gozzi had already won his theatrical battle by the Carnival–autumn season of 1762, the moment of his greatest creativity. In the April of that year, Carlo Goldoni had made up his mind to accept an offer from Paris and leave Venice, disappointed, among other things, by a significant fall in the number of spectators in the San Luca theatre, where he was employed as author. Pietro Chiari had also left Venice in April the same year. These were not, however, good conditions for an author who had built his own theatre work on open rivalry with others.

Nevertheless, Gozzi did not lay down his arms. Deprived of his stimulating adversaries, and having concluded what, in a passage in his *Memorie inutili* ('Useless Memoirs'), he would call his 'homogeneous path', he set off anew with the same aim as before: to help the Sacchi company in the daily grind of winning approval. In a climate which was becoming more uncertain and confused by the day, but was still enlivened by theatrical polemics and initiatives, Gozzi was determined that his actor protégés would not lose their identity, and that he would not renege on the central principles of the *Fables*. For that reason, he turned to the rich theatrical heritage of seventeenth-century Spain, with its plethora of works with a strong dramatic, narrative drive. Gozzi began to work on such authors as Calderón de la Barca, Tirso de Molina and Matos Fragoso. His many adaptations include: *La donna vendicativa* (1767, 'The Vengeful Woman'); *La Caduta di donna Elvira* (1768, 'The Fall of Donna Elvira'); *La punizione nel precipizio* (1768, 'Punishment in the Ravine'); *Il pubblico segreto* (1769, 'The Secret Audience'); *Le due notti affannose* (1771, 'Two Nights of Torment'); *I due fratelli nemici* (1773, 'Two Enemy Brothers'); *La malia nella voce* (1774, 'The Spell in the Voice'); and *Il moro di corpo bianco* (1775, 'The White-Bodied Moor'). These 'tragi-comedies,' equipped with the customary counterpoint of space for improvisation, employ an apparel of elaborately decorated backcloths to suggest exotic remoteness – palaces in Saragossa or Aragon, countrysides in Navarre or coastlines near Salerno – where princes or dukes are involved in adventures interwoven with intrigue or dark psychology and which are, then, rigorously distinguished from the equally complex but everyday cases featured in the hated post-Goldoni drama. The special attention paid to the actors' demands meant that Gozzi gave way more and more frequently to their requests. The most unexpected of these demands was for the partial abandonment of performance with masks, justified by the progressive exhaustion of the players, the changed composition of the company and the heightened competition from works based on the exploration of character. As early as 1762, Sacchi had asked the writer for two comedies *Il cavaliere amico* ('The Friendly Cavalier') and *Doride* without roles requiring improvisation 'so as to allow for a few evenings' rest'.

In 1771, with the willing backing of Gozzi, the troupe transferred to the San Luca theatre, but Darbes, the popular Pantalone, left them, and Teodora Ricci, a highly temperamental actress, joined the company as lead actress. The following year Carlo Coralli arrived to take up the role of Truffaldino in direct opposition to the ageing Sacchi, but his relative lack of success did not hide the power shift inside the company. Gozzi and Ricci embarked on a personal and professional relationship which was to last six years and which would provoke open, even comic, clashes with other pretenders for her hand. Gozzi promised her 'theatrical pieces built round her'. The first fruit of this promise was *La donna innamorata di vero* (1771, The Woman Deeply in Love') a comedy with a 'bizarre plot' which saw the actress grappling with a tricky switch of roles which convinced neither actors nor audience. Intent on developing roles of greater and greater depth for Ricci – even to the extent of translating specially for her in 1771 a hated French play, *The Fajel* by F. Th. D'Arnaud – Gozzi wrote in 1772 *La Principessa filosofa* ('The Philosopher Princess'). In this work, the masks are definitively abandoned, establishing a practice Gozzi would follow in his later output *Il metafisico* (1778, 'The Metaphysician') or *Bianca contessa di Melfi* (1779, 'Bianca, Duchess of Melfi') after his separation from Ricci.

Ricci's departure was hastened by the rivalry of her colleagues and the jealousy of Sacchi, but above all by the aftershock of a theatrical and society scandal in which she and Gozzi played leading parts. A new production, entitled *Le droghe d'amore*, ('Love Drugs') was staged at the San Luca on 10 January 1777, and it required little effort from the audience to recognise in the figure of don Adone, an 'affected young gentleman', a caricature of Pietro Antonio Gratarol, who had been for some time Ricci's lover. The incident could not be disregarded, and Gratarol, a Secretary of State viewed with some distrust by the nobility on account of his Masonic affiliations, felt compelled to leave Venice. If the political and biographical ramifications of the affair gave much meat to gazetteers and chroniclers, the implications for the theatre were less helpful. The break with Ricci was not final, and Gozzi wrote further plays for her: the comedy, *L'amore assottiglia il cervello* (1782, 'Love Softens the Brain'), and two other works which proved difficult to stage – *La figlia dell'aria* ('The Daughter of the Air') and *Cimene Pardo*. The latter two works appeared in 1786, but by then the Sacchi company had been dissolved. It is worth recording that in these productive years, Gozzi finally accepted the invitation to publish the theatrical *Fables* and the Spanish-inspired works he had written earlier. The eight volumes of the Colbani edition were completed in 1775. Later, between 1801 and 1803, he prepared a fourteen-volume edition for the Zanardi presses. This edition was completed in 1805 with a volume of non-theatrical works. One year later, on 4 April 1806, he died in Venice.

Note

1 Both texts in P. Bosisio (ed.), *Carlo Gozzi e Carlo Goldoni: una polemica letteraria con versi inediti e rari.*

Bibliography

Editions

Gozzi, C. *Fiabe teatrali,* ed. A. Beniscelli, Milan, 1994.

Five Tales for the Theatre, trans. Albert Bermel and Ted Emery, Chicago, 1989.

Critical works

Alberti, C. (ed.), *Carlo Gozzi scrittore di teatro,* Rome, 1996.

Beniscelli, A. *La finzione del fiabesco: studi sul teatro di Carlo Gozzi,* Genoa, 1986.

Bosisio, P. (ed.), *Carlo Gozzi e Carlo Goldoni: una polemica letteraria con versi inediti e rari,* Florence, 1979.

Luciani, G. *Carlo Gozzi: L'homme et l'œuvre,* Lille and Paris, 1977.

17 Metastasio and the *melodramma*

COSTANTINO MAEDER

Pietro Metastasio (1698–1782) was the most successful author of *dramma per musica*, as the *melodramma* was commonly called in the eighteenth century.[1] Throughout the century, his poetic works, mostly written for the stage, were set to music by almost every important composer in Europe. He attained a peak of popularity during a century when Cartesian rationalism was succeeded by the Enlightenment, Arcadia by a cult of Sensitivity, of *Sturm und Drang* and early Romanticism, when absolutism was challenged by revolutionary ideas and emergent nationalism, and when monarchy was threatened by democratic tendencies. Metastasio created *libretti* which enjoyed an immediate contemporary success but which also survived changes in aesthetic creeds, and which retained their fashionable appeal in the most disparate cultural and political contexts. His model of the *melodramma*, although subject to frequent criticism, remained dominant, with only slight modifications, well into the nineteenth century.

The genre of musical theatre for which Metastasio wrote emerged in the late sixteenth and early seventeenth centuries. He inherited the legacies of the Camerata Fiorentina (or Camerata de' Bardi), an academy of scholars, musicians, poets and aristocrats who set themselves the task of reinterpreting Greek tragedy, *feste teatrali* and *intermezzi* for court performance, and of those other scholars of the same period who sought to devise a style of music which was less complicated and which lent itself more easily to performance. The central aims of the new musical style were to enhance the poetry, to speak directly to the heart of the listener and to permit more direct communication. Many academicians of that age were convinced that classical tragedy had been sung throughout, and that it was the combination of text and musical interpretation which produced the perlocutionary and emotional effect on the audience, a phenomenon described by ancient authors but missing in contemporary performances of tragedies. Metastasio, almost two centuries later, was of the same opinion. In a letter of 29 January 1766 to F. G. de Chastellux in Paris, he argued that his *libretti* complied with the practice of the ancients:

> It will not have escaped your attention that the characters themselves [of the early writers of tragedy] sing either solo or among themselves, and chant in turn strophes, antistrophes and epodes with the chorus, metres which by their very nature require that kind of music used by us in the arias . . . whereby you will conclude, as a necessary consequence, that in the custom of flattering the delicate ears of our spectators we have ancient, illustrious and authoritative predecessors, to whom beyond all doubt we owe the *aria* and the *recitative.*[2]

The development of polyphonic music led poets and musicians to conclude that a more sober style could enhance the relationship between text and music, and facilitate communication. They opted for a clear distinction between melody and accompaniment (*monodia*). While in polyphonic music, vocal exuberance, harmonic boldness, embellishments, repetition of syllables and words, the elongation of a syllable over several notes made it difficult to follow a text-line (if that had ever been intended in the first place), the music in the new manner, referred to as the *seconda prattica* (second practice) or *stile rappresentativo* (performance style), was designed to accompany more closely, or even serve, the text. Plainly, even in polyphonic music the poetic content, if not every single word, was important, but the syntax and discourse were secondary to the musical expression of a general theme. The *seconda prattica,* on the other hand, followed and interpreted a text-line step by step, often mimicking and exaggerating normal pronunciation, or including if necessary disharmonies or irregularities of rhythm.

The first significant poet of this new trend was Ottavio Rinuccini (?1562/4–1621), whose *Dafne,* set to music by Jacopo Peri and premiered in 1598, is the first *libretto* for a fully fledged opera. Early musical theatre was performed either in aristocratic palaces or before groups of scholars, but by 1637 the first opera houses for paying audiences had opened their doors in Venice. From that point, a production had to be successful and please its audience. Purely literary or humanistic considerations were insufficient for attracting mass audiences. From the outset, music was dominant, and often the logic of an opera plot was unintelligible; this approach was inimical to Arcadians or rationalists, engaged in a struggle against the 'bad taste' of the Baroque. Such *libretti* as those of Matteo Noris (?1650–1714), illustrate the intricacy of plot that seems to predate Hollywood movies in their penchant for cliff-hangers, unrelated side plots, unexpected twists, duels, war scenes, sinking vessels, exotic locations, frequent changes of scenery and episodes of tragedy followed by comedy.

Towards the end of the seventeenth century, complaints were voiced about the poor quality of *opera seria*. Whereas originally musicians, poets, architects, engineers and scholars had worked collaboratively, now writers attempted to establish the dominance of text over music. Leading poets offered more sober, clearer libretti, based on their interpretation of Aristotelian or 'Arcadian' principles. Silvio Stampiglia (1664–1725), one of the founders of Arcadia, Apostolo Zeno (1668–1750) and Antonio Salvi (1664–1742) were among the principal exponents of the new school. Others, including Ranieri Calzabigi (1714–95) and Lorenzo Da Ponte (1749–1838), attempted a wider reform of opera. Many of these served as 'Caesarean' poets at the Imperial court in Vienna, the most important centre for opera during the eighteenth century. The most celebrated and significant poet and reformer working at the Austrian court was, however, Pietro Metastasio.

Pietro Trapassi, whose name was translated into the Arcadian 'Metastasio', was born in Rome in 1698. Gian Vincenzo Gravina, jurist, author of a treatise on theatrical matters and co-founder in 1690 of the Roman Academy of Arcadia, took charge of his education. He introduced the young poet to the Cartesian philosopher, Gregorio Caloprese, who gave him a thorough grounding in rationalist thought. This familiarity with Descartes was a vital element of Metastasio's personal culture.

It is easy today when, apart from Mozart's *Il re pastore* or *La clemenza di Tito,* operas based on Metastasio's *librettos* are rarely performed, to overlook his former popularity and influence. During the eighteenth-century, such works as *Didone abbandonata* (1724, 'Dido Abandoned'), *Siroe* (1726), *Semiramide riconosciuta* (1729, 'Semiramis Recognised'), *L'Olimpiade* (1733, 'The Olympiad') or *Attilio Regolo* (1750) were standard fare in the opera houses of Europe and America. His libretti, like those of Apostolo Zeno, his predecessor at the Viennese court, were not written for a single composer, as would later be the case with Da Ponte and Mozart, Calzabigi and Gluck, or Piave and Verdi. They were set to music by virtually all the important composers of the century – Hasse, Vivaldi, Galuppi, Porpora, Caldara, Paisiello, Cimarosa, Mozart and Handel – some more than a hundred times. More than ninety scores for *Artaserse* are known, but precise calculations of the number of settings of other scripts is impossible since few scores were published. Important centres like Vienna, Venice, Milan or Naples required new productions and new music, but not necessarily new libretti, for every new season. Metastasio was a guarantee of success. His works were also staged as tragedies on their own, without music.

Metastasio's plot-structures are highly repetitive. Two principal types of drama can be distinguished: those featuring Roman heroes, for instance *Catone in Utica* (1728, 'Cato in Utica') or *Attilio Regolo*, and intrigue-based plays like *Semiramide riconosciuta* or *L'Olimpiade*. While the former end with the tragic death of the protagonist, the latter frequently end with a double marriage. Invariably, in a Metastasian *melodramma*, the script predominates over every other aspect of performance. Music, scenery, plot, even performance are all secondary to text, an approach for which Elena Sala di Felice coined the term 'logocentrism'. Metastasio adopted different devices to achieve this goal:

1. *Elimination of all comic elements*: the attention of the audience is focused on a single dimension, and is not to be distracted by laughter or 'vulgar' considerations which might distract attention from the main themes of the drama.

2. *Diversity of action is drawn together in final unity*: Metastasian *libretti* are in appearance extremely complex, with various strands intertwining, but the dénouement demonstrates that all subplots originate from one central, core situation.

3. *The scenery provides background but is independent of plot development*: scenery may be luxuriant and exotic, but once the curtain is lifted, it will not be altered and will therefore not influence the unfolding of the action, as may happen in Baroque opera.

4. *The relationship between recitative and aria highlights the semantic and narrative élan of the music*: the deft segmentation of the plot into recitative and aria enables the poet to exploit music to the full to enhance the text.

5. *The plot is secondary*: most *dénouements* are known from the opening of the play, so there is no suspense over the evolution of plot. After a few scenes, the audience knows virtually everything about the drama, and more than any character on stage.

6. *The spoken text contains all pertinent information*: even the captions or stage directions are, often unnecessarily and redundantly, inserted into the spoken dialogue.

These features compel the audience to focus on the text, on the dialogue between the characters, on their expressions of emotion and, crucially, on their psychological response to events. The stage is the locus of the word, not of action: action takes place offstage, in the 'space of death', to adapt a phrase used by Roland Barthes on Racine's theatre.

The drama had to conform to rationalist notions of verisimilitude: what happens on stage must be made to seem possible or plausible in real life. Kings, princesses or heroes are confronted by problems experienced in life by everyman: clashes of duty, conflicts involving citizenship, betrayal, friendship, love, hate. Plots may be situated in the past and could be based on historical documents. However, many ancient accounts contain elements of fantasy, for which Metastasio, like Goldoni, had little taste. In an *argomento* (prologue) to the *libretto*, he explained away those 'irrational' parts, in order to create verisimilitude. In his *argomento* to *Semiramide riconosciuta*, he writes: 'it was believed that [Semiramis] had a nymph for mother and doves as nursemaids . . . The principal action of the drama is the recognition of Semiramis, but to give rise to this event, and to *remove at the same time the inverisimilitude* in her fabled origins, we pretend that she was daughter of Vessore, king of Egypt.'[3]

The setting in the past and the verisimilar approach serve to create an atemporal dimension: values are eternal and not subject to change. Virtually no difference exists between the performance time and the represented historic time, just as there is no difference between the audience and the onstage heroes of the past. This serves the didactic purpose of offering the audience lessons on how to deal with life, while having their values confirmed by history.

Most *melodrammi* by Metastasio, continuing the tradition of baroque tragedy, are based on the dialectical opposition of duty and volition, of (civil) responsibility and passion. Of the various antimonies in Metastasio's theatre, none is deeper than the clash between reason and passion. Passion and the unreasoning will, signs of egotism and of the frailty of human nature, divert the individual from the path of reason, from truth, from social integration and participation in community goals. Most Metastasian dramas stem from the preference of an individual, driven by instinct and passion, to pursue his private ends, causing disorder. The conflict is resolved by the intervention of another, usually a monarch, perhaps himself riven by opposing emotions and desires, who re-establishes order by imposing the rule of reason, including compassion, and who therefore dispenses forgiveness. In *La Clemenza di Tito,* the emperor initially plans to marry Berenice, thereby arousing the jealousy of Vitellia, who convinces Sextus, who is in love with her, to lead a conspiracy against Titus. Matters become more complex when Titus alters his plans and decides to marry Vitellia, but she is now fully committed to the plot. Titus escapes death at the hands of the plotters, and at the close displays his compassion by issuing a pardon to all the conspirators.

However, Metastasian dramas are not as simple (and 'pleasing') as might appear. What is the final judgement on those passions, apparently criticised in the dramas? A closer look reveals that the positive outcome of every drama has itself its origins in the passions and emotions: without them, injustice, conflicts or clashes would be irresolvable. They are necessary to life and are therefore not opposed to reason: there is no reason without passion, and only passion can guarantee a happy conclusion. This paradoxical outcome is in conflict with certain of his arias. Arias allow characters, for example tutors or fathers, to express opinions in the guise of proverbs which refer to shared values and which are seemingly based on common sense and experience, but these apparently reasonable arias, often built on comparisons, are contradicted by the dénouement. In an attempt to find a *reason* for what is happening, a character explicitly creates a link between the outer world of experience and his own situation. Metastasio is deeply ambiguous and this heuristic drive often fails. The course of events often shows that all human reasoning is doomed to fail.

In an aria in *L'Olimpiade,* the lyrics suggest that in the woods, that is, in nature, betrayal and deceit are not possible, but the thrust of the drama as a whole undermines any facile trust in nature, for the plot features acts of deceit and betrayal conceived in the same woods. Another character sings that life is like a ship in a storm: you may see the coast, the haven, but ultimately the vessel will sink. Passions are, the same opera suggests, like a storm, but in the end it is these selfsame passions which ensure that everyone will finally reach a safe haven and happiness. This ambiguity underwrote Metastasio's success: the text is subtly layered and capable of multiple readings and interpretations. Frequently, no one character can be unequivocally identified as protagonist. In the 'intrigue' plays, such as *L'Olimpiade,* there are often two couples of lovers, who can equally appear as the main characters, but in the dénouement the true protagonist appears, often a regal figure who, by virtue of his office, displays the magnanimity needed to take a decision opposed to his own private wishes and desires.

In *L'Olimpiade,* Licida, a young prince from Crete, has fallen in love with Aristea, the daughter of King Clistene, but she has been promised in marriage to the winner of the Olympic Games. Licida is not an athlete but a warrior, and persuades his friend, Megacle, who owes his life to him, to take his place in the games. However, Megacle discovers that Aristea is the woman he had loved but had been forbidden to marry. To complicate matters, Licida had previously promised to marry Argene, and the spurned woman is also at the Games. Driven by his new passion, Licida refuses to recognise the wrong he has done Argene, while Megacle cannot speak of his own dilemma without betraying the person who saved his life, and Aristea herself is in despair. Licida makes a wild, reckless attempt to kill Clistene in an attempt to resolve this self-created chaos, but at this juncture solutions begin to emerge. Each character discovers a willingness to sacrifice themselves for their friends and to accept punishment for their misdeeds, and each is prepared to act in accordance with society's laws. The situation now moves to a climax: the oracle discloses that Licida is the lost son of Clistene, making Aristea his sister. Clistene alone is wretched. His son has committed crimes for which the punishment is execution, and being king, Clistene cannot defy the law, even though it conflicts with his wishes. However, a new player now enters the story: the people, until now a non-participant, appeal for clemency. A formal error is discovered, allowing Clistene to embrace his long-lost son, Licida to marry his abandoned fiancée and Megacle to wed Aristea.

In the first act, the main characters are Megacle and Aristea, the unhappy lovers: in the second act, however, the focus is on the progressive isolation of Licida, while in the last act attention is centred on King Clistene, symbol of accord with the eternal rules of social behaviour, but also on the people who, at the end, judge the king's actions. With slight directorial changes (lengthening or elimination of one character's arias, altered musical interpretation), Licida, Clistene or the Megacle/Aristea couple can be made protagonists. In the deep structure of the work, the people too are a protagonist.

Metastasio perfected a system, still in use at the end of the nineteenth century, which offered composers a flexible framework, and writers a device for exploiting music for their own ends. Metastasio's musicality resides not, as many believe, in a florid style, rich in vowels and harmonic cadences: he created an efficient framework of conventions and exceptions, in which the plot is developed through a succession of recitatives and arias. He believed that for *opera seria* to succeed, it must be sufficiently rational and limpid to permit easy comprehension, meaning that only two characters can converse onstage. The others are spectators, awaiting their turn, intervening only via occasional asides, even if the events onstage concern them directly. The recitative is the preferred means of communication, giving characters the opportunity to try and exchange information rationally. Every aspect of a complex situation is evaluated, but at the end one of the characters will be given an aria in which he expresses his understanding that communication has failed, or in which his passions simply overwhelm rationality.

Metastasio brought this structure, which had previously been present in a rudimentary form in Rinuccini's operas, to perfection. This rational structure, suited to the musical limits of the age, is frequently broken by a carefully chosen transgression: a character sings an aria but is interrupted and will not leave the stage, or an aria has three couplets. The absence of arias, often toward the end of a drama, shows that the time for expressing emotions or thought is past, that the dramatic climax is at hand. The *melodramma* offers a simple and straightforward integration of text, music and dramatic development. The distribution of the plot between recitative and aria is simple but effective. The Metastasian *libretto* held sway in Italian opera over a lengthy period: the recitative may be shortened, the form of the aria may vary, but the intrinsic dialectic of rules and exceptions, or clash between rational communication and overwhelming passion was not abandoned until very late in the nineteenth century.

Notes

1 Metastasio himself used the term '*melodramma*' only on one occasion, in his correspondence, preferring to refer to his work as *opera*. However, since '*melodramma*' is currently used when the reference is to text rather than to music, it will be employed in this volume. The Italian spelling is retained to distinguish it from Victorian melodrama, with which it has no connection.

2 P. Metastasio, *Lettere*, in *Tutte le opere*, ed. B. Brunelli, Milan, 1943–54, vol. CXI, p. 702.

3 P. Metastasio, 'Semiramis', in *Tutte le opere*, vol. I, p. 397.

Bibliography

Beniscelli, A. *Felicità sognate: il teatro di Metastasio*, Genoa, 2000.

Fucilla, J. G. *Three Melodramas by Pietro Metastasio*, Lexington, KY, 1981.

Gallarati, P. *Musica e maschera: Il libretto italiano nel Settecento*, Turin, 1984.

Maeder, C. *Metastasio, L'Olimpiade e l'opera del Settecento*, Bologna, 1993.

Miggiani, M. G. (ed.), *Il canto di Metastasio*, Bologna, 2004.

Sala di Felice, E. *Metastasio: ideologia, drammaturgia, spettacolo*, Milan, 1983.

Strohm, R. *L'opera italiana nel Settecento*, Venice, 1991.

18 Vittorio Alfieri

GILBERTO PIZZAMIGLIO

When in 1773 Vittorio Alfieri wrote his first tragedy, *Cleopatra*, he had almost reached the mid-point of his life and the end of what he calls in his *Autobiography* the third period of his existence, the conclusion, in other words, of the sequence of childhood, adolescence and youth: he was now on the threshold of a thirty-year period of 'virility'. These were his most active and productive years when he produced some twenty tragedies and six comedies, in addition to various other tragedies and comedies left in draft form, and a succession of poems and political-literary works closely linked to the dramas.

The connection between biography and literary activity is already apparent in *Cleopatra*, which Alfieri tells us was closely related to his 'third youthful love-affair', between the end of 1773 and the beginning of 1774. *Cleopatra* was his first attempt at tragedy, later rejected and excluded from the published editions of his works, but providing nevertheless a fairly accurate foretaste of the main features of his poetic inspiration and revealing the distinctive methods of composition to which he later remained faithful: initial conception of plot, first draft in prose, subsequent versification, still hesitant at this stage but showing quite clearly his concern to avoid melodramatic excess – hence his continual, unquestioned attachment to the *endecasillabo sciolto* (hendecasyllable blank verse). The process of composition is split up into various phases, sometimes of several months each, with interruptions and revisions, and is complicated in the initial stages by his translation of the French original into Italian, reflecting the cultural ambivalence that marked his exposure to literature, first with his tutor at home and then during his eight years as a pupil at the Royal Academy in the conservative environment of Vittorio Amedeo's Turin.

Alfieri leaves us with a negative impression of this period, without however concealing that it did provide an opportunity for him to cultivate his musical tastes and to begin reading the Italian classics from Dante, Petrarch, Ariosto and Tasso, to his contemporaries, Goldoni and

Metastasio. He remained distinctly dubious about *melodramma*, following in this L. A. Muratori, but this led him, significantly, to examine closely the theoretical principles underlying the Arcadian reform of the theatre. The strong impact of French literature, thanks to his strong partiality for French novels, is of great significance for his early development, and this can be viewed as the earliest of a series of cosmopolitan influences which developed during his lengthy travels in Italy and the rest of Europe, and his various periods of residence in England, Russia and Sweden, where he made several visits between 1766 and 1772. He was thus able to see some of the major figures of the Enlightenment at work and to assess, sometimes approvingly, sometimes not, the effect of their writing on practical politics.

Cleopatra was premiered in Turin on 16 June 1775 by the Medebach company, which had been so closely involved with Goldoni. It was the only one of Alfieri's tragedies to be performed with his consent, and its favourable reception set him off on the first phase of his dramatic career. His tragic method seems at this stage to lack adequate stylistic support but already in the protagonist-queen the outlines of the tyrant can be seen, as can those of the yielding antagonist in Anthony. In order to improve his style and give it the classical flavour he wanted, Alfieri embarked on an extensive and feverish programme of reading in the Greek and Latin classics, both tragic and otherwise – the Greek in translation, the Latin in the original – and on a study of tragic verse. This led him to disparage Metastasio and the early eighteenth-century writers, as well as Scipione Maffei's tragedy *Merope*, and to discover instead sublime splendour in *Ossian* as translated by Melchiorre Cesarotti. He carefully selected thirteen Ossianic poems and made *Estratti* ('Extracts') from them, or more precisely, rewritings dramatised and transformed into dialogue form, putting life into his hybrid script with substantial revisions for dramatic and emotional effect. He also eliminated Cesarotti's decorative metaphors with the intention of creating lean and essential tragic verse.

The consequences are apparent shortly after this in his *Filippo* (1776), still conceived in French but showing a significant advance in dramaturgy. Alfieri is now clearly aiming at a reform of the structure of tragedy, involving a drastic reduction in the number of characters and eliminating the *confidants*, who until then had been considered indispensable to tragedy. The action is reduced to a single subject with an increasing concentration on the dominant, often soliloquising figure of the tyrant, prey to an unquenchable thirst for power, suspicious of everyone and everything and hence involved in a crescendo of cruelty which causes him to sacrifice all human and family feeling to his dark obsession. The blind violence of Filippo the king leads to the suicide of his wife Isabella and, more importantly, of his son Don Carlos, and finally provokes an explosive outburst where his torment of anxiety (like the ambiguously destructive anguish in the later *Saul*) concerning the true effects of his tyranny produces a highly dramatic finale. Don Carlos will be the archetype of future Alfieri creations, the sacrificial victim who asserts his own human dignity, unyielding in the face of approaching death:

> ISABELLA: See your wife die. . .
> And your son . . . both innocent . . . both at your hands
> I follow you, my beloved Carlos. . .
> FILIPPO: Now flows a river of blood (and what blood!). . .
> Now in this dread slaughter I gain my full revenge. . .
> But am I happy? . . . Gomez, conceal
> This grim deed from everyone – your silence
> Will save my name and your life.   (v. iv. 279–83)

Filippo also demonstrates the marked evolution of Alfieri's dramatic style from a clearly, and necessarily, Petrarchan mode – as in other late eighteenth-century writers – via a distinctly lyric phase (which can be seen as an experiment in the expression of intimate feelings) to a tragic style where the verse is often broken and halting in the search for increasingly dramatic and incisive effects.

Filippo was set in a comparatively recent period, the Spanish court in the late sixteenth century, and may seem superficially a historical play. This is not, however, the dimension that interests Alfieri, who wants to give his characters universal, non-historical significance. Confirmation comes with his simultaneous use of subjects from Greek tragedy in a series of works starting with *Polinice,* conceived between 1776 and 1777, where the eponymous hero is overcome by his antagonist brother, Eteocles. Polynices is a less complex protagonist than Filippo but is equally greedy for power. He is duplicated here by the young Creon, the aspiring tyrant who takes advantage of the rivalry between the two brothers in order to gain the throne for himself. *Antigone* was the first of Alfieri's tragedies to be drafted in Italian, with a heroine confronting the tyrant, and Creon now facing the conflict between ambition and fatherly affection. This first phase of Alfieri's dramatic production ends with his *Agamennone* and *Oreste*, which were conceived the same day, and followed the same creative process. *Oreste* employs the dominant, obsessive image of blood to convey to the spectator the particular nature of tyrannical abuse.

Alfieri's discomfort with established cultural models increases at this stage and he now seems eager to pursue independently his own ambitions as tragic writer and to create a radically new form of tragedy. In 1776, after having dramatically given up all claims to his inheritance in exchange for a pension that allowed him to dedicate himself entirely to literary activity, he took up residence in Tuscany, thus coming into direct contact with the main source of the Italian language. This can be seen as both the crowning moment of his career to date, and as an acceptance of new and totally different ways of acting and thinking. He now definitively eliminated all Gallicisms from his writing and abandoned certain snobbish attitudes for which he had been a mouthpiece. Under the influence of his close friend, the Sienese Francesco Gori Gandellini, who introduced him to Machiavelli and to the radicalism of those *philosophes* who opposed tyranny, Alfieri adopted a democratic, Enlightenment ideal, close to Republicanism. This tendency was evident in his early tragedies but it now became more sharply defined, and a new objective of social utility appeared in such tragedies as *Virginia*, *La congiura de' Pazzi* ('The Pazzi Conspiracy') and *Timoleone*. All these works share the common theme of the clash between the tyrannical prince and the freedom of the individual, and use catharsis to expound a programme of political and civil redemption which the spectator is expected to support.

These 'tragedies of liberty' written in 1777 express the central nucleus of Alfieri's tragic ideology, with subjects connected to Republican Rome in the first phase, to Medicean Florence and the modern city-state in the second and returning to the ancient world in the third. Plutarch's *Lives* and the *Florentine Histories* of Machiavelli provide the bases for the creation of characters who illustrate the failure of individual or collective aspirations to liberty in the face of various kinds of tyranny, mostly in the confined and oppressive settings of royal palaces. This tragic model is characterised by the intensely passionate speeches of the heroic protagonists, while the author's attention is focused on the one, or at most two, points of interest on which the action is deliberately centred. Very few characters appear on stage; they are isolated in their greatness by the skilfully paced succession of insistent, tense dialogues or by their introspective, self-questioning soliloquies. This is evident in *Timoleone*, one of Alfieri's favourite tragedies, which he considered superior to the other two 'liberty-plays' by virtue of the very starkness of the action and the sharp contrast between political absolutism and individual freedom. It may equally be that the treatment of these themes here is so schematic as to constitute a weakness.

Alfieri's theatre may therefore seem timeless and remote from history, but this impression is untenable in view of its strong metaphorical charge and the reflection it offers of the contemporary world where the European revolutions would shortly afterwards mark the end of the absolutist *anciens régimes* and expose tyranny as the cause of the failure of mankind's highest aspirations. The contemporary treatise *Della tirannide* ('On Tyranny') was begun in 1777, but only completed in Paris ten years later. Written in the style of an Enlightenment pamphlet, it upholds the same views and represents the more reflective, theoretical side of Alfieri, who was, however, set on directing his political energies not towards any practical commitment but towards tragic writing. The treatise *Del principe e delle lettere* ('The Prince and Letters') was also begun in 1778 and completed in 1786, and discusses the view that the economic independence of the writer is indispensable to ensure the quality of his work, and that in republican regimes he will find the best conditions to express himself.

The concentrated, almost frenzied activity of this crucial period is followed by a phase of quieter creative energy between 1778 and 1781, when the intensity of Alfieri's output seems to slacken and he returns to the themes and characters, duly reconsidered and refined, of his earlier career. It is thus possible to find elements of *Filippo* in the complicated *Don Garcia,* and of *Oreste* in the barbaric fury of *Rosmunda,* a tragedy characterised by an overwhelming and obsessive thirst for revenge. This is not of course a mechanical process, and if Alfieri himself found the results unsatisfactory in some cases – as in the uninspired *Maria Stuarda,* written to satisfy his lover Luisa Stolberg, Countess of Albany – there are nevertheless frequent touches of novelty in *Ottavia,* with its gentle heroine who has dedicated herself to a liberating death. *Ottavia* also anticipated some aspects of *Mirra,* the final masterpiece of the following period, 1782 to 1786, which opened with the other undoubted masterpiece of Alfieri's theatre, *Saul.*

Saul was written in 1782, the same year as *Merope,* and the two plays were, explicitly, a response to works of the same title by Scipione Maffei and Voltaire, the great tragic models of early eighteenth-century Italy and Europe. Alfieri replies with a hesitant heroine and with a concession to the Arcadian happy ending in the death of the tyrant. *Merope* and *Saul* illustrate the passage from the tragic rationality of the first half of the century to a new emphasis on the portrayal of passion, and to this can be added the themes of the clash between liberty and tyranny, and of the incurable internal conflict within the individual torn between an overwhelming lust for power and the anguish of an inability to achieve happiness. This is the case of Alfieri's Saul, a complex portrait of a tormented tyrant who yields to the violence of his passions and who sees suicide as an extreme act of liberty that will allow him to escape the divine will. The story is taken from the Bible and concerns the hatred of the King of Israel for David, the husband of his daughter Micol. Since David is God's elect, Saul accuses him of treachery and sends him into exile. Pulled between feelings of affection and esteem on the one hand and a paranoiac fear of losing power on the other, he then nominates David as commander of his army in the battle against the Philistines, at the end of which Saul, defeated, commits suicide. A comparison of the ending of this tragedy with those of the preceding *Filippo* and *Mirra* makes possible a deeper appreciation of the author's attempt to delve into the inner psychology of his characters and to convey a drama which springs not just from an external conflict between tyranny and liberty but also from an internal conflict within an individual as he struggles with his conscience:

> SAUL: . . .O my children! . . . I was a father. –
> Now here I am, a king, alone; not one remains
> of all my friends and servants. Are you satisfied,
> inexorable God of anger?
> But I still have you, my sword: for one final service
> come now, my trusty minister. Hear now the howls
> of the insolent conqueror: now before my eyes
> I see the flash of their blazing torches
> and their swords in their thousands. . .Wicked Philistine,
> here you will find me, dead. . .but still a king –
> (*As he falls on his sword the swarms of victorious Philistines bear down
> with flaming torches and bloody weapons. As they rush over to Saul with
> piercing screams the curtain falls.*)   (v. v. 216–25)

Subsequently in *Mirra*, composed in 1784 and revised over the next two years, the hidden depths of passion, the inadmissible and irrational forces that oppose reason and once again lead to death, are explored. Taking its theme from Ovid's *Metamorphoses*, the tragedy depicts the incestuous love that Mirra, as a consequence of the revenge of Venus, feels for her father and which she hides from everyone, including her fiancé Pereo and her nurse Euriclea. At her wedding, which she has welcomed as an escape from her guilty conscience, Mirra is overcome with horror at her sacrilege and confesses her sin, driving both Pereo and herself to suicide in a climax that is both tragic and pathetic, and which reveals all the author's compassion for his heroine, a symbol of the unhappy destiny of all humanity:

> MIRRA: When I begged you, Euriclea. . .
> then you should have handed me the sword. . .
> then I would have died an innocent woman. . .
> now I die a sinner. (v. iv. 218–20)

Between 1782 and 1784 Alfieri's theatre acquires its definitive form and distinctive features: it is no accident that we now find the earliest evidence of the author's direct intervention in performance but, in typical eighteenth-century fashion, this intervention is made primarily in public and private readings rather than in actual theatrical productions, which Alfieri authorised only rarely and approved even less frequently. In 1777 he had read *Antigone* to the Accademia Sampaolina in Turin; in 1782 he read *Oreste*, and on another occasion *Virginia*, both in Rome. The same year he staged *Antigone* in Rome in the private theatre of the Spanish ambassador, taking the part of Creon; then in 1783 *Saul* was recited before the Arcadian Academy in Rome. These dramatised readings before select, specialist audiences allowed him to test the effectiveness of the instructions he intended to give to professional actors whom he considered incapable of meeting the demands of his dramatic roles. He required them to be fully lucid in performance and capable of conveying the finest nuances of characterisation.

> If a tragedy or a comedy that deserves to be performed properly is to be less mangled on the stage than is usually the case, I would tell the actors: first read it carefully and get its meaning, then study

it and rehearse it in front of me, and don't worry about anything else in the world except your own part. The first principle is, of course, that they have the education and are in a context that allows them to understand and to feel what they are saying. I attend the first rehearsal, without prompters; the actors recite their parts slowly, meaningfully and with the correct pronunciation. They are not really good actors but they are the best Italy has at present. I have plenty of criticisms to make. Then I attend the second rehearsal and make more criticisms; and I attend and criticise the third and the fourth, and the tenth. So the actors, without being under pressure, feeling some degree of rivalry towards each other, moved perhaps by a sense of shame, after some ten rehearsals have made the part their own and have spoken so slowly that they have had time to reflect on what they are saying, and so have gradually managed to say it so much better. Then at last they go on the stage and people listen to them because they are really acting their parts, rather than singing them: they know their parts properly and they actually fill their roles because they know them.[1]

This was in 1785 when Alfieri's tragedy-writing career might be considered at an end, but his subsequent output is still, if not invariably, of interest, as for example when he returns to political subjects in *Agide*, which presents the figure of the just and liberal monarch who is a victim of his own patriotic ideals; or in *Bruto primo*, dedicated to George Washington, which emphasises the moral strength of the protagonist and the superiority of republicanism over other forms of government; and in *Bruto secondo*, dedicated to 'the future Italian people' who are yet to attain liberty.

The comic and satirical works written at this time are equally interesting, perhaps even more so. They owe much to his experiences from 1785 onwards while resident in Alsace and Paris, where he led a largely solitary life but did make friends with various intellectuals such as André Chenier. This period came to a dramatic halt when he fled France with the Duchess of Albany after the events of 1792 leading up to the Terror. The impressions left by these events caused Alfieri to reconsider his political position and led to a tetralogy of comedies which examine satirically the various possible forms of government: monarchy in *L'uno* ('The One'), oligarchy in *I pochi* ('The Few'), democracy in *I troppi* ('The Too Many'), and in

L'antidoto ('The Antidote'), a mixed form, moderate and constitutional, capable of remedying the defects in these different systems and providing a solution. His two other comedies – *La finestrina* ('The Window') and *Il divorzio* ('The Divorce') – are works of social criticism connected to his earlier writing by the recurrence of a moderate, almost benign vein of satire which he had always possessed. They are in keeping with the criticism of contemporary society first sketched in 1773 in his youthful *Esquisse du jugement universel,* drafted in dialogue form and containing a gallery of caricatures of various human types as they face Divine Judgement, and which continued with his seventeen *Satire*, marked by wide-ranging moral criticism and a rising Francophobia. This anti-French feeling received its most systematic expression in that curious mixture of poetry and prose, the *Misogallo*, started in 1793 but completed only in 1798.

There are late flashes of originality in some of the experiments Alfieri made during the last fifteen years of his life, when he went to live in Florence and undertook a study of Greek tragedy, making a number of translations and new versions of the originals, including for example *Alcesti prima* and *Alcesti seconda,* both inspired by Euripides. He also oversaw various reprints and new editions of his own works. From this miscellany of collections and revisions emerged the tragedy/melodrama *Abele*, which has to be considered in the context of the prevailing taste for the 'contamination' of the classical theatrical genres found among nearly all *fin de siècle* dramatists, from Alessandro Pepoli to Giovanni Pindemonte and Francesco Albergati Capacelli.

This was a period of continuing intellectual activity, calmer than before and ending with the author isolating himself from his fellow writers and reflecting anew on his own physical and spiritual identity and his ideals, as is evident from the partial reorganisation into a sort of spiritual diary of his *Rime*, principally the sonnets which he went on composing throughout his creative life. From 1790 onwards he busied himself with the drafting and revising of his autobiography, *Vita scritta da esso* ('Life Written by Himself'). Alfieri merges his own figure with that of his dramatic characters, creating the image of a man of heroic and determined will, never satisfied and always ready to confess his failings, fighting permanently against any form of conformity and in support of the political and moral rebirth of his country through the medium of literature. This is the reading of his work which gained ground in the nineteenth century and has persisted in some form to the present time. It has led to a critical assessment of Alfieri as a pre-Romantic rather than what he was, a child of the late eighteenth century, an accurate interpreter of the lights and shades of neo-classicism with its faithful adherence to a classical tradition set midway between a forward-looking Enlightenment outlook and a Romantic longing for a return to primitive nature.

The silence of Alfieri's final years was broken by the extraordinary success which his tragedies, especially the 'liberty-tragedies', enjoyed on stage in the Jacobin period in Venice, Milan and Florence, creating a myth of the man and his work which persisted into the nineteenth century, and thanks to which he became a principal point of reference, morally and poetically, for young men like Ugo Foscolo, who saw him as a beacon of intellectual and political freedom. This notion was passed on to the patriots of the Risorgimento and provided the basis of the widespread appreciation of his work in Italy and elsewhere in Europe during the liberal and independence movements in various countries from Germany and Spain to Poland and Romania.

Note
1 Alfieri, V. *Parere sull'arte comica in Italia,* p. 243.

Bibliography
For Alfieri's works see the critical edition by the Centro Nazionale di Studi Alfieriani, begun 1951 and now complete.

'Parere sull'arte comica in Italia', in *Parere sulle tragedie e altre prose critiche,* ed.
  Morena Pagliai, Asti, 1978.

Critical studies
Barsotti, A. *Alfieri e la scena. Da fantasmi di personaggi a fantasmi di spettatori,* Rome,
  2001.
Camerino, G. A. *Alfieri e il linguaggio della tragedia: verso, stile, topoi,* Naples, 1999.
Di Benedetto, A. *Le passioni e il limite: un'interpretazione di Vittorio Alfieri,* Naples,
  1994.
Joly, J. *Le Désir et l'utopie: études sur le théâtre d'Alfieri et de Goldoni,* Clermont-Ferrand,
  1978.
Masiello, V. *L'ideologia tragica di Vittorio Alfieri,* Rome, 1964.
Scrivano, R. *La natura teatrale dell'ispirazione alfieriana,* Milan and Messina, 1963.

PART V

The Risorgimento and united Italy

19 The Romantic theatre

FERDINANDO TAVIANI

The masterpieces of Italian Romantic theatre were not plays, not even ensemble productions. They were characters, not the characters in the scripts but the characters on the stage, masterpieces of discontinuity. These characters on stage, the protagonists, while encapsulated in the spectacle like jewels in a ring, were autonomous works of art, elaborated autonomously, independently of the rest of the performance, by the actor-creator. Only when the character was ready did the rehearsals with the whole company begin, and then the protagonist was fitted into the stage-work. Italian theatre is famous for the masterpieces created by its actors and for its concern to redefine the parameters of theatre. The innovations in terms of scripts are far less impressive, although these too, on closer inspection, often prove to be significant.

The 'Romantic' period as discussed here comprises the first decades of the nineteenth century when the debate between the new 'Romantic' and 'Classical' schools was at its height. During those years the foundations were laid of the great Italian theatre of the Victorian age, which would make its mark on the European stage thanks to the exceptional ability of its actors and actresses, particularly those of the latter half of the nineteenth and the early decades of the twentieth century – Adelaide Ristori, Tommaso Salvini, Ernesto Rossi, Giovanni Grasso, Ermete Zacconi, Ermete Novelli, and including the solitary, disturbing genius of Eleonora Duse. These were the main contributors to a theatrical culture equal in strength to the tradition of Italian opera. Nothing that Italy produced before or since in the field of dramatic literature or stagecraft possessed the same depth or breadth of inspiration.

The masterpieces of the Italian Romantic theatre, that is, the protagonists on the stage, contradict some of the criteria by which we are accustomed to judge the art of drama, in part because they compel us to consider the separate components of drama as self-contained units, and in part because they rely on memory weakened by incomprehension. They are not founded on works which have stood the test of time, and can therefore be based only on the sparse records of a now vanished art. Further, the masterpieces under discussion employ written texts, classical or otherwise, as the raw material for the creation of another art. They deny therefore in practice what is always maintained in theory, and that is the primacy of literature.

The gap between the clichés of criticism and actual stage practice is a constant source of concern, but theatre history rarely conforms to the programmes presented by aesthetic doctrines and literary movements. This was even more the case in the nineteenth century when the everyday life of the theatre, at least as it appeared to the devotees of high culture, seemed no better than commercial entertainment, compelled to abase itself to meet the taste of the majority of the spectators, and leaving seats empty when the play being performed turned out to be too serious or difficult. It was a profession in which the finest of artists mingled and collaborated with the most vulgar and uncultured of players. The operations of the business meant that even for the best artists there was no great difference between mere trickery and genuine creativity. Finally, since the achievements of actors vanish while the scripts of performed plays survive, and since these scripts were for the most part of very poor quality from the literary point of view, the world of the stage seemed secondary or culturally inferior.

The theatre and the novel

Stage practice has never conformed to principles considered appropriate for legitimate or ideal theatre, but with Romanticism the very notions of what is legitimate or ideal undergo change. In the early years of the nineteenth century, boundaries crumble and the ideal theatre ceases to be organised and sub-divided according to immutable cultural distinctions. Legitimacy is thus given, in theory as well as in practice, to various kinds of theatre which were already accepted in professional and commercial terms, so that theatre can be seen as a cultural open space, often barren and despised, but at least potentially free. In this space, theatrical time is synchronised more and more openly with the time of the novel.

Theatre and novel no longer belong to two distinct branches of expression. They had begun to come together in the eighteenth century and the marriage was given theoretical underpinning by the Romantics. The novel becomes the principal touchstone for the theatre, and the

Aristotelian distinction between the epic and the drama is eroded, both on practical and the conceptual levels.

For the entire Romantic movement in Europe the novels of Walter Scott were the main starting-point for the various journeys to Shakespeare and from Shakespeare. Shakespeare, interpreted and staged according to the standards of eighteenth- and nineteenth-century theatre, complete with realistic sets and divisions into acts and scenes, was the high road along which the novel-based theatre progressed. The heated debates, refined or pedantic as they may have been, on the so-called Aristotelian unities were a screen behind which the disappearance of any clear demarcation between staged and narrated action was implemented, and with it the idea that drama should have a specific language of its own (an idea which had previously held sway, at least in theory if not in the varied practice of the stage).

When Alessandro Manzoni discussed the unities of time and place in tragedy with Victor Chauvet, he did not argue that tragedies were better without the rigid classical rules, but that they were more interesting and closer to the principles underlying a truthful narrative of unfolding events. His *Lettre à M*C*** sur l'unité de temps et de lieu dans la tragédie* (written in 1820, published three years later in Paris) was a distillation and development of the arguments that had been put forward by Schlegel in 1808 and further discussed by Giovanni Berchet in his *Lettera semiseria di Giovanni Grisostomo al suo figliuolo* ('Semi-Serious Letter from Giovanni Grisostomo to His Son'), published in Milan in 1816. In March 1819, the Romantic journal *Il conciliatore* published a long article in two instalments by Giovanni Berchet comprising an imaginary lecture on Kalidasa's drama *Shakuntala* in which the lecturer declared: 'This is a drama where the unities of time and place are not observed, but in spite of that it is as fine a drama as any other.' He imagined that at this point some of the audience would leave the theatre, hands clasped over their ears to avoid hearing blasphemies. Berchet proposed the classic Indian drama as an alternative model of classicism, to rank with Shakespeare and Calderón, in opposition to the model provided by Racine and the classicists. Then he narrated *Shakuntala* as a love-story adapted for the stage.

The admission to the ranks of classics of theatrical models considered irregular in terms of the Western tradition was the most powerful weapon in the Romantic armoury. It turned the normal hierarchy of values upside down, and for that reason *Shakuntala* is particularly significant. So long as attention was focused on Shakespeare and Calderón, the revolution remained within the confines of European culture. The admission of Oriental elements, as the Germans had been doing for some time, suggested that the theatre itself needed refashioning according to criteria independent of tradition and capable of assessment exclusively according to contemporary values. If the models to be followed were so numerous and disparate, it meant that the choice between them would depend on the individual needs of the writer and not on some intrinsic aesthetic principle.

The less polemical, apparently more moderate Alessandro Manzoni, who refused to admit comic characters or incidents in tragedy, was however more radical in matters of principle. In his Letter to Victor Chauvet and in various handwritten passages in the manuscript of his *Moralità delle opere tragiche* ('Morality of Tragic Works'), he maintained that the purpose of theatre was not to give aesthetic pleasure or to move the spectators through the characters' feelings and passions but to provide rational pleasure, that is, the pleasure to be gained from knowledge, the stirring of conscience, the study of the relationship between cause and effect and the analysis of facts which could lead the spectator to make a judgement and hence take a stance on the problems and the contradictions inherent in the story being performed.

It was this line of argument, apparently indifferent to aesthetics but intent on providing theatre with a practical purpose, that separated Manzoni from the young, gifted Victor Chauvet. Chauvet believed that the restraints imposed by squeezing the whole action into the space of one day and one place served to give focus to the characters and to avoid making the performance the staging of a displaced action, or the straightforward viewing of 'different moments in the life of the protagonist'. He added that 'constraints in art provide energy and impetus for the imagination. Signor Manzoni should grasp this idea. Breaking down these constraints produces not great, but infantile art.'[1] In other words, as he said in his essay published in Paris in 1820 in the *Lycée Français* on Manzoni's tragedy, *Il Conte di Carmagnola*, it deprives art of its own specific, individualised language.

A sort of regression to the infancy of art, with no individuality or rebelliousness – this was the fear expressed by the great Italian poet, Ugo Foscolo, a combatant and libertarian in exile in London, in an article on 'The New School of Italian Drama' intended for inclusion in a pamphlet *On Literary Criticism* which would be published only after the author's death. Foscolo opposed the idea of theatre as staged narrative. Theatre, he said, should be like poetry 'which tends to make us feel our existence more fully and intensively', not like history which teaches us 'to lead our lives in such a way that we can enjoy the world as it is'.[2]

Before he went into exile Foscolo had composed three tragedies. The classical *Tieste*, written on the Alfierian model when he was seventeen, enjoyed considerable public acclaim and was performed on nine successive nights in Venice in January 1797. The more accomplished *Ajace*, completed in 1811 but not performed until 1828 after the poet's death, when its classical stance perhaps no longer chimed with a new mood in the theatre, enjoyed only modest success. *Ricciarda*, however, completed in 1813 and performed in Bologna the same year, was well received. It had a medieval setting, a story of a Romantic love on the pattern of Romeo and Juliet, and an impassioned despairing heroine.

Victor Chauvet and Ugo Foscolo demonstrate that the champions of the new theatre were not confronted only by reactionaries, pedants or elderly, myopic traditionalists. The real point of the debate was not the freedom to write and perform according to one's choice, but the defence of some of the peaks of the Western theatrical tradition, or rather of its hierarchies. The Romantics were engaged in dismantling the very ideals of the theatre. They attacked and conquered not so much working theatre as its image and orientation: they were intent on undoing its standards. They insisted that their way of creating theatre was replacing what until then had been considered the acme of dramatic art. (This was the crux of the battle over Victor Hugo's *Hernani* in Paris in 1830, one of the most important dates in the history of the theatre in Europe.)

For this reason Manzoni's tragedies, *Il Conte di Carmagnola* (1820), and *Adelchi* (1822) are key events in Italian theatre history. They may have been only rarely performed, and then only experimentally and never successfully, but they provided a model, a theatrical prototype. In dramatising two prominent events in Italian history (the execution of their *condottiere* by the Venetians in the fifteenth century in *Il Conte di Carmagnola*, and the struggle between Franks and Lombards for control of the peninsula in the eighth century in *Adelchi*), Manzoni broke with the unities of place and time, stretching the actions over years rather than hours and making frequent and drastic changes of scene. He exploited history to underline some key contemporary issues dear to his heart: the misfortunes arising from the disunity of the Italians and the need for brotherhood and trust in God. From these works, actors often selected as recital pieces for gala evenings monologues or choruses similar in structure to symphonic passages in opera, but which had been conceived by the author as lyric intervals where he could let his own voice be heard. In a theatre permeated by the tempo of the novel, drama was perceived as staged novel and was arranged as fragments which could have separate life, so that, as with opera, independent pieces, 'arias' or choruses, could be detached and performed separately.

Contrary to what might be expected, this lack of cohesion was a sign of vitality and made it possible to escape temporarily from the bounds of the fiction. It made for a flexible and articulate rapport with the audience. The emotional, ethical and political effectiveness of the production often depended on it, and the actors were able to exploit it creatively. One of Manzoni's Choruses, perhaps the most famous, in the interval after Act III of *Adelchi,* tells the story of an enslaved people raising their heads and pricking up their ears as they hear the distant rumble of a new war. They feel the surge of the impossible pride of their ancestors, long forgotten in the midst of their humiliations. They are compelled to recognise its 'impossibility' because they are a scattered race, entrusting again their hopes of freeing themselves from foreign domination to another foreigner. At the very moment when their rebellion emerges as a force, they are prepared to trade their freedom for a new slavery.

The protagonists of the tragedy were remote figures – Desiderio, King of the Lombards, his heir Adelchi, Charlemagne, the Pope (who did not, however, appear in person) – but in the years of insurrection and repression, of conspiracies for freedom and independence put down by the forces of the Holy Alliance, that Chorus was read and performed on its own in salons, halls, private theatres and commercial stages. In May 1821 Napoleon, who had been exiled to the outskirts of the civilised world, had only just died on his tiny island.

In a world of splendid ruins and startling poverty, the characters created by actors and actresses stood out as sublime and mocking exceptions, as if a tribe of sculptors, with its Michelangelos and Canovas, had dedicated themselves to resurrecting the great art of sculpture fashioning statues of mud.

A theatre of different levels

Produced in 1818, Gioacchino Rossini's *Mosè in Egitto* provided a powerful image of the drama of liberation. Music, *libretto* and production rose to a climax with the apparition of a contradiction in terms, a path opening through the raw might of the sea. Mazzini wrote that Rossini was 'the Napoleon of music'. He achieved the impossible, he rescued a world which had seemed in thrall to 'merchants of notes' and placed it at the service of liberty. In August 1829, from Paris where he had been resident for four or five years, the fame of Rossini's *Guillaume Tell* echoed down to Italy. On those foundations, Verdi was to create an alternative Italy, a musical and theatrical homeland more glorious than the real land.

If that was the world of opera, the situation of the companies of actors and actresses who travelled the different states of the Italian peninsula playing their characters on unimpressive stages was very different: they seemed to operate on a different level. Unlike opera, their theatres were on the margin of the great artistic movements of the age, not benefitting from the attention of the élite or of popular acclaim and often cut off from close contact with the main currents of Italian culture. It was a theatre lacking in music because it was a spoken theatre, but also lacking in poetry because it generally worked with poor quality scripts.

There was a conspicuous gap in Italy between performed and written theatre, and on a more general level between drama as a literary genre and the culture and practice of the stage. In the first decades of the nineteenth century, the only drama capable of both meeting the demands of serious literature and of simultaneously holding a prominent position in the contemporary theatre repertoire was *Francesca da Rimini* by Silvio Pellico, a man of letters who began to show sympathy for the Romantic school and joined the circle of writers around *Il conciliatore*, the most important mouthpiece of Italian Romanticism. Pellico's tragedy was performed in August 1815, shortly after Waterloo, and at the beginning of the dismal Restoration period when Ugo Foscolo, a friend of Pellico's, went into voluntary exile. (Foscolo thought his young friend's tragedy was worthless.) *Francesca da Rimini* was published in 1818, when *Il conciliatore* was born, and it was considered Romantic in respect of its context and content (the proverbial story of love and death immortalised by Dante in one of the most famous passages in the *Divine Comedy*), but not for its form. It observed the unities of time and place, just like Alfieri's tragedies; it could not be labelled a historical drama and it made no attempt to mingle tragic and comic.

Its author soon became an emblematic figure in Risorgimento Italy. He was arrested for conspiracy in 1820 by the Austrian authorities and suffered ten years of harsh imprisonment. Freed in 1830, he retired into silence and religion, but in 1832 he published a slim but powerful volume, *Le mie prigioni* ('My Prisons'), which was all the more effective as a vehicle of political propaganda because it was in style and tone so distant from propaganda. *Francesca da Rimini*, thanks to its literary qualities, its story of a love stronger than the will or moral principle, its allusions to the ideal of a united Italy (but subdued allusions strike home in an age of censorship), the constantly fluctuating emotions of its characters and, above all, thanks to the fame of its author, became the paradoxical masterpiece of a non-existent repertoire, that longed-for but never achieved repertoire of high quality dramas capable of gaining the applause of a paying public in a professional theatre.

In reality, the markedly national colours sported by Italian theatre in the Napoleonic period and the years immediately following the Congress of Vienna, the years of the *carbonari* and independence movements, do not correspond to the provenance of the material. Indeed, when the Italian Romantic theatre finds its 'contemporary' author, he will be neither Italian, nor a contemporary, nor a Romantic, but William Shakespeare.

In the spring of 1820 Victor Emmanuel I, King of Piedmont, Savoy and Sardinia, the provisional head of the dynasty destined to unify Italy politically, founded in Turin the Compagnia Reale Sarda, which survived until 1852. Some of the greatest Italian actors of these years performed there, from Carlotta Marchionni to Giuseppe de Marini and Luigi Vestri. In the second half of the century Adelaide Ristori, Ernesto Rossi and Tommaso Salvini established their reputations there, and they will be the actors mainly responsible for Italy's international theatrical fame. The greatest actor of the period, Gustavo Modena, as a Mazzinian and a Republican was unwilling to accept the patronage of the monarchy, and declined to join. The Company had been founded with the aim of promoting the Italian language and of providing a model theatre of high cultural standing. Its repertoire consisted of more than a thousand works, but less than half of these were Italian, and less than half of those showed any literary merit.

Although in theory theatre was seen as a branch of literature, in practice theatrical and literary culture did not coincide. An actor-creator could fashion his masterpiece from a play by Alfieri or Goldoni or from scripts that were workmanlike but of little literary merit, for example *The Two Sergeants* by Aubigny, Maillet and Roti, or the dramas of Francesco Antonio Avelloni, the so-called *poetino* (little poet), an itinerant playwright attached to several different companies. Further, the panorama of Italian theatre was split into two halves, each with separate lives: theatres that used Italian, and those employing regional languages, or dialects.

The dialect theatres alone used the language actually spoken by the spectators. 'Italian' was almost a dead language, employed by educated people for writing and reading, even when they spoke in their regional languages. The dialects were not 'popular' languages but, like all languages, had different levels corresponding to the different social classes. Theatres, therefore, were one of the few places where Italian was actually spoken. The establishment of this distinction between a theatre for the whole of Italy but not based on an actually spoken language, and theatres which provided a voice for languages that were actually spoken but were peculiar to a region, would have profound and lasting consequences for the history of Italian dramaturgy and theatre.

From the literary point of view the dialect theatres could be considered marginal and 'minor', but from the point of view of theatrical impact they were as strong as the theatres employing Italian. Among the characters on stage, the Florentine Luigi del Buono's *Stenterello*, the Milanese Giuseppe Moncalvo's *Meneghino*, the Neapolitan Antonio Petito's *Pulcinella* and *Pascariello,* and the Turinese actor Francesco Torelli's *Gianduia* were masterpieces and just as authoritative as those created in Italian by their major contemporaries. The Venetian theatre constitutes a special case since, although it used a regional language, it was based on the works of Carlo Goldoni, one of the mainstays of the repertoire of the Italian language companies.

The dialect actors and the characters they played were not confined to their particular regions. When Italian actors conquered European audiences in the second half of the nineteenth century, after the 'Romantic' period in its strict sense, the dialect companies too began to travel and to gain success all over Europe. It is true that they were generally settled in one city with a loyal, popular audience, but for that very reason as much as for any picturesque sights or famous architecture, these cities became obligatory stops for travellers, and in this way too Italian dialect theatres made their presence felt in the outside world. Their fame was spread by travel-books and *conversazioni* in the salons of Paris, London, Vienna or the Russian and German capitals. This was especially (but not exclusively) the case with Naples.

The existence of the regional theatres, with their individual languages, their stock characters and distinctive masks led European theatregoers to believe that the Italian *commedia dell'arte* tradition was still alive, but the regional theatres were really the reverse and the negation of that tradition: the plurilinguism of the *commedia dell'arte* had been replaced by a regional monolinguism which was as uniform as theatre in the national language. The trans-regional unification of the different masks in a single dramatic system which had characterised *commedia dell'arte* had been abolished, and each mask was associated with a particular city or region.

The masterpieces

The actors may have lived in a sort of cultural imbalance but inside it some of them acquired their own particular greatness. The history of the theatre is generally studied alongside literary history, but the statement that the masterpieces of the Romantic theatre were the characters created *on the stage* by the actors and actresses means that accounts of theatre normally given in the histories of literature, with the appropriate literary criteria, have almost no connection with the real history of the stage. We should also stress that Italian dramatic literature in the Romantic period is not of great importance in the European context. The achievements and innovations of the actors, however, were in the vanguard, comparable in quality and effect to the achievement of the Italians in the field of opera.

But if we were to say that the names of some of these great artists, the creators of characters, should be set alongside the famous figures in other genres, if for example we maintained that in our imaginary pantheon Carolina Internari, Luigi Vestri, Gustavo Modena and Carlotta Marchionni could quite reasonably stand with Foscolo, Rossini and Manzoni, that Giuseppe Moncalvo could be set on the same plane as the great Milanese dialect poet Antonio Porta, or that, later in the century, the genius of Tommaso Salvini could be ranked alongside that of Verdi, if we were to make a claim of that sort, we could expect to be written off as over-zealous fanatics. And perhaps with good reason.

However, in the process of composition, we ought to consider the work of the actor-creator as similar to that of any other artist, but since that work was created to achieve an effect in the course of a transitory action and not to leave any permanent record, the fame of the actor-creator was bound to fade away as time passed. To obtain an idea of the actors' masterpieces we have to follow a badly marked pathway, an effort which is extremely trying for conventional historians of the art.

Carolina Internari (1794–1858), a member of an acting family, alternated tragic with light, sentimental and comic roles such as those from the comedies of Carlo Goldoni and Alberto Nota, who was seen in the nineteenth century as a rival, almost an equal, to Goldoni. Among the hundreds of roles she played, she created her masterpieces with the characters of Mirra (the protagonist of Alfieri's eponymous tragedy), Phèdre (from Racine's tragedy), Pia de' Tolomei (from a tragedy by Carlo Marenco, now considered a very second-rate writer) and Medea (from a tragedy by an even more obscure author, the Duke of Ventignano). Carolina once found herself competing with the French actress Rachel in the role of Phèdre in Trieste when Rachel arrived in the city on tour, and Internari was considered to have held her own. Rival performances of this sort were not regarded in the nineteenth century as competitions so much as wonderful opportunities for audiences to see two different performances of the same original role on different stages within a few days of each other – a good example of art reaching new heights under the stimulus of competition and commerce.

Antonio Morrocchesi (1768–1838) was a teacher of 'Declamation' at the Royal Academy of Fine Art in Florence from 1811, and the teaching manuals he left us, if carefully interpreted and stripped of their rhetoric and scholarly frills, allow us to understand the methods he adopted to produce his effects with the characters he portrayed. Spectators have given the impression of an impetuous actor, always on the verge of a fit or a swoon, apparently reliving the tempestuous moods of his characters, but Morrocchesi shows us that behind the apparent paroxysm or unrestrained outburst of passion, he built up his effects carefully, detail by detail, accompanying every phrase and every word in the climactic scenes with a particular stance, similar to the poses chosen by painters and sculptors to make their subjects expressive and 'capable of speech'. When the sequences of images were presented at speed, the individual photograms were no longer distinguishable and the action seemed like a volcanic eruption, a restless flame, but inside that flame there was order, a sequence of measured, counterpoised effects and of miniature fragments as complex and articulate as the elements that bring a poem to life and prevent it becoming a mechanical exercise in metre.

In similar ways the modulations of the voice were varied so as to produce different levels of intonation which would hold the attention of an audience and create a sort of descant to the syntax, the metrical form and semantics of the text. The very existence of such a descant with its variously soft and sharp tones was sufficient to open up unexpected routes into the spectators' consciousness. In some cases it could shed light on fragments of the text which in themselves were of secondary significance, or it could raise the tone of rather opaque or mediocre literary compositions, as happens with the interaction of song and text in an opera *libretto*.

For the actors and actresses of those times it was generally important to have for the creation of their characters plots based on contradictions: personalities at odds with themselves, involuntary or unacceptable emotions, deception, double-meanings. The characters of Orestes and Saul, and later those of Hamlet and Othello, were as paradigmatic for actors as Mirra, Phèdre, Medea and Mirandolina had been for actresses since the beginning of the century. To these female characters we must add, after 1815 and following the performances of Marchionni, the figure of Francesca, whom Silvio Pellico had portrayed through a series of contrasts: she hates Paolo, her brother-in-law, who has killed her brother in a war, but she falls in love with him; she lives by a code of nobility of spirit and aristocratic chastity but she marries out of duty; she feels the vocation of a nun but she is murdered because of her adultery, and only in adultery and betrayal does she discover the profound sanctity of love and the value of liberty.

The erosion of the boundaries between the tragic and the comic was the other side of a stage conceived as the site of the appearance and materialisation of the unknown. One of the dreams of European Romanticism and of its search for the grotesque, as is apparent from various experiments, particularly by the Germans, was to overturn the traditional hierarchy of genres and to establish above comedy and tragedy a sort of comedy that follows after tragedy. The abolition of the distance between comedy and tragedy is easy to enunciate as an idea but almost impossible to realise with words. The achievement is easier with music, as for example with Mozart, or even Paisiello or Rossini. In some of their masterpieces of characterisation, Italian actors managed to do this.

The masterpieces of Luigi Vestri (1781–1841) were of this nature. His parents were not actors, and by entering theatre, he abandoned his middle-class origins and his destined place in the higher professions. He developed a passion for the stage as a student and acted alongside Vittorio Alfieri in one of the private performances organised by the poet. He was an unarmed rebel who took refuge in the theatre, and as a professional actor he began with tragic heroes, then devised a means of bringing tragedy into the comic theatre. This undertaking was different from what happened when a comic character showed the dramatic or pathetic aspects of a situation, bringing a tear to the eyes of spectators who had previously been crying with laughter. It was as though Luigi Vestri displayed the impact of Tragedy where it was least expected: in a caricature of everyday life, in adventure novels, even in farce. He was extremely funny ('too funny' some of his refined admirers said wryly), and could suddenly twist a comic scene in such a way as to terrify spectators. He played characters from highly respected authors, especially Goldoni, and many from adaptations of romantic intrigues created by Giovan Carlo Cosenza, Eugène Scribe, and Kotzebue. He practised on the stage what the serious Italian Romantic writers generally refused to do, what Alessandro Manzoni had barred from his Romantic tragedies, what the Germans and Victor Hugo liked, and what Shakespeare continued to teach: the mixture of comic and tragic, of light and shade, of squalor and nobility of spirit, of clowning and suffering.

Parallel lives

The two actors who made the most coherent attempt to link the itinerant life of the theatre with the great currents of Italian culture were Alamanno Morelli and Gustavo Modena, the former by giving the stage an aura of distinction and cultural authority, the latter by demonstrating the potential of theatre for reflecting the voice of the people, as opposed to the myths and ideologies of holders of power. Morelli tried to endow theatre with the prestige enjoyed by art or music, Modena with the prestige of free thought. In reality, they were complementary rather than opposing figures. Their lives initially followed similar courses: they served their apprenticeships in the same company, directed by Gustavo Modena's father, and grew up almost sharing out the jobs between them – or so it appears with hindsight. For the art of opposition which Modena undertook, Morelli provided a solid departure point.

Unlike Modena, Alamanno Morelli (1812–93) enjoyed a long life, in the latter part of which he organised encounters between actors and intellectuals, founded a prize for Italian playwrights and tried to summarise the principles of stagecraft in publications that would be of use to beginners.

In the course of his career he enlarged the current repertoire with unusual works like *Kean* by Alexandre Dumas *père* and the 'new classics' which innovating theorists talked about but which theatres declined to stage, Shakespeare above all. If his adaptations of *Macbeth* and *Hamlet* raise a smile today, in those days they were bold experiments. He also put on Schiller's tragedies, Goethe's *Faust* and Calderón's *Life is a Dream*. He devoted a lot of time to teaching acting to amateurs, an activity despised by professionals as a last resort for a retired actor needing to earn a bit extra and considered a waste of time from an artistic point of view. Amateurs, they said, do not have to worry about earning a living, or taking risks: they may be enthusiastic but are unadventurous. Morelli saw amateurs differently: to him they were living proof that the art of the theatre was a dignified one which amateurs could practise for cultural improvement in the same way that many of them engaged in music and *bel canto*.

Gustavo Modena (1803–61) cared little for the proprieties of his profession. He made great play of the contrast between its lowly condition and its concealed, jealously guarded grandeur. He spoke of acting as 'moral gymnastics' that often had to be satisfied with 'physical gymnastics'. Because he tried not to compromise in the theatre, because his artistic excellence allowed him to decline the outward signs of fame and success, because he had the courage to risk his life and well-being in political struggle, in insurrectionary movements and the wandering life of the exile and the conspirator, he could take satisfaction in laughing at intellectual friends who admired his art while arguing that it was only one of the lesser trades that served to earn enough to live on and pay debts. He is remembered today not just as a great actor, but also as one of the most interesting and original prose-writers of the first half of the nineteenth century in Italy.

Unlike the majority of actor-authors Modena never wrote an autobiography, memoir or acting manual, but he has left us satirical works, polemical pamphlets, paradoxical dialogues and, especially, letters. His correspondence is a formidable monument to an eternal 'winter of our discontent', rendered tragic and farcical by the continual interaction of his political activity and the exercise of his profession. Modena alternated his theatrical activity with his clandestine political life, his participation in Giuseppe Mazzini's 'Young Italy' movement and his republican intransigence. He remained true to his principles and refused the comfortable position and generous stipend of Professor of Declamation in Florence when it was offered him at the beginning of 1860. He attracted a considerable following in the theatre world while avoiding academic rules by creating companies of young actors in which some of the best-known performers of the new generation were trained, including two of the major figures in nineteenth-century theatre: Tommaso Salvini and Ernesto Rossi.

He could make people laugh and had a very extensive and wide-ranging repertoire, but what he liked best was to stir spectators with his grotesque, monstrous portrayals of tyrants. His masterpieces were characters from famous eighteenth-century tragedies: Alfieri's *Saul* and *Filippo*, Schiller's *Wallenstein*, Voltaire's *Mahomet* and Delavigne's *Louis XI*. To accompany the historical action, he had the skill to weave a web of reflections and comparisons linking it to contemporary political events and to the struggles against fanaticism and monarchy. To achieve this he broke up the individual character into a multiplicity of different elements and viewpoints, so that the figure on the stage came to constitute a broad, varied and contradictory world of his own, made up of numerous fragments and ingredients. The individual character became a kind of ubiquitous reality, on the one hand a component of the story and on the other an independent microcosm in which numerous minuscule elements elided and intermingled.

The actual performance as a whole was more than a simple presentation of the text, but could be seen as an enactment of the text's three parallel lives: firstly as a piece of poetry, composed and fixed once and for all; secondly as a fluid composition, seemingly unfolding of its own accord at the moment of performance and apparently not yet having decided on which among various alternatives or possible directions it would take; and thirdly as a creation witnessed by a contemporary observer passing judgement on the story, not seeking to excuse it, but smiling at it or gazing at it in a state of shock, dismay or aversion. Modena's greatness lay in his ability to recreate a coherent and credible unity out of the complex mass of different fragments that emerged from his vivisection of character, and this became the basic strategy underlying the art of the great actors and actresses of Italian theatre in the nineteenth century, a strategy based on the complementary processes of fragmentation and re-unification.

It is not difficult to see here, behind all the rhetoric, a germ of Romanticism capable of evolving beyond the boundaries of the Romantic schools, and to see this as a possible solution to the problem of rescuing Italian theatre from the wretched condition it was in at the beginning of the nineteenth century. Gustavo Modena showed people how to combine love and hatred of the theatre without endowing it with a false grandeur. He showed how the reaction to the decadence of the stage was another facet of its greatness. He identified the underlying and persistent weakness of the theatre as he attempted to transform it into a serious art-form. It was a course which only Eleonora Duse among the acting community was to pursue with comparable single-mindedness, and along which the reform of the European stage at the beginning of the twentieth century was to advance.

Notes

1 Quoted in Alessandro Manzoni, *Tutte le opere*, ed. M. Martelli, 2 vols., Florence, 1973, pp. 1654–72.
2 Ugo Foscolo, 'Sulla nuova scuola drammatica in Italia,' in *Saggi Critici*, p. 853.

Bibliography

Scripts

Berchet, G. *Opere*, ed. R. Turchi, Naples, 1972.
Foscolo, U. *Saggi critici*, ed. E. Bottasso, Turin, 1950.
Manzoni, A. *Tutte le opere*, ed. A. Chiari and F. Ghisalberti, 10 vols., Milan, 1916. *Tragedie*, ed. G. Bollati, Turin, 1965.
Pellico, S. *Opere scelte*, ed. C. Curto, Turin, 1954.

Criticism

Alonge, R. and Davico Bonino, G. (eds.) 'Il grande teatro borghese. Settecento e Ottocento', in *Storia del teatro moderno e contemporaneo*, vol. II, Turin, 2001.
Buonaccorsi, E. *La recitazione del 'grande attore'. Da Gustavo Modena a Tommaso Salvini*, Genoa, 1974.
Gatti, H. *Shakespeare nei teatri milanesi dell'Ottocento*, Adriatica and Bari, 1968.
Meldolesi, C. *Profilo di Gustavo Modena: Teatro e rivoluzione democratica*, Rome, 1971.
Meldolesi, C. and Taviani, F. *Teatro e spettacolo nel primo Ottocento*, 4th edn, Bari and Rome, 2000.
Orecchia, D. *Il sapore della menzogna. Rossi, Salvini, Stanislavskij: un aspetto del dibattito sul naturalismo*, Genova, 1996.
Pandolfi, V. *Antologia del grande attore*, Bari and Rome, 1954.
Pardieri, G. *Ermete Zacconi*, Bologna, 1960.
Petrini, A. *Attori e scena nel teatro italiano di fine Ottocento: Studio critico su Giovanni Emanuele e Giacinta Pezzana*, Turin, 2002.
Salvini, C. *Tommaso Salvini nella storia del teatro italiano e nella vita del suo tempo*, Bologna, 1955.
Viziano, T. *Il palcoscenico di Adelaide Ristori: Repertorio, scenario e costumi di una compagnia drammatica dell'Ottocento*, Rome, 2000.
Zacconi, E. *Ricordi e battaglie*, Milan, 1946.

20 The theatre of united Italy

PAOLO PUPPA

In the culture of united Italy, theatre takes on a double role, didactic, ideological and socially instructive on the one hand, sublime and ethereal on the other, but remaining always true to a clearly defined strategy of consent-building for the newly formed state. The stage, it is tempting to conclude, acts in a complementary way to military service, reducing linguistic diversity by undermining dialect use and giving an impetus to the integration of different regional cultures and traditions. In addition, theatre has to educate as well as delight, meaning that the stage enjoys a higher status than the stalls, to which it presents conflicts between the old aristocracy and the nouveaux riches as well as a version of the great popular forms of entertainment and performance. An evening at the theatre could often be confused with a judicial hearing, and was the more successful the more closely it resembled the national-popular genres par excellence: melodrama, with its arias and plots of raw passion, and the *feuilleton* with its piquant, picaresque tales of adventure. In his *Prison Notebooks* dated 1932–5, Gramsci time and again stresses the centrality of the nineteenth-century, court-style address which was capable of drawing together large crowds of 'supporters' who would 'absorb turns of phrase and solemn language, digest them and commit them to memory'.[1] This was the only age when Italian writers did not retreat into castes of men of letters remote from the needs of the people and at the service of the court or regime, as is confirmed by the constant presence of lawyers in bourgeois, turn-of-the-century theatre, either as the previous profession of the playwright or as dramatic protagonist, an omnipresence that reflected the pre-eminence of jurisprudential matters in the constitution of the new state and its institutions. The dramaturgy of such plays is marked by speeches, lengthy debates and analyses of ideas, in accordance with discursive techniques adopted in the so-called 'discussion' or 'well-made' plays in vogue in France, for example in Scribe, Dumas *fils* and Augier. Their tried-and-tested technique of alternating phases of discussion and action confirmed the rights and cohesion of the 'good family', or economic and emotional unit, in such a way as to guarantee the inevitable reconciliation of husband and wife typical of the most popular plots. The principal aim of these works was to offer reassurance and edification to the audience. Thanks to the centrality of this one master-image of life, the new state managed almost to identify itself, in the imaginary dimension created by theatre, with family, home and hearth, even if drama also reflected worries and concerns affecting the audience.

In *La morte civile* (1861, 'Civil Death'), a work set in Calabria and a celebrity vehicle for three generations of actors and actresses up to the First World War, the Ligurian author, Paolo Giacometti (1816–82, frequently called on to supply Adelaide Ristori with historical sketches which she freely adapted to display her star-quality), put into the mouth of the imprisoned Corrado a closing tirade against the indissolubility of marriage as enshrined in law. Corrado had escaped from gaol and gone back to his wife, Rosalia, who in the meantime had made a new life for herself as servant to her daughter (who is ignorant of her parentage) and to the doctor who had accepted her into his house and who loves and respects her in spite of being aware of her status as wife of a prisoner. In a final speech before committing suicide, thus liberating the unfortunate trio and allowing the couple to regularise their union, Corrado addresses the audience:

> Unhappy, magnanimous woman! I tore her from the arms of her parents, I killed her brother, I made her mother die of anguish, I covered her in misery and shame, I exposed her to abuse, I pierced her to the heart. She loved the noblest of men who would have raised her from the mire in which I had buried her . . . But a corpse kept them apart . . . well, that corpse shall disappear because I shall bury it. . . Oh you champions of a law that some blasphemers call sacred . . . Look now at this murderer who accuses you, this prisoner who teaches you charity.[2]

The tone, with its sententious, overblown style, is that of the serial novel, and the atmosphere reminiscent of a crude translation of *The Count of Montecristo,* with additional overtones of the *libretti* of Bellini or Verdi.

It is worth underlining the mood of opera that hangs over such prose. The cultural and social primacy of the great opera singers affected the delivery of their theatrical counterparts, from Adelaide Ristori to Tommaso

Salvini, and from Ernesto Rossi to Giacinta Pezzana. Their oratorical fervour is complemented by the hesitancy of the conversation-scenes, as is evident in the works of the Modenese dramatist Paolo Ferrari (1822–89), from *Goldoni e le sue sedici commedie nuove* (1853, 'Goldoni and his Sixteen New Comedies') to *La satira e Parini* (1858, 'Satire and Parini'). Ferrari is compelled to place characters from the past in colourful historical contexts in order to justify dialogue made heavy by the absence of the substratum of dialect. On the other hand in the last twenty years of the century, thanks largely to French models, Italy is home to experiments in naturalistic theatre in which the actor does not have to face the audience like an orator or singer, but is free to turn his back on them as though ignoring them or making them voyeurs peering at events on stage through a keyhole. No mirroring of society, in the sense of a systematic sense of fellow feeling with a subaltern world, is really possible in a theatre where the slices of life on offer are all of an exotic nature. Nothing demonstrated this better than the success in Northern Italy of *Cavalleria rusticana,* complete with the Sicilian folklore apparatus of bites to the ear, drawn knives and murders, a triumph for Eleonora Duse in the part of Santuzza in Turin in 1854, as against the contemporary failure in Milan of Vittorio Bertolazzi's realistic Turinese-dialect plays, or of Giovanni Verga's *In portineria* (1885, 'In the Porter's Lodge') adapted from *Il canarino del numero 15* ('The Canary in Number 15'), a short story from his collection *Per le vie* ('In the Streets') which featured a proletarianised petty bourgeoisie.

At any dramaturgical crossroads of this nature, novelties risk appearing dated. Before his triumphs with his Shakespearean *libretti* for Verdi's operas, Arrigo Boito (1842–1918) had tried his hand at fashionable upper-class drama with a drawing-room comedy, *Le madri galanti* (1863, 'The Gallant Mothers'), jointly authored with Emilio Praga (1839–75). In a letter dated 3 June 1890, Boito begs his secret mistress Eleonora Duse to stay clear of 'the old Norwegian chemist who has been distilling rhubarb for the theatre, real botches. You can't like them.'[3] In the same letter the author of *Mefistofele* also refers to the enormous, recent success of *Ghosts* at the Théâtre Libre in France. How can such open hostility to Ibsen be explained in a man who was among the most cultured of Italian intellectuals, one of the most European-oriented and most deeply committed to the reform of the Italian stage? Any reply which attributes this attitude to Idealist philosophy, or to a hatred of all that smacked of flat, mechanical imitation of reality would be merely facile, but there can be no denying that Ibsen was introduced to Italy as part of a trend towards strongly naturalistic, psychological drama. In addition, it is essential to take into account imprecise objections advanced by conservative Italian impresarios and directors, among whom notions of abstraction, unduly cerebral drama and abstruse rambling of sick minds appear regularly in their refusal of Ibsen and all his works. Yet it was precisely plays like *Ghosts* that should have set Boito thinking about the potential of a mixture of such different codes as naturalism and symbolism, considered antithetical prior to Ibsen. Duse herself seems to mark her approval of this compatibility in her own Ibsenite itinerary from *A Doll's House* in 1891 to the 1906 *Rosmersholm* directed by Edward Gordon Craig. In her rivalry with Sarah Bernhardt's repertoire, Eleonora Duse also gave a strong impetus to the widening of the range of female characters in Italian bourgeois drama. An actress more suited to the role of the neurotic sinner than of ingenuous lover, Duse made a particular sort of female character acceptable on Italian stages by the sheer power of her performances, whether it was the harrowing image of the daimonic Cesarina in Dumas' *Claudio's Wife* (1882), or Giulia, the perfect adulteress in *La moglie ideale* (1890, 'The Ideal Wife') by Marco Praga (inspired by Clotilde in Henry Becque's *La Parisienne*), in other words, the type of the restive, non-conformist woman in search of autonomy, the figure who finds her highest expression in Ibsen's Nora or in the redemptive suffering of Marguerite Gautier in *La dame aux camélias,* played by Duse from 1882 onwards.

So the playwright of a united Italy is, among other things, a preacher and chronicler of *mores*. A graph could be constructed to trace debates on the family. There is a revealing play by the Neapolitan Achille Torelli (1841–1922), *I mariti* (1867, 'The Husbands'), which centres on a young and serious bourgeois lawyer, Fabio, married to Emma, a spoilt aristocrat and aspiring provincial Madame Bovary, who entertains dreams of romantic love and is tired of her work-obsessed husband. In the predictable and optimistic ending, the wife realises that the most sincere form of love is that of the productive head of the family. In the moving closing scene, the husband learns that his wife is pregnant, and by him! The curtain falls on a united holy family grouping, with the wife accepting both her husband's moral leadership and the effective passage of hegemony to the new class. Civil code, moral law and personal feelings all fall into line. How often are the good wives of the newly united Italy honoured in these displays of ideological moderation by such writers as Torelli, Ferrari and the Piedmontese Giuseppe Giacosa (1847–1906), at least in the latter's early career when he was partial to whimsy, proverbs and the medieval kitsch of *Partita a scacchi* (1871, 'The Chess Match'). Twenty years later the enthusiasm for the new state and the happy family begins to fade. *Tristi amori* (1887, 'Sad Loves'), written by Giacosa and played by Duse, is emblematic in this sense. The leading man is a lawyer with an unfaithful wife, but far from being either a naturalist drama of duels and revenge killings or an ambiguous farce, this is a work of unusual and disconcerting half-lights. The wife, Emma, whose name may be a reference to her Neapolitan namesake, betrays her lawyer-husband with his best friend and partner, but loves her husband even though she allows passion to drive her into the younger man's arms. At the final curtain, the husband is fully aware of the affair but for the sake of the children does not chase his wife from the house. The title underlines the lessons on conduct. The curtain comes down not on a kiss and promise of pregnancy, as in the earlier *I mariti,* but with a sort of negotiated settlement. The couple will content themselves with a formal cohabitation arrangement which permits the wife to bring up her daughter to be more dutiful than she herself had been. The marriage will continue, but lovelessly, and the wife, who has already renounced her lover, will stay on solely as mother.

There followed a flurry of these depressing and disillusioned plays on the foundations of marriage, such as *La trilogia di Dorina* (1889, 'Dorina's Trilogy') by the Brescian playwright Gerolamo Rovetta (1851–1910), featuring a simple governess seduced by her employer but finally married off to her first love; or *Le Rozeno* (1891) by the Milanese Camillo Antona Traversi (1857–1934) where the fragile Lidia, who has been brought up by bad parents, falls, is redeemed by love and dies when she discovers her lover will offer her no more than indifference.

Pathos and delicacy of treatment can mitigate the impact of adultery and remove it from the sphere of comic or dramatic climaxes, even in dialect theatre. Guilt for the past may resurface, as in Ibsen's *The Wild Duck*, premiered in Milan in 1891 with the Venetian writer Giacinto Gallina in the audience. This experience encouraged him to write and stage the following year *La famegia del santolo* ('The Godfather's Family'), which in its turn inspired Renato Simoni's *Tramonto* (1906, 'Sunset'). Dialect theatre is discussed elsewhere in this volume, but it should be stressed that the relationship between husband and wife in any such context, in a business-marriage which has ceased to be a loving home, brings out the essential ontological disjunction between all human beings. The language exchanged between the self and the other varies in tone from the confession (postponed until the end of the play) to the impenetrable, hermetic self-justification, as though the self were conscious of the simultaneous occurrence of confession and end of performance. In this sense, plays on the bourgeois stage on the subject of marriage mirror the conflict in the script between what is spoken and what is left unspoken, a process particularly evident in those styles of theatre denominated 'intimist drama' or 'theatre of silence', which were invariably of French origin (Jules Renard, Charles Vildrac, Henri René Lenormand). As the century wore on, this trend merged with the influence of Chekhov, which was to remain strong on the Italian stage until the years following World War I. Examples include the Dickensian *Sperduti nel buio* (1901, 'Lost in the Dark') and *Piccolo santo* (1910, 'The Little Saint') featuring a young priest with a sublimated love-affair behind him, both written by the Neapolitan Roberto Bracco (1861–1943), who would later be persecuted by the Fascists; *Tignola* ('Bookworm'), featuring a humble bookshop assistant, which in 1908 brought fame to its author, Sem Benelli (1877–1949), a year before his highly successful *kitsch* masterpiece, the pseudo-medieval *Cena delle beffe* (1909, 'The Supper of Practical Jokes') brought him wealth; and the delicate *Fiore sotto gli occhi* (1921, 'The Flower Beneath Their Eyes') by the Roman playwright Fausto Maria Martini (1886–1931).

The compact, allusive speech of these plays was an oblique way of compensating for the lack of a conversational, bourgeois language. The moment an intimate exchange between lovers or husband and wife took place, or even when a conversation between friends round the dinner-table was struck up, the audience, being dialect-speakers, was made immediately aware of the gap between their own normal mode of expression and the language heard on the stage, between the language written and spoken on the other side of the footlights and their ordinary speech. It was an age-old problem for Italian theatre, which has always been badly limited by its refusal of dialect and the prevailing self-censorship backed up by the strong, normally conservative, role played by certain influential reviewers. The role of the theatre critic in his judgement seat observing the play, script in hand, determining its success or otherwise on the basis of his own moral and aesthetic criteria should not be underestimated. Succeeding generations of opinion-makers, whatever their different tastes and ideologies, have concerned themselves with the safeguarding of morality and decorum on the stage. Among the more prominent were the Florentine Ferdinando Martini (1841–1928), who considered Italian theatre to be simply deficient in great writers and could see no sense in the endless plans to provide state grants and subsidies, and the Milanese Ettore Albini (1869–1954), whose savage reviews were greatly feared. A longer list of publications and critics included: in *La Nazione,* first 'Yorick', the pseudonym of the Florentine Pietro Coccaluto-Ferrigni (1836–95) and later 'Jarro', the pseudonym of the Tuscan Giulio Piccini (1849–1915); in *La Stampa* and *La Gazzetta del Popolo,* Domenico Lanza (1868–1949), and in the *Giornale d'Italia* Domenico Oliva (1860–1917), both from Turin; in the *Corriere della Sera,* there was first Giovanni Pozza (1852–1914) and then the highly rated Renato Simoni, whose column appeared from 1914 to 1952; *Il mondo* employed the Liberal Adriano Tilgher (1887–1941); *L'Illustrazione italiana* had Marco Praga, a harsh reviewer but also a restive playwright and a regular supporter of writers' associations, and finally the Catholic Silvio D'Amico (1877–1955) from Rome, who brings us to the mid twentieth century. The exceptions, in that they were genuinely open to European culture and to innovation, were Antonio Gramsci (1891–1937) in *Avanti,* and Piero Gobetti (1901–26) in *L'Ordine nuovo,* both of whom were victims of Fascist tyranny.

Italian post-Unification drama owed its very being to the fact that it was controlled and managed by great performers, the real authors in the period in question: it is they who did onstage rewriting of scripts that are now often quite unreadable, at best only fit to raise a laugh – like the heavy, late Romantic dramas of the Milanese Felice Cavallotti (1842–98), or the sombre classical-style plays of the Roman Pietro Cossa (1830–81), whose *Messalina* (1872) and *Nerone* (1876) lie somewhere between operatic *libretti* and embryonic cinema scripts. In the same way as the scripts of some of Verdi's or Bellini's sublime works are painful without the music, so the texts of these plays seem no better than caricatures or skeletons of the taste of other days when separated from the body and voice of the actors. However, to complain of the lack of playwriting in Italy in the latter half of the nineteenth century is to invert various factors, to confuse cause and effect and mistake a deliberate choice for a general weakness. It displays the Idealistic fallacy of origin, it smells of the midnight oil, it overlooks the great onstage creations by the actors under discussion. It is not too much to suggest that the more mediocre and stereotyped a published script, the greater dramatic freedom the actor, in the days before the advent of the director, had for the creation of character. Deprived of any standard conversational language, under pressure from the charisma of the big-name performer and beset by a nostalgic impotence in the face of the demands of 'literature', the playwright in the best, or most theatrical, of cases could do no more than restrict himself to the subordinate but still useful role of provider of the *canovaccio* (outline script), following in the ancient and noble tradition of *commedia dell'arte*.

However, the theatre of nineteenth-century Italy proved capable of exporting models and techniques that everyone drew on, including such great theatre reformers as Stanislavsky, who learned so much from seeing Salvini and Duse on tour. For overseas tours, these performers had often to assume quasi-industrial managerial roles: the employment prospects of hundreds of families depended on the initiatives of such figures as Adelaide Ristori (1822–1906). Onstage, in the interest of audibility, they adopted the grand, stately poses of opera singers, but we have also the testimony of their numerous privileged and enthusiastic admirers to tell us that they also invented new material and gestures. Further, with the passing years they could not fail to respond to the attraction of a natural and true-to-life style of acting, in line with naturalist reforms, which they bent to their own aesthetic and emotional demands. An examination of the iconographic documentation of late nineteenth-century Italian stage reveals finely sculptured, frontal poses and sweeping gestures redolent of a grandiose, romantic atmosphere, aimed directly at the audience from the proscenium where the actors took up the stances which, making allowance for the poor lighting at the time and an unexpected swiftness of gesture, enabled them most easily to be seen. The long-standing and deep-rooted legend of the gesticulating Italian arose partly from the masterful performances of Italian actors on stages all over the world.

From France to the USA, from Britain to Russia, these actors spoke a language unknown abroad, even if they did occasionally venture into the local tongue, Ristori in English and French, or Pezzana in Spanish. The same is true of the voice itself, which could sound clear and musical, alluring and seductive but which could also darken and become broken and breathless, as it did for a long line of actresses from Pezzana to Duse. The flexible, elegant voice and musical diction of Adelaide Ristori had little in common with the babble of nervous sounds backed by trembling hands grasping for invisible supports which marked performances by Eleonora Duse.

Figure 11: Adelaide Ristori on her 80th birthday.

In the case of the actors, one can trace an age-old diachronic line involving use of head rather than chest notes, producing a cerebral sound like a falsetto. Ruggero Ruggeri, the actor from the Marches who in 1904 created the part of Aligi, the dreamy, unhappy lover in D'Annunzio's *Figlia di Iorio* ('Daughter of Iorio'), also performed between 1917 and 1922 in plays by Pirandello centred on the role of the *raisonneur,* a tradition in which he was followed by the Florentine Renzo Ricci and his son-in-law Vittorio Gassman. Carmelo Bene, from Puglia, was a sort of offshoot of the Tuscan Ernesto Rossi (1827–96), who excelled as Hamlet and whose piping, tenor voice contrasted with the more controlled, sober baritone of the Milanese Tommaso Salvini (1827–1915), whose Othello was considered unrivalled for rage and despair. Such creatures, however firmly identified with the twentieth century, really belong to the previous century in the emphasis they put on the construction of their roles and the creation of their own myths before audiences enthralled by their charisma.

In the biographies of nineteenth-century actors, and often also of actresses, we regularly come across pathetic tales of the rise from obscure social or moral origins to acceptance in the highest levels of society. For instance, Adelaide Ristori at the age of twenty-five married the Marquis of Capranica, a member of a distinguished Roman family with cardinals and popes in its lineage. She then settled comfortably into aristocratic society and found herself teaching etiquette in the royal household, training the young princesses in comportment at table and in the reception of visitors. Eleonora Duse herself (1858–1924), who belongs to the next generation and came from a company of itinerant players in Lombardy and Veneto, eagerly pursued *liaisons dangereuses* with poets and intellectuals from Boito to D'Annunzio so as to compensate for the moral and cultural deficiencies of her origins. *Il fuoco* (1900, 'Fire'), D'Annunzio's novel about her, is a mixture of harsh truths and admiring compliments, together with a searching exposé of the great actress's basic inferiority complex.

Scholars have identified three generations of actors and actresses in nineteenth-century Italy: first, in the years of the Risorgimento, a patriotic group represented above all by the Venetian Gustavo Modena (1803–61), an admirer of Mazzini, a reader of Dante and discoverer of Shakespeare; second, the canonical generation of the *grande attore,* represented by the classic trio Ristori–Rossi–Salvini, all born in the 1820s; and third the generation of the actor-artist exemplified by the isolated figure of Duse, with her leaning towards poetry, her acceptance of the reforms ushered in by the rise of the director but with her roots firmly in the native Italian traditions of touring theatre. In this, she was largely similar to Giovanni Emanuel (1848–1902), Giacinta Pezzana (1841–1919), also active in the movement for female emancipation, and Ermete Zacconi (1857–1948). The latter claimed to have consulted medical treatises when, thirty years after Salvini's premiere of *La morte civile* ('Civil Death'), he successfully revived it and made a radical switch of interpretation. Salvini, so as not to leave the family guilt-stricken, preferred to have Corrado, the prisoner, die of a heart-attack rather than commit suicide, while Zacconi, after visiting asylums, gaols and hospitals, revived the poison option.

However, it is in theatrical form and the concept of the sublime that the main changes occur in the years between 1860 and 1900. The move away from the poetical and lyrical approach and the treatment of the daily life of the middle classes in the stalls in terms of clinical pathology and existential neurasthenia became more frequent. The beauty/truth dialectic which in the first generation gave, through deftly chosen dramatic gestures, a privileged position to the sublime, alters in the second generation, under the pressure of naturalism, so as to put truth before all else, while beauty, if it has a place at all, occupies second place after the insignificant, the anti-aesthetic and the unharmonious. The last generation was a witness to the rise of the early avant-garde, when war broke out. At the same time, the company structure, which had been at the beginning of the century as straightforward and predictable as in opera, began to disintegrate in favour of the *brillante* (comic actor) and the *promiscuo* (character actor). The latter took up position in the auditorium, overseeing the rehearsal, so that people like Ermete Novelli and Virgilio Talli can be seen as proto-directors. The Great War sanctioned this revolution.

The birth of the silent cinema, centred on images and on inevitably dream-like montage, the emergence of new disciplines like anthropology and psychoanalysis with their focus on primitive cultures and the subconscious, the explosive arrival of avant-garde movements and, in the case of Italy, of Futurism, brought the post-Unification period to a close, and with it experiments in naturalism and the search for an everyday stage-language. The focus of theatre is no longer the space, or the place, where individuals come into contact or collision with each other but time, the dimension in which the Ego comes into contact and collision with itself. The *other* then becomes a mystery and the way is open for the Pirandellian revolution. The change of horizon and motivation in theatre brings with it a change of actors and authors. A harsh revolutionary dawn breaks, but theatre loses forever its centrality.

Notes

1 Antonio Gramsci, ed. V.Gerratana, *Quaderni dal carcere,* vol. III, p. 1677.
2 Paolo Giacometti, *La morte civile,* in *Il teatro italiano,* vol. V, ed. Siro Ferrone, p. 203.
3 Eleonora Duse–Arrigo Boito, *Lettere d'amore* (ed. Roberto Radice), pp. 705–6.

Bibliography

Scripts

Faccioli, E. (ed.), *Il teatro italiano: La tragedia dell'Ottocento,* 2 vols., Turin, 1981.
Ferrone, S. (ed.), *Il teatro italiano: La comedia e il dramma borghese dell'Ottocento,* 3 vols., Turin, 1979.

Criticism

Alonge, R. *Teatro e spettacolo nel secondo Ottocento,* Rome and Bari, 1988.
Antonucci, G. *Storia della critica teatrale,* Rome, 1990.
Camilleri, A. *I teatri stabili (1898–1918),* Bologna, 1959.
Ferrone, S. (ed.), *Il teatro dell'Italia unita,* Milan, 1980.
Gramsci, A. *Quaderni dal carcere,* ed. Vittorio Gerretana, Turin, 1973.
Livio, G. *La scena italiana: Materiali per una storia dello spettacolo dell'Otto e Novecento,* Milan, 1989.
Monti, S. *Il teatro realista della nuova Italia:1861–1876,* Rome, 1978.
Puppa, P. *Parola di scena:Teatro italiano tra '800 e '900,* Rome, 1999.
Radice, R. (ed.), *Eleonora Duse–Arrigo Boito: Lettere d'amore,* Milan, 1979.
Tinterri, A. (ed.), *Il teatro italiano dal naturalismo a Pirandello,* Bologna, 1990.

21 The dialect theatres of Northern Italy

ROBERTO CUPPONE

The use of dialect has played an important role in professional Italian theatre from its origins, making Italy unlike other countries where the decisive factor in the development of theatre was the emergence of a unified national language. From the second half of the nineteenth century until the early twentieth century, particularly in Piedmont, Lombardy and the Veneto, dialect theatre constituted, paradoxically, one of the first significant chapters in the history of theatre in the newly United Italy.

Although there were previous works like *'L cont 'Piolet* ('Count Piolet') by Carlo S. B. Tana (1784), Piedmontese theatre can be dated from 1859 when the actor Giovanni Toselli, a disciple of Gustavo Modena, opened the first official season at Turin's *Teatro D'Angennes* with *La Cichina 'd Moncalè,* ('Franceschina from Moncalieri') adapted from *Francesca da Rimini* by Silvio Pellico. This was essentially a commercial venture, with a company originally made up of unknown actors, some of whom were or would become writers. The actresses Marianna Moro Lin and Giacinta Pezzana joined later. The success of the venture was aided by publicity and support given by three journalist-writers: Federico Garelli, already known as a translator of French scripts, who wrote about thirty pieces for the new company, most notably *Guera o pas?* ('War or Peace?') which dealt with the imminent war with Austria; Luigi Pietracqua, later to be influenced by Zola, whose writing focused on the working classes and their frustrated hopes; and Giovanni Zoppis, a craftsman versed in the art of creating vernacular characters, who wrote fourteen works between 1860 and 1861 including *Marioma Clarin,* ('We Shall Marry Clarin') which was performed many times. The most representative creative figure for this repertoire was yet another journalist, Vittorio Bersezio (1828–1900), a veteran of the early battles of the Risorgimento. Although initially opposed to dialect theatre, on the grounds that it was anti-unitarian, he later took up the challenge, writing under the pseudonym *Beneficenssa,* and almost became the 'official' writer. His work culminated in *Le miserie d' monssù Travet* (1863,

'The Misfortunes of Signor Travet'), the portrait par excellence of the petty civil servant in the throes of an identity crisis. The play won generous acclaim from Manzoni when performed in Milan, but shortly afterwards Bersezio himself wrote a pamphlet declaring *The Death of Piedmontese Dialect Theatre*. After flourishing for ten years, the Toselli troupe disbanded.

There were several short-lived ventures, until Toselli was asked to direct a new Turinese company which relaunched the Piedmontese repertoire with various works, most notably *I mal nutrì* ('The Starving') by Mario Leoni (a pseudonym for Giacomo Albertini). The play was inspired by Zola's *Germinal,* and was later translated into Sicilian by Giuseppe Rizzotto, into Milanese by Ferravilla and Venetian by Benini. The period between 1870 and 1890 saw a flowering of actor-authors such as Teodoro Cuniberti and Alfonso Ferrero, who adapted Hugo, Rostand, Cavallotti, and authors such as Quintino Carrera, Oreste Poggio, Fulberto Alarni, Oreste Mentasti and, Pezzana's favourite, Sergio Domenico Beccaro (*Marghera 'd Cavôret*). Cuniberti's company was still performing at the turn of the century, and in 1911 they celebrated fifty years of Italian unification with Leoni's *La bella Gigogin* ('The Fair Gigogin'). In 1912 Dante Testa (formerly of the Cuniberti troupe) and Federico Monelli took over the Teatro Rossini, which had replaced the Teatro D'Angennes, where they opened with *La Regina d'un re* ('The King's Queen') by Ferrero. With the theatre's closure, the actors dispersed, moving on to vaudeville, operetta and variety shows – where the soubrettes Isa Bluette and Milly and the comedian Erminio Macario excelled – and the cinema, Turin being the forerunner of this genre in Italy. The dialect repertory was left to amateurs.

The Milanese theatre laid claim to a longer and more important theatrical tradition, including various stock characters such as Nicolò Barbieri's *Beltrame* and the *Meneghino*, devised by the writer Carlo Maria Maggi and actor Gigi Moncalvo. As with Piedmont, its beginnings were heralded both by individual initiatives (*El cioccon de grappa* ('Drunk on Grappa') by Giovanni De Toma and *I misteri de Milan* ('The Mysteries of Milan') by Giuseppe Telamone and Carlo Dossena), and by a press campaign, orchestrated in 1867 by journalist-writers Camillo Cima (1827–1908) and Carlo Righetti (1830–1906). The latter is better known as Cletto Arrighi, the pseudonym he assumed as member of the Milanese *fin de siècle* group of artists, the *Scapigliatura*. In 1869, ten years after the Toselli group was formed, the first resident company, the Accademia del Teatro Milanese, a group of amateurs directed by Pietro Tanzi, opened with *El zio scior*

('The Rich Uncle') by Cima. The troupe moved soon afterwards to the Carcano theatre, where they performed scripts by Giovanni Visconti Venosta and others. The following year it moved to the ex-Cattaneo pavilion, rechristened the Teatro Milanese, where it became the resident, professional company, with Arrighi as director. It opened with *El barchett de Boffalora* ('The Little Boat from Boffalora'), based on Eugène Labiche's *La Cagnotte*, which was badly received at first but went on to become a huge success and ran for 2,380 performances. The company performed scripts adapted from the French and new works by Lorenzo Carati, Policarpo Campagnani and Giovanni Duroni. Arrighi himself wrote thirty-five plays including *El divorzi de chi a cent'ann* ('Divorce in a Hundred Years'), *Foeura de post* ('Out of Place') and *El milanes in mar* ('The Milanese in the Sea'). Originally viewing himself as belonging to the realist school, Arrighi later settled for translations, adaptations and parodies. The musical side developed and would remain a distinctive feature of Milanese theatre.

Worthy of note within the company was the actor Edoardo Ferravilla, an ex-accountant with a keen eye for observation and exceptional comic ability. Between 1872 and 1880 he created a gallery of memorable characters such as *el sciur* ('The gentleman') Pedrin, the mayor Finocchi, *el sciur* Panera, the 'Gigione' ('The swank') and the much imitated Tecoppa. He devised, adapted and wrote the scripts which became the mainstay of the Teatro Milanese. Between 1876 and 1890, after Arrighi's departure, the company (first Sbodio-Ferravilla-Giraud, then later Sbodio-Carnaghi) was enriched by great actors like Ferrucio Garavaglia and Dina Galli. It staged works by Cima, Ferdinando Fontana of the *Scapigliatura*, Camillo Antona-Traversi, Giulio Ricordi and Luigi Illica (*L'ereditaa del Felis* ('Felice's Inheritance') was a huge success), and adapted works by Marco Praga and Bracco Lopez Rovetta. More importantly, Carlo Bertolazzi (1870–1916) made his debut with *Ona scenna dela vita* ('A Scene from Life'), followed by *La povera gent* ('Poor Folk'), which was conceived as the first part of an intended trilogy, *El nost Milan* ('Our Milan'). Bertolazzi was noted for his urban realism and his connections with Italian and French naturalism, and the second part of the trilogy, *I sciori* ('Gentlefolk'), confirmed him as a leading figure within theatre. Giorgio Strehler revived *El nost Milan* to great acclaim in 1956 at the Piccolo Teatro. *La guèra* ('War'), a socialist response by Pompeo Bettini and Ettore Albini to the Risorgimento rhetoric of Rovetta's *Romanticismo,* was premiered in 1901. A new company directed by Francesco Grossi opened with *Ol Carlin e la soa dona* ('Carlino and His Lady Friend'), by Corrado Colombo and with *Donna Fabia* by Antonio Curti. The Teatro Milanese officially closed in 1902 and its leading figures died over the following years: Arrighi (1906), Grossi and Cima (1908), Giraud (1912), Ferravilla and Bertolazzi (1916), Sbodio (1920). The post-war period saw a series of 'renaissances' promoted by Colombo, Alberto Colantuoni and Paolo Bonecchi, and, as had happened in Turin, some actors moved on to variety shows and burlesque.

The theatre of the Veneto, the last region to be annexed to the Kingdom of Italy, was perhaps the most experimental from a linguistic point of view, and the most 'Italian' in distribution of scripts and national debuts. It perhaps boasted the longest theatrical history of any Italian region, and this gave rise to an awareness of its autonomous identity. It could trace a continual history from such sixteenth-century authors as Ruzante and Calmo, through eighteenth-century writers like Goldoni and Gozzi, on to the nineteenth century, where actors like Luigi Duse and Francesco Augusto Bon flourished, the latter being also author of the *Trilogia del Ludro* ('Ludro's Trilogy'). Among other Venetian dialect writers of that century, Domenico Pittarini is worthy of note for continuing in *La politica dei villani* ('Country Politics') the linguistic experimentalism of Ruzante.

As had happened in Turin and Milan, the most significant event occurred when Angelo Moro Lin and his wife Marianna formed the first Veneto company in 1868. The fact that the couple had worked with Toselli influenced not only the choice of repertoire (initially texts were translated from Piedmontese) but also the acting technique of Marianna Moro Lin and even the works of the authors who wrote for her. After a difficult start, the company successfully reopened the Teatro Camploy (known as San Samuele in the days of Goldoni and Gozzi), then moved to the Apollo (ex-San Luca), which from 1875 became known as the Goldoni. The writings of Riccardo Selvatico (1849–1901) were particularly influential (*La bozeta de l'ogio* ('The Cruet of Oil'), *I recini de festa* ('Earrings for the Feast Day')) as were those of Giacinto Gallina (1852–1897), who between 1872 and 1879 guaranteed the theatre's growing success in Italy as a whole, as well as in the Veneto region.

After Marianna's death, the company drew plaudits with such productions as Ernesto Andrea De Biasio's *Prima el sindaco e po' el piovan* ('First the Mayor and Then the Parish Priest') and *Nobiltà de undez'onze,* ('The Twopenny-Halfpenny Nobility') and the anti-clerical Libero Pilotto's

Dall'ombra al sol ('From Shade to Sun') which, in terms of setting and language, marked the definitive transition from urban Venetian to regional Veneto theatre. In 1883 Emilio Zago, already a member of the company, became actor-manager in partnership with Guglielmo Privato. He freshened the repertoire, took the lead roles and in the period until the end of World War I staged a range of works including Goldoni and Gallina, adaptations from the Florentine writer, Augusto Novelli and from the Bolognese Alfredo Testoni, new works by Giuseppe Ottolenghi (*In pretura* ('In the Police Station')) and Pilotto (*L'onorevole Campodarsego* ('The Honourable Campodarsego'), translated from a previous version in Italian, as well as the irreverent *I pelegrini de Marostega* ('The Marostica Pilgrims')). Luigi Sugana authored for the company an ambitious heptology on the decline of Venice. Other companies too began to make a name for themselves with a Veneto repertoire, in particular the Corazza-Marzollo company with its use of the traditional Goldonian mask, and the Italian-Veneto Benini company, which staged Sugana's *Le fortunate metamorfosi de Arlechin* ('Harlequin's Fortunate Metamorphoses'). In 1890 Ferruccio Benini, one of the leading spirits of the Veneto stage, took the role of actor-manager, and this persuaded Gallina to return to the theatre after a period of silence. They made their debut with *Serenissima*, where the actor created the character of the Nobilomo Vidal ('the Nobleman Vidal'), and *La famegia del santolo* ('The Godfather's Family'), a masterpiece written by Gallina after he had seen Ibsen's *The Wild Duck*, which imbued the writer's proverbial Goldonian composure with a new, modern sense of angst. Benini convinced some of the leading writers of the age to write for his company, including Bertolazzi, who wrote *L'amigo de tuti* ('Everyone's Friend') directly in Venetian and translated his *L'egoista* ('The Egoist'), and Testoni, with whom Benini had a ten-year correspondence. Between 1902 and 1910 Renato Simoni entrusted him with his four plays, *La vedova* ('The Widow'), *Carlo Gozzi*, *Tramonto* ('Dusk'), *Congedo* ('Farewell') in a dialect which had by then become 'national'. The Baldanello (1906–10), Corazza-Brizzi (1908–11), Bratti (1910–19) companies were still performing at the outbreak of the First World War.

The inter-war period saw the emergence of such outstanding figures as Carlo Micheluzzi, Gianfranco Giachetti, Gino Cavalieri, Emilio Baldanello and Cesco Baseggio, who at different times collaborated or competed with each other. This period also produced such writers as Arturo Rossato, who with Gian Capo wrote *Nina, non far la stupida!* ('Nina, Don't Be Silly'),

Figure 12: Portrait of Ferruccio Benini.

one of the most frequently performed plays of the twentieth century, Arnaldo Boscolo, Primo Piovesan, Giuseppe Bevilacqua, Enzo Duse and above all Eugenio Ferdinando Palmieri, who was also a campaigning theorist and critic and the first historian of the Veneto Theatre. Gino Rocca wrote about ten scripts in dialect for Giachetti, while other works of his were translated into Roman by Ettore Petrolini, into Milanese by Anna Carena and into Neapolitan by Eduardo De Filippo. It is worth noting that the role of the Old Man, the successor to Goldoni's Pantaloon, has always been central to the Veneto repertoire, encouraging promising actors to take on the role while still in their youth. Other matters worthy of note include the revival of the work of Ruzante. *Bilora* ('The Weasel') in 1927 was something of a flop, but was followed by more successful productions by Cesco Baseggio in 1949 and 1950. The emerging Biennale made its contribution to the enormous vitality of the years following World War II, and more recently the dialect repertoire has been taken up by Veneto amateur groups, still the most numerous in Italy.

Although similarities and exchange of ideas meant that dialect theatre was largely concentrated in the three regions already discussed, it is also true that dialect theatre, with resident companies and repertoires of their own, was also popular in other regions, albeit on a slightly different timescale.

The Bolognese theatre, which had had the stock character of the Doctor at its core since the days of *commedia dell'arte*, veered in the second half of the nineteenth century towards realism and sentimentalism. Its central interests were the insurgents of 1848, and *I facchèin ed Bulògna* ('The Porters in Bologna') by Giuseppe Muzzioli can be taken as the prototype of this repertoire. Others, such as Luigi Brighenti, took this work as model, while Alfredo Testoni (1856–1931) sought to update the tradition. Once again, the origins of this theatre lay in the activities of amateur groups and campaigning journalists, such as Gino Roncaglia. After some early successes (*Instariari, Pisuneint* and *Scuffiareini*), Testoni, with the support of the actor Adriano Pagani, set up a permanent company at the Teatro Contavalli (1888) where he staged his own works (*La sgnera Tuda* ('Signora Tuda')), an adaptation from *Una famegia in rovina* ('A Ruined Family') by Gallina) and works by lesser-known authors. In 1891 the company was taken over by the actor Goffredo Galliani, who performed some of his own scripts as well as works by others, and continued until 1909. In 1911 only works by puppeteers were seen at the historic Contavalli theatre, but the season of great Bolognese theatre was not quite over. Testoni joined up with the actress Argia Magazzari, and the Principe Amedeo Theatre was opened in the working-class suburbs by Goffredo Galliani and his leading actor, Oreste Dozza. In 1923 another press campaign in the newspaper *Il Resto del Carlino* promoted a 'renaissance'.

As director, Testoni promoted new works, while Galliani bought over the Contavalli and, in the absence of new plays, adapted Tuscan texts. With the death of Testoni and Galliani in 1931 and 1932 respectively, the repertoire, as elsewhere, was taken up by amateur groups.

The Genoese theatre was also significant within this framework of exchange of ideas. Despite having its own *commedia dell'arte* stock characters and theatrical tradition (*La locandiera de Sampé d'Arenna* ('The Innkeeper of Sampierdarena'), adapted from Goldoni by Stefano De Franchi), it had survived throughout the nineteenth century thanks to amateur groups or isolated authors (Nicolò Bacigalupo, *I manezzi pe' majà na figgia* ('The Trouble with Marrying off a Daughter')), until Davide Castelli at the end of the century and Gilberto Govi in the post-World War I period produced a genuine repertoire of new works and of adaptations from the Italian and from the dialect theatre of the Veneto and Tuscany.

At its height, dialect theatre, with its conflicts between tradition and innovation, sentimentalism and condemnation, caricature and symbolism, is the link between a representation of the *polis* and of an emerging *demos*. However, its distinctive feature is the centrality of the choice of language, since its so-called realism is only a kind of congruent relationship with, or one of the consequences of, linguistic realism. It is further characterised by a relationship, both genetic and generative, with amateur theatrical activities *and* with the highest acting tradition. It was open to misunderstanding, primarily because it was in conflict with Italian-language theatre, as though theatrical Italian and dialect were real languages rather than constructs. At the Volta Congress in 1934, during a period of full-blown Fascist anti-regionalism, the debate between the nationalist critic Silvio D'Amico and the cosmopolitan director Edward Gordon Craig proved once again that dialect theatre was more 'international' than Italian-language theatre. The reasons for this are varied, to be found in part in the history of declining autonomy. Turin, Milan and Venice had long been national capitals, enjoying independent relations with the rest of Europe: it was not by chance that in Turin, for example, the first manifesto in support of dialect theatre was issued by a group of intellectuals the day after Florence replaced Turin as capital of Italy. Other factors include the lack of a national theatre, the equivalent of the Comédie Française, which in Italy did not exist then, nor today, and a literary realism which found in the dialects an intact and more powerful narrative instrument than was available in other European countries. To these factors could be added the purely practical one, that small to medium-sized companies needed to define the organisation, production and distribution of their productions. They needed to achieve immediate consensus, hence the use of dialect for performance to largely regional audiences; they needed a balance in their casts, hence the sight of the great actors of the period developing *within* the company; they needed to create new repertoires, hence the return of the 'company poet' and translations from one dialect to another.

Nevertheless, in spite of inconsistencies, dialect theatre should not be seen as a palliative for the much-lamented, non-existent national theatre, but as an organised and often conscious expression of some of the most authentic and deeply felt work in the history of Italian theatre. It occupies a space between writing and performance, between characters and audience, between writers and actors, and has inspired important work in Italian by writers from Verga to Pirandello, from De Filippo to Dario Fo. At the same time, it has inspired amateur productions which are true to its spirit.

Bibliography

Enciclopedia dello Spettacolo, the relevant entries on dialect theatre under *Bolognese t.d.[teatro dialettale]*, *Genovese t.d.*, *Milanese t.d.*, *Piemontese t.d.*, *Toscano t.d.*, *Veneto t.d.*; and theatres of *Bologna, Genova, Milano, Torino, Firenze, Venezia*, Rome, 1954–62.

Mangini, N. *Il teatro veneto moderno 1870–1970*, Venice, 1993.

Palmieri, E. F. *Il teatro veneto*, Milan, 1947.

Puppa, P. 'Teatro e teatri a Venezia dal primo dopoguerra ai giorni nostri', in M. Isnenghi (ed.) *Storia di Venezia, Il Novecento*, Rome and Venice, 2002, pp. 2077–127.

Scaglione, M. *Storia del Teatro Piemontese da Giovanni Toselli ai giorni nostri*, Turin, 1998.

Zoppello, M. 'Carlo Bertolazzi, Cronache drammatiche', *Ariel*, 2, (1991), 6–71.

22 Neapolitan theatre

GAETANA MARRONE

Theatrical production in Naples began relatively late, at least compared to Rome, Venice, Florence or Milan. Opera remained the city's dominant form of entertainment throughout the nineteenth century, although King Ferdinand I gave support to the spoken drama by attracting troupes of actors to enrich the city's cultural life. In 1818 the Compagnia Reale Italiana, directed by Salvatore Fabbrichesi (1760–1827), was invited to move from Milan to Naples, where it would successfully produce a repertoire of comedy, farce and classical drama at the Teatro Nuovo and at the Fiorentini. The Teatro dei Fiorentini was for many years the home of spoken drama, while the Teatro Nuovo specialised in *opera buffa*, the popular comic form developed in Naples at the beginning of the eighteenth century. When Fabbrichesi left Naples on tour, the court invited a former member of his troupe, Alberto Tessari, to take up residence at the Fiorentini. Prose theatre was kept alive by some forty touring companies.

The tradition of dialect drama: the actor-author from Petito to Scarpetta

The history of Neapolitan dialect theatre from the creation of the Italian state can be divided into two periods: a phase of reform (1860–1900) during which actor-authors such as Antonio Petito and Eduardo Scarpetta dominated the scene, followed by a period of national expansion with Raffaele Viviani and Eduardo De Filippo. In the second half of the nineteenth century, dialect theatre demonstrated its ability to produce actors worthy of being ranked among the best in the country, and with Eduardo, it was able to claim that distinction in playwriting as well. By mid twentieth century, Naples could be counted among the principal centres of theatrical creativity in Italy and abroad.

Benedetto Croce claimed that 'the craft of the Neapolitan *commedia dell'arte* actors was so universally recognized, particularly for their salacious gestures and mimicry, that in order to redefine a good comic act, a new proverb was formed: "Neapolitan *lazzi* and Milanese scenarios"' (*I teatri di Napoli*, p. 34). Pulcinella, the Neapolitan mask or stock character from *commedia* (who became the English Punch), had been the popular mask at the Teatro San Carlino for more than a century.' Founded in 1770, the San Carlino housed the traditional popular theatre until it closed its doors in 1884. Two noted actor-authors continued its repertoire: the more conventional Giuseppe de Martino (1854–1918), and Eduardo Scarpetta, whose career began under Antonio Petito and who became the advocate of a more realistic style.

The most revered Pulcinella of his time was Antonio Petito (1822–76), the archetypal actor-author who, like most of his breed, had full entrepreneurial power in his company. Petito had the ability to revive old plays and represent them with his own personal interpretation. He was also the recognised creator of a new form of performance in which the actor is a master of his craft, and at the same time a convincing interpreter of the written word. Scarpetta observed that Petito was an admirable and protean artist who tried and excelled in many things. In his hands, Pulcinella became 'a singer, a mime, a lover, a comic actor, and an acrobat' (*Cinquant'anni*, p. 52). In the heyday of *verismo* and bourgeois comedy, Petito proposed popular adaptations and parodies of classic 'high art', ranging from melodrama to tragedy and historical plays. He offered irreverent versions of high culture, observed from 'below', and subverted all aspects of the performance, by relying on what the *commedia* actors called the skills of 'playing the mask'. Caricature and melodramatic parodies replaced conventional middle-class behaviour, disguise replaced standard costume, the fragmentary plot of one-act plays replaced the three-act structure and regional dialect was presented without sentimental lyricism. Salvatore Di Giacomo defined Petito's Pulcinella as 'a good husband and an honest worker, generous, somewhat courageous, witty, not subservient, not malicious, not egotistical, shrewd, not a clumsy suitor, a keen observer, an intelligent *popolano*, or commoner' (*Storia*, p. 311). In his theatre, his main character is a valet whose many functions involve typical city jobs, while the supporting role, in the person of Feliciello Sciosciammocca, is an incompetent petit bourgeois figure, at a loss in a world he cannot fully comprehend.

Eduardo Scarpetta (1853–1925) became a protegé of Petito at the San Carlino. He transformed the mask of Pulcinella into an individualised character and ventured beyond the *canovacci* of the *commedia dell'arte*, which he found increasingly limiting. The *commedia* performers, who perfected one role in a lifetime's practice, spoke a language of physical gestures. They were mime experts as well as improvisational actors and were allowed to improvise from a vast repertoire of learned speeches and antics, but this freedom had its limitations in character development. Scarpetta pioneered reforms of the older tradition to keep up with changing tastes. In an introductory note to the published version of *Don Felice* (1878), he set out his ambitions: 'Naples too must have its good dialect theatre, with written texts and scenes built up from within. We need to create truth and not juggling tricks: (we need) to want to be men and not marionettes' (*Don Felice*, p. 125). Scarpetta is a supreme example of the comic actor's evolution from the inhuman machinery of farce. In 1876, he created Felice Sciosciammocca, a character on whom he built his reputation, initially in the farce *Feliciello mariuolo de na pizza* ('Feliciello, Pizza Thief') by Enrico Parisi. Sciosciammocca was originally a naïve country student who played alongside the more sophisticated Pulcinella, but in Scarpetta's reform programme, this semi-mask slowly evolved into the embodiment of petit-bourgeois values, resembling the Venetian Brighella, with upwardly mobile aspirations. He became 'a good fellow, crafty and impudent, a hedonist and a ladies' man, selfish and stingy, yet very charming and shameless. A little chubby kid, with the looks of a mummy's boy' (Scarpetta, *Don Felice*, p. ix).

Another of Scarpetta's innovations was the reform of stage design: 'I would, first, take away as gently as possible all those old worn-out scenes, all those tattered rags, all those machines for apotheoses, those flying devices, those resurrections, those appearances and disappearances' (*Don Felice*, pp. 125–6). His national tours helped promote the ideals of the Italian dialect theatre, and after Petito's death, Scarpetta joined a dialect company in Rome, but returned to the San Carlino in 1878 to present his *Don Felice*. In 1880, he returned definitively to Naples and founded his own dialect company, which opened with his adaptation of the French vaudeville *Bébé* by Najac and Hennequin, a production which astonished audiences for the naturalness of performance. The influence of contemporary French farce and comedy was marked, and the rise of the number of performances staged by the major Italian troupes of this period was due in part to the number of adapted works presented.

Scarpetta's popularity was unchallenged because his rivals insisted on pursuing traditions of *commedia* dating from the sixteenth century.

Contemporary critics disagreed on the validity of his reforms. Some thought that, by working with a repertoire of foreign adaptations, he was betraying the very nature of Neapolitan dialect theatre: others felt he had paved the way for the realist drama of such writers as Achille Torelli (1841–1922), whose *I mariti* (1867, 'The Husbands') achieved a dazzling success, or for the Neapolitan poet-playwright Salvatore Di Giacomo (1860–1934) who made his debut with *'O voto* (1888, 'The Vow'). If the actor-author was born with Petito, he achieved full recognition with Scarpetta, who had created a character more popular than the stock masks of the typical *commedia dell'arte* play. Eduardo Scarpetta can be said to have invented Neapolitan-style comedy.[2]

Di Giacomo focused his attention on the city's sub-proletariat. His dialect dramas are colourful studies of an old Naples, filled with criminals, beggars and prostitutes. The sonnets of *A San Francisco* (1895, 'In San Francisco Prison') became a play in 1897 about the jail inmates. In *'O mese mariano* (1900, 'Marian Month'), he captures a tragic world of poverty in all of its emotional nuances: a mother is forced to give up her eldest son to the poorhouse. Di Giacomo carefully chose the venue in which to stage his works, the San Ferdinando, the popular arena of the Neapolitan picturesque tradition, whose *capocomico*, Federico Stella, he admired for his acting virtuosity. Di Giacomo's naturalistic approach is somewhat tempered by a lyrical, compassionate vein. The premiere of *Assunta Spina* at the Teatro Nuovo in 1909 caused an uproar with Di Giacomo accused of depicting Naples as a socially and politically backward city at a time when the local working class was organising three strikes.[3] The play was a defining moment in the history of Neapolitan theatre, and can be considered a manifesto for the 'art theatre'.[4] The influence of Salvatore Di Giacomo and his *verismo poetico* (lyrical realism) upon Eduardo De Filippo was decisive. Eduardo's first major success as a young actor was in the part of Tittariello in *Assunta Spina* in 1909. He was nine years old.

The Neapolitan theatre from Raffaele Viviani to Eduardo De Filippo

By the turn of the century, the dialect theatre of Naples, unlike 'serious' drama and bourgeois comedy, had evolved into a form capable of reflecting social realities. The remarkable actor-author Raffaele Viviani (1888–1950) abandoned Scarpetta's style, or the San Carlino tradition, for a more modern, naturalistic epic drama. Viviani portrays the Naples of the alleyways and the slums, a city whose problems included the progressive decline of the aristocracy and the economic marginalisation of the poor. He avoids the melodramatic sentimentality of Di Giacomo and the psychological, Ibsenite realism of his fellow Neapolitan, Roberto Bracco (1862–1943), a writer more concerned with deeper, more personal feelings. In an introductory note to *Il piccolo santo* (1912, 'The Little Saint'), Bracco writes that if 'the characters do not explain what they think, what they feel, what agitates them, then there is no way of getting to know them, nor to understand what their true intentions are', and adds that it is essential to adopt 'a combination of synthetic signs that can offer the stage the necessary transparency in order to render all that is not *truly* expressed' (*Teatro*, p. 8). One of the major objections made by realists to nineteenth-century melodramas and farces was that they never faced real problems.

Viviani learned his trade within the traditions of the touring companies, interacting with the others in the ensemble. His father, also named Raffaele, was a small-time, music hall impresario, who made his son perform at the age of four-and-a-half in a puppet show. By the time Raffaele was twelve, he had already learned how to compose words and music for his original character parts. At an early age, after the death of his father, he worked in a circus and toured Italy with the composers Bova and Camerlingo. His first official engagement was at the Teatro Petrella in 1904, where his distinctive interpretation of *Scugnizzo* ('Urchin'), a musical poem by Giovanni Capurro, attracted favourable comment. His most original role, Fifi Rino, a puppet-like aristocratic character with resemblances to a musical *zanni*, represents the anti-*scugnizzo*. Viviani used a pliable mask in order to produce the most diversified facial mimicry, and made his body a dynamic instrument capable of conveying character attitudes and nuances. Raffaele Viviani is the creator of the histrionic marionette theatre.

In November 1890, the first *caffè sciantà* (*café chantant*) was inaugurated in Naples, at the elegant Salone Margherita, located in the Galleria Umberto I. Viviani embraced the *Teatro di varietà* and became a central figure in the *avant-garde* debates on variety theatre staged by the futurists, particularly F. T. Marinetti and Francesco Cangiullo. The critic Eduardo Scarfoglio praised the *sintetismo mimetico* (mimetic synthesis) of chaos, shouting and loud noises achieved by Viviani in his sketch *Piedigrotta* (V. Viviani, *Storia*, p. 818). The new genre required some adjustments in the professional techniques of traditionally trained actors: the performer was forced to display his craft alone on the bare stage, in direct contact with the audience, relying on his own skills and ability. Variety theatres officially closed in 1917 when the military defeat of Caporetto led to censorship of irreverent farces and comedies, causing Viviani to rent the Teatro Umberto and to turn to writing dramas with music and song. In 1917, he premiered *O vico* ('The Lane'), with a cast of non-actors from the slums, mixing the comic-grotesque made popular by the Parisian *bistrot* with a realistic *mise-en-scène*. During the first decades of the twentieth century, it is in the dialect theatre that one finds authentic portrayals of real life.

During the 1920s, Viviani toured Italy with his new variety company, La Rosea. In the meanwhile, the *sceneggiata*, a combination of vaudeville, drama and variety show originally inspired by the songs of Libero Bovio, had become Naples's most popular form of stage entertainment. By 1925 it had reached its height of success with Gaspare Di Majo at the Teatro Trianon, but Viviani ridiculed this hybrid genre as 'the whore of art'. At the same time, he began to voice his frustration with the managers of certain national theatres and became critical of their requests for a renewal of his repertoire to please audiences increasingly manipulated by the commercialism of cinema. He spoke out in favour of artistic freedom, and held up as an example the old *commedia dell'arte* actors who had combined innovation with the reinterpretation of the various stock characters. Eventually he was silenced during the 1930s and 1940s when Fascism, under the prompting of Benito Mussolini himself, promoted a campaign against dialects, but he was invited to play the role of Don Marzio (a Neapolitan gentleman) in Goldoni's *La bottega del caffè* ('Coffee House') in 1934 during the first theatrical Venice Biennale.

Viviani's reputation is based on his audacious productions which celebrated the typologies of the variety theatre as well as of social outcasts: from *Porta Capuana* and *Tuledo 'e notte* (1918, 'Via Toledo by Night') to *Circo equestre Sgueglia* (1921, 'The Squeglia Equestrian Circus') and *La figliata* (1924, 'The Brood'); from *La tavola dei poveri* (1936, 'The Poor Man's Table') to *I dieci comandamenti* (1950, 'The Ten Commandments'), a series of sketches which he completed with the collaboration of his son Vittorio shortly before his death.[5] Although tradition was important to Viviani, invention is the key to his acting roles. His vigorous *verismo,* with its combination of comic routines and tragic representation of daily life, brought about a fundamental innovation of Neapolitan theatre. His characters are not just hilarious *scugnizzi*, but deeply imagined portraits of destitute youth, who embody, with their passionate spirit born of hunger and desperation, the afflictions and hopes of the urban sub-proletariat. Viviani endowed them with extraordinary linguistic inventiveness and showed an eye for meticulous detail.

> The beauty of a work lies in its minutest details, in fidelity to the scene, in the gradation of the tones, in the complexity of transitions, in the sound of the spoken word, in the humanity of the events as they unfold. The creation of live characters not literary ones is essential. Fluid action must first relate to the main audience rather than the boxes, and must cut off at the appropriate time. When one has no more to say, one must have the courage to stop: does it really matter whether a play is divided into one act and a half or into two acts and three quarters? (*Dalla vita alla scena*, p. 154)

It was this theatre which inspired Eduardo De Filippo (1900–84) to innovate further and to bring to the stage themes from contemporary society. Eduardo continued the old tradition of Neapolitan popular comedy, which typically involved three interacting sets of characters. His works are set in his native city, and depict a wide spectrum of characters mainly from a lower middle-class background. The theatrical figures he created were more universal than the traditional masks. He succeeded in developing roles that turn to advantage the inherent weaknesses of *commedia dell'arte,* and in forging a form of theatre that holds a mirror to the lives of contemporary audiences.

Eduardo's own life was lived completely in theatre. His father, Eduardo Scarpetta, put him onstage at the age of four in his own work *La geisha.* Under Scarpetta's guidance, he honed the skills of improvised action and dialogue, learned how to interact with other actors, how to 'listen' to them and represent farcical caricatures and imitations. Scarpetta had his own approach to making his son understand theatrical works. 'My father used to tie me up in a chair, forcing me to rewrite scripts, word by word. He used to say: "Today you copy Bracco, tomorrow Viviani." And so I sat there with calloused hands and ink on my fingers' (Cirio, 'Filumena Garibaldi', p. 79).

In 1913 Eduardo made his official debut in *Babilonia* ('Babylon'), a musical review by Rocco Galdieri, and not long after he performed with the great dramatic actor Enrico Altieri in a sprawling piece which included elements of farce, *sceneggiata* and melodrama. In 1914, together with Peppino and Titina, he joined the company of his half-brother Vincenzo Scarpetta (1876–1952), and during the 1920s he built on his repertoire of dialect theatre and reviews by performing with various companies. In 1929, he made his authorial debut, under the pseudonym of Tricot, with a one-act play, *Sik-Sik, l'artefice magico* ('Sik-Sik, the Magician'), the story of a poor circus magician, whose pregnant wife remains locked up in a trunk. The play had started life as a sketch for Mario Mangini's *Pulcinella, principe in sogno* ('Pulcinella, the Dream Prince').

In 1931, together with his brother Peppino (1903–80), who was also an influential playwright, as well as his sister Titina (1898–1963), he set up the Teatro Umoristico De Filippo. It developed a genre that drew on the *commedia dell'arte* and its range of professional skills, but was no longer limited to regional theatre. The company initially toured Italy from Palermo to Milan, with mixed reactions, and a year later, returned to the Teatro Nuovo in Naples, where they staged comedies by Eduardo (*Farmacia di turno* ('The On-Duty Pharmacy')), and such works by Peppino as *Tutti insieme canteremo* ('We'll All Sing Together'), *Don Rafele 'o trumbone* ('Don Rafele, the Braggart'), *Miseria bella* ('Splendid Poverty') with great success. On Christmas Day 1931, the troupe performed a one-act play, *Natale in casa Cupiello* ('Christmas in the Cupiello House'). Their engagement, originally scheduled for one week, was extended until May 1932. Peppino described the reason for their success: 'Our theatrical sense of humour was never before seen on the Italian stage. We had a unique way of describing unhappy things with a sad smile by presenting sadness and pain, disappointment and sorrow through a veil of comedy' (P. De Filippo, *Una famiglia difficile*, p. 254). In several interviews, Eduardo defined humour as the bitter side of laughter originating not from everyday life, but from the disappointments of man who by nature is an optimist.

The transition from variety shows and one-act plays to full-length plays was promoted by impresario Armando Arduino who, in 1932, brought the De Filippos to Naples' most elegant theatre, the Sannazzaro, with Eduardo's *Chi è cchiù felice 'e me?* ('Who Is Happier Than Me?') and Peppino's *Amori e balestre* ('Slings and Loves'). Eduardo, Peppino and Titina were applauded for their performances but their artistic accomplishments too began to be recognised. Pirandello was sufficiently impressed to give Eduardo permission to adapt for the Neapolitan stage his play *Liolà* and his short story *L'abito nuovo* ('The New Coat'). *Liolà*, with Peppino in the

Figure 13: Luca De Filippo and Mariangela D'Abbraccio in *Napoli Milionaria!* by Eduardo De Filippo, directed by Francesco Rosi, 2003 production.

title role, was an overwhelming success. The Company's repertoire regularly included plays by Peppino and Titina, Ernesto Murolo, Luigi Antonelli, F. M. Martini and Ugo Betti. Actress-author Maria Scarpetta (Mascaria), Vincenzo's sister, also wrote for the company.

During the 1930s, the company continued to perform in their own way, in spite of the Fascist regime's stated hostility to the use of dialect. During the early 1940s, Eduardo realised that the vogue of dramatic plays was diminishing and boldly returned to traditional farces and comedies. However, Eduardo and Peppino were confronted by the repeated threats of Fascist sympathisers, who often interrupted their performances, as happened with *Basta il succo di limone!* ('Lemon Juice Will Do!'), *In licenza* ('On Leave') and *La fortuna con l'effe maiuscola* ('Fortune with a Capital F'), the last of which was co-written with Armando Curcio. In 1944, due to artistic differences, Peppino's collaboration with Eduardo came to an end. For many years the two brothers had played memorable *zanni*, one the shrewd servant type, the other the blundering fool. Eduardo remained largely faithful to the vernacular, while Peppino dedicated himself to Scarpetta's tradition of farce.

Eduardo formed with Titina in 1945 the Teatro di Eduardo, and the new company opened with *Napoli milionaria!,* a play presenting through the experiences of one family the sufferings and dilemmas of defeated and occupied Naples. Gennaro, played by Eduardo, is initially viewed with contempt by his own family, but after being captured and taken to Germany as part of a slave labour detachment, returns to Naples as the judge of the degeneration and opportunism of his family. Eduardo recorded that when, at the end of Act III, he recited the last line, which became famous – *ha da passà 'a nuttata* ('the night must pass') – 'there was a complete silence which lasted between eight to ten seconds, followed by an exploding applause with unrestrainable weeping, everyone held a handkerchief . . . everyone was crying, even I was crying. Raffaele Viviani, while running up towards me, was also crying. I had expressed everyone's sorrow' (Di Franco, *Eduardo*, p. 52). In the subsequent *Questi fantasmi!* (1946, 'These Ghosts!'), he depicts the fortunes of the enigmatic Pasquale Lojacono, a pathetic, impoverished husband and father, who may or may not know that his wife is being unfaithful to him. He rents a house believed to be haunted so as to make the money indispensable to the dignity he craves. *Filumena Marturano,* written for Titina, was presented in November the same year. Filumena was born in the slums of Naples and her position as mistress to the wealthy Domenico Soriano is threatened when he takes a new lover, but she has one ace: she reveals that she has three children, one of which is Domenico's, but she refuses to say which one. All children deserve respect.

For Eduardo, Peppino and Titina theatre was life itself, their art deeply rooted in human suffering, rather than in the virtuosity of performance and verbal dexterity. Eduardo's primary goal was to represent the realities of the people, in a language that reflected the everyday vernacular, with specific Neapolitan inflexions. In 1954 Eduardo, draped in the garb of Pulcinella, inaugurated the San Ferdinando, which he had bought and restored, with a farce by Antonio Petito, *Palummella zompa e vola* ('Palummella Leaps and Flies'). The symbolism of play and costume, the dedication to the traditions of Naples were unmistakable. By the mid-1970s, exorbitant taxes forced him to sell the theatre and to concentrate on cinema and television. After his retirement from the stage in 1981, his son Luca formed the Compagnia di Teatro Luca De Filippo, whose first production was Vincenzo Scarpetta's *La donna è mobile,* directed by Eduardo.

While remaining faithful to the tradition of dialect theatre, Eduardo developed a modern type of comedy in which the characters assume a

Figure 14: *Christmas in the Cupiello House* by Eduardo De Filippo, 1976 production.

specific personality. His theatre offers a mixture of dialect with high language, while retaining native sounds and accents: with Eduardo, Naples enters the age of mass media. During the nineteenth century, Naples had been perceived as the city of philosophers and critics, the city of Giambattista Vico and Benedetto Croce, a view which overshadowed the achievements of the Neapolitan theatre. By the time of Eduardo's birth, modern dialect theatre was well established. Under his leadership, the Neapolitan comedy began to build a repertoire which would charm national and international audiences. His career is a poetic parable of the spirit that produced the *commedia* characters.

Notes

1 The 'mask' the actor played was his dominant theatrical image and the embodiment of the soul of the character.
2 For Scarpetta's beginnings as a *cerretano* (charlatan), see his first contract at the Teatro San Carlino. He was hired as an all-round actor (*generico di secondo filo*) whose obligations included playing the least significant roles as well as 'dancing, painting his face, and being suspended in mid-air' (Scarpetta *Cinquant'anni*, pp. 91–92).
3 The influential Neapolitan critic Ferdinando Russo attacked Di Giacomo's characterisation of Assunta Spina because of her alleged lack of truly Neapolitan attributes. (V. Viviani, *Storia*, pp. 727–8).
4 Andrea Bisicchia, Introduction to Di Giacomo, *Assunta Spina*, Milan, 1986, p. 23.
5 For Viviani's performances see Introduction to *Teatro*, 1987–94, and Mario Martone's Introduction to *I dieci comandamenti*, 2000.

Bibliography

Bracco, R. *Teatro: Il piccolo santo*, Lanciano, 1935.
Cirio, R. 'Filumena Garibaldi', *L'espresso*, 13 January 1980, pp. 78–85.
Croce, B. *Pulcinella e il personaggio del napoletano in commedia*, Rome, 1899.
    I teatri di Napoli, Bari and Rome, 1916.
De Filippo, E. *Cantata dei giorni pari* and *Cantata dei giorni dispari*, 3 vols., Turin, 1973.
De Filippo, P. *Una famiglia difficile*, Naples, 1977.
    Farse e commedie, 12 vols., Naples, 1984.
De Filippo, T. *Il teatro*, Naples, 1993.
Di Franco, F. *Eduardo da scugnizzo a senatore*, Rome and Bari, 1983.
Di Giacomo, S. *Storia del Teatro San Carlino*, Milan, 1935.
    Assunta Spina (introduction by Andrea Bisicchia), Milan, 1986.
Frascani, F. *Burle atroci di Antonio Petito*, Naples, 1998.
Grano, E. *La sceneggiata*, Naples, 1976.
Leparuolo, W. *Raffaele Viviani: Momenti del teatro napoletano*, Pisa, 1975.
Petito, A. *Palummella zompa e vola d'int' 'e bbraccia e' nenna mia*, ed. Enzo Grano, Naples, 1975.
    Io, Pulcinella: L'autobiografia e quattro commedie originali, ed. Vittorio Paliotti, Naples, 1978.

Puppa, P. *Teatro e spettacolo nel secondo Novecento*, Rome and Bari, 1998,
     pp. 134–41.
Scarpetta, E. *Don Felice: Memorie*, Naples, 1883.
     Cinquant'anni di Palcoscenico, 2nd edn, Rome, 1982.
Viviani, R. *Dalla vita alla scena*, 2nd edn, Naples, 1977.
     Teatro, ed. Guido Davico Bonino, Antonia Lezza and Pasquale Scialò, 6 vols.,
          Naples, 1987–94.
     I dieci comandamenti, introduction by Mario Martone, Naples, 2000.
Viviani, V. *Storia del teatro napoletano*, Naples, 1969.

23 Sicilian dialect theatre

ANTONIO SCUDERI

Bourgeois and aristocratic theatre in nineteenth-century Sicily was in many ways indistinguishable from its counterpart on the Italian mainland. Lyric opera was popular, as were plays coloured by romanticism and melodramatic tones. There was a continual movement of Sicilian performers to the mainland and of Italian touring companies to the island to perform in the theatres of the main cities. Review and variety theatre flourished alongside the tired remnants of the *vastasata*, a slapstick-farcical genre which had seen its heyday in the eighteenth to nineteenth centuries.

Sicilian dialect theatre, *teatro dialettale siciliano,* made its mark in the late nineteenth century, before going on to achieve international acclaim at the beginning of the twentieth century. The initial objective was to perform plays with Sicilian characters and settings in the Sicilian language. Many of the plays were in a *verista* register, some written by the most important *verista* authors, including Giovanni Verga, Luigi Capuana and Federico De Roberto. This theatrical movement, along with *verista* literature and opera, represents an important aspect of the greater Italian *verismo.* Two of its most important exponents, Nino Martoglio (1870–1921) and Giovanni Grasso (1873–1930), also brought naturalism and *verismo* to cinema. Sicilian dialect theatre was also where Luigi Pirandello began his successful career as a playwright.

The birth of this movement is marked in 1863 in Palermo by the production of *I mafiusi di la Vicaria*, written by two Sicilian actors, Gaspare Mosca (1825–?) and Giuseppe Rizzotto (1828–95). The play follows Iachinu as he enters prison and asserts his dominance over the other incarcerated thugs, thus establishing his right to a cut of all transactions. It presents a microcosm of Mafia society and a rather romanticised view of its codes and ethos, as, for example, when Iachinu protects a non-Mafia friend whom he deems worthy of respect. The folklorist Giuseppe Pitrè noted how the play, based on the experiences of inmates in Palermo's Vicaria prison, accurately portrayed the habits, culture and speech patterns of the Palermitan Mafia. *I mafiusi* and, more importantly, its *verista* mode were taken up by a group of talented actors based in Catania. In Rome, 1902, the Catanese troupe, led by Giovanni Grasso and including actress Marinella Bragaglia, performed *I mafiusi* along with *La zolfara* ('The Sulphur Mine') by Giuseppe Giusti Sinopoli (1886–1923), a play dealing with the working conditions of miners. They also produced a dialect version of Giovanni Verga's *Cavalleria rusticana*, with Grasso as Alfio and Bragaglia as Santuzza. The production received glowing reviews, and it seems that the qualities inherent to the Sicilian troupe enhanced the sense of *verismo* for viewers and critics. The technical simplicity of the provincial actors worked in their favour, with one review hailing their 'sense of truth' and 'rejection of all theatrical pretences'. The actors came primarily from various modes of popular performance and had no professional training or experience in literary theatre. Many even lacked a formal education and were semi-literate. Their simple style of acting, the cultural affinity they shared with the characters they portrayed, together with the use of their authentic Sicilian language conveyed a strong sense of genuine realism.

Despite the enthusiastic reception of its Rome debut, the company was unable to progress much beyond its initial success, due primarily to the lack of a substantial repertoire and to their lack of experience in the theatre business. This was resolved by the enterprising genius of Nino Martoglio. He took control of the troupe and set out to make it a world-class theatrical company. The Compagnia Dialettale Siciliana made its debut in Milan in 1903 and toured other major Italian cities. It was received warmly by audiences and critics. A great compliment was paid by Gabriele D'Annunzio, who saw the troupe perform *La zolfara* in Milan. He was so taken by the performances of the Catanese actors, in particular that of Grasso (as he expressed in a letter to Martoglio), that he commissioned Giuseppe Antonio Borgese to translate his play, *La figlia di Iorio* ('The daughter of Iorio'), into Sicilian and have it performed by Martoglio's troupe. In fact the Sicilian theatre was instrumental in inspiring D'Annunzio to write the play in the first place.

Martoglio approached the best Sicilian writers of his day, starting with Giovanni Verga, who, although not enthusiastic, consented to have some of his works, including *La lupa* ('The She-Wolf') and *Dal tuo al mio* ('From Yours to Mine'), translated into Sicilian and performed by the dialect troupes. Martoglio obtained commitments from Luigi Capuana, whose works for the company included dialect versions of his plays *Malia* and

Figure 15: Portrait of Nino Martoglio.

Giacinta (based on his novel). More importantly, Martoglio persuaded his friend Luigi Pirandello, already an established author of novels, short stories and poetry, to write for the theatre. Other authors who contributed plays for dialect performance included Federico De Roberto and Rosso di San Secondo. Martoglio worked with several troupes as director, and authored many dialect plays himself. His endeavours gave the Sicilian dialect theatre its momentum. Not long after its inception new companies were formed. Besides those led by Giovanni Grasso and Nino Martoglio, Angelo Musco (1872–1937), the other great actor from the original group, formed and led his own troupes. Over the years there were also companies under the leadership of Grasso's brother, Domenico, Giovanni Grasso junior, Rocco Spadaro, Virginia Balistrieri, Turi Pandolfini and others. The Sicilian companies received great international recognition, performing all over Europe and in North and South America.

Prior to their international venture, Grasso, Musco and the other actors who formed the original core group performed plays and review shows, often written by Martoglio, in Catania's Teatro Machiavelli. Most of them had their training in various types of popular performance. In nineteenth-century Sicily *l'opra 'i pupi*, the puppet theatre based on Carolingian lore, along with the *cuntastori* (epic storytellers who performed Carolingian tales in the piazzas) were the most important forms of popular entertainment. In this period it began to share the stage with variety performance and plays. Grasso was from a famous family of Catanese puppeteers who brought to life the beautifully crafted Catanese *pupi*, which stand about four feet tall and weigh over one hundred pounds. Musco's first experiences in performance were also in *l'opra 'i pupi*, where he sang and provided the voice for the puppet characters. Other actors began their careers in variety and cabaret. The company was used to performing plays and review-style sketches at the Machiavelli by improvising their lines around a given scenario, and found it nearly impossible to memorise scripts verbatim. Their flexibility with a given text became legendary, and sometimes entire scenes were added impromptu. This approach often undermined the authority of the text. Verga was outraged when he saw a performance of *Cavalleria rusticana* altered by Grasso's company. Whereas in his original version Turiddu dies offstage, Grasso had him staggering back to die dramatically before the audience. Verga subsequently withdrew permission for performance.

However, some theatre critics at the time, including Antonio Gramsci, considered the improvisational skills of Grasso's company as a continuation of the *commedia dell'arte*. Contemporary scholarship on the techniques of *commedia* improvisation, which were apparently akin to those used in other oral traditions, substantiates this notion. Giovanni Grasso's performance style was marked by a raw, earthy quality, described in terms such as 'savage energy'. Along with illustrious admirers, such as D'Annunzio and Vsevolod Meyerhold, Grasso's detractors included Verga, and even

Pirandello, who at times considered his acting coarse and heavy-handed. The latter found inspiration instead in the somewhat more refined and versatile Angelo Musco, whose admirers were to include Antonio Gramsci and Edward Gordon Craig. Some of Pirandello's earliest plays were written for him.

Nino Martoglio, the primary force behind the Sicilian theatre movement, is now considered one of the most important Italian dialect authors. In addition to being a playwright, he was poet and editor of the Catanese dialect newspaper *D'Artagnan*. In all of his literary and theatrical activities he championed Sicilian language and culture. Around 1907, Martoglio decided that the Sicilian dialect theatre needed to be redefined. He was concerned that through an overemphasis on violence and themes of betrayal and revenge, a distorted image of Sicily was being presented. He wanted the dialect theatre to convey a broader picture of Sicilian ethos, including folk humour. With some of his best comic pieces, such as *San Giovanni decollato* (1908, 'Saint John Beheaded') and *L'aria del continente* (1915, 'Continental Airs'), which became standards for the major Sicilian troupes, Martoglio helped to expand the thematic scope of the Sicilian repertoire. This endeavour was greatly assisted by Pirandello, whose plays were not limited to the conventional principles of *verismo*.

Martoglio's interest in dialect was part of a greater interest in folklore, shared by many intellectuals of his day. His genius for capturing the cultural and linguistic panorama (anticipating socio-linguistics) is demonstrated in his earliest play *I Civitoti in pretura* (1893, '*Civitoti* in Court'). Several *Civitoti*, from Catania's Civita neighbourhood, are in the magistrate's court as plaintive, accused and witness. The *Civitoti* speak only Sicilian while the officials from the peninsula speak only Italian. The other characters, including the bailiff, the registrar, the attorney and the police officer each demonstrate a different combination of passive and active competence in the two linguistic codes. The humour created by the resulting miscommunications and malapropisms and the attempts of the closed community to resist outside authority, reflects the historical reality of an Italy which was far from being culturally and linguistically unified. (There are moments of a similar linguistic humour in *I mafiusi*, when a non-*mafioso* takes the coded criminal language literally, or when an uneducated *mafioso* utters malapropisms in an attempt to speak standard Italian.)

Martoglio also made a venture into the young art of the motion picture, directing four films. In 1914 he became art director of Morgana films in

Figure 16: Scene from *Continental Airs* by Nino Martoglio, 1988 production.

Rome, and directed two of the most important films in Italian cinema history. Though both films were lost during the Second World War, stolen along with other film treasures by the Germans, photographs and comments from the critics of the time are extant. *Sperduti nel buio* ('Lost in the Dark', 1914) was based on a play by the Neapolitan playwright Roberto Bracco (1862–1943). The film, starring Giovanni Grasso and including other actors from the Sicilian theatre, recounts the relationship between a blind musician and an abandoned girl, the illegitimate child of a nobleman. Critics commented on how Martoglio skilfully juxtaposed and contrasted the worlds of rich and poor and pronounced the film a masterpiece. The other film, also starring Grasso, was *Teresa Raquin* (1915), based on Zola's novel. Along with *Assunta Spina* (1915) by Francesca Bertini and Gustavo Serena and *Cavalleria rusticana* (1916) by Ubaldo Maria Del Colle,

Martoglio's films constitute a small core of *verista* films that would help to define realism in Italian cinema and would eventually inspire the neo-realist movement. Although these films were made about thirty years before the birth of neo-realism proper (marked by Rossellini's *Rome Open City* in 1945), film critic and teacher Umberto Barbaro exalted *Sperduti nel buio* in his essays, urging Italian filmmakers not to lose sight of their own artistic tradition. *Sperduti nel buio* and *Assunta Spina* featured in the courses he taught at the pre-war Centro Sperimentale di Cinematografia in Rome, which were attended by many who would later become neo-realist filmmakers, including Rossellini and Visconti.

Pirandello's interest in Sicilian dialect is evident from his doctoral dissertation, *Laute und Lautentwickelung der Mundart von Girgenti*, a philological study on the dialect of his native Agrigento dialect, written for the University of Bonn. However, when Martoglio first approached him for contributions for the Sicilian theatre, he initially showed scepticism about dialect performances. His first plays for Martoglio's company, *La morsa* ('The Vice'), an earlier work, and *Lumìe di Sicilia* ('Sicilian Limes'), based on a short story, were in Italian, and both were first performed in 1910. Later, finding inspiration in the dialect performances of Angelo Musco, *Pensaci, Giacuminu!* (1916, 'Think it Over, Giacomino!'), *Liolà* (1917), *A' birritta cu i ciancianeddi* (1917, 'Caps and Bells'), and *'A giarra* (1917, 'The Jar') were written in Sicilian, *Liolà* specifically in the dialect of Agrigento. There is epistolary evidence to indicate that, on occasion, Pirandello entrusted Martoglio with the task of modifying certain scenes of his plays while on tour. The two men also collaborated on several plays, including *A' vilanza* ('The Scales') and *Cappiddazzu Paga Tuttu* ('Cappiddazzu Pays for Everything'). The latter, whose title is the name of a Catanese folk character, interestingly involves a play within a play, with characters from Sicilian folktales and puppet theatre, such as Giufà and Peppi Nnappa. Although accounts vary, Martoglio's *L'aria del continente* was most probably initiated with the collaboration of Pirandello.

Besides being his first major venture into playwriting and first theatrical experiences, Pirandello's activities with the Sicilian theatre represent an important development in the art that would so greatly impact on Western theatre. Although these early works suggest some *verista* tendencies, his theatre quickly evolved towards the idiosyncratic complexities of character and plot, and play of illusion and reality that would come to define the Pirandellian outlook. *A' birritta*, along with *Liolà*, and *Pensaci,*

Giacuminu! demonstrate a complexity of plot and character that make them unique in the greater Sicilian dialect repertoire. *A' birritta*, for example, presents an in-depth look at the Pirandellian concept of the tenuous balance between insanity and the social mask an individual must present. These plays exist in both Sicilian and Italian versions.

Sicilian dialect players worked in a mostly oral tradition, which entailed approximating the utterances of written text to the possibility of variations from one performance to the next, and not memorising lines verbatim. The inability, or even resistance, to conveying the text as written by the playwright often infuriated Pirandello. In his memoirs, Musco recounted how in Rome, at the dress rehearsal of *Liolà*, Pirandello, furious with the actors' inability to memorise their lines, stormed out with the script, with the intention of stopping the performance. Musco called after him, 'It's useless taking the manuscript. Tonight we'll just improvise'! However, it is also reported that Pirandello sometimes incorporated Musco's improvisations into his scripts. These early experiences with the Sicilian actors, particularly with Musco, are germinal to understanding Pirandello's seeming ambivalence with regard to actors' interpretative autonomy and creative license, as expressed in his essays. In *Illustratori, attori e traduttori* (1908, 'Illustrators, Actors and Translators'), the actor is seen as no more than a necessary barrier between the playwright's text and its realisation on stage. However, in the later *Primato del teatro italiano* (1935, 'The Primacy of the Italian Theatre'), he praises actors of the *commedia* tradition, whose improvisational skills and interpretative licence make them authors as well as actors. In his plays the issue of improvisation is at the basis of *Stasera si recita a soggetto* ('Tonight We Improvise'), while the instantiation of the author's text informs *Sei personaggi* ('Six Characters').

Capuana died in 1915, Pirandello abandoned dialect theatre around 1917 and Martoglio himself died in 1921. The Sicilian dialect companies continued for a while to build on the momentum they had gathered during their heyday. The death blow was delivered by the Fascist regime, which attempted to discourage the use of dialects in favour of the national language. In 1936 legislative measures were passed blocking state funds and subsidies to dialect companies. Eventually the art form became primarily a local phenomenon. Sicilian dialect plays continue to be performed, particularly in Catania, and are sometimes brought to communities of Italian origin abroad, but with the renewal of interest in regional cultures, it could be said that a revival of dialect theatre is happening all over Italy.

Bibliography

Barbaro, U. 'Un film italiano di un quarto di secolo fa', *Scenario*, November 1936.

Barbina, A. *La mantellina di Santuzza*, Rome, 1983.

Mafiosi, baroni, ereditieri: Teatro minore siciliano tra Ottocento e Novecento, Rome, 1996.

(ed.). *Teatro verista siciliano*, Bologna, 1970.

Meldolesi, C. and Taviani, F. *Teatro e spettacolo nel primo Ottocento*, Bari and Rome, 1991, ch. 6.

Musco, A. *Cerca che trovi*, ed. Domenico Danzuso, Catania, 1987.

Sambataro, G. (ed.). *Il teatro di Nino Martoglio*, 3 vols., Rome, 1982–4.

Scuderi, A. 'Code interaction in Nino Martoglio's *I Civitoti in Pretura*', *Italica*, (69.1) (1992), 61–71.

Zappulla Muscarà, S. *Nino Martoglio*, Caltanisetta and Rome, 1985.

Zappulla Muscarà, S. (ed.). *Carteggio Pirandello–Martoglio*, 2nd edn, Catania, 1985.

PART VI

The modern age

24 Actors, authors and directors

JOSEPH FARRELL

The foundation of the Piccolo Teatro in Milan on 14 May 1947 is the central date in twentieth-century Italian theatre. Others might prefer to give that primacy to the 1921 première of Pirandello's *Sei personaggi in cerca d'autore* (*Six Characters in Search of an Author*), but however deeply that play affected European playwriting, the reforms introduced by the establishment of the Piccolo changed the very nature of Italian theatre. In the aftermath of the Liberation, the climate was propitious for change, and in no sphere was the need to break with the past more strongly felt than in the theatre. The establishment of the first *teatro stabile* (fixed venue) in Milan provided the model for other such theatres, and by enshrining the position of the director, it permanently and radically altered the balance of power in Italian theatre.

The main advocate of change had been Silvio D'Amico (1887–1955), writer, director, critic, broadcaster, official in various ministries, including the Commissione per l'Arte Drammatica, first editor of the *Enciclopedia dello Spettacolo* and later founder of the Drama School in Rome which now bears his name. He believed that the energy associated with the mainstays of the Italian tradition – touring theatre and the centrality of the actor – was spent, and advocated the introduction of the director and the establishment of the *teatro stabile* as the quickest paths to his El Dorado.

D'Amico damned the *grande attore* with the faintest of praise for his competent stagecraft, and argued that the touring companies, still the mainstay of much theatre production, had not the time to perfect the quality of their shows. The traditional *capocomico* could never be any more than a tradesman, deficient in the techniques or sensibility to graft on to his craft that elusive quality called, in the terminology of Benedetto Croce, poetry or art. D'Amico called for a new figure whose task would be to bring order to the prevailing, unsatisfactory *anomie* and artlessness. The redeemer was the director, already glimpsed in territories from which redeemers always descended on Italy – the northern side of the Alps. Lugné-Poe, Georges Pitoeff, whose Paris production of Pirandello's *Six Characters* galvanised

Italian theatre life, and Louis Jouvet, who would later make a substantial contribution to the young Piccolo in Milan, were already active on the French stage, as was Max Reinhardt in Germany and Meyerholdt in Russia. For D'Amico, the director was visionary and coordinator, whose principal aim was to ensure coherence and balance between elements of an ensemble, to impose narrative flow and pay due attention to the psychological and emotional consistency of the individual character. His prose could rise to heights of lyrical passion on the subject:

> Yesterday's theatre was entrusted to the performer, who even if he was director, sought his means of expression in his speech and writing, as well as in that of his actors. Today, however, through a phenomenon similar to that which in opera has seen 'bel canto' replaced by the orchestra, personal virtuosity has given way to a taste for the ensemble, the individual to the group . . .
>
> The co-ordinator has arrived, the *metteur-en-scène.* Yesterday it was the *grande attore,* the *mattatore* who relegated the poet to second rank to put himself on display (and there is not knowing yet in which rank the author has finished.)

The director was to be 'the head, the despot, the supreme artist of the stage: the one who takes in hand the literary word, or the written script, and transforms it into theatrical action.'[1]

The unwillingness of leading actors to surrender their position of prestige and power had caused the director to emerge as an independent force some fifty years later in Italy than in other European countries. While D'Amico in the passage quoted was unsure of the future role of the playwright in Italy, he gave elsewhere the need to protect the author from the excesses of the *grande attore* as one of the factors which made a countervailing, directorial presence indispensable. There were other factors. Perhaps there was simply an exhaustion among the *figli d'arte,* as D'Amico suggested, and undoubtedly the growing complexity of the trade of theatremaking required a new professionalism and division of labour. The greater sophistication of lighting techniques, advances in sound engineering, the introduction of complex mechanisms for revolving stages, demands for greater authenticity from theatrical *costumiers,* quests inspired by naturalism for a more accurate reflection of public values and for more intricate psychological depth all required coordinating skills which could not, it was felt, be met by any of the existing theatre operators.

The Italian language did not even have a name for director, so D'Amico consulted the respected linguist, Bruno Migliorini, who coined *regista,* and the word gained acceptance. The first directors to operate in Italy were either foreign directors on tour, like Pitoeff, Copeau and Reinhardt, or Tatiana Pavlova (1896–1975), who took up residence. Among Italians, Anton Giulio Bragaglia (1890–1960), Virgilio Talli (1858–1928) and Dario Nicodemi (1874–1934) can be regarded as proto-directors. Talli was a veteran *capocomico* who set up his company in 1909, and staged Pirandello's *Così è (se vi pare!)* ('Right You Are (If You Think So!)') in Milan in 1917, while Nicodemi's company was established in 1921, and premiered *Six Characters in Search of an Author* that same year. Bragaglia aligned himself with the Futurists, and by the 1920s was writing that theatre was different in kind from literature, so requiring to be entrusted to someone other than the writer. His productions included in 1931 the first Brecht seen in Italy, as well as other European authors of the new theatre including Strindberg, Schnitzler and Jarry.

Like so much else in Italian life, theatrical development was complicated by the advent of Fascism, but in theatre even if there was rupture in the content of plays tolerated by the censors, there was also considerable continuity. Many of the generation who came to prominence after the war did their apprenticeship within the structures of Fascist theatre, particularly in GUF, the Fascist University Group, but few had the candour of Vito Pandolfi, later attracted to Marxism: 'Yes, we who are between twenty and thirty years old, who were drawn to some art or who have embarked on some non-manual work, we almost all believed in Fascism, for a greater or lesser period.'[2] Giorgio Strehler, Paolo Grassi, Vittorio Gassman, Giorgio Albertazzi, Gianfranco De Bosio and Luigi Squarzina were among those who could have written similar words, although the allegiance to Fascism, as distinct from the willingness to operate within the structures of the time, would have varied from one to the next. Silvio D'Amico's life and active career straddled Fascism.

The director began to gain that acceptance which comes not from forceful assertion but from custom and familiarity. With some qualification, it can be said that the birth of the director in Italy occurred in the 1940s, under Fascism. In January 1941, the periodical *Scenario* was able to carry an article squarely entitled *La nascita della regia in Italia* ('The Birth of Directing in Italy'). Not all these early directors deserve to be remembered for pioneering or visionary work but they were able to do routine work under the dictatorship. Of special interest were the productions mounted by Corrado Pavolini with a company associated with the Royal Academy, a body of Mussolini's own making, and by Enrico Fulchignoni, whose version of Thornton Wilder's *My Town* (1939) in Milan and Rome caused a furore for its inventive brilliance, especially the staging of the problematic third act when the dead re-emerge.[3]

These developments did not meet with the unqualified approval of Luigi Pirandello. His views on actors may have been influenced by his own experiences with the Sicilian actors Giovanni Grasso and Angelo Musco, although they may also have had deeper philosophical roots. In his 1909 essay *Illustratori, attori e traduttori* ('Illustrators, Actors and Translators'), he viewed actors as comparable to inessential artisans like translators or illustrators, being at best an obstacle to the direct communication between the author and the audience. For similar reasons he was ambivalent about the director. His theatre-in-theatre trilogy constitutes not only an extended meditation on identity, the nature of truth, communication and personality, but is also a series of reflections on questions on the state of Italian theatre, and on the various figures involved. The *capocomico* of *Six Characters*, still so called because the newer term had not yet been coined, abrogates to himself the right to mould from the lived experiences of the mysterious characters the substance of a work of theatre, to the outrage and derision of the characters themselves. Pirandello makes the figure slightly, but not totally, ridiculous, but in his behaviour the *capocomico* was performing precisely the function D'Amico had allotted his ideal director. 'The *metteur-en-scène* is then the real author of the performance for which he uses as *materia prima*, the actors, the lights, the script (which is reduced to *one* of the elements of the thing which, transformed and given life, will be born of his imagination)' (D'Amico, *Tramonto*, p. 21).

There can be even less dubiety over the scorn with which Pirandello treats the *regista,* as he can now be called, who makes his appearance in *Questa sera si recita a soggetto* (1930, 'Tonight We Improvise'). In the intervening period, Pirandello had deepened his own experience of production and directing through the management of his own company, the *Teatro d'arte* and through seeing *Six Characters* produced in Germany. The life of the *teatro d'arte,* Pirandello's personal fiefdom, was short (1925–8), and although intended as a 'stable' theatre in Rome, economics meant that it had to undertake a touring programme. In all, some fifty productions were mounted by the troupe, of which around twenty were written by

Pirandello. Directorial notebooks from that time demonstrate the level of Pirandello's involvement with the works he himself directed, and he was not free of vanity over his own abilities. In a letter to Marta Abba, he expressed his irritation at Georges Pitoeff's judgement that 'the great Pirandello was no more than a mediocre *metteur en scène*.[4] The collapse of the company left him embittered, and he left immediately for Germany, where he wrote *Tonight We Improvise*. The play *Six Characters* had been staged in Berlin in 1924, directed by Max Reinhardt, and some have been tempted to see in the choice of a German name, Dr Hinkfuss, for the director character in *Tonight We Improvise* a swipe at Reinhardt. The evidence is inconclusive, but the animus towards the director is inescapable. Almost the last words spoken by him – 'Magnificent! Magnificent tableau! You have done just what I asked you to' – are a caricature of all that Pirandello loathed in the *homo novus*. He had made himself the focus of theatrical creativity, reducing everyone else to a state of servility.

D'Amico recalled a speech at a conference after the fall of Fascism at which there was a call for the abolition of the director as a relic of Fascism, but in the post-war era his position was made secure.[5] While the foundation of the Piccolo is inseparable from the energy and optimism of the Liberation whose epicentre was Milan, it was also the culmination of debates on such questions as touring theatre and *teatro stabile*, the role of the actor and the potential of the director, the value of private theatre and the prospects for public theatre, and the intervention of the state. The new course was largely set by two men, Paolo Grassi and Giorgio Strehler, the first of whom became the administrator and the second the artistic director of the Piccolo, but both of whom were galvanised by a shared vision of public theatre. Grassi believed that theatre should be viewed as a 'public service', like transport or education, and invited theatre professionals and city councillors to consider theatre as a 'collective necessity'. The two men chose an ex-cinema in Via Rovello as a possible venue, so the new theatre was a 'Little' theatre of necessity, but the manifesto stated that it was not to be chamber theatre, nor experimental theatre, nor theatre for an elite. The spectators would be recruited in workplaces and factories, and the theatre was to be 'a place where the community, meeting in freedom, will reveal itself to itself: the place where a community can listen to words which it is free to accept or reject. These words, even when the spectators are unaware of it, will help them to plot their individual lives and social responsibilities.' Only on one crucial point were the drafters of the manifesto guilty of prevarication, when they wrote: 'the ideal centre (of theatre) was the writing of the author . . . at others, the actor prevailed'. They lacked the courage to add that the core of their theatre would be the director, opting instead the more anodyne statement that for them the centre would be 'the spectator'.[6]

The Piccolo was Italy's first *teatro stabile,* with its own civic roots, venue and links to the life of one city, but the model proved popular: Genoa in 1951, Turin in 1955, and thereafter, Bolzano, Trieste, and later still Catania and Aquila all had their own *teatro stabile.* The tone and style of each theatre were set by the director, the Piccolo by Strehler, Genoa by Ivo Chiesa and Turin by Gianfranco De Bosio. The director became a shaman or demi-urge, imposing style and unity of vision, and guaranteeing adherence to certain artistic criteria. In single productions, he led the quest for authenti-city of character, and his was the selection of the perspective through which an incident, an epoch, an ethic or a political viewpoint should be represented. If his prestige rested on personality, charisma and insight, his power was founded ultimately on the ability to hire and fire actors and to choose the repertoire. Actors came and went, and even when they remained over long periods and asserted themselves in particular parts, as did Marcello Moretti as Harlequin in Goldoni's *Arlecchino, servitore di due padroni* ('Servant of Two Masters') at the Piccolo, neither the theatre nor even the production was primarily associated with him.

It may be no more than chance that so many directors of high talent appeared in the same generation when the structures were in place to give free rein to their vision. The achievements of the trio Luchino Visconti (1906–76), Giorgio Strehler (1921–2000) and Luigi Squarzina (1922–) consolidated the position of director as cardinal figure. Visconti, who directed film and opera as well as theatre, came to public attention in the immediate post-war period with his production of Jean Cocteau's *Les Parents terribles,* followed by works by Hemingway, Anouilh and Sartre. In 1946, he took over the running of the Morelli–Stoppa company, with whom he achieved his greatest successes, beginning with *Crime and Punish-ment.* Critical judgements were not uniformly positive, since some critics abhorred both his taste for decadence and the mechanical, clockwork style of acting he was alleged to impose. D'Amico was among the unenthusiastic.

Squarzina, the most politically motivated of the three, was also a writer and theorist of some versatility and depth. He started out with Vittorio

Figure 17: Scene from *The Impresario of Smyrna* by Carlo Goldoni, director Luchino Visconti (1957).

Gassman, who starred in Squarzina's productions of *Hamlet* and *A Streetcar Named Desire* in 1952. The impact of Artaud was apparent in a production of Seneca's *Tieste* in Siracusa in 1953, and Squarzina continued to make an impact when he joined Chiesa in Genoa from 1962–76. Strehler remains the most influential and eclectic. After an early period when he directed up to eight productions a year, he subsequently opted for lengthy rehearsal periods and the repeated production of a few cherished masterpieces. He did four separate versions of *Servant of Two Masters* over forty years, and returned several times to Pirandello's *I giganti della montagna* ('Mountain Giants'). However, working with new Italian authors was not central to the directorial activities of any of the new breed. Only Visconti worked with modern authors, and they were from abroad. The great triumphs of those years were all achieved with revivals of classic works. De Bosio reclaimed Ruzante for the stage, Brecht, Shakespeare and Goldoni were the mainstays of Strehler, while Squarzina too preferred reworking and remoulding, as with his celebrated version of Pirandello's *Ciascuno a suo modo* ('Each in His Own Way') (1961), to the efforts of nursing a new repertoire. Even when Strehler returned to the Piccolo in 1970 after a time in exile, he launched his new career with *King Lear, The Cherry Orchard* and the poetic production of Goldoni's *Campiello*. Similarly, when Luca Ronconi came to international fame in 1966, it was with an adaptation of *Orlando Furioso,* performed in free spaces – an ex-church in Spoleto, and then Piazza Duomo in Milan, Les Halles in Paris and an ice rink in Edinburgh. He continued with Kleist's *Pentesilea* on a lake in Switzerland, Aristophanes in a one-way street, and when he was drafted in to work inside the structure of the *teatro stabile,* his repertoire included Seneca's *Phaedra* in Rome and *Richard III* in Turin. New writers were still *de trop* in Italian theatre.

By 1968, the generation of the Liberation had grown into respectable gentlemen and holders of power, and consequently, in the eyes of the Young Turks of the sixties, into bourgeois protectors of bourgeois interests. Instant revisionism had it that the Piccolo had been bourgeois from its very inception, that its policies had been paternalist and colonialist until the fraud was uncovered by the more attentive eyes of the New Left. Giorgio Strehler heard, literally, the voice of the mob calling for his resignation. He left to set up the Gruppo di teatro e azione, whose aim was to perform in alternative venues. It was a time of symbolic walk-outs in theatre. De Bosio left his charge in Genoa, and Dario Fo abandoned 'bourgeois theatre' to establish a co-operative. The new watchword for the suddenly dated institution of the *teatro stabile* was *decentramento,* and productions were done in tents or cinemas in suburbs so as to bring culture to an excluded class. The theatre buildings themselves were opened for activities which ranged from 'happenings' to non-specific experiments involving school parties.

Some of the new co-operatives, like Parma's Teatro 2, rejected the role of the director, now seen as a tyrant who had overridden the creativity of others. Reforms were urged in the name of Antonin Artaud, whose name became shorthand for the right to universal creativity, actors' theatre and thus, by extension, for co-operative structures and collectives who would fashion theatre-work of their own. This trend was not universal, in part because the writer still could not find a place in the new order. The words of author and critic, Mario Prosperi, are illuminating: 'Official and avant-garde theatre both took up the same stance towards the writer: he was expected to provide thematic material for the authorial work of the director and for the system of communication which is the remit of the director and which, both with the *stabili* and the experimental groups, is integral to the production.'[7]

Parma's Teatro 2 produced a memorable 'Shakespearean' trilogy based on *Hamlet, Macbeth* and *Richard III*, but any connection with work found in the Folio edition was purely accidental. Newer co-operatives manufactured their own work after sessions of research and improvisation.

It was, in any case, only a brief interlude. The unarmed prophets of 1968 did not build structures or institutions that could last, so the old/new order of the *teatro stabile* re-established itself once the storms died down. The century ended with the opening of the new Piccolo in Milan, with individual theatres named after Strehler and Grassi, both by now dead. The symbolism of the choice was unmistakable.

Notes

1 Silvio D'Amico, *Tramonto del grande attore,* pp. 19–20.
2 Quoted by Claudio Meldolesi, *Fondamenti del teatro,* Florence, 1984, p. 59.
3 Claudio Meldolesi, 'Atti di fede e polemiche al tramonto dei teatriguf', *Biblioteca teatrale,* III. 2 (December 1978), 34–53.
4 Luigi Pirandello, *Lettere a Marta Abba,* (edited by Benito Ortolani), Milan, 1995, p. 38.
5 Silvio D'Amico, *Il teatro non deve morire,* p. 23.
6 David Hirst, *Giorgio Strehler,* pp. 23–7.
7 Mario Prosperi, 'E poi venne il sessantotto', in Pietro Carriglio and Giorgio Strehler (eds.), *Teatro Italiano 1,* Bari, 1993, p. 295.

Bibliography

Bentoglio, A. *Invito al teatro di Strehler,* Milan, 2002.
Bertani, O. *Parola di teatro,* Milan, 1990.
D'Amico, S. *Tramonto del grande attore,* Milan, 1929.
    Il teatro non deve morire, Rome, 1945.
Hirst, D. *Giorgio Strehler,* Cambridge, 1987.
Ortolani, B. (ed.), *Pirandello: lettere a Marta Abba,* Milan, 1995.
Puppa, P. *Teatro e spettacolo nel secondo Novecento,* Bari and Rome, 1990.
Tessari, R. *Teatro italiano del Novecento: fenomenologie e strutture 1906–1976,* Florence, 1996.

25 Innovation and theatre of the grotesque

JOSEPH FARRELL

The period around World War I was a moment of impatience, renewal and innovation in Italian theatre. Pirandello had already started writing for the stage, although his acknowledged masterpieces appeared only post-1916. The Futurist manifestos, notably the 1913 manifesto on Variety Theatre, added to the vitality of the debates, as did their own anarchic performances, or *sintesi,* in various Italian cities in 1915–16. Grotesque theatre, which can be dated from 29 May 1916, the premiere in Rome of Luigi Chiarelli's play, *La maschera e il volto* ('The Mask and the Face'), made its own idiosyncratic contribution to this process. The choice of adjective is unrelated to the richer and deeper traditional meaning of 'grotesque' in, for example, Shakespeare's drama, where it involves misalliances and distortions of convention, reason and expectation, or even to its connotations in Victor Hugo's preface to *Cromwell,* where it implies a rejection of Romantic ideas of the sublime. At a time when the very word *commedia* was inimical to a new generation of dramatists, Chiarelli chose to subtitle his play 'a grotesque in three acts', and the term became the generic tag for a theatre which derided the established conventions of society and theatre, and which sought to merge laughter and seriousness.

There was never any manifesto of grotesque theatre, nor agreed definition nor even, as is the case with virtually all artistic movements, any canonical list of exponents. Its life was meteorically brief and its energy was spent by the mid-1920s. Nevertheless, while there is no doubt that what divides them is at least as significant as what unites, Luigi Chiarelli (1880–1947), Enrico Cavacchioli (1885–1954), Luigi Antonelli (1882–1942) and Rosso di San Secondo (1887–1956) are commonly identified as writers of the grotesque, with Massimo Bontempelli (1878–1960) and Luigi Pirandello (1867–1936) having more tenuous connections with a club whose existence was in any case purely imaginary. All of these writers were 'grotesque' for only part of their career, most obviously in the case of Pirandello, but also of Antonelli, whose first major production, *La campana d'argento* ('The Silver Bell') was staged in 1909, and who had a long and commercially successful career as writer. The same could be said of Bontempelli, who was described as displaying traits of 'magical realism' in the 1920s, long before the term was applied to South American writers. Enthusiasts for the theatre of San Secondo are anxious to underline the idiosyncratic nature of his poetic theatre and his debts to the Sicilian tradition and to German Expressionism, while Antonelli did the job of dissociation for himself by writing that anyone 'who had put him among the grotesques or assigned him to other groups had not followed, read or understood (his) theatre'.[1]

The grotesque writers operated under the, benign, shadow of Pirandello. *Pensaci Giacomino* ('Think It Over, Giacomino') and *Liolà* were staged in 1915, with *Così è (se vi pare!)* ('Right You Are (If You Think So!')) premiered in the same year as *La maschera e il volto*. His now universally accepted superior status was not always apparent to contemporary critics, and there is much, for instance in the fascination with the concept of masks, that links him to the grotesque writers. He shared the distaste for nineteenth-century, or bourgeois, playwriting which is perhaps the most immediately identifiable trait of the grotesque. The decorum, the gentility, the endorsement of codes of ethical, political, social and sexual assumptions which marked plays such as *I mariti* (1867, 'The Husbands') by Achille Torelli (1841–1922), where Emma learns her obligations to her husband, were now the subject of ironic treatment. The rebelliousness of the grotesques should not be overstated. G. K. Chesterton spoke of the culture of the turn of the century as the 'Victorian compromise', and perhaps that remains the best description of a theatrical output based not on corrosive satire, scorn or rejection but on a detached irony and disbelieving humour that suggested that old attitudes are passing but have not entirely disappeared. The self-assured Victorian patriarchs who ruled their homes like their factories may have given way to a more irreverent breed, but the characters who represent the new generation on stage were unsure of how to rid themselves of old nostrums. The mood marks such English plays as Arthur Wing Pinero's *The Second Mrs Tanqueray* as much as Italian grotesque drama.

It is in such a climate that the notion of conflict between 'the face and the mask' gained strength. In Pirandello, the clash indicates a profound existential dilemma, suggesting that behind the mask there is no more than another mask, and that it will never be possible to reach any authentic face, or personality: personality is a series of guises, some assumed by the individual, others imposed on him by circles surrounding him, but none can be judged any more genuine or definitive than the other. The climactic closing scene of Pirandello's *Così è* invites spectators to set aside common-sense views and believe the veiled woman, whose identity had been the cause of dispute, when she declares she has both the identities previously regarded as mutually exclusive: she can be, in her own words, 'who she is believed to be', and also 'for herself, no one'. For the writers of grotesque theatre, however, the mask is a more contingent matter. It primarily denotes the dominance of social convention and the enforced deference to society's civic code, etiquette and attitudes, as distinct from the concealed, authentic face which expresses private conviction. The clash is deeper than sincerity versus hypocrisy, but those in this theatre who experience this conflict lack the heroic, dissenting vision of Ibsen's or Shaw's rebels. The 'Victorian compromise' may have included a recognition that, in Yeats's words, 'the centre cannot hold', but it also allowed space for the awareness that those who wished to continue to live in society had to defer outwardly to its canons, an attitude displayed by those who frequent the salons of Oscar Wilde's *Lady Windermere's Fan* or *A Woman of No Importance*. They know that new standards are being proposed, especially for women, but since they cannot quite comply with them, their dilemma over the contradictory demands of both the mask and the face is real and dramatic. It was partly for this reason that Gramsci wrote that grotesque theatre was a negative rebellion: it had no new code to propose. And here it would be worth noting the contribution of critics to the profile of grotesque theatre, since several high-calibre critics, including Silvio D'Amico (1887–1955), tireless theatrical reformer; Adriano Tilgher (1887–1941), the philosophical critic who influenced Pirandello by his interpretation of his plays; and the playwright Marco Praga (1862–1929) were all working as reviewers at the time. So too were important thinkers such as Antonio Gramsci (1891–1937), the Marxist thinker, and Piero Gobetti (1901–26), the theorist of Liberal Revolution. Criticism and creativity often overlapped, and such grotesque playwrights as San Secondo, Antonelli and Chiarelli were later to earn their living as critics.

The 'woman question' dominated grotesque theatre as it had the bourgeois theatre it scorned. The conflict in Chiarelli's *Mask and Face* concerns the eternal triangle of husband–wife–lover, and the appropriate treatment of the wife guilty of infidelity, this being a more serious problem in

Mediterranean society than in Edwardian England. It is intriguing that Chiarelli, Cavacchioli and Antonelli were all from Southern Italy, where the grip of the code of honour was stronger and had led to the spilling of theatrical blood in Verga's play, and Mascagni's opera, *Cavalleria rusticana*. Count Paolo Grazia makes the casual statement that if Savina, his wife, were caught *in flagrante* with another man, he would of course kill her, this being something which 'everyone knows is required' (1.1). His motivation is not the code of honour itself, but a fear of ridicule. Almost by accident, he discovers that his wife had been unfaithful, but he cannot bring himself either to carry out his threats or to face repudiating them in public. The couple connive to allow Savina to flee to London, leaving him free to claim that in a fit of passionate jealousy, he had drowned her in Lake Como. No jury is willing to convict a man for a crime of passion, so later Paolo returns home a hero, to discover that a woman's body has been found in the lake. The body is duly identified by Paolo as his wife's, but then Savina herself returns. Having been cleared of murder, Paolo now finds himself facing imprisonment for having made false reports to the police. The couple rediscover their old love, and run off together, so that, in however paradoxical a way, family values are upheld even if the iron demands of honour are undermined.

Chiarelli is no Ibsen: Savina does not demand the right to behave as she sees fit, but in its more moderate way, the play ridicules previous standards of social and sexual morality, and the cuckolded husband accepts a new modus vivendi. In theatrical terms, the originality of the work lies in the merger of dramatic genres and categories. Comedy and tragedy come together in a way the Romantics had never quite achieved, but there are elements of compromise in this position, which is far from 1950s black comedy. There are even doubts over Chiarelli's original intentions. Marco Praga, a traditional-minded, 'bourgeois' playwright and no friend of theatrical reform, wrote in his memoirs that Chiarelli had written the play as a serious work, until Virgilio Talli, director of the second production in Milan, drew his attention to the vein of iconoclastic comedy present in his writing. This anecdote has been challenged, but even if Chiarelli sleep-walked into the new mixed style, he caught the mood of the moment with a humour which wards off tragedy and is deep enough to accommodate what were once seen as tragic themes and impulses. Rosso di San Secondo too would insist that the tone of *Marionette, che passione!* ('Puppets, What Passion!') should be one of 'tragic, not comic humour'.

This authorial dominance was itself innovative, making grotesque theatre one of the few moments when playwrights, not actors or directors, were dominant in the collaborative process which is theatre. A reaction to the undue power of actors was in the air, and it is not surprising if Silvio D'Amico, who railed against that power in his 1929 pamphlet *Tramonto del grande attore* ('Twilight of the Great Actor'), was an enthusiast, even if a critical one. The plays themselves show a self-conscious theatricality in line with what would later be tagged 'metatheatricality'. The characters are conscious of playing roles, of being part of some fiction, of acting out roles in a life comedy which is not altogether coherent, while attention is drawn to the writer's perspective. The *raisonneur,* a figure borrowed from French theatre, makes his appearance, but is as much the onstage *motor immotus* as ironic commentator, and perhaps the ubiquity of the *raisonneur* is a sign of impatience and of a knowing irony towards the theatrical conventions the grotesques had inherited. Cavacchioli's *L'uccello del paradiso* (1919, 'The Bird of Paradise') contains a character known simply as Lui (He), a creator figure who moves in salons among men and women, offering advice and judgements but seemingly detached, in a dimension of his own. The heavy imagery and overblown poetic diction of the play express the sense of bewilderment his characters feel in an unfamiliar cosmos. There is no avoiding the obvious symbolism of the activities of Giovanni Ardeo, the taxidermist who lives in a museum surrounded by artificial creatures. Life, as Pirandello would express it, has been forced into inappropriate forms, and this inappropriateness weighs heavily on Ardeo's estranged wife as she visits him and their daughter once a week. On one occasion Ardeo recounts the legend of the bird of paradise, an exotic creature in some oriental island, whose feet have been ripped off to prevent it touching ground, but which can fly above storms. Cavacchioli started his literary career with volumes of Futurist verse, but his characters in his grotesque period are not so much supermen as superior beings, continually striving for poetic effects.

The characters in grotesque drama would often be more at home in a puppet booth than on stage. Interest in puppets and their potential use in theatre was widespread at the time and was encouraged by the Futurists and by Edward Gordon Craig, who settled in Florence in 1908, and whose writings were enormously influential in this regard. He founded and edited a journal with the significant title *The Mask,* propounding ideas which were given definitive form in his book, *The Marionette* (1918). The notion that theatrical characters could aspire to no more than the status of puppets was reinforced by the grotesque reaction against the quest for psychological depth which had been one of the cornerstones of nineteenth-century theatre. In some ways, the new characters, and not only in the theatre of the grotesque, were fashioned in accordance with the principles laid down in the visual arts by the Cubists, for whom a painting was a work depicted on a flat surface, hence bereft of any sense of depth or perspective. The figures who people grotesque drama are robotic, like puppets on a string, responding to stimuli they do not fully comprehend. Silvio D'Amico described them as an 'expulsion of an art in decomposition', before making the acute point that the new dramatists 'are no longer capable of believing in their own creatures'.[2]

This robotic quality is most evident in Rosso di San Secondo's *Marionette, che passione!* (1919). San Secondo, as well as trying to create a poetic theatre, drew on German Expressionism, and in a prefatory 'note to the actors', felt it necessary to insist that 'although the protagonists are like puppets, and passion is their pull-string . . . they are still human beings, and therefore profoundly pitiable'.[3] None of the characters is given a name: the three principal figures are identified only as the Woman in the Blue Fox Fur, the Man in Mourning and the Man in Grey. While still strangers to each other, the three gather in a telegraph company office, where the first two strive in vain to compose messages to the errant partners who have abandoned them. They propose forming a new relationship with each other, but are roundly mocked for this idea by the third. All three remain together, ending up in a restaurant where they have the waiters set an extra table for '*those who will not come.*' The woman's husband does come and takes her uncomplainingly off, causing the Man in Grey to choose suicide. Inner motives are sketched out with the superficiality of a Punch and Judy show, for if these characters have an inner life, it is impenetrable. They act, they perform in ways which are mysterious and unaccountable, all the while speaking in forced lyrical tones. The themes, the pain and anguish the characters suffer may have been those experienced by figures in naturalist theatre, but naturalism and *verismo* have been consigned to the past.

The most theatrically interesting and deftly imagined work, which was also an attack on received ideas, came from Luigi Antonelli, once viewed as being on a par with Pirandello. A later play, *Il maestro* (1933, 'The Master'), was directed by Pirandello with Marta Abba as female lead, but with the

'grotesque' *L'uomo che incontrò se stesso* (1918, 'The Man Who Met Himself')
Antonelli removed conventional 'bourgeois' topics from their expected
context and placed them in a wholly original fantasy dimension. His
subject too was adultery, but there is a touch of fantasy in his writing
reminiscent of J. M. Barrie, so that while the magic island where the action
evolves has been compared to Prospero's island, it more strongly resembles
an adult version of Never-Never-Land. Dr Climt presides over an island
outside time, where Luciano meets Sonia, his now dead wife, whose
infidelity he had discovered only when her body and that of her lover
were dragged from the wreckage of a building. His efforts to warn his
younger self of the impending adultery are futile, although the elder
Luciano had himself managed to seduce the younger Sonia after their first
meeting on the island.

Antonelli is free of doctrinaire dogmatism, has a lightness of spirit and
demonstrates the deft knack of combining a misty tale of fragile individuals
stranded in a borderland between the present and the past with a critique
of responsibilities and irresponsibilities. But the task of finding genuinely
innovative theatrical approaches was left to Luigi Pirandello.

Notes

1 Luigi Antonelli, *Lo scrittore si confessa*, p. 270.
2 Quoted in Gigi Livio, *Teatro grottesco*, p. 17.
3 *Ibid.*, p. 45.

Bibliography

Albini, E. *Cronache teatrali 1891–1925*, Genoa, 1972.
Antonelli, L. 'Lo scrittore si confessa', introduction to *L'uomo che incontrò se stesso*
 and other plays, Rome, 1943.
D'Amico, S. *Teatro dei fantocci*, Florence, 1920.
Davico Bonino, G. *Gramsci e il teatro*, Turin, 1972.
Ferrante, L. *Teatro grottesco italiano*, Bologna, 1964.
Livio, G. (ed.) *Teatro grottesco del Novecento* (anthology), Milan, 1965.
Pullini, G. *Teatro italiano fra due secoli 1850–1950*, Florence, 1957.
 Cinquant'anni di teatro in Italia, Bologna, 1960.

26 The march of the avant-garde

DONATELLA FISCHER

There is no wholly acceptable definition of what constitutes the theatrical avant-garde beyond saying that it is self-consciously distinct from mainstream theatre, that it sets itself in opposition to the status quo in artistic and, often, socio-political terms, that it is dedicated to experimentation and takes as its target, in general terms, a 'bourgeoisie' seen as the repository of conservative values. In its anti-establishment stance, avant-garde drama challenges the fundamental credo of institutional theatre and privileges underground venues that lend themselves to more radical performance styles. Often it rejects patterns of coherence in favour of anti-narrative performance structures, through which it undertakes a debate with the 'canon' and a quest for the new. Inspired by surrealism, dada, symbolism and Antonin Artaud's concept of the 'theatre of cruelty', the poetics of the avant-garde, while never uniform, tend to highlight the metaphorical qualities of a theatre where gesture and performance rather than text are the favoured means of communication.

There have been various waves of the avant-garde in Italian theatre since the outburst of Futurism in the years immediately preceding and including the Great War. As the term indicates, Futurism set itself against traditions. The artistic objectives of Futurist theatre, whose major representatives were Filippo Tommaso Marinetti (1886–1944), Enrico Prampolini (1898–1975) and Giovanni Papini (1881–1956), were uncompromisingly stated in a series of 'manifestos'. In the 1911 *Manifesto dei drammaturghi futuristi* ('Manifesto of Futurist Playwrights'), the Futurists affirmed their 'contempt for the audience' and their 'horror for immediate success' in favour of 'an absolute creative originality', but their stance remained paradoxically indebted to an old-fashioned poetics of the theatre and to traditional literary genres.[1] Perhaps more importantly, the manifesto dealt specifically with the 'playwright' rather than with the overall scope of the theatre. Profoundly influenced by French symbolist poetry, Marinetti was author of *Roi Bombance* (1905), inspired in some ways by Alfred Jarry's

1897 *Ubu Roi* (itself an irreverent parody of *Macbeth*), and widely regarded as the first manifestation of the avant-garde spirit in Europe. Marinetti's play was received with considerable indifference by the French audience, as it appeared to be little more than a diluted version of a much more subversive European experimental avant-garde. The straightforward production of plays was not, however, the only form of Futurist theatre. From 1910, Marinetti's 'Futurist evenings' set out to present the audience with an altogether new concept of theatrical art. The low cost of tickets was intended to attract non-traditional audiences, while theatre became a much wider 'spectacle' as Marinetti's productions pulled down the 'fourth wall', thus establishing a stronger relationship with the audience. These 'evenings' included music and poetry recitals as well as some anarchic, irreverent acts borrowed from the variety theatre; their intent was subversive and vocally anti-establishment. The first 'Futurist evening' at the Teatro Politeama in Trieste, in 1910, triggered off strong anti-Austrian sentiments on the part of the audience: the Futurists' concept of 'war as the hygiene of the world' found a fertile ground, but the Futurists were generally reactionary in their politics (Marinetti later joined the Fascist party).

The genre of the Variety Theatre was enthusiastically embraced by the Futurists as representing the opposite of bourgeois drama, and of the precepts of the well-made play. It is traditionally a 'lower' and popular genre, where satire and farce are important components, and where the division between audience and actors is blurred by the suppression of the 'fourth wall'. Spectators are addressed directly and often provoked by comedians and can, in turn, respond. In 1913 the periodical *Lacerba*, edited by Giovanni Papini, reiterated the relevance of Variety to Futurist thinking by publishing the second manifesto, *Il teatro di varietà* ('Variety Theatre'), where the artists advocated a type of theatre which must constantly surprise the audience by blending comical, farcical, satirical, absurd as well as disrespectful elements. The emphasis was no longer simply on the playwrights, as in the first manifesto, but on the relationship with the audience as the focal point of any performance. Futurist experimental theatre was to move further still. In 1915 a third manifesto set out the precepts of the Futurist Synthetic Theatre. Its intention was first and foremost to criticise such 'innovators' of nineteenth-and twentieth-century theatre as Ibsen, Maeterlinck or Shaw, and all the traditional aspects of such drama. The Synthetic Theatre was transgressive in its refusal of old-fashioned acting techniques, and advocated non-realistic, anti-narrative structures, free cues, recitals of poems, discussions and simultaneous dialogues. One *sintesi* entitled *Feet* consisted of seven brief scenes in which the audience could hear dialogue but could see only the performers' feet.

Futurist theatre had a strong impact on other writers, such as Rosso di San Secondo, Alberto Savinio, Massimo Bontempelli, as well as on Luigi Antonelli, Luigi Chiarelli, practitioners of the Theatre of the Grotesque, and on the theatre director Anton Giulio Bragaglia, who was among the first to challenge the concept of 'actor's theatre' and to promote 'director's theatre'. Bontempelli's 1916 play *La guardia alla luna* ('Watching the Moon') deals with the ancient myth of motherhood, and experiments with symbolism and expressionism. Here, a mother who is mourning for the death of her daughter reaches hallucinatory and visionary states. Still pursuing a vividly symbolical and metaphorical level, in his 1928 play *Minnie la candida* ('Candid Minnie') Bontempelli depicts reality as an inauthentic artificial construction.

After the bold avant-garde movements of the first two decades of the twentieth century, the avant-garde scene in Italy all but disappeared during the period of Fascism. Theatre at this time, apart from the work of Pirandello and Eduardo De Filippo, was very much a vehicle for political propaganda, or a means of mild entertainment. The state had wide control over their theatre companies, funded through the Ministry of Culture, and therefore over their repertoires. In this climate, the subversive voices of underground avant-garde drama were forcefully suppressed by the regime. Neo-avant-garde reappeared only in the sixties, matching similar trends both in Europe and in America. The impression is of an exceptionally fragmented situation, where a plethora of alternative and often fashionably subversive groups attempted to take a stand against the status quo, both from a political and an artistic perspective. Ironically, some of these groups would later make their mark in the very mainstream theatres they had so fiercely opposed, as some of their predecessors among the Futurists had done. On the whole the Italian avant-garde of the sixties had the features of a tentative movement, seeking more a way of expressing itself than contributing constructively to innovating the theatre scene. It was also considerably derivative since the mentors of many of these new artists were gurus of theatrical art such as Bertolt Brecht, Vladimir Mayakovsky, Peter Brook and, most importantly, Antonin Artaud. The arrival of Julian Beck's Living Theatre in Italy in 1964 was a highly influential event. Beck was profoundly indebted to Artaud's concept of the 'theatre of

cruelty' and contributed to the trend towards a physical style of performance. In Artaud's theory, the scene should 'assail' the spectator from an
intellectual, emotional and physical point of view, transforming the gesture
into the most powerful means of communication, and the word into pure
sound.

The focal point of the Italian avant-garde was the Conference of Ivrea
in 1967. Theatre practitioners such as Carmelo Bene, Carlo Quartucci,
Giuliano Scabia and Luca Ronconi subscribed to the project for a New
Theatre based on a manifesto reminiscent of Marinetti's almost five decades
before. The fundamental objective of this enterprise was to create a theatre
of protest, unconditionally against all 'dominant structures', and here
perhaps lay its inherent weakness, as the propensity for unconditional
protest sometimes hindered a genuine drive towards artistic renewal. The
Conference of Ivrea provided primarily an arena for discussion, but the
variety of contrasting voices gave rise to a cacophony of disparate ideas.
Franco Quadri recalled how in Ivrea radical views against all mainstream
theatre clashed with more moderate positions which preferred compromise to confrontation so as to minimise a loss of audiences. Among the
main influences on the manifesto were British documentary theatre,
German conscience theatre, American protest theatre, and Third World
revolutionary theatre.

Quartucci was primarily interested in reassessing the role of the actor,
of the director and of the stage-manager, with a view to renewing the
overall concept of theatre. He worked with a company known at different
times as Teatro della Ripresa, Teatro Studio and Teatro Gruppo. The
emphasis was on experimentation and theatre research involving the whole
company. Quartucci's troupe started work in 1965 at Genoa's Teatro
Stabile with Beckett's *Waiting for Godot* and *Endgame,* but his second
company best reflected his concept of the relationship between actors
and theatrical space. Avoiding all use of recognisable imagery, actors and
objects merged into shapeless figures, the word was linked to the actor's
gesture and changed with it to create new phonetic sounds which de-
fied any traditional representation of the text. Not only Artaud, but also
the idiosyncratic features of much Futurist theatre emerged through
Quartucci's works. His theatrical experiments continued with the Teatro
Gruppo in a collage of texts by Brecht, Calvino, Parise and Rabelais, where
the director used other media such as film projections at the back of the
stage to illustrate the action.[2] The multi-media technique became central

for the avant-garde, both nationally and internationally, as the different media converged increasingly in theatrical performances.

Mario Ricci pioneered experimental work of a different type, with the emphasis on theatre as a ritual game, a concept which predated avant-garde and could be traced back to classical times and to the anthropological roots of theatre. Distancing himself from the visual aggressiveness of Artaud and his followers, Ricci returned to the ritualistic origin of drama in works such as *Gulliver's Travels* and *Building Sacrifice*, where actors moved large cubes on stage in a ritual manner.

The avant-garde as a protest against existing theatre forms found other representatives in Leo de Bernardinis and Perla Peragallo, who in the mid-sixties experimented with Shakespeare's plays. Among their works, *La faticosa messinscena dell'Amleto di Shakespeare* ('The Difficult Staging of William Shakespeare's Hamlet') was one of the most provocative. Theatre and cinema met to underline the complex and competitive relationship between screen and stage as actors on stage frantically chased the actors projected on the screens. At the heart of the performance there seemed to be the impossibility of representing Shakespeare and of finding an oral and physical language to allow such representation. The ultimate message was profoundly nihilistic and self-indulgent.

Other groups, such as Teatro 101, the Comunità Teatrale dell'Emilia Romagna, which focused on the actor's role as someone who 'elaborates' culture,[3] or the theatre of Giancarlo Nanni, who saw theatre as a 'great surface to be filled in', left their mark on the avant-garde of the sixties. Many groups were created post-1968, when protest and strong anti-establishment sentiments flourished and a number of companies established themselves as 'democratic' collectives (most notably Dario Fo's co-operative *Nuova Scena*), where actors, directors and technicians shared the various stages of production. The shortcoming of many of these companies, however, was that often they used theatre as a means for political propaganda, allowing political militancy to overshadow theatrical creativity.

Within the panorama of the avant-garde in Italy in the 1960s and 1970s, one artist, Carmelo Bene (1937–2000), came to be seen as an *enfant terrible* of the stage. Bene's career was launched in 1960 when he presented his own work, *Spettacolo Majakovskij*. His main purpose being to create an anti-establishment theatre that questioned authors, repertories and theatrical rules, he pioneered the idea of the ideological and philosophical actor who provokes the audience into exploring ambiguities. As an actor, Bene adopted techniques inspired by the theatre of Artaud, Mayakovsky, Brecht and Elizabethan theatre. Acting was always represented as a fictional and artificial occurrence which often verged on the pantomime. His transgressive, provocative and frequently outrageous adaptations of plays by Shakespeare (with Laforgue often providing a crucial subtext), Wilde, Marlowe and Collodi routinely provoked outrage. Bene's *Hamlet*, first produced in 1961 and subsequently restaged in six different versions, is a parody of the original based on a collage of operetta, music, farce and pictorial arts. Through his dissection of the original text, Shakespeare's play is lampooned and reduced to a grotesque parody of itself with Horatio reading some of the most famous speeches from scraps of papers served to him on a tray. Parallels with the biblical iconography of Salomé, with the Baptist's head served on a silver plate, are underlined by the portrayal of a Horatio being presented with a torn text from Shakespeare. Through monologues which ridicule any attempt at poetry and are wilfully obscure in their juxtaposition of words, the play affirms uncompromisingly that the old tragedy is dead, and the canon is only good for being torn apart. For all its iconoclasm and its subversive rereading of Shakespeare, Bene's works, dependent as they were on his presence, are unlikely to be much performed in the future but his influence on the development of the avant-garde was profound.

The avant-garde of the seventies saw the birth of many regional companies that experimented with new and provocative forms of theatre, influenced by major avant-garde theorists such as Eugenio Barba, whose mentors were Jerzy Grotowski and Tadeusz Kantor. Barba founded in Oslo in 1964 the Odin Theatre, which was at the forefront of international avant-garde, while his variation of 'poor theatre', a concept borrowed from Grotowski, opened up new ideas on dramatic art in Italy. Barba limited the number of spectators to maximise involvement and include the audience in the action onstage. His performances rejected all canonical techniques and realism, and strove to achieve a 'pure form', in a Platonic sense. By the seventies, Barba was advocating a 'third theatre', separate from both mainstream theatre and the avant-garde itself which, he felt, had become another fashion.

Carmelo Bene's deconstruction of Shakespeare was adopted by other artists, for example by the Gruppo Teatro Vasilicò, headed by Giuliano Vasilicò. In 1971, the company staged a production of *Hamlet* which was reminiscent of Bene's and saw the number of characters reduced so as to concentrate the focus on the four main characters: Hamlet, Ophelia, Gertrude and Claudius. Vasilicò claimed that such a reduction would not only sharpen the drama of those characters but would also, by heightening the allure of, and struggle for, power, facilitate the emergence of a clearer political meaning.

Very much as during the sixties, the theatrical avant-garde of the seventies was fragmented into many different groups with no one single vision for the future of Italian theatre dominant. The influential group, Il Carrozzone, believed in an 'analytical theatre' and in the 'theatre of silence', strongly influenced by the visual arts, while the Teatro Maschera, directed by Memè Perlini, embraced existentialism and produced work based on 'fragments' as if to stress the uncertainty and the contradictions of life. What undoubtedly united all these artists was the fundamentally metatheatrical and transgressive perception of theatre. The past represented something unconditionally negative, even ridiculous, and the only purpose of theatre was to bring about a *Götterdämmerung* of tradition.

After such heterogeneous theories and performances, post-seventies avant-garde theatre, or 'post-avant-garde', has moved in a new direction. The aim of such new theatre is less an attempt to ridicule the past than to explore the interrelation of art and the media in the modern world. Groups such as Magazzini Criminali (the former Carrozzone), or the theatre of Mario Martone, work in this direction. At the core of Magazzini Criminali's performances lies Federico Tiezzi's articulation of a 'theatre of poetry' where rhythm is the basis of movement,[4] whereas Martone, especially in his later work, has operated a 'theatricalisation of cinema', showing the two media as inseparable elements of contemporary culture. The same trend towards a multi-media theatre is present in other groups, such as the Compagnia Teatrale di Barberio Corsetti, which makes deft, intertwining use of video material and live performance.

Avant-garde drama has remained a live force in Italy long after it withered elsewhere, perhaps because it appeals to the taste of a public accustomed to a theatre based on the primacy of actors and directors, not authors. The predominance of the 'director's theatre' has opened up infinite possibilities of experimentation. The old divide between stage and screen, already undermined by the Futurists, has been blurred. Contemporary Italian avant-garde has moved away from the militancy and political engagement of the sixties and the seventies to focus instead on the multi-layered reality of the present, and on the power, intrusion and ubiquity of the mass media and virtual reality. Of its very nature, avant-garde theatre in each generation is closely linked to its own time and historical period, and outside that context, avant-garde works date rapidly, especially in an age when politics and political allegiances have proved to be much more complex than those portrayed by the theatre of the 'protest' generations. It remains to be seen whether the post-avant-garde will be able to use theatre as a means of profound artistic inquiry, rather than as a vehicle for political or aesthetic declarations.

Notes

1 Luciano Bottoni, *Storia del teatro italiano,* p. 56.
2 Franco Quadri, *L'avanguardia teatrale,* p. 158.
3 *Ibid.,* p. 315.
4 Giannachi and Kaye, *The Post-Avant-Garde,* p. 62.

Bibliography

Bottoni, L. *Storia del teatro italiano 1900–1945,* Bologna, 1999.
Giannachi, G. and Kaye, N. *Staging the Post-Avant-Garde: Italian Experimental Performance after 1970,* Oxford, 2002.
Kirby, M. *Futurist Performance,* New York, 1971.
Puppa, P. *Parola di scena,* Rome, 1999.
Quadri, F. *L'avanguardia teatrale in Italia (Materiali 1960–1976),* 2 vols., Turin, 1977.
    Il teatro degli anni settanta: Invenzione di un teatro diverso, Turin, 1984.
Tessari, R. *Teatro italiano del Novecento 1906–1976,* Florence, 1996.

27 Luigi Pirandello

PAOLO PUPPA

Premise in form of paradox

I'm only asking to find out if you really see yourself now in the same way that you saw yourself, for instance, once upon a time, in the past, with all the illusions you had then, with everything inside and outside yourself as it seemed then – and not only seemed, but really was! Well then, look back on those illusions, those ideas that you don't have any more, on all those things that no longer seem the same to you. Don't you feel that not only this stage is falling away from under your feet, but that so is the earth itself, and that all these realities of today are going to seem tomorrow as if they had been an illusion?[1]

These are the famous words which at the première on 9 May 1921 of *Sei personaggi in cerca d'autore* ('Six Characters in Search of an Author') the Father addressed to the Director to undermine the certainties and presumptions which the latter, believing himself fully alive, entertained with regard to his superiority to the phantasm standing in front of him. Every statement is to be seen in an existential flux, leaving only vertigo, the labyrinth and the void behind the infinite multiplication of opinions produced by the Subject in time. The principle of contradiction, in other words, drains ideologies and patterns of behaviour.

Pirandello's brand of relativism was wrapped in a humorous style, where 'humorous' stands for that language of playfulness and joy which fails to shut out the shadow of tragedy, and which is enclosed in his unchanging framework of a deliberately chosen uncertainty of judgement.[2] The same will occur in his dramatic writing, pulled in opposing directions, and showing the influence of the birth of cinema and the arrival of the culture industry which will lead to the progressive marginalisation of theatre even although, in the years following World War I, theatre remained the dominant form of middle-class entertainment. At the outset, Pirandello dressed his work in the costumes of the well-made play, and in that disguise managed to introduce dissent into the system. What the Futurists had contrived to do for brief periods, Pirandello succeeded in doing systematically, from inside the professional circuits, altering writing styles, performance habits and expectations, all with the help of the leading companies and stars of the age. Pirandello's gradual sabotage of the rigid hierarchies of roles inside the drama companies with whom he worked should never be overlooked. He transformed a secondary part like the *brillante* (comic role) into the protagonist, downgrading in the process the lead-actor, the hero-lover, who more often than not found himself humiliated and ridiculed by the plot. Normally, Pirandello, who had little patience in the early days of his career with the vanity of his actors (as instanced by his exhausting conflicts with Angelo Musco at the perform-ance of his first dialect works), constructed his theatre in contact with the actors of the day, showing himself attentive to the grammar and syntax of the companies, even being prepared to produce a fixed script *after* and not *before* the production. Recent studies have enabled us to have a clearer idea of the close relationship between theatre of this kind and the voice and body of its actors.

This revolutionary impulse has not been, perhaps cannot be, brought fully to fruition. Pirandello's approach is still far from being fully put into practice and appreciated by the majority of the theatre community in Italy and elsewhere. His radicalism is as little recognised now as in his own times. Indeed, productions tend, paradoxically, to underscore the psychic unity of the dramatis personae, aided in this by the contribution made by leading actors whose charisma can have a tranquillising, comforting effect which makes for the reinstatement of the human figure. However, it is beyond dispute that the Pirandellian theatrical character, exactly at the point at which he or she is most closely linked ideologically and linguis-tically to the twentieth-century tradition, is a decentred form divided against itself. The character is split apart by the author's vivisectionist examination. The twin of the Pirandellian theatrical character who appears in the great narrative trilogy that spans the period from *Il fu Mattia Pascal* (1904, 'The Late Mattia Pascal') to *Uno, nessuno e centomila* (1924–5, 'One, No one and One Hundred Thousand') tends see the body and physical being dissolve into an entity which disintegrates in a euphoric epiphany. Towards the end of *Uno, nessuno e centomila*, Vitangelo declares emphatic-ally, in an explicit homage to Gabriele D'Annunzio's *Meriggio*, that he will die and be reborn every day to become a thing – water, air or sky. A metamorphosis of that kind will permit him to overcome private angst or private defeat, to undergo the process of depersonalisation which, by making him view himself in the third person or submit to a quasi-Brechtian process of alienation from the self, enables the hero of the printed page to ward off every kind of pathos. What performer could incarnate a theatrical character who is multiple and experiences the separation of the head from the innards of the body? What adaptation or stage transcription could ever realise this epic selfhood in its endless process of self-epiphany? Perhaps only on an abstract stage could such a journey into night be realised.

From dialect to dialectic

Pirandello was born on 28 June 1867, in Girgenti – now Agrigento – into a well-off family. In 1894, he married a young, introverted girl, Antonietta Portulano, who brought him a rich dowry invested by the writer's father in a sulphur mine which was later destroyed, in one sense by flooding and in a wider sense by the industrial development of the newly formed Italian state. Reduced to poverty and compelled to transform himself from an intellectual *rentier* into a conventional middle-class teacher, he came to the stage at the relatively late age of almost fifty. It might be more appropriate to talk of his theatres in the plural, so as to take account of a discontinuous trajectory which smashed barriers in its movement from one phase to another. His journey led from the dialect productions of the 1910–15 period to the dialectic drawing-room of the 1916–20 period, and from the metatheatrical trilogy of 1921–30 to the myths of his final phase. It is an adventure which brought him alongside the experimental stage of his own day, whether the transgressive soirées of the Futurists or the dream-dimension outpourings of the Surrealists, the Symbolist *imagerie* or the enigmatic metaphysical works and monumentality of the new neo-classicists. Especially at the outset of his career, all his initiatives were compromised by the adoption of codes which were to all appearance unobjectionably naturalistic.

Today, thanks to recent philological research, we know that Pirandello's vocation for the stage dates from his earliest youth, and yet there can be no denying that theatre was peripheral to the intellectual tastes of the young writer. From *L'azione parlata* ('Spoken Action') in 1899 to *Illustratori, attori e traduttori* ('Illustrators, Actors and Translators') in 1908 and even as late as *Teatro e letteratura* ('Theatre and Literature') in 1918, Pirandello evinced a distinct distaste for any transfer to the stage, since he viewed the performer's interpretation as a mere act of betrayal which could not fail to be unfaithful to the original poetic vision.[3] The footlights, in their crude materiality, could not but debase the author's hidden, and therefore invisible, poetic inspiration. Nevertheless, the bulk of his stage scripts were born as short stories on the written page, therefore from books.

In the first phase, even if the regional or local idiom was hardly loved by their author, his characters tend to express themselves in dialect, perhaps because the performer of these early works was the Sicilian actor-manager, Angelo Musco. In the early repertoire we encounter scenarios with a strong anthropological vein and an eccentricity of approach which refine the Sicilian background. *L'altro figlio* ('The Other Son') and *Lumie di Sicilia* ('Limes of Sicily')[4] employ grotesque twists which act as ambiguous distancing mechanisms. In the first, the shift of stance does not exclude even the myth of motherhood, normally the one value invariably upheld in Pirandello. The relativism of outlook and the brutal discovery that all is illusion drain of all worth the ageing Maragrazia's wait for the sons who have long since emigrated and forgotten her, but cause her to ignore the other son, the bastard offspring born of a rape by a satanic bandit, even though this son has remained at her side and offers her every show of affection. *Lumie di Sicilia* sees the protagonist, Micuccio, armed with nothing more than a bunch of fragrant local oranges and his own obsessions, undertake the initiation rite that is the journey from Sicily to some far-off city in the north, only to discover that Teresina, who could have emerged from some *fin de siècle* idyll or poem by Leopardi, has been transformed into Sina Marnis, a *diva* of dubious morality and an empty shell celebrated by impresarios and protectors. Similar considerations apply to the lawyerly dispute involving the shattering of an earthenware pot and the trapping of an elderly, demonic restorer inside it which constitute the plot of *La giara* ('The Jar') (adapted in 1917 from a 1909 story), or to the revenge of the man with the evil eye who, in *La Patente* ('The Licence') (staged 1918, original story 1911), turns to his own advantage the boycott imposed on him by the malice of village gossips and sets himself up as a rustic sorcerer.

Shortly afterwards, the curtain rose not on naturalistic scenarios but on the anxieties of the drawing-room. The objects of a parody sharper than that of the contemporary theatre of the grotesque concern questions of conjugal honour and fidelity. The most characteristic writers of the grotesque movement, Luigi Chiarelli, Luigi Antonelli and Enrico

Cavacchioli seemed committed, at least in the years around the Great War, to playing down the melodrama that accompanied adultery in late nineteenth-century theatre and that underlay the conduct of civil society and the provisions of criminal law. The topic of infidelity had been previously the subject for boulevard farce or for realist dramas of jealousy, but in the drama of the 'grotesques' and Pirandello these approaches merged. The renunciation of woman and property, the attack on bourgeois ambitions and the philistinism of the nouveaux riches – these being objects of intolerant impatience and suspicion as expressions of the dominant culture in the 1920s – are evident in, for instance, the physical disfigurement of Signor Lavaccara in the nightmarish, baroque–Expressionist feast of the pig in *Sagra del Signore della nave* ('Festival of Our Lord of the Ship'), directed by Pirandello himself in the presence of His Excellency Mussolini at the inauguration in 1925 of the Teatro d'Arte in Rome. The impact is heightened by the presence of notaries, lawyers and assembled representatives of the law with their consorts in the parade which is the central point of the play, where they are treated to a ferocity of derision scarcely surpassed in the caricatures of Georg Groz.

Similar characters in stories appearing around the same time as the stage works are placed by the author in unsustainable situations, or in an angst-filled existence. Death is the spectre which circulates in these ironically macabre pages, death which determines the impulse towards the *beyond*, death as the only form of revenge or vindication. Some of his short stories operate as a metaphysical laboratory, or a *via crucis* marked out by stops for derision and humiliation, each stop representing deepening torment and disgust with life and a move away from its values and seductions. Between 1904, the year of *Il fu Mattia Pascal*, and 1915, the writer Pirandello moves gradually towards the stage, perhaps by way of the study where the author-character, often in the guise of a lawyer, gives audience to the most odd human types. Three stages, or stations of the cross, can be identified in three short stories corresponding to three metaliterary or metatheatrical narratives: *Personaggi* (1906, 'The Characters'), *La Tragedia di un personaggio* (1911, 'The Tragedy of a Character'), and *Colloqui coi Personaggi* (1915, 'Dialogues with Characters'). During his journey, the writer-advocate shows a growing intolerance with his petitioners, becoming increasingly acid and impatient with their petulance. In the first stage, the writer makes use of a serving-maid dressed in black, a character who is, in anticipation of her more celebrated colleague who introduces *Sei personaggi*, both an allegory of Imagination and a somewhat sadistic version of the Goldonian domestic servant. She takes pleasure in showing the petitioners into the study in any order, delighting in the confusion and conflict she creates and even giving a touch of libertinage to the writer's inspiration. The visitors are not dead but creatures who oscillate between being imprecise projections of the narrating subject and paper characters read and ruminated on by the author during the night-time hours, or appearing unheralded in search of a more gifted writer than the one who has rejected them. These shadows tend to become obsessively a-historical and take on the dimensions of eternity, and for that reason they stand in contrast to human beings in flesh and blood, beings born of women and therefore condemned to die. For the same reason, they are wholly distinct from the series of corpses who present themselves one last time before their dissolution.

Let us at this point reconsider the theatrical character. The only one to whom Pirandello extends explicit sympathy is the man who dallies with death and frequents burial grounds, such as the philosopher at the centre of the profane mystery play, *All'uscita* (1922, 'At the Exit', short story 1916). Never having felt any kind of desire, the dead man will continue reasoning for all eternity, and by giving vent to sophistical disappointments will become the first of a long series of cavilling *raisonneurs* who do not so much live on stage as watch others live, who become not *dramatic* but *epic* subjects, implacable and transgressive commentators dedicated to sabotaging all attempts at constructing a respectable mask, or existential safety net, or indeed any form of coherence acceptable in a bourgeois drawing-room. Lamberto Laudisi in *Così è (Se vi pare!)* (play and short story 1917, 'Right You Are (If You Think So!)'), his contemporary Angelo Baldovino in *Il piacere dell'onestà* (1917, 'The Pleasure of Honesty', from a short story 1905), Leone Gala in *Il gioco della parti* (1918, 'The Rules of the Game', from a short story 1913), Luca Fazio in *L'imbecille* (1922, 'The Imbecile', from a short story 1912), each gifted in his own way with an alienating, vertical glance at the world, are the heroes of dialectic theatre, bodiless heads, empty shells narcissistically revelling in their refusal of the heroic role, dizzying pyrotechnic engineers of argumentation who toss grenades into sitting-rooms (as Antonio Gramsci put it in one of his reviews) in the hope of smoking out contradictions between public roles and secret impulses. These characters, icons of problematic relativism, shatter the institution of marriage, undermining its very foundations, exposing skeletons stuffed into cupboards for possibly retroactive sins, as with *Tutto per bene* (1920, 'All for the Best', from a story published in 1906), drawing up curious contracts, as in *Pensaci, Giacomino!* (dialect version 1916, rewritten in Italian 1922, 'Think It Over, Giacomino!'), or destroying the standards of married life with acts of animalistic indecency, as in *L'uomo, la bestia e la virtú* (1919, 'The Man, the Beast and Virtue', from a short story 1906). The drawing-room is the site of action as it had been in the French-inspired theatre of Marco Praga. In the early plays written not in dialect but in standard Italian, the subjects are to all appearance immersed in the atmosphere of nineteenth-century respectability, where the adulterous wife, hounded by her husband's suspicions, must pay for her guilt by suicide, as in *La morsa* (1910, 'The Vice', based on an earlier, 1892 draft), or where the adulterous husband must die, as in *Il dovere del medico* (1913, 'The Doctor's Duty', based on a short story 1902). However, from *All'uscita*, the institution of marriage and its accompanying adulterous triangle undergo a process of abstract expansion, in that the lover has no wish to see his lover's husband die lest he become, in his turn, victim of the treacherous activities of the female with another partner. In *Bellavita* (1927, from a short story 1914), the relationship between the two men has ambiguous homosexual overtones reminiscent of the Dostoevskyan eternal husband. The woman having conveniently died in the meantime, Bellavita, heedless of the scandal this might arouse among the *bien pensants* of the community and keen to torment his ex-rival, has himself theatrically registered as cuckold. It may be disease that acts as the prime agent – cancer in *L'uomo da fiore in bocca* (1923, 'The Man with the Flower in His Mouth', original short story 1918), tuberculosis in *L'imbecille* – urging speech before the final silence, and giving the victims both the opportunity of a wry look at human ambitions and the capacity to grasp the latent fascination of the insignificant detail.

When he emerges into the open, the *raisonneur* seems to take on the part of the *brillante,* the comic character or anti-lover, a canonical role in nineteenth-century Italian theatre. It is no surprise if in Pirandello's theatre this figure attained his apotheosis in the performances of Ruggero Ruggeri, the century's most celebrated performer of that role. In this guise, the *raisonneur* figure does not content himself with parodying bourgeois prudery or limit himself to mocking the sexual and economic possessiveness of the hapless, smug participants in the Vanity Fair unfolding before him, each obsessed with private appetites, with the satisfaction of the self, with honour or with possessions. He goes well beyond that point. His ferocious pursuit of stereotypes, of the facile labels which regulate civil society both on and off the stage causes him to extend his apocalyptic quest into the interstices of the drama, into the mechanisms which underlie interpersonal communication and which guarantee the endurance of conflicts. The task of the *raisonneur* is to shake from the inside the Pirandellian score, based as it is on a precise scansion of monologue arias and syncopated recitative, or on a language pitched at a sustained, feverish level, and to send it tumbling towards chaos. It should not be forgotten that the *Sei personaggi* was first brought to the stage by the most elegant company of the day, directed by Dario Nicodemi, a writer of comedy of manners, with a cast of refined performers accustomed to operating in an atmosphere that prefigured the 'white telephones' and red roses of theatre and cinema in the Fascist era, in other words in a climate, or better a fragrance, in which an Italian Noel Coward would have been perfectly at home. But the mystery of the characters introduced into that atmosphere a sinister sense of deviation and the foul stench of the cemetery.

Metatheatre

Pirandello's dialectic theatre owed its irresistible movement towards metatheatrical solutions to the disturbing presence of its *raisonneur*. *Il berretto a sonagli* (dialect version 1917, Italian version 1923, 'Cap and Bells') signals not only the genesis of the philosopher – in this case, Ciampa, a humble clerk – but also the allusive intrusion of the metascene. Ciampa's wife, Nina, is involved in an affair with his manager, Fiorica, which Fiorica's wife, Beatrice, threatens to make public, but thanks to the stratagem of compelling Beatrice to feign madness, Ciampa is able to avoid the familiar *grand guignol* ending, with its accompaniment of penitential mourning and punitive killings. Ciampa becomes the 'onlie begetter' of the final outcome and the spokesman for the author in his awareness that life is a stage, enlivened by the fiction of what he denotes 'puppets' and by the varying force of the three 'chords' of human expression. It is he who suggests to the other characters the appropriate acts and words to silence gossip and bring down the curtain. In the midst of the havoc which removes from him every shred of dignity and respect as a human being, he finds consolation in the status of the cunning, wily servant devoted to his master, familiar from the theatre of Plautus or the Atellan farces. Being jealous, being emotionally attached to others brings with it the risk of being reduced to the puppet state and being manipulated by situations no longer controlled by the self but dominated by hackneyed scripts which are dangerous for the freedom of the subject. The clown's grin with which Ciampa takes his leave from his adversaries and exits from the story, consigning the wife (of his manager in the metamorphoses of the script, but Pirandello's own in life!) to the mental asylum, is in some ways the sneer of *Enrico IV* (1922 'Henry IV'), since in both plays we come close to the loneliness of the creator in his pseudo-triumphant farewell to everyday life.

The male hero, bereft of body and the materiality of life, in the absence of the female, can now venture forth into tangled labyrinths where the dramaturgy has been cleared of recognisable codes or functions. Interruptions and digressions have the upper hand over plot. If *Enrico IV* reveals the impossibility of penetrating the mystery of the other, of finding a way round the enigmatic wall with which everyman defends his own ineffable interiority, if even earlier Lamberto Laudisi in *Così è (Se vi pare!)* dialogues in front of the mirror with himself as though with another, it is in *Sei personaggi* that autism reaches its disconsolate culmination. Here all reasoning on theatre is the death of theatre itself and undermines all possibility of interpersonal conflict. Since actions do not represent the character, according to the bitter, enraged claims of the Father who had just been caught in a brothel on the point of copulating unknowingly with his stepdaughter, and since the gulf between sound and significance for speaker and listener means that words can no longer carry the same semantic weight for participants in a conversation, the consequence is that all possibility of interpreting other people's drama has been cancelled, leaving nothing except the slow descent into aphasia and the recognition that scenes based on conversation, or on slyly misleading chatter, must give way to the alternation of the howl and the silence. Subjectivity is shattered by a combination of fantasy images made up of delirious confessions and of horrors belonging to the dream state. *Questa sera si recita a soggetto*, (premiered in Germany in 1930, based on a short story of 1910 'Tonight We Improvise'), is a statement of the validity of a systematic disunion which destroys stage protocols and which affects even the aspirations of Symbolism or the Wagnerian total work of art. Now, cinema, jazz, religious processions and cabaret all mix and clash with each other. Opera can be celebrated on stage, at least in the form of an outsize gramophone exhibited as a scratchy acoustic prop, while filmed scenes from the same opera are silently acted out on a screen at the back of the stage, all to the accompaniment of the chatter of the main characters and the indignant protests of the minor parts. The influence of the Futurists is evident in various aspects, particularly where the sounds produced are in conflict with what is going on, where all semantic strategy is denied to what is being articulated, or where the contradiction between signifier and signified is clear.

In the same way, the earlier *Ciascuno a suo modo* (1924, but based on aspects of the 1915 novel, *Si gira . . .,* ('Shoot! '), 'Each in this Own Way') exults in its ability to expand beyond its own performance space, in line with the theatrical 'syntheses' of F. T. Marinetti and his Futurist companions. There are traces of Futurist influence too in the anti-pedantry expressed in the struggle against teachers in the college story *Pensaci, Giacomino!*, and in the satirical drama *L'uomo, la bestia e la virtù*, a work where, with chairs as characters, a kind of animism can be detected, as it can in *L'uomo dal fiore in bocca*. Improbably, *Enrico IV* contains acts of homage to the contemporary entertainer Ettore Petrolini, who can be viewed as representing a popular version of Futurism. In a grandiloquent scene worthy of D'Annunzio or Sem Benelli, two medieval footmen are made to speak in Roman dialect, lowering immediately the grand tone of the exchanges: 'Do us a favour. You don't have a match, do you? / What? A pipe in here?' Even if Pirandello's script is wholly successful in weaving a way between the quarrelling parties and in managing the dismantling of the montage, the scene is nonetheless redolent of forms of popular entertainment for the urban masses. Dr Hinkfuss, the eccentric director in *Questa sera si recita a soggetto*, acts as vendor of commercialised images and irresistible sensations as he addresses an audience dazzled by the astonishing, sensuous but superficial novelties on offer. He regulates the criss-crossing movement of rapt trances and redemptive reawakenings which bind the stage and the stalls, and acts as the deus ex machina of postmodern theatre from which the very form of theatre must be expelled.

The reverse side of the Pirandellian script, especially in this metatheatrical strategy which is by no means confined to the celebrated theatre-in-theatre trilogy, reveals planned chaos and the transcription of an unresolved decentring movement which sets the forces producing the event one against the other – actors versus characters, directors versus audience, street versus theatre building, story recounted in the past versus repetition of present action. Often, actor and character find themselves cohabiting in a difficult relationship inside the same part. Again in *Enrico IV*, it is worth drawing attention to the significant remark about clothes 'on top of other clothes', that is, both those used in the medieval perform-ance and those used in the generational switch between mother and daughter when Matilde, the mother, tries to shock the 'Emperor' out of his insanity by presenting him with an image of herself and of him as they had been. She finds the clothes she once wore but which, with the passing of the years, no longer fit her but which are perfect for her daughter. The gulf between actor and part also emerges forcefully in the fictional company's prologue to such works as *Questa sera si recita a soggetto* and *I giganti della montagna*, ('The Mountain Giants'), notably in the Arsenal of Apparitions in the latter play, where the puzzled actors drag their characters behind them, suffusing them with elements of their own dreams and liberating the unconscious.

However, the metatheatrical change of direction does not consist in a mere intellectual superfluity induced by traumas more suspect and troub-ling than those brought on by adulterous unions. In *Così è (Se vi pare!)*, for example, the unknown woman in the upper apartment, whose plight is in some ways similar to the tale at the heart of *Questa sera si recita a soggetto*, casts a shadow over the strange couple of daughter-in-law and son-in-law, whose status, rendered more mysterious by the destruction of all identity cards in an earthquake, simultaneously reveals and conceals dark, terrifying forces whose power transcends all trite consideration of relativism of viewpoint. And in *Sei personaggi*, the incestuous tension, hinted at in the core scene, is redeemed by the slaughter of the innocents, by the sacrifice in the garden of the two children as though in expiation of the sins of the adults, while the continual reminders of convention and of the falseness of the production serve to downplay the taboos of the image. In any case, the theatre is no longer central in the modern city of mass culture and totalitarian regimes. Drama seems to vanish from sight in the chaotic Babel of the metropolis, where the crisis of the self seems to require other, swifter and more drastic techniques of resolution.

Theatre of myths

All that remained was retrogression towards enchanted but fatal land-scapes, a journey over well-trodden paths with the daring of street per-formers in search of an unknown public. This is the fortune and misfortune awaiting the tattered troupe lost on the mysterious island in *I giganti della*

Figure 18: Scene from *The Mountain Giants* by Luigi Pirandello, director G. Strehler (1947).

montagna, the unfinished work left as last will and testament. Pirandello's theatre now becomes, in its mixture of Dionysiac and Apollonian themes, mythic.

The closing phase of his work as writer of short stories covers a similar range of registers, and coincides with the re-presentation of symbolist bric-à-brac, but now in a surrealist version. From the stories *Una sera, un geranio* (1934, 'One Evening, a Geranium') to *Effetti di un sogno interrotto* (1936, 'Effects of a Disturbed Dream'), from *I piedi sull'erba* (1934, 'Feet on the Grass') to *Una giornata* (1936, 'One Day'), the indeterminacy of perception narrated on the page reaches its peak: mirrors, windows, paintings are the magic agents of a playful, numinous bedlam where it is no longer possible to distinguish between observer and observed. Life and dream, present and past, reality and fiction exchange and confuse their respective dimensions. The arsenal of apparitions, the court of miracles of the unhappy and yet privileged Scalognati (literally, 'Luckless') who find themselves the unwilling guests of the Giants, is the site where, inspired by celestial music or by inexplicable fragments of some vision, desire itself can be represented, or where the depths of human shame can come to the surface. Private insanity, archaic magic, occult rites are imprinted on the internal walls of this strange habitation, as they are in the mixture of whimsy and nightmare that is *Sogno (ma forse no)* (written 1928, premiered in Lisbon 1931, 'Dream (But Perhaps Not)'), or in the subliminal adultery of *Non si sa come* (staged 1935, based on stories written in 1913, 1914 and 1932, 'You Don't Know How'). The work of art, in an age when technology made its reproduction possible and when competition from the cinema was intensified (1929 was also the year when Pirandello became involved with silent cinema, in spite of the reservations previously expressed in the novel *Si gira . . .*), is revived by this return to animism filtered through Pirandellian humour. In the trilogy of myths, *I giganti della montagna*, *La nuova colonia* (1928, but based on a 1911 short story, 'The New Colony') and *Lazzaro* (1929, 'Lazarus'), Pirandello experiments with mystical shamanism and a blend of prodigious, baroque *coups de scène*. The philosopher vanishes, the *raisonneur* of the dialectic theatre falls silent, and the metalinguistic rage of poor Ciampa fades away. Pirandello's theatre no longer has any truck with the dialect excess of Angelo Musco nor with the shrill falsetto of Ruggero Ruggeri but aims at a bombastic lyricism, at the sublimity of the oratorio. The father-author is definitively erased, either condemned to sterility, as in *Quando si è qualcuno* (1933, 'When You Are

Figure 19: Portraits of Pirandello.

Somebody'), or to suicide, like the poet in the prologue to *I giganti*. The word becomes poetry in its ritualistic, etymological sense of 'fabrication', of sound which evokes and creates a reality, and can therefore cure the legs of the paralysed girl in *Lazzaro*, or make disappear under a tidal wave the island of the wicked in *La nuova colonia*. At this point, the stage must be on show: it is no longer a descent into ontology, a compromise between taboo and desire but something which corresponds to a religious practice requiring rigid protocols, sacred gestures and the speech of the miracle worker.

It is the female, not the male, actor who performs the tasks which make possible the miraculous impact. The actress Marta Abba became Pirandello's own emblematic *Nostra Dea* ('Our Goddess') after he saw her in Massimo Bontempelli's eponymous play as he was about to embark on the Teatro d'Arte initiative, an encounter that led to the enigmatic relationship and collaboration between the two. Pirandello wrote his last female roles for Abba – Tuda in *Diana e la Tuda* ('Diana and the Tuda'), Marta in *L'amica delle mogli* ('The Wives' Friend') (both 1927), Sara in *Lazzaro*, the unnamed woman in *Come tu mi vuoi* (1930, 'As You Desire Me'), Donata in *Trovarsi*

(1932, 'Finding Oneself'), the Russian Veroccia in *Quando si è qualcuno* and perhaps Ilse in *I giganti della montagna*. These may be viewed as steps in a coded public and private correspondence between two lives which came together for a time, laying bare a tension between animal and spiritual feeling, between physiological and aesthetic motherhood. Actress characters had previously appeared in Pirandello's productions, but in the conventional guise of the femme fatale, for instance Nestoroff in *Si gira . . .* or Moreno in *Ciascuno a suo modo*. Now the plots are deepened by a new complexity of motivation: fickleness, impulsiveness, intolerance of bourgeois decorum and male authority, self-giving, overwhelming and disdainful sensuality, physical frustration, anxious inspiration, despairing quest for something transcendental and disgust with the body are constituent notions of the new culture of the mythical actress.

Motherhood, a frequent obsession and recurrent theme in Pirandello, becomes the dominant motif and dramaturgical form. The quasi-devotional mother–child couple, as it appears in the euphorically catastrophic climax of *La nuova colonia* or in the voyage of initiation and regression featured in *La favola del figlio cambiato* (set to music by Piero Malipiero, and staged in Germany in 1934, 'The Changeling') is a means of overcoming the isolation to which a person, or individual mask, is condemned, and hence of seeing the other as something more than blankness. Whether for a prostitute, like Spera in *La nuova colonia* or for a rebellious adulteress, like Sara in *Lazzaro*, the metamorphosis of the protagonist-actress means that the process of transformation of matter into spirit takes place at ever higher levels. What is needed is a special kind of motherhood, no longer confined to a prosaic or neurotic solitude, as was still the case with *O di uno o di nessuno* (1929, based on a 1912 story, 'Either of One or of No One'), nor blocked by arguments between mother and adulterous lover of the type found in *La ragione degli altri* (final version 1915, 'Other People's Reasons') or even *Come prima, meglio di prima* (1920, story 1904, 'As Before, Better Than Before'). There now emerges an assertive femininity capable of victory or at least of poetic portrayal, unlike the suffering, tortured heroines of earlier plays, such as Ersilia in *Vestire gli ignudi* (1922, 'Naked'). It may even be that demographic propaganda and Fascist incentives for a theatre open to the masses played their part in the creation of a feminist, Mother Ocean mythology. Be that as it may, thanks to Marta Abba, Pirandello's late theatre seems to find a new élan and inspiration in the tormented dedication to the other that only a woman, and only an actress,

Figure 20: Scene from *Think it Over, Giacomino!* by Luigi Pirandello, director N. Rossa (1987).

can offer. This context makes possible the appearance of motifs borrowed from Expressionism, including the male–female conflict and the Madonna–whore dualism, as well as the revolt against paternal authority already present in *Sei personaggi*, where the discovery of fatherhood in a brothel led to the dethroning and expulsion from the stage of the role of the father-author. The idea of father-killing will later find a kind of consecration in the nihilistic request contained in Pirandello's will where he asked for his body to be burned and the ashes scattered in the sea.

Let us return, then, to the explosive energy contained in *I giganti della montagna*, the final summing up of the themes of his entire work. The theoretical tension is multi-faceted, with prime place given to the Hegelian idea of the death of art in the modern metropolis (even if Pirandello in all probability never came to grips with the totalitarian dimension of the Fascist regime). Extra weight is given to this sociological factor by the author's private vicissitudes. Art dies because the poet kills himself, in part because of the exhaustion of his professional functions and in part for personal reasons. A despairing love story with no possibility of physical expression with the beloved daughter-muse, Marta Abba, is one element of the metaphorical fullness of the script, which is another way of saying that her rejection of Pirandello led him to compensate imaginatively with the melodramatic end. In addition, the metatheatrical element makes a reappearance, since the play contains in itself a second work – *La favola del figlio cambiato*. The metatheatrical element of the script also resides in the phenomenology of the theatrical apparatus, in the sense that in *I giganti della montagna*, as much as in the theatre-in-theatre trilogy, light is shed on the encounter between performers and spectators, while the official audience, that is, the Giants themselves, make their presence felt only by the noises-off during the closing, mythical cavalcade.

For her part, the complex character of the countess Ilse unites in her being various forces: she is an echo of the sacred prostitute of antiquity, a creature now reduced to sexual ineptitude and perhaps an anticipation of the elderly Sgricia of the Scalognati group. If she had not been torn apart, as appears to have been her intended fate in the hypothetical finale of the uncompleted play, Ilse could have remained as a guest in the Villa of the Scalognati as a second Sgricia, in other words, another demented relic endowed with useless magic powers, reduced to autistically retelling her own tale. Ilse is a schizophrenic, part charismatic *prima donna* and part mother-figure compelled by a sense of guilt to keep acting, part wife in a failed relationship with the count-impresario and part lover *manquée* of the suicide poet.

The other group in the work are the Scalognati, who recall in their own way the pariahs of *La nuova colonia* in that they too are a socially defenceless group, an embarrassing presence for Fascist censorship. They can be viewed either as monsters created from Romantic inebriation with the 'infinite' and surreal imagery so dear to the Symbolists, or as freaks born in Pirandello's private library, where residues of positivism are filed alongside Idealist culture. Cotrone, the coordinator of the Scalognati group, is a new version of Hinkfuss from *Questa sera si recita a soggetto* but one purged of corporal disfigurement because free of all temptation to sell the products of his imagination on the theatre market; his imagination is for private, internal use. A demiurge or shaman whose word can make the image flesh, he is the relentless animator of dream reality, of the prime matter which underlies the principle of individuality. The villa has an internal wall on which the elderly residents project the free associations which rise from the depth of their spirits, and on which emotions can be printed and audiovisual pleasures prepared. In this room of apparitions, Eros dissolves as soon as it is clothed in language, but the chaos of dreams unleashed in the night of the villa casts light on the work of the actor. What is an actor but the history of his own performances? In the dream dimension, the actors and the roles allocated to them in the unfolding tale multiply, while together they act as sounding board for anthropological motifs where the dream is a physical journey beyond the body. The dramatis personae include puppets and robot characters, the petrified and terminal stage of the process of isolation of the private imaginative dimension. Abandoned in the room of transparent walls, these are the adaptable walk-on parts available for an infinity of uses but which click back into immobility in the presence of outsiders. These animated figures permit Pirandello not only to quote himself but also to sack the work of such contemporaries in the avant-garde as Bontempelli, who cooperated in the Teatro d'Arte and whose *Siepe a nordovest* (1923, 'Hedge on the North East') listed actors and puppets in the cast, or Rosso di San Secondo, who in the early stages of his career owed much to Pirandello and whose *Marionette, che passione!* (1918, 'Puppets, What Passion!') was staged after the intervention of Pirandello with the director, Virgilio Talli. As for the production pyrotechnics, the ludic innovations and the disconcerting epiphanies in the script itself, it is worth recalling Pirandello's experiences as director of Teatro d'Arte and his enthusiasm for experimentation. It may all seem a remarkable reversal of the author's initial literary creed, but life for Pirandello is an, often happy, contradiction.

Notes

1 Luigi Pirandello, *Six Characters in Search of an Author,* trans. John Linstrum, London, 1982, p 45.
2 Luigi Pirandello, *L'umorismo,* first edn, 1908; now in *Saggi, poesie, scritti vari.*
3 The Italian word *interprete* can mean both interpreter and performer. These essays are included in *Saggi, poesie, scritti vari.*
4 *The Other Son* was staged in 1923 but is based on a short story from 1905, while *Limes,* based on a short story published in 1900, was produced in 1910 but revised in dialect for production in 1915.

Bibliography
Editions of Pirandello
Pirandello, L. *Maschere nude,* ed. M. Lo Vecchio-Musti, 2 vols., Milan, 1958.
   Saggi, poesie, scritti vari, ed. M. Lo Vecchio-Musti, Milan, 1977.
   Maschere nude, ed. A. D'Amico, 3 vols., Milan, 1986–2004.
   Pirandello: Collected Plays, ed. R. Rietty 4 vols., London, 1987–94.
   Tutto il teatro dialettale di Luigi Pirandello, ed. S. Zappulla Muscarà, 2 vols., Milan, 1993.
   Lettere a Marta Abba, ed. B. Ortolani, Milan, 1995.

Criticism
Alonge, R. *Luigi Pirandello,* Bari and Rome, 1997.
Angelini, F. *Serafino e la tigre. Pirandello tra scrittura teatro e cinema,* Venice, 1990.
Borsellino, N. *Ritratto e immagini di Pirandello,* Rome and Bari, 1991.
D'Amico, A. and Tinterri, A. *Pirandello capocomico: La compagnia del Teatro d'Arte di Roma 1925–1928,* Palermo, 1987.
Gioanola, E. *Pirandello e la follia,* Genoa, 1983.
Giudice, G. *Pirandello,* Turin, 1963.
Macchia, G. *Pirandello o la stanza della tortura,* Milan, 1981.
Puppa, P. *Fantasmi contro giganti. Scena e immaginario in Pirandello,* Bologna, 1978.
   Dalle parti di Pirandello, Rome, 1987.
   La parola alta: Sul teatro di Pirandello e D'Annunzio, Rome and Bari, 1993.
   Parola di scena, Rome, 1999.
Vicentini, C. *L'estetica di Pirandello,* Milan, 1985.
   Pirandello. Il disagio del teatro, Venice, 1993.

28 Italo Svevo, dramatist

PAOLO PUPPA

Italo Svevo's very considerable dramatic talent was never fulfilled. The thirteen scripts which he composed without any hope of seeing them performed in his lifetime and without the support of theatre companies, circuits, commissions or the attention of public or critics were almost totally ignored in his day.[1] This is not of course the only example of a dramatist being neglected by the theatre establishment of his time, but in the case of Ettore Schmitz, the name on Svevo's birth certificate, the bare stage mirrors his abortive literary career, producing a painful double failure. A novelist can, technically, continue writing even in the absence of publication, but for a dramatist the refusal of a stage constitutes a death-sentence. Svevo's habit of continuously modifying his scripts and effect-ively treating them as work in progress makes their dating very difficult: some estimates put them at the end of the nineteenth century, others in the years following World War I. *Un marito* ('A Husband') is a special case since the manuscript is dated 1903, when the author was forty-two (he was born in Trieste on 19 December 1861). The language of these 'armchair plays'[2] sounds odd, never having been actually spoken by actors who could make it natural and speakable. The diction is laboured, not really authen-tic, a mixture of the German prevalent in commercial circles in Habsburg-dominated Trieste, the English which he studied for business purposes, and the dialect spoken in his home and traces of which remain in the bitter-sweet rhythms of his lively *Atto Unico* ('One-Act'), with its domestic scenes in the style of Giacinto Gallina.

Svevo's cultural horizon when he begins to 'imagine' plays is still naturalistic, that is, aimed at a close reproduction of everyday life, but in spite of, or perhaps because of, this dilettante background and complete absence of any demand from an audience, his 'amateur' works are genu-inely reflective of developments in the European theatre of the time, and are in certain respects more so than with any other Italian dramatist of the early twentieth century, including Pirandello. This remains true in spite of the many deficiencies in plot construction and typologies of situation forced on him by current convention: it remains true in spite of the mismatch between the interpersonal, objective structure of drama itself and the tendency towards the subjective in Svevo's narrative work, and even in spite of the chaotic interweaving of overlapping time-frames in his plots. The brief, amusing Schnitzlerian monologue, *Prima del ballo* ('Before the Ball'), in which the young female protagonist waiting at the door for her carriage to take her to the ball muses over the suitors proposed by her family and her own romantic fancies, is a good example of Svevo's 'stream of consciousness', but is far removed from the rhythms of dialogue. Ettore Schmitz may seem quite unsuited to the stage yet he had a genuine vocation for the theatre, even if we ignore the welter of anecdotes about his precocious talent, about his acting ambitions despite a stammer and lisp and his willingness as a young journalist to take on theatre reviews for the local, mildly irredentist, *Indipendente.*

All of Svevo's work is centred on the motif of the failed artist, around whom he created a gallery of portraits of *fin de siècle* characters, each one condemned to anonymity and disappointment, unlike the happy, dissipated and spoiled young men of D'Annunzio's theatre. This theme recurs in Svevo's narrative works where such characters find themselves strangely paralleled by medical practitioners of all kinds (as happens in *La coscienza di Zeno* ('The Confessions of Zeno'), peopled as it is by psychoanalysts, directors of clinics, specialists and/or ordinary doctors, not to mention lowly nurses, and which gives off an odour of ether or iodine which, in its obsessive intensity, is equalled only by Molière's farces). By the very use of a nom de plume (firstly E. Samigli and then Italo Svevo), Ettore Schmitz gives evidence of the disapproval of the economic environment (the Stock Exchange!) in which he moved.

His abandonment of writing parallels his move away from his inherited Judaism, similarly suppressed but surviving not least in the persistently macabre and grotesque tones in his work. Many of the conflicts within the family circles in his plays can be traced back to his own family situation as son-in-law to the Veneziani family, wealthy, assimilated Jews, or more precisely converts to Catholicism who were unswerving in their observance of Catholic rites. We find such a situation in *L'avventura di Maria* ('Maria's Adventure'), possibly written in the period immediately preceding World War I, where the male protagonist talks of 'repatriating' after business trips between Florence and Trieste which are in reality pretexts for erotic escapades. Maria is a variant of a recurring prototype, a nervous violinist who is expelled from the bourgeois household after capriciously falling in love with Alberto, the head of the family, a businessman married to her childhood friend. The triangle is eventually broken and normality restored, thus preventing the bourgeois/artist couple realising their love-dream. This sounds like a rather sad allegory for the formal prohibition imposed on Ettore Schmitz's writing by his full-time job at his underwater-paint factory, as well as a general allusion to the incompatibility between art and middle-class work.

Un marito and *La rigenerazione* ('Regeneration'), both structured on interlocking relationships, are his most ambitious plays. The former follows the ideological swings of the protagonist, the lawyer Federico Arcetri, who in the distant past had stabbed to death his unfaithful wife, Clara, after finding a number of letters indicating her *probable* infidelity. Meantime he has taken a second wife, Bice, and when the curtain rises the mother of the first wife strides on to the stage carrying other letters, this time belonging to the second wife and proving that she too is *perhaps* unfaithful, and demanding that the husband repeat his act of murderous revenge. At the same time, in a parallel situation, one of Federico's clients has also killed his wife, whom he had caught *in flagrante*. Federico at first undertakes to defend him but later, tired of 'serving as an example of untainted honour', declines the uxoricide's case. At first sight this is no more than a straightforward tale of cuckoldry, but the social status of the characters, upper-middle class, is significant. Even when writing a play in the knowledge that it will not be performed, the author to some extent adjusts to the expectations of the stalls by providing characters of an elevated social status, similar to his own personal position following his marriage.

On first reading, the play seems to fall into the category of nineteenth-century *pièces bien faites*. Svevo, an enthusiastic theatregoer, was certainly familiar with the repertoire of Dumas *fils* and Scribe, who were very popular in Trieste at that time. Scribe regularly makes use of mislaid letters, handkerchiefs and eavesdropping from behind screens. (The central element in another of Svevo's plays, *Una commedia inedita* ('An Unpublished Play'), is the screen from behind which a potentially cuckolded husband checks on the adulterous tendencies of his wife, who is involved with an aspiring lover, who happens to be a playwright). There is no shortage of letters in *Un marito,* both in the traumatic memory of the motive for the killing and the newly discovered correspondence of the second wife. Clearly, this is no longer a well-made play: by 1903 these devices had worn thin. In keeping with the rejection of action in late nineteenth-century drama, nothing actually happens on stage. If reality is uncertain, if identity and guilt gradually disappear, feelings of jealousy, the urge to commit murder, the Othello complex are also bound to decline. Svevo's work anticipates a wider movement, a peaceful protest against the crime of honour, which finds its fullest expression in Pirandello's *Cap and Bells* some fourteen years later.

On the other hand, there is no shortage of vaudeville touches in Svevo's play, which contains dialogue and situations worthy of Feydeau, or reminiscent of some witty central-European operetta sparkling with smart repartee: for example, the brother-in-law, a doctor, tells Federico that he will have to 'take the bull by the horns', before remembering that 'horns' are a synomym for cuckoldry. In the third act, Bice convinces Federico that the letters he has found were just an innocent attempt on her part, after being neglected and humiliated by her husband for so long, to distract him from his infatuation with the dead Clara, leading us to expect a happy ending, such as Svevo often contrived elsewhere. In the already mentioned *Una commedia inedita*, the protagonist forgives his wife whom he has caught with her lover, because he realises he has been a neglectful husband, too wrapped up in his business affairs, and so must share the blame. In *La verità* ('The Truth'), Silvio Arcetri, who has the same surname as the Federico of *Un marito*, uses a blatant lie backed up by zealous witnesses to persuade his wife, who has caught him in bed with the dressmaker, to come back to him. In *Le ire di Giuliano* ('Giuliano's Rages') the couple overcome the problems caused by tension and incompatibility of character and stay together in order to carry on their business and maintain their property. In *Le teorie del conte Alberto* ('Count Albert's Theories'), the protagonist gradually abandons his adherence to rigid Darwinian convictions in matters of heredity and, in spite of initial doubts about her family origins, marries Anna. In *L'avventura di Maria,* Alberto and Giulia decide to stay together, partly for the sake of their only child but in spite of Alberto's affair with a touring violinist.

However, in a sudden shift of plot in *Un marito*, the wife of the couple's friend Paolo claims to have seen Bice in a carriage letting Paolo caress her hand. Federico, finding himself once more compelled to assume the executioner's part, declines to face the truth and takes on a new role, that of the trusting friend: 'I know, Bice, that you were ready to betray me, and I also know that you didn't, but not out of any virtue of yours. I forgive you.' From a case of actual cuckoldry actually punished in the past, the script moves to one of hypothetical cuckoldry in the present, accepted by the victim with a resignation worthy of Hamlet. This equivocation, a disconcerting departure from the binary logic of realist plots where the truth or falsity of a real act leads to the condemnation or forgiveness of the supposedly guilty party, undermines both the playful and the opposing, complementary (or dramatic) dimension involved in adulterous situations, and steers developments towards an ambiguous outcome. Federico resorts to various legalistic arguments to persuade his wife to fall in with his theatrical display of noble feelings, his 'peace-offering', and drags her along to the sick-bed of his dying mother-in-law, thinking that in her confusion she might mistake Bice for her dead daughter Clara – a sort of ghost of his first wife who has been symbolically present from the opening of the play and whose portrait has been hanging in the lawyer's severe office, like an Ibsenite fetish, or a lugubrious Fury whose presence hangs over the action.

The intrusion of the dead on the stage creates a murky, funereal atmosphere in *Un marito. Terzetto spezzato* ('A Broken Trio'), which seemingly unfolds in the style of farce, is similarly conceived, and is yet another variant of the clash between the economic and artistic sides of the author's life. The script seems to promise nothing more than another spiritualist séance set up to evoke a dead wife. The séance is arranged by the widower, who is worried about the coffee-merchandising business where his partner is his best friend, obviously his wife's former lover, as well as an aspiring man-of-letters now inconsolable because he has lost his inspirational Muse. Both men need the woman for their own professional purposes, but she derides them in a very unmetaphysical way. The situation in *Un marito* is of a different order. In killing his wife for an obsolete 'question of honour', Federico has transformed her into some sort of superior reality, an icon of unattainable desire, a saint to be worshipped. Married love has vanished with his first wife, the murdered Clara, and he is now totally inhibited sexually.

The plot hinges on the disturbed relationship between husband and wife, as in Ibsen and Pirandello. If he really married Bice in a vain attempt to dispel the ghost, she took him for a great romantic hero, the violence of whose passion could lead him to commit murder, only to find that he is a spent force, interested only in making money. Earlier in his life when he fell in love, he was committed to the study of law and of great juridical ideas based on the humanitarian spirit and tolerant solidarity. Later he moved quite cynically into civil law, taking on not merely administrative but financially remunerative cases. Federico now seems almost a double of Ibsen's master-builder, Solness, who gave up building churches to God in favour of producing simple houses where couples lived out their loveless lives. In Svevo's case, it may be that lawyers and architects are metaphorical allusions to his own thwarted literary ambitions. There is a fundamental ambiguity in the relationship between man and woman, as in any exchange of affection or power, making it a mere tangle of attraction and repulsion. This is also the case in the unfinished *Con la penna d'oro* ('With a Golden Pen') where the two cousins, the rich Alberta and the unfortunate Alice, each interpret in her own way the reciprocal, constantly changing feelings of love and hatred that bind them together, each taking in turn the roles of persecutor and victim; as again in the almost Hegelian relationship between master and servant in *Inferiorità* where, after a bizarre drawing-room game, the naïve but spiteful waiter kills Alfredo Picchi and then puts on his hat and coat.

While attending the consulting rooms of the analyst, Edoardo Weiss, and considering those of Freud, Svevo seemed to veer in the direction of the Scandinavian dramatists, Ibsen and Strindberg. At the end of *Un marito,* Federico undergoes a regeneration of an ontological nature. The play demonstrates the absurdity of the crime of honour from both a moral and a juridical point of view, but it also underlines the lack of any consistency or coherence in the individual. There is no need to destroy yourself, as Ignazio does literally in Svevo's youthful *Il ladro in casa* ('The Thief in the House'), when he falls from the roof almost as though to compensate for the trouble he has caused his family through his repeated irresponsibility. It is sufficient to fall silent, to leave things unsaid, to let strange symptoms and inconsistent conduct reveal the inner self. The rejection of the myth of male honour coincides with the humiliation of the ego. Federico discovers in practice the ambiguity of the self. At the end, as he and Bice go off to give their performance at the bedside of the aged Arianna, all relationships seem to demonstrate the impossibility of being defined or of assuming a distinct identity. Law has been abolished, lawyers put to flight, fathers deprived of their power. In any case, the couple have no children. The spoken word has now lost all authority, all credibility. All that remains is an area of lawlessness, confirmed by one significant statement made by Paolo, the only father in the play, to clarify his pedagogical methods:

> My Guido is accustomed to the strictest injustice. When he be-
> haves well I always manage to punish him for some trivial reason;
> when he behaves badly I do the same, but not always. I praise him
> only when I myself feel well, physically and morally. He has
> learned from this that he is not in charge of his own destiny but
> has to submit to capricious and unreasonable chance . . . con-
> fronted with this gloomy prospect, with this harshness and injust-
> ice, he despairs, and in a few years he will have lost most of his
> congenital illusions.[3]

Before Federico kills Clara, we learn that he had dreamed about her death. The homicidal impulse resurfaces in *Rigenerazione*, where dreams have a more literal sense. The principal character aspires to return to the past and accepts the possibility of rediscovering his youth. If the earlier play had a tight, compact structure, like a sonata with interlocking motifs, the later work is a prolix and, in many ways, unfinished symphony, a choreo-graphed, multi-figured fresco, focused on the theme of regression. How-ever, the parental roles remain as confused as before. The protagonist is husband, father, grandfather, lover and, now that the function of the dominant father in the earlier play has been suppressed, interacts continu-ally with the others in each of these roles according to external stimuli and his attempts to subdue them. The wealthy, retired textile merchant, Giovanni Chierici, leads an apathetic existence. All passion spent, he lives quietly in the loving care of Anna, his wife-nurse who looks after his sleep and his digestion in the way she does with the numerous pets in the house and garden. Boredom rules over his forgetful universe (he cannot remember people's names), and his only pleasure is taking a walk with his grandson. In this twilight world the protagonist suddenly agrees to undergo an operation to recover his youth, though the author himself appears uncertain of his age.[4] What Zeno attempted with his writing, Giovanni attempts with his body, his skin, making the Faustian journey not metaphorical but literal. He will not be having the surgical operation for sexual reasons, according to his honourable claims. If the other old men, the prying merchants from the Stock Exchange who scurry along to see the physical effects of his operation, reduce the motives of this central-European Frankenstein to an attempt to seduce the maids, Giovanni has his own agenda. He intends nothing less than to 'see one more time' his past lovers, now long gone, to rediscover the vision now lost but once aroused by those exuberant girls he later abandoned, particularly the lovely Pauletta.

Behind his craving to evoke the ghosts of the past, behind this spiritualist voyeurism, we sense the obsessions that haunt Svevo, the obsession with ageing, or the obsessive need to end the eternal conflict between fathers and sons, that gulf which, in so much proto-Expressionist drama at the turn of the century, is the substitute inside the family for class conflict, but which also humanises it. Giovanni is not a lawyer (unlike Federico in *Un marito*), and not even a writer, but his real difference from Federico is that he surrounds himself with a multiplicity of women, starting with Anna, the wife with whom he has played out the pleasant but exhausting charade of middle-class family solidarity, overlaid with a touch of Epicurean hedonism, or at least absence of tension. But behind the tepidity and torpor of married life there is a brooding resentment (a hint of the uxoricide of *Un marito*) surfacing in the second intermezzo, where the serving maid Rita urges uxoricide but only in the safe dimension of dream. Giovanni returns to his wife in the end, in a sort of twilight farewell, making repeated but enigmatic declarations of love:

GIOVANNI: I loved you so much.
ANNA: Will you kiss me?
GIOVANNI: Kiss? No, certainly not. I love you. I never wanted to kill you. I love you. For your sake I will love all your pets, birds, cats, dogs. And I will work for you. I will gladly work for you. For your sake I will save people and care for them. That is the duty of us youthful old people.[5]

Rita herself, the Goldonian maid, is the bodily representation of the myth of guiltless Eros, the embodiment of the fantasies of Giovanni's youth, the sentimental relic of times past. Giovanni gives life to private associations, mixing time and desire, indulging his own visions, depriving the others of any objective existence, making them clusters of associations inside his own being. Rita miraculously becomes Pauletta, a parody of Goethe's Gretchen, caught up in an episode which causes our hero to sink briefly into the low comedy of the Atellan farce. With Rita, Giovanni constructs a *mise-en-scène* of a stolen but interrupted kiss, complete with legalistic bickering and attempts to outflank her feigned defences: the

saddest of seductions. It is melancholia that, as in *Un marito,* connects this
scene with others, connects Rita the actress and Pauletta the character, as
previously Bice and Clara. The ambiguous rapport between the girl and
the old man parallels that between father and daughter so common in
Scandinavian and Pirandellian theatre. Rita's mother's name is Giovanna, a
name similar to Anna, the name of the protagonist's wife. The girls who
ought to flourish in the figure of the maid were never actually possessed
in the past, because of their very availability and their overwhelming
desirability. Giovanni makes this confession to his wife:

GIOVANNI:	I found the whole world turned upside down. Kissing didn't mean anything any more. I kissed Rita. . .
ANNA:	Yes, like a father kisses his daughter.
GIOVANNI (*impatiently*):	OK – like a father kisses someone else's daughter.

(p. 561)

There is, however, a third woman on the stage, Emma, Valentino's
widow, a daughter in mourning like the stepdaughter in *Six Characters in
Search of an Author.* An unloving father and a daughter without a husband –
an odd couple! When she finds her father sunk in his biblical (therefore
Jewish) sleep, like Lot, in a state of, she believes, post-coital drunkenness,
she immediately decides to marry the awkward Enrico, the dead man's
friend (and yet another Zeno-surrogate) so that he will protect her against
her rejuvenated father. The peaceful, bourgeois drawing-room cannot fail
occasionally to evoke another scene, the adjacent cemetery. There is an
anxious link between the two, the Futurist automobile that has replaced the
horse-drawn carriage but has multiplied its ancient destructive power.
Often in the later Svevo, as though prophesying his own demise, there
are buses or cars that bring metaphysical or baroque tremors to the *Ville
industrielle.* Rather than doctors, it is the car that expresses fear and desire
for death, its dark form casting a shadow over Giovanni's senseless
operation. The nightmarish fear of losing Umbertino, the spoiled grandson, of seeing him crushed under the wheels of a car, the ritual of dressing
him in preparation for going out, the insistence that he hold his grandfather's hand are in reality obscure sacrificial formulae. As in *Il buon vecchio
e la bella fanciulla* ('The Old Man and the Pretty Girl'), the novella written
at the same time as *Rigenerazione,* loving the girl implies for the old man

the urge to annihilate her, to get her out of the way so that he can then possess her completely in his grief, perhaps even through writing (even if on this occasion he is a boy). At the end of the play, freed of the temptation to repossess his old ghosts, Giovanni advances the dismal proposal of conjugal friendship.

In a contemporary story, *Vino generoso*, similar tensions appear, ineffable in the sense that they stem from impulses that are not confessable but are the very essence of dreams. Here an old man who gets drunk at his daughter's wedding dreams he is in a cave and condemned to be put to death in some strange ritual. In this modern version of Euripides' *Alcestis*, no one is prepared to take his place. The old man has no hesitation in calling for his young daughter to save him, and does this so loudly that when he sobers up, his wife (the usual ingenuous wife of all Svevo's œuvre) in a paradoxical flash of insight interprets these screams of death as expressions of love. The ancient myth of Iphigenia or, in the Christian tradition, the myth of Jacob, with allusions to the already mentioned biblical Lot, are all in evidence here, with Bacchus not far off to help overcome the moral resistance of the elderly protagonist. Pointedly, in the *novella*, the old man at the end experiences an acute feeling of guilt for having brought into the world creatures condemned in their turn to die and be devoured, a fate like being possessed by one's father, as in the myth of Chronos, the cruel god who devoured his children.

There are many flashes of Jewish humour in the witty thrusts and sophistry of *Rigenerazione*. In addition to denying the univocal meaning of words, to oscillating between the mendacity of every confession and the authenticity of every deceit, Svevo's witticisms explode in a stunning display of paradoxes and rhetorical figures that turn the Trieste drawing-room into a sophisticated Wildean comedy set. The spectator is embarked on a journey towards a ground zero of logic, with sketches equalling anything produced by such contemporary comics as Achille Campanile, featuring doctors who bury their mistakes and thieves who steal everything other than a second head. The script is sprinkled with popular sayings, as for example the now obsolete 'going to the well' as a metaphor for sexual initiation. Speaking no longer guarantees winning a case, or imposing an outlook. Speaking is a means of resisting drawing-room nihilism, and if it brings the stage to life, it ends up nevertheless by invalidating it, as in the central crisis of the child who is thought to have been killed by a car but is resurrected to make a farcical reappearance moments later. While still in full mourning, people manage to make jokes in an effort to overcome their grief. The driver who was believed to have accidentally killed the child is dismissed with a ridiculous joke to the effect that he is somebody who 'careers through the streets with his tongue out, flattening people' (*Teatro*, p. 479).

However, Giovanni's satanic attempt at sublimating the Oedipal complex and other parental obsessions, at reconciling offspring with their parents and seeing anew lost Sphynxes does not end in total failure: there remains language, a healer of wounds and a means of putting together broken pieces and of regenerating faith in life, and there remains too the humble ability of what is left of the self to face the shame of its own disintegration.

Notes

1 Only one work, *Terzetto spezzato*, was performed, for one week in April 1927.
2 The image is taken from the *Caprices* of De Musset who, in his disgust with nineteenth-century Parisian theatre, refused to allow his stage works to be circulated. Svevo did not make that choice.
3 Italo Svevo, *Un marito* in *Teatro e saggi*, p. 296.
4 In Act 1, scene 5, the wife declares that her husband is seventy-four, but in the following scene, Guido and Enrico state he is seventy-six while in Act 1, scene 20, the protagonist himself insists he is only seventy-four.
5 Italo Svevo, *La rigenerazione*, in *Teatro e saggi*, pp. 763 and 767.

Bibliography
Scripts
Svevo, I. *Teatro*, ed. G. Contini, Milan, 1986.
  Teatro e saggi, ed. F. Bertoni, introduction by M. Lavagetto, Milan, 2004.

Criticism
Camerino, G. A. 'Svevo e il teatro di prosa', in R. Scrivano (ed.) *Contributi sveviani*, Trieste, 1979, pp. 75–85.
Chia Romonte N. 'Svevo e la commedia', in Romonte (ed.), *Silenzio e parola*, Milan, 1978, pp. 167–74.
Gatt-Rutter, J. *Italo Svevo: A Double Life*, Oxford, 1988.
Guidotti, A. *Zeno e i suoi doppi: le commedie di Svevo*, Pisa, 1990.
Moloney, B. *Italo Svevo: A Critical Introduction*, Edinburgh, 1974.
Puppa, P. 'Svevo e le metamorfosi della scena', in *Parola di scena: Teatro italiano tra '800 e '900*, Rome, 1999, pp. 23–5.
Rimini, R. *La morte nel salotto: Guida al teatro di Italo Svevo*, Florence, 1974.
Saccone, E. *Il poeta travestito (otto scritti su Svevo)*, Pisa, 1977.
Vigorelli, G. 'In atto la riscoperta del teatro di Svevo', *Il Dramma*, 44. 3 (1968), 37–49.

29 D'Annunzio's theatre

JOHN WOODHOUSE

Gabriele D'Annunzio (1863–1938) composed fourteen tragedies, seventeen if his operatic *Parisina*, the silent-cinema captions of *Cabiria*, and the sketches for four acts of the *Crociata degli innocenti* ('The Innocents' Crusade') are also taken into account. In his dramatic productions, as in his short stories, novels and poetry, D'Annunzio sought to appear inimitable, though, as in his other writings, the plays sometimes echoed the work of others, notably the recent productions of French playwrights. Though less successfully than in his other literary endeavours, D'Annunzio experimented with most dramatic forms, including opera and ballet, and, by 1914, with silent cinema. Thanks to his forceful personality and the uninhibited expression of his drama, Italian theatre after 1915 could no longer return to the banal entertainment that it had earlier provided.

1895 was a crucial year for a literary change of direction for D'Annunzio, already famous throughout Europe for five major novels, anthologies of harrowing short stories and collections of poetry. D'Annunzio's dramatic turn that year was motivated by a series of apparently unconnected events: a trip to Greece, a meeting with the actress Eleonora Duse and an address to the first of what would become the Venice *Biennale*. In 1895 D'Annunzio had gone to Greece on the luxury yacht of his publisher friend, Edoardo Scarfoglio. At Mycenae, beneath the Lion Gate, he had read the plays of Sophocles and Aeschylus; his first tragedy, *La città morta* ('The Dead City'), inspired by Mycenae, was written the following year. On his return from Greece, D'Annunzio was invited by the organising committee of Venice's new festival to give the concluding address in November 1895. The occasion provided him with his first major experience of addressing a large audience in a grand public room. The importance of his speech, entitled *L'allegoria dell'autunno* ('Allegory of Autumn'), was highlighted when he reproduced it almost verbatim in *Il fuoco* ('The Flame'), the novel he was writing at the time. There the autobiographical protagonist, writer-musician-speechifier Stelio Effrena, rouses his

Figure 21: Portrait of Gabriele D'Annunzio.

audience's passions, and muses at various points on the dramatic qualities of the orator's power: 'in that hour he was simply the go-between, the means by which Beauty presented the divine gift of forgetfulness to people gathered together in a place consecrated by centuries of human glories'.[1]

What particularly thrilled D'Annunzio was the instant rapport between speaker and audience. It was a discovery which returned in the speeches he gave during his successful parliamentary election campaign of 1897, notably in the *Discorso della siepe* ('Speech on the Hedge'), in which he experimented with the crowd's reactions. It also foreshadowed his later rabble-rousing speeches before and during World War I. D'Annunzio stopped work on *Il fuoco* in 1896 to devote himself to his Mycenaean drama, and to his new paramour, Eleonora Duse, Italy's greatest actress, whom he had met apparently coincidentally in an autumnal Venice, shortly before delivering his *biennale* address. During this time, D'Annunzio also illustrated the effect of his words upon the mob in *La tregua* ('The Truce'), the opening poem of the important *Alcyone* collection begun about 1900. Theatrical productions presented him with the possibility of an instant rapport, without the attendant aggravation of a political contest, or without risking dignity at a public lectern. Effrena's words in *Il fuoco* also seemed to imply that he wished to hold up to a decapitated world its own horrors and imperfections, a Gorgon's head that would stun the body from which it had been cut, perhaps a wildly idiosyncratic idea of Aristotle's view of pity and fear. Certainly D'Annunzio's plays would reveal a darker, grotesquely harrowing side of humanity and may be seen to illustrate a philosophy of drama all his own. But the use of rhetoric to sway a crowd had obvious political implications. D'Annunzio was a nationalist, and political ambition often shows through in his plays. Significantly, Effrena also reveals in *Il fuoco* D'Annunzio's preoccupation within his dramas to establish an Italian national theatre akin to his idol Wagner's *Festspieltheater* at Bayreuth.

Eleonora Duse (1858–1924) was in great demand as Italy's leading actress by the time she met D'Annunzio in 1895. Until that point, her fame rested on performances of mainly traditional bourgeois drama, largely in translation, but by mid 1894 these had begun to bore her. In correspondence with her protector Arrigo Boito she speaks of the tedious artificiality of acting in contemporary theatrical productions, 'amongst those papier mâché trees padded with green canvas' (8 May 1894). The theme of tedium returns throughout their exchanges, notably when she writes that she is 'terrified of taking up so-called work again with the eternal *Dame aux Camélias*; my very mouth by now refuses to say those words! Boredom, boredom, more deadly to the artiste than any physical danger.'[2] Her letters also contained requests for copies of D'Annunzio's latest fiction. D'Annunzio would supply the need for a new and often shocking type of drama, which would satisfy Duse's immediate desire for novelty, and she in turn would provide another catalyst for D'Annunzio's new literary direction, not least because she began to pour her wealth into his ever more glamorously exotic stage productions.

At the turn of the century, Eleonora Duse was second only to Sarah Bernhardt in her European reputation and D'Annunzio's celebrity on the stages of London, Paris, and Berlin would be enhanced by her performances of his plays. She would also take D'Annunzio's plays on tour to Russia, the United States, South America and Egypt. In this way Eleonora's young protégé was able to consolidate his reputation with littérateurs of the standing of Anatole France, Romain Rolland, Jean Moréas and J. K. Huysmans. Even James Joyce, who became an aficionado of D'Annunzio's plays, made the tedious journey from Dublin to London to see Duse perform. Before that generous publicity, however, and unfortunately for Eleonora's initial ambition to have the first Dannunzian play as a vehicle for herself, the author had determined to give his *Città morta* ('Dead City') a European launch of his own design. D'Annunzio secretly negotiated with Sarah Bernhardt to produce and act in the play. In the event it meant waiting a further two years before Bernhardt's busy schedule allowed her to do as he asked and put on his *Ville morte* in Paris.

Eleonora, understandably angry that she had been passed over for her French rival, had to be assuaged by a play written purely for her. In fact in 1897 D'Annunzio's *Sogno d'un mattino di primavera* ('Spring Morning's Dream'), a one-act drama dashed off hurriedly (in just ten days) preceded *La città morta* in a production in June 1897 by Duse and her company at Bernhardt's own theatre, La Renaissance, in Paris. It was a slightly inauspicious beginning to D'Annunzio's dramatic career, not helped by the quality of his plot. In this first *Sogno,* set in a Tuscan villa, Giuliano, adulterous lover of Isabella, is murdered by Isabella's husband. After hugging Giuliano's dead body to herself all night, Isabella emerges next morning, drenched in his blood and insane. Her sister Beatrice is in love with Giuliano's brother Virginio, who loves the mad Isabella: in collusion with her doctor, he impersonates the dead Giuliano in order to shock her out of her insanity. Virginio's scheme fails and both he and Beatrice remain desolated by the situation. Duse was applauded by the Parisian critics for her performance as Isabella, but the play itself was not well received; it had a similarly disappointing reception in Italy. In London the Lord Chamberlain's office banned it. One reason for its lack of success, and for the similar fate of its partner *Sogno d'un tramonto d'autunno* ('Dream of an Autumn Sunset'), written in 1898 but not performed until 1905, was perhaps the improbable theme. Furthermore the intricacy of the plot forced the audience into difficult calculations and hypotheses concerning action offstage, and whereas in classical tragedy the public could be relied upon to know the mythical antecedents to a given drama, in the case of the first *Sogno* they had to intuit what had happened before curtain-up.

In the second *Sogno*, set near Venice, on the Brenta, the ageing Dogoressa Gradeniga, in order to further her affair with an unnamed younger man, kills her husband the Doge, only to see her lover fall into the arms of the young courtesan, Pantea. She casts a spell on Pantea's ceremonial barge, the *bucintoro*. The curse is worked out when the noble Priamo Gritti and others in rival groups attack the barge and incinerate Pantea and her lovers. It was a play in which critics were not slow to see the association between the ageing Duse-Gradeniga, the younger D'Annunzio and the even younger companion of Eleonora, Giulietta Gordigiani-Pantea. The plays, their titles deliberately echoing Shakespeare's *Midsummer Night's Dream*, and their static qualities akin to the *drames statiques* of Maurice Maeterlinck, had been written too quickly, and their themes were too improbable even for an audience desirous of a revolutionary new theatre.

La città morta was a much more thoughtful, even intellectual, composition. D'Annunzio had taken the newspaper stories of Schliemann's discoveries of a few years previously, added his own reaction to the priceless finds which he had been able to examine in the Archaeological Museum in Athens and transferred all these elements to a contemporary archaeological dig at Mycenae. The team-leader of D'Annunzio's fictional group is a poet, Alessandro, married to the blind Anna, but in love with the chaste Bianca Maria. The hypersensitive Anna perceives their love, and her consequent emotional suffering adds to the pathos of the story. The passionate turmoil is further deepened by the remorse and compassion of Bianca Maria, who has in her turn fallen desperately in love with Alessandro. Anna plans to drown herself, in the hope of cutting short her own grief and leaving the way open to the two lovers. In the meantime the professional archaeologist Leonardo, Bianca Maria's brother, directs the excavations which bring to light the Mycenean tombs. Those discoveries infect him with a germ of ancient voluptuousness. He is driven to an incestuous passion for his sister, and partly to prevent her from falling into Alessandro's bed, partly to free himself from his illicit love, he kills her.

Stated baldly the themes appear outlandish to a modern audience, but there is no doubt that D'Annunzio's plot reflects obliquely the tragic history of the ancient Mycenean dynasty. To that mythical and classical lore, he fashionably attached Europe's then current fascination with the new and barely credible archaeological discoveries. He also inserted the theme of the intrusion of the inquisitive present into a solemn and untouchable past, with the baleful consequences that such desecration brought in its train. Almost every Italian critic adduced the lack of action as a major defect in the play, and it is true that the murder of Bianca Maria, the only violent action, takes place offstage: probably it is better thus, and possibly more in keeping with the way D'Annunzio was thinking at the time about the Orestes myth, which is also present here in ghostly form.

D'Annunzio's theatrical productions reached a peak in April 1899 with two new plays: *La Gioconda* in Palermo's Teatro Bellini and *La gloria* at the Mercadante theatre in Naples. The former play continued on a successful tour in the major Italian cities, while *La gloria* by contrast received such a mauling from its Neapolitan audience that D'Annunzio withdrew it permanently from his repertoire. In the first of these tragedies, Gioconda Dianti is the beautiful young model and mistress of sculptor Lucio Settala, who is married to the conventional but loving Silvia. Lucio has some of the characteristics of D'Annunzio's earlier aesthetic heroes, regarding himself as above the law of normal mortals and considering it his duty and function to create beauty: 'when a substantial form has come from my hands with the imprint of beauty, the duty assigned to me by Nature is, for me, completed. I am within my own law, beyond goodness though it may be' (II.I). Nevertheless, Lucio is torn by the emotional conflict between feelings of tenderness for his devoted wife and his sexual passion for the girl who at the same time provides him with necessary artistic inspiration. He attempts suicide, is nursed back to health by Silvia, but chooses Gioconda. In an argument between the two women, Gioconda overturns one of Lucio's heavy statues and Silvia, ever the victim in this drama, has both hands hideously crushed in an attempt to save the work of art. As in the second *Sogno*, critics again saw allusions to the poet's relationship with Eleonora Duse, this time represented by the character of Silvia, whose self-sacrificing attempt to save Lucio's masterpiece reflected a feature for which Duse was renowned, her beautiful hands and the dramatic gestures which helped show them off during her performances.

La gloria, the second play of the season, was the drama which D'Annunzio told his brother-in-law Antonio Liberi was destined to rouse the frogs in the putrid bog which was Italy. It proved to be a political counterpart to the artistic *Gioconda*. The plot concerns the competition for power between the old conservative politician Cesare Bronte and the bright new political orator Ruggero Flamma, eager to reconstruct Rome, the fatherland and source of vitality of Latin civilisation. The setting was D'Annunzio's contemporary Rome, corrupt and decadent, and the play's two politicians represented the old statesman Francesco Crispi and his rival Felice Cavallotti. Flamma succeeds in usurping not only Bronte's political power, but also in taking his beautiful, passionate and ambitious mistress, Elena Comnèna. Following the decline in Bronte's influence, Elena (with Flamma's connivance) poisons him, and spurs Flamma to achieve his political goals. Her aspirations and her sexual prowess are, however, too overwhelming for her new lover, who sees that he is falling short of his political dream and losing the support of his party and the favour of the people. With a death-wish akin to that of other Dannunzian heroes, Flamma finally begs Elena to kill him; she obliges, stabs him to death and abandons his body to the hostile mob. Critics were unanimous in judging *La gloria* the worst of D'Annunzio's plays. It was never performed again. Nevertheless, it is remarkable for certain semi-prophetic statements; one such is made by Bronte just before he dies, when he suggests he would die happy if he could see amongst his fellow politicians 'a true man, suited to the great emergency, a vast, free, human spirit, a son of the earth, rooted deeply in our soil'. Flamma's acolyte, Giordano Fauro, believing him to be that man, declares unswerving allegiance to him for 'the reconstruction of the City, the Fatherland and the Latin Force' (1.2). D'Annunzio might have seen himself as such a messiah, others saw Mussolini adumbrated. By a curious coincidence Flamma's political slogan, *Chi si arresta è perduto* ('He who hesitates is lost'), was one later adopted by Mussolini himself, along with many other phrases and gestures he also cribbed from his older rival.

By October 1901 D'Annunzio had written a new play, his first experiment in verse drama, *Francesca da Rimini*. Published in 1902 by Emilio Treves, the opening page of the volume made it clear that this was to be the first in a trilogy of plays entitled *I Malatesti*, of which only one other, *La Parisina*, was ever written (and that an operatic piece set to music in 1913 by Pietro Mascagni). *Francesca da Rimini* was D'Annunzio's version of the adulterous, if humanly justifiable, love of Francesca for Paolo, her brother-in-law, the discovery of their love by Paolo's grotesque brother, Gianciotto, aided by an Iago-like figure, Malatestino, and the bloody deaths of the couple, impaled upon Gianciotto's sword. The plot contains other sado-masochistic touches of a Swinburnian mode. The play was in effect a dramatisation of the events which Dante had made famous in Canto v of the *Inferno*, and was intended to break new frontiers in D'Annunzio's revolutionary verse drama. For once one of his tragedies received a friendly reception from an Italian audience at its première in Rome's Costanzi theatre on 9 December 1901. The staging of the play cost more than any previous production on the Italian stage, and its very sumptuousness, relying as it did on genuine medieval antiques for props and furnishings on the sets, may have astonished critics and audience into taking a more positive attitude, though some critics considered it a medieval pastiche. For Eurialo De Michelis, usually one of D'Annunzio's most supportive critics, this was 'a fake antiquity which can be compared to the bric-à-brac of (the novel) *Piacere*'.[3] In January 1914, set to music by Riccardo Zandonai with Tito Ricordi's *libretti*, a version of *Francesca da Rimini* was produced at Turin's Teatro Regio, where it was generously treated by audience and critics.

A more successful play from every point of view was the second major tragedy of this period, *La figlia di Iorio* ('Iorio's Daughter'), another verse drama written in just over a month during the summer of 1903, and generally regarded as D'Annunzio's masterpiece. Set in an undefined but remote period of time in the countryside of the author's native Abruzzi it makes use of the superstitious lore and primitive instincts of a tribal community. The drama was inspired by a real incident, witnessed by D'Annunzio and his friend Francesco Paolo Michetti twenty years earlier in the painter's birthplace, Tocco Casauria. There one summer's day they had seen a dishevelled but beautiful woman running across the square, pursued by a group of lecherous, half-drunk peasants. Michetti later used the incident as inspiration for his best-known and prize-winning canvas, exhibited at that first *Biennale* in 1895. The plot of the play depends upon D'Annunzio's distantly remembered folklore, the reality of primitive villages in the mountains of the Abruzzi and upon his great imaginative gifts. Aligi, the protagonist, a shepherd newly betrothed to a decent local girl, has saved Mila di Codra, Iorio's daughter, from a crowd of drunken yokels, providing her with sanctuary in his family home. In the primitive

Figure 22: Performance of *La figlia di Iorio* by Gabriele D'Annunzio, Vittoriale, 1927.

superstitious atmosphere, Mila's presence is seen as a profanation of Aligi's betrothal rites, and a source of dishonour for the house. Aligi's gifts as a woodcarver set him apart from his cruder fellow villagers, while his disregard for their superstitions marginalises him further. Breaking his vows he leaves home for a cave in the hills, where he and Mila live a wholesome, apparently sexless, existence. When his enraged and overbearing father Lazaro arrives to have his way with Mila, by then regarded even more as a public woman, Aligi uses his sculptor's axe to kill him. The final act sees Aligi condemned to a barbaric death, but he is saved when Mila declares to Aligi's accusers that she had bewitched him and that it was she who had killed Lazaro. She leaps into a funeral pyre, and the tragedy concludes. The play was an immediate success at its première on 2 March 1904 at the Teatro Lirico in Milan. Naturally enough there were few peasants in the audience; the Milanese bourgeoisie found in that cruelly primitive world a picture of southern peasant life which they suspected was not far removed from late nineteenth-century reality. Audiences in Italy still regard the play as reflecting some of the primitive quality of life in southern villages and such a feeling at the turn of the last century would have been even stronger.

La fiaccola sotto il moggio ('The Light under the Bushel'), his third drama in verse, was a further vehicle to exploit D'Annunzio's knowledge of Abruzzese folklore. The plot blends a potentially realistic contemporary situation with the passion and superstition which characterise even nowadays some of the more remote parts of the region. The plot also contains something of the atmosphere of the classical Clytemnestra–Electra conflict. Angizia, the former housekeeper of the Sangro castle, has (initially unknown to all) killed the wife of Tibaldo de Sangro, in order herself to become the mistress of the house. Simultaneously she is carrying on an affair with Tibaldo's stepbrother Bertrando, and planning with him to murder the sickly adolescent Simonetto, heir to the dynasty. Gigliola, Tibaldo's daughter, provokes Angizia into confessing to the murder, and resolves to avenge her mother's death by killing Angizia and then committing suicide. Gigliola plunges her hands into a basket of snakes, intending, while the poison is working, to slay Angizia before she herself dies. Before killing Angizia, she tells Tibaldo of the affair which Angizia is having with Bertrando. Tibaldo anticipates Gigliola's plans by himself killing Angizia and then committing suicide. Gigliola discovers this too late as she dies from the inevitable end she has prepared for herself. The play had a mixed reception at Milan's Teatro Manzoni on 27 March 1905, not least because of the poor performance of D'Annunzio's son Gabriellino, playing the role of Simonetto with hysterical cries and mad gestures. The audience, well aware of the relationship between Gabriellino and Gabriele, yelled 'Patricide, patricide!' Nevertheless the tragedy has proved one of D'Annunzio's more lasting dramatic achievements.

The atmosphere of *La fiaccola* may seem more melodramatic than a Renaissance horror tragedy, yet the staged drama has a strange power and fascination which maintains a sporadic commercial appeal even today. D'Annunzio knew the area and the local folklore very well and even an audience in northern Italy would be willing to accept the authenticity of the atmosphere, which tourists find it still possible to sample. Thus every year, on the first Thursday of May in the area of Cocullo (part of the play's setting) local snake-catchers, like the *Serparo* of the play (the renegade father of Angizia), bring in from the fields a rich harvest of serpents, both to demonstrate their *machismo* and also to adorn the statue of St Dominic, whose feast day falls around then. Decorated in this bizarre way, the plaster saint stands during the Mass at the high altar, writhing with snakes, before being paraded around the town square to be shown to the people. The serpent lore of the region, noted centuries before by Virgil, here finds its modern form, and is still very much alive in our twenty-first century.

Dramatically speaking *Più che l'amore* ('More than Love'), written and produced in 1906, plumbs the depths of *La gloria*. The theme of the superman, above ordinary human morals, returns in the person of Corrado Brando, an explorer who had shown his courage by resisting torture by African tribesmen, and who was now planning another expedition. Brando is defended by his faithful friend Virginio, as Flamma had been supported by Fauro: here is the new Exemplar about to reappear from the deep roots of his race. While making his plans to reinvestigate Africa, Brando seduces Virginio's sister, Maria, who becomes pregnant. Despite her pitiful state she insists that he ignore her problems, continue with the project and fulfil his splendid vocation. Unfortunately Brando does not have the funds to pay for his great new venture. Reasoning that as a superman he is above ordinary moral laws, he decides to kill his gambling companion, the money-lender Paolo Sutri, and steal the necessary cash. His scheme fails when he is detected by the police, and the curtain falls on the heroic explorer and his faithful retainer as they load their hunting rifles, ready to do battle with the forces of the law. To any objective spectator or reader,

Brando is anything but a heroic superman. His great aim to go on further expeditions is reduced to personal and trivial ambition, while his willingness to abandon his best friend's sister, along with the wretched murder of Sutri, adds to the impression of a selfish criminal mind.

A political epic drama in verse, *La nave* ('The Ship'), was premièred in Rome's Argentina theatre on the evening of 11 January 1908 in the presence of the King and Queen. The mood and theme of the new play caught the mood of D'Annunzio's audience, nationalistic and imperialistic, a factor which explained the initial enthusiastic reception, and an invitation for D'Annunzio to the Royal Box. The drama has its setting in Venice, where the city is building a great ship. The year is AD 552, a period when Venice was attempting to assert its independence from the Byzantine empire. In the community itself the reins of power are held by the two Gratico brothers, Marco and Sergio, the first a tribune, the second a bishop. Between them they have broken the power of their imperial rulers in Venice by slaughtering the powerful Faledro family. The scene in which this is carried out is worthy of the most horrifying Renaissance tragedy: the four rival brothers are blinded and have their tongues torn out. The beautiful Basiliola, survivor of the family feud, appears as an avenging angel (or demon), causes the two Gratico brothers to fall in love with her and incites them to a duel in which Marco kills Sergio. To expiate his sin, Marco decides to take the great ship and sail into exile, where he will perform heroic deeds, including the transportation of the body of St Mark to Venice. Realising too late how Basiliola has tricked him, Marco has her arrested and in the final scene of Act III is about to have her nailed to the prow of the ship in lieu of a figurehead, praising God for having revealed this splendid way of punishing the wanton. Freed temporarily from her ropes, Basiliola hurls herself, like Mila di Codro in *La figlia di Iorio*, into the flames of an altar. Basiliola is a nightmarish *belle dame sans merci* who causes men to burn with masochistic desire to have her plunge her jewelled sword between their ribs, or to die from the arrow to which she has given a final kiss. Add to these delights Basiliola's striptease, which finally entraps the Gratico brothers, and other more or less shocking interludes in those Edwardian days, and some of the popularity of that first performance is explained. The production was also one of the most lavish ever seen in Italy. The tragedy ran until 1 March and was taken to other Italian cities, including Venice and the Italian enclave of Fiume, where its nationalistic message had a profound effect on the local populace.

In Rome alone the run produced 110,000 lire, an enormous sum for the time, and a useful boost to D'Annunzio's crumbling finances.

Between December 1908 and February 1909 D'Annunzio wrote his final Italian tragedy, *Fedra*, another verse play and a reworking of the classical Phaedra theme. Following the classical myth, Queen Phaedra is in love with her stepson Hippolytus, who rejects her advances, and whom she falsely denounces to her husband, Theseus. Theseus believes her, curses his son and calls upon Poseidon to avenge his honour. The god hears the king's prayer and causes Hippolytus' horse to rear, throwing its rider, prior to attacking him. Phaedra, in turn, is slain by the arrow of Artemis, guardian deity of Hippolytus. On the surface the plot conforms to tradition, but D'Annunzio introduces a new sensuality and new sado-masochistic elements. Phaedra, for instance, declares her love to her stepson, kisses him passionately and when rejected challenges him to split her body with his axe and reveal her heart burning with passion for him. In the third Act, the messenger's speech describing Hippolytus' death engenders greater horror by his account of how the horse gnaws and bites at his master's body, and tears out his innards. When Phaedra is finally killed she dies heroically, affirming her will, proclaiming her superiority to the forces which have destroyed her, and triumphantly claiming the dead Hippolytus as her own in death. Once more, as with Basiliola in *La nave*, D'Annunzio replaces the notion of a superman with that of a superwoman.

Driven out of Florence and Italy by his many creditors in 1911, D'Annunzio spent the next four years in exile in France, living in Arcachon and Paris. On 3 March 1911 he completed *Le Martyre de St Sébastien*, a verse 'mystery' in five 'mansions' with a prologue. It was produced by Michel Fokine at the Chatelet theatre in Paris on 21 May 1911. The main intention of the drama was to illustrate the conflict between pagan and Christian belief during the first century AD, but in effect it is another celebration of D'Annunzio's delight in spectacle and voluptuousness, with elements of sado-masochism thrown in to spice the performance. Surrounded by the totalitarian might of pagan Rome, the Christian twins Marco and Marcellino are about to be put to death for their faith, while their mother and her five daughters plead tearfully with them in an attempt to make them abjure their God and save themselves. Sebastian, captain of archers, revealing himself to be Christian, strengthens the youths' resolve to keep their faith, not only by his words but also, in a practical demonstration

of the power of God, by walking barefoot on the live coals laid ready for
the two brothers. In turn Sebastian is condemned to death, and though his
men attempt to save him by allowing him a way of escape, the future saint
insists on his own martyrdom, invoking their arrows almost voluptuously;
the archers fire at him with a mixture of love and despair. Sebastian dies,
but as his body slumps away from the tree to which the arrows have
pinned him, he is at once taken up into heaven and gathered with the saints
in paradise. Unintentionally guaranteeing D'Annunzio a good audience at
least for its first week of production, the Archbishop of Paris issued a
decree prohibiting Catholics from attending the performance, not least
because the part of the saint was played by a woman, and a Jew at that, Ida
Rubinstein, well known for her stage striptease. Rubinstein had been
chosen by D'Annunzio after an inspection of her fabulously long legs,
but in the play she was required to have them bound. Her speaking voice
was weak, and the play, with incidental music by Debussy, was taken off
after nine days. It had to wait for its Italian debut at the Scala, and an
orchestra under Toscanini in 1926 (by which time D'Annunzio had
become a national hero in Italy) before it obtained its maximum success.
Recent productions include Peter Weigl's 'updated' version of 1984, subsequently shown on BBC television, and Robert Wilson's lavish restaging
of the original at the Châtelet theatre in 1988. Of interest as historical
curiosities, for most critics such productions have left an impression of
baffling longueurs, probably more closely reflecting the original five-hour
performances given at the Châtelet in 1911.

D'Annunzio attempted to write other French dramas during his period
in France, including *La Pisanelle ou la mort parfumée* ('Pisanella or Perfumed
Death'), another family intrigue of a sado-masochistic kind written in
verse, famous for the scene where Sainte Alétis is suffocated beneath an
avalanche of rose petals. Disappointed with its outcome, D'Annunzio
published the original text only in 1935 and withdrew the play after three
performances. Similar disasters awaited another verse tragedy, *Le chèvre-
feuille* ('Honeysuckle'), produced in Paris in 1913, and, in translation as *Il
ferro* ('The Weapon'), in Rome, Milan and Turin in 1914. It was immediately translated into unreadable English by two non-native-speakers and
left unread; D'Annunzio, realising its lack of merit, published the work in
Italian only in 1935.

Throughout his career D'Annunzio had been desperately short of the
sums of money necessary to maintain a lifestyle worthy of a Renaissance

prince, and often his theatrical disasters were attributable to attempts to make money quickly. Possibly the worst example was *La Parisina*, written in March 1912 to placate a publisher-creditor. This was a hasty compilation in verse, publicised as one of the *Malatesti* trilogy, which exploited material not used for the much earlier *Francesca da Rimini*, and which, to save time, contained some text copied shamelessly from two medieval poems recently edited by Giosué Carducci and Severino Ferrari. The play itself had a *Phaedra*-like plot and was destined to be set to music by Pietro Mascagni. At its one performance at La Scala on 15 December 1913 the opera was jeered off the stage as the audience roared instead for Mascagni's *Cavalleria rusticana*.

D'Annunzio had tried to exploit the nascent silent cinema by selling the copyright on some of his more literary works and by writing the captions for other films. In June 1913 he began to collaborate with Giovanni Pastrone, proprietor of the Turinese film company, *Itala Film*. He set to work revising a silent film, already shot in large part, taken from the original novel by Emilio Salgari, *Cartagine in fiamme* ('Carthage in Flames'). D'Annunzio altered the title to *Cabiria*, changed the names of some of the characters and rewrote the captions, using more grandiloquent expressions than those originally employed by Pastrone. D'Annunzio assumed responsibility for the screenwriting, and pocketed 50,000 lire for his pains. The importance and originality of the film lay in the grandeur of its proportions and its cast of thousands; it became a pioneering example of epic screen production, lasting an unprecedented three hours, and created a sensation in Turin, Milan and Rome, before beginning a world tour. The technical improvements invented by Pastrone added to the vastness of the enterprise, which foreshadowed the work of Eisenstein, D. W. Griffith and others. It may be that, however unconsciously D'Annunzio created the phenomenon, since he had no faith in the artistic merit of films, his most lasting dramatic legacy lay in that forerunner of such epics as *Ben Hur*. With the exception of the sketch for four Acts of *La crociata degli innocenti* ('The Crusade of the Innocents'), of 1920, another projected play in verse, *Cabiria* was the last of D'Annunzio's dramatic compositions.

Still impecunious, D'Annunzio gave up the unequal struggle of trying to remain solvent in the French capital. By 1915 the rhetorical gifts which had in part persuaded him to launch his dramatic career thirty years earlier now served him again politically, and helped him persuade popular audiences in the squares of Rome, Genoa and Venice to back the Italian government's decision to declare war against the Central Powers on behalf of the Allies. His dramatic roles as submariner, aviator, cavalry officer and autocratic regent of Italian Fiume would more than satisfy his dramatic ambitions during the coming four years.

Notes

1 G. D'Annunzio, *Il fuoco,* Milan, 1975, p. 85.
2 Duse–Boito, *Lettere d'amore,* pp. 85 and 197.
3 E. De Michelis, *Tutto D'Annunzio,* p. 225.

Bibliography

D'Annunzio, G. *Il fuoco,* ed. G. Ferrata, Milan, 1975.
Bisicchia, A. *D'Annunzio e il teatro tra cronaca e letteratura,* Milan, 1991.
De Michelis, E. *Tutto D'Annunzio,* Milan, 1960.
Duse, Eleonora and Boito, Arrigo. *Lettere d'amore,* ed. R. Radice, Milan, 1979.
Klopp, C. *Gabriele D'Annunzio,* Boston, 1988.
Pontiero, G. *Eleonora Duse in Life and Art,* Frankfurt, 1986.
Valentini, V. *La tragedia moderna e mediterranea: Sul teatro di Gabriele D'Annunzio,* Milan, 1992.
Woodhouse, J. R. *Gabriele D'Annunzio, Defiant Archangel,* Oxford, 2nd edn, 2001.

30 Theatre under Fascism

CLIVE GRIFFITHS

At the time of the March on Rome and of the Fascist seizure of power in 1922, theatre in Italy appeared to be in a rude state of health, both in an artistic and commercial sense, but appearances were misleading and Italian theatre was struggling to come to terms with problems and challenging new developments. Ownership of theatres was concentrated in the hands of a relatively small number of commercial enterprises, creating mono-polistic pressures, while growing competition from the less cerebral en-tertainment of the cinema tended to persuade theatre owners, company managers and even dramatists to move from experimentation towards works which were considered safe and unchallenging. Although box office receipts continued to grow until the second half of the twenties, they were being outstripped by the sales of cinema tickets from as early as 1924, and the few who tried to encourage experimentation in drama, for example Anton Giulio Bragaglia through his Teatro degli Indipendenti (1922–30), were fighting a constant, and generally ultimately unsuccessful battle.

The Fascist authorities initially appeared somewhat dismissive of the theatre and more interested in the cinema as a means of propaganda, but belatedly came to recognise the need to channel some measure of financial support towards the sector. In 1925, they revived a system of subventions similar to the one they had abandoned on coming to power in 1922, to be administered through the Ministry of Education. However, these interventions were relatively small scale and lacked any systematic direction. There was a clear reluctance on the part of government to commit the funds required to set up the state-funded, national theatre which was increasingly being talked of as a possible solution to some of the problems of the sector. State financial support for theatre during the 1920s was never generous, either in absolute terms or in comparison with that which was directed towards opera and institutions like La Scala. It was very limited, too, in its reach and was unable to prevent a decline in the number of professional acting companies in the second half of the twenties.[1] Even Fascist sympathisers like Pirandello and D'Annunzio had to be content largely with moral, rather than financial, support for their high-profile theatrical initiatives. Both Pirandello's Teatro d'arte, launched in 1925 with the Duce's blessing, and the Istituto nazionale per la rappresentazione dei drammi di Gabriele D'Annunzio, launched to great acclaim in 1927, had to content themselves with relatively modest state support, and despite, in the former case, a cash contribution from Mussolini's own pocket, and in the latter case, free rail travel for the company on its tour round the peninsula, neither initiative succeeded in establishing itself on a long-term basis.

In 1927, perhaps with the intention of trying to shock a response from competent authorities, the influential critic and theatre historian Silvio D'Amico published an article entitled 'La crisi del teatro' in *Comœdia*. D'Amico's analysis focused neither on any lack of quality nor on competition from the cinema, but on the low levels of professional competence among contemporary actors and on the lack of state support. If standards of acting could be raised, both through the setting up of dedicated training establishments for actors and through the creation of an adequately resourced national theatre, then, according to D'Amico, audiences would return, and the theatre could take its rightful place once again in the cultural life of the nation.

While there appears to have been no direct response to pleas for special state support, it does appear that the regime, towards the end of the twenties, was finally coming to take more of an interest in the theatre as an instrument of cultural policy and a means of reaching out to the masses. In 1929 the regime's after-work agency, the Opera Nazionale del Dopolavoro (OND), launched its touring theatre initiative (Carro di Tespi), which aimed to take drama to the people, or at least into those parts of the peninsula which did not benefit from permanent theatre buildings. The venture was promoted and initially directed by Giovacchino Forzano (1884–1970), a well-known figure in contemporary theatrical circles. Forzano's earliest claim to fame was as a librettist who had written for Puccini and most of the other major operatic composers of the day, but he had also made a name as a director. He had worked at La Scala alongside Toscanini and in other major opera houses including Covent Garden, and had directed a notable open-air production of D'Annunzio's *La figlia di Iorio* at the author's home on the shores of Lake Garda in 1927. In 1929 he was perhaps more well known as a prolific writer of light-weight, but

Figure 23: Giovacchino Forzano on the film set of *Villafranca*, with Prince Umberto di Savoia and Annibale Bertone as Vittorio Emanuele II, in 1933.

well-crafted dramas. Forzano's plays, having both historical and contemporary settings, greatly appealed to audiences for the clarity of their generally unpretentious plots and to professionals for the strong characterisation of the protagonists and for the almost cast-iron guarantee of commercial success the plays afforded. Prior to his involvement with the OND's mobile theatre, Forzano had not been especially prominent as a supporter of the regime, and his plays, although generally supportive of the status quo and broadly conservative in social outlook, had been largely apolitical in content. However, his involvement with the OND directly led to an artistic collaboration with Mussolini in the composition of three plays (*Campo di Maggio, Villafranca* and *Cesare*) in which the Duce sought in part to define his role in history through drama. From the early thirties, Forzano came to be closely identified with the regime in general and Mussolini in particular, something that did nothing to harm the already considerable popularity of his works, but which presented him with problems after the fall of Fascism.

The first Carro di Tespi season was inaugurated in the presence of Mussolini in Rome in the summer of 1929 before going on tour, and the venture proved so successful that eventually four such theatres were created, including one dedicated to the performance of opera. The theatres were based on a design by the theatrical architect and set designer Antonio Valente (1896–1975). They were technically sophisticated, easily dismantled structures, specifically designed to accommodate large audiences in the open air. The repertoire was a fairly conservative mix of classic Italian drama, including plays by Goldoni and Alfieri, and works by late nineteenth-century and contemporary playwrights, such as Ferrari, Marengo, D'Annunzio, Morselli, Chiarelli, Rosso di San Secondo and Sabatino Lopez. Forzano's name figured prominently, and indeed his *libretto* for Puccini's opera, *Gianni Schicchi*, had been one of the works performed at the inauguration, but Pirandello's was notable by its absence, in part because of the 'difficult' nature of his drama. Forzano acted as artistic director for the first few years, and the venture was extremely successful and well received in the more than one hundred communities visited each season. It generated interest and favourable comment abroad, but absorbed throughout the thirties and into the early years of the Second World War a significant proportion of the OND's finances, much to the regret of those like D'Amico who, perhaps ungenerously, felt that the money could have been better spent on quality drama.[2]

However, even if mainstream theatrical activity continued to suffer from a lack of state support, a lively amateur dramatic movement grew up, sustained, co-ordinated and promoted for propagandistic ends throughout the thirties by the OND. State funds also appeared to be readily available to support the presentation of Greek and Roman drama in suitable historical sites such as the Roman Forum and the classical theatres at Paestum and Syracuse. Although such open-air theatrical performances had a long tradition going back to the early years of the century, the Fascist authorities were clearly attracted by the idea of mass spectacle and participation, and by the nationalist and cultural propaganda potential of such large-scale events in historically significant locations. They became regular features on the Fascist cultural calendar from the late twenties onwards.

Alongside these initiatives designed to broaden the appeal of drama, the regime also sought to introduce some degree of regulation to the world of entertainment in general, and in 1930, the Corporazione dello spettacolo was set up with the aim of bringing managements, artists and practitioners together in a single forum to foster the worlds of drama, opera and film. Although it met regularly during the thirties, the Corporation lacked any real effectiveness in resolving the problems of the theatre, in part because its interests were so broad, and in part because of the presence amongst its membership of powerful interests, such as representatives of theatre owners, who were disinclined to give up any of their power. The regime was more effective in exerting ideological control. In 1931, after having tinkered with existing systems of censorship over a number of years, it finally introduced a new, highly centralised system of censorship, which for the rest of the Fascist period, with a considerable degree of success, dictated, at least in a negative sense, what issues could be explored through drama. Ideas that challenged or were out of tune with the perceptions that the regime sought to encourage and develop through its propaganda machine or its control of the educational system were unlikely to find expression on the stages of Italian theatres.

Talk of crisis in the theatre persisted, and in 1931 Giuseppe Bottai, the Minister of Corporations, asked D'Amico to prepare a report on the state of Italian theatre and to make recommendations for its future development. D'Amico, who had turned down the offer of the presidency of the council of the Corporazione dello spettacolo a year earlier on the grounds that his competence was restricted to the world of drama, but possibly on account of a desire not to become too closely involved with the regime, accepted the commission. His analysis and conclusions, contained in a *Progetto per la creazione di un Istituto nazionale di teatro drammatico*, were similar to those of his earlier article: proper training for professional actors and a state-funded national theatre. His proposals found favour with Bottai, who reported them to Mussolini the following year, but to no great effect.[3]

It seems that Mussolini, still basking perhaps in the limelight of his first two authorial collaborations with Forzano, the recreation of Napoleon's last days as Emperor in *Campo di Maggio* (1930) and the presentation of Cavour at a moment of crisis in 1859 in *Villafranca* (1931), had his own analysis of the problem and plans for its solution. In a widely reported speech celebrating the fiftieth anniversary of the Italian Society of Authors and Publishers (SIAE) delivered at the Teatro Argentina in April 1933, he called on all writers to become interpreters of the new age, that of the Fascist revolution. He briefly referred to the talk of crisis, which he acknowledged was real, but which he refused to blame on competition from the cinema. In his view the problem was twofold: a lack of theatres of sufficient size, and the tendency of authors to recycle tired old dramatic formulas. To address the first problem, he suggested the creation of a *teatro di masse*, with theatres capable of holding fifteen or twenty thousand people. As for the content of drama, he was looking for something which would realise the full educational potential of drama and would move contemporary audiences in a way which the 'eternal triangle' of bourgeois drama would not. However, his words seemed to have had little effect and one of the few practical responses to the Duce's entreaties came in the form of Antonio Blasetti's *18BL* (1934), which sought to present on the banks of the Arno a truly mass drama outlining a Fascist view of contemporary history, with the participation of hundreds of actors, to an audience of mass proportions, many of whom were bussed in from all over Tuscany. This experiment was widely judged as a failure, both in terms of execution and content, and it remained an isolated example of such spectacle.

Precisely what Mussolini had meant by 'mass theatre' and whether this related solely to the size of the audience with no bearing on the content of the drama itself, was the subject of heated debate at the Convegno Volta the following year in Rome, with interventions on the subject by leading theatrical and cultural figures, such as Massimo Bontempelli and F. T. Marinetti. This high-profile conference, organised by the Accademia d'Italia under the chairmanship of Pirandello and with D'Amico as secretary, was devoted to issues affecting the contemporary European theatre, such as the level and desirability of state intervention and the consequences for the theatre of the world economic situation. Many major writers, directors and theorists from the world of Italian and European drama attended, although actors were notable by their absence. Some leading participants such as Edward Gordon Craig were left a little puzzled as to what had been gained from it, but D'Amico used the occasion to propose once more the creation in Italy of a state-funded national theatre.

The conference clearly reflected the regime's growing interest in the theatre, and this led in 1935 to the creation of the Ispettorato generale del teatro, a centralised instrument of state intervention in, and control of, theatre, to which were devolved all the roles and responsibilities, including those of censorship and financial support, previously fulfilled by a variety of state agencies and ministries. This new department, headed by Nicola De Pirro, who was then joint editor with D'Amico of the journal *Scenario* and who survived the fall of the regime to continue to exercise his sometimes controversial influence over the sector within the Direzione generale dello spettacolo well into the 1950s, was created within Galeazzo Ciano's

burgeoning Sottosegretariato della Stampa e Propaganda. This was transformed into a full ministry later the same year, before its apotheosis in
1937 as the Ministero della cultura popolare, familiarly known as Mincul-
pop. The Ispettorato was charged with general responsibility for theatre in
Italy, and De Pirro and his ultimate boss Ciano were clearly prepared to
do almost anything to further the development of theatre as an instrument
of Fascist cultural policy, even to the extent of crushing the powerful
Suivini-Zerboni trust, a company directly controlling some of the main
theatres in Milan, Rome and other major cities, and long unpopular with
authors and actors alike for its stranglehold over the repertoire. The attack
on the Suivini-Zerboni trust was exceptional, and the principal means of
intervention employed by the Ispettorato were the fairly crude devices
of financial subventions to companies and control of the repertoire with
the imposition of limits on the number of productions of plays by foreign
authors and of pre-1900 works. Many companies and individuals benefited
from the considerable *largesse* at De Pirro's disposal, but the true effectiveness of this policy remains a matter of debate. The privileging of contemporary over pre-twentieth-century drama did little, if anything, to bring
into existence the new drama of the Fascist era called for by Mussolini and
others.

While the much vaunted 'triumphs' of the regime, notably the successful war in Abyssinia and the subsequent proclamation of the Empire,
prompted many amateur authors, usually writing specifically for the amateur dramatic groups of the OND, to celebrate these achievements, the vast
majority of such works proved to be almost totally worthless exercises
in propaganda. Professional playwrights could do little better. While an
accomplished dramatist like Forzano was able to give a reasonably authentic voice to the genuine emotions shared by many Italians during the
months of the Abyssinian conflict in his 1937 play *Racconti d'autunno,
d'inverno e primavera* ('Tales of Autumn, Winter and Spring'), which sets
the story of a small family-run business against the experiences and
changing fortunes of the war, even he struggled to maintain dramatic
credibility in his monumental eulogy to the Duce, *Cesare* (1939), the last
of his plays written with Mussolini's collaboration. This latter work
comprises a series of *tableaux* which portray Julius Caesar first as the man
of destiny called to save Rome from decadence, then as the hero who
safeguards the imperial destiny of Rome through the defeat of the decadent
Egyptians and finally as the architect of a new Rome whose work is

tragically cut short. Although critics understandably vied with each other in their praise of Forzano's (and Mussolini's) achievement, Ciano condemned the work's excessive adulation which he suggested was counterproductive to its intent, and he dismissed it in his diary as a failure both as drama and as propaganda.

Playwrights increasingly found the regime's propagandistic demands for social and ideological conformity well-nigh impossible to reconcile with the essence of true drama, which challenges and questions perceived social and political conventions. Creativity and artistic liberty were circumscribed not only by the strings attached to the financial support offered by the Ispettorato and by the operation of the official censorship, but also by hot-headed Fascist supporters who were likely to disrupt performances of plays by authors considered, rightly or wrongly, to be out of sympathy with the ideals and aspirations of the regime. Reputations of authors counted for little, neither with the censor Leopoldo Zurlo nor with the Fascist mobs. Even distinguished dramatists such as Pirandello suffered the indignity of seeing the performance of their works obstructed in some or all of these ways. The net result of such intervention, both official and 'unofficial', appears to have been a drying up of the creative talents of Italian playwrights during the 1930s and a decline in the number of new plays coming forward, given the reluctance of companies or theatre owners to risk the financial consequences of trying to present anything that might be considered in any way unsuitable in ideological terms. Boulevard drama, lightweight social comedy (the theatrical equivalents of the cinema of 'white telephones') and nationalistic costume drama came to dominate the repertoire. Popular though such works undoubtedly were, and there were some playwrights like Forzano who certainly enjoyed a healthy income from the performance of their works, theatre ticket sales continued to shrink both in absolute terms and in comparison with cinema. Not even the popular initiative of the *sabato teatrale* (theatre Saturdays), launched in 1936 and offering cut-price tickets for matinée performances to disadvantaged social groups, could reverse this trend.

Nonetheless, despite all the problems associated with and caused by the heavy hand of state control, despite ongoing competition from the cinema and new societal pressures affecting the world of art in general which tended to transform all cultural products into items for consumption, there were some pointers to a better future for Italian theatre evident in the closing years of Fascist rule. The spirit of such dramatists as Ugo Betti and Eduardo De Filippo was not snuffed out, and there were some notable directorial achievements by Renato Simoni, who directed the first performance of Pirandello's *Mountain Giants* in 1937, Guido Salvini, Tatiana Pavlova and others, clearly influenced by some of the most notable European directors of the time such as Jean Copeau and Max Reinhardt, and in their turn provoking comment and healthy debate in theatrical circles. Even direct state intervention could produce positive outcomes for the sector, such as the establishment at long last of a national theatre school, the Reale Accademia Arte Drammatica (Royal Academy of Dramatic Art). Under D'Amico's direction from 1935, the academy had its own professional company from 1937 and began to develop the talents of a new generation of theatrical professionals, actors, directors and technicians, who would make their contributions to theatrical life after the end of the war. Bragaglia's small experimental theatre, the Teatro delle Arti, set up in Rome in 1937, benefiting from state financial support and, thanks in part to Mussolini's personal interest, was accorded an element of freedom from the censor and was able to give young directors a chance to develop their talents. It also brought into the Italian repertoire important foreign contemporary drama by playwrights such as Wilder and O'Neill.

However, as far as the Fascist authorities were concerned, the content and style of contemporary Italian drama remained as unsatisfactory as ever. In 1939, Dino Alfieri, Minister of Culture, speaking to the Chamber of *Fasci* and the Corporations, was reported in *Scenario* as bemoaning the absence of plays which would give voice to the ideals and values of the 'Fascist spirit'. Fascists wanted a drama that was celebratory and helpful in reinforcing the consensus that the regime tried to achieve. Criticism and confrontation were attitudes the regime did its best to discourage. Even the most politically sympathetic playwrights found it difficult to produce anything of real and lasting value, and Italian drama sank towards a sterility of content and political subservience from which it was freed only with the end of World War II.

Notes
1 Walter Pedullà, *Il teatro italiano nel tempo del fascismo,* pp. 85–6.
2 Emanuela Scarpellini, *Organizzazione teatrale,* p. 250.
3 Pedullà, *Il teatro italiano,* p. 123.

Bibliography

Berghaus, G. (ed.). *Fascism and Theatre: Comparative Studies on the Aesthetics and Politics of Performance in Europe, 1925–43*, Oxford, 1996.

Griffiths, C. E. J. *The Theatrical Works of Giovacchino Forzano: Drama for Mussolini's Italy*, Lampeter, 2000.

Pedullà, G. *Il teatro italiano nel tempo del fascismo*, Bologna, 1994.

Scarpellini, E. *Organizzazione teatrale e politica del teatro nell'Italia Fascista*, Florence, 1989.

Schnapp, J. *Staging Fascism; 18BL and the Theater of Masses for Masses*, Stanford CA, 1996.

31 Pier Paolo Pasolini

ROBERT S. C. GORDON

The theatre of Pier Paolo Pasolini (1922–75) represents something of an anomaly within his own multi-layered œuvre, and even more of an anomaly within the panorama of post-war Italian theatre. His interest in theatre was only sporadic, and he had little passion for the techniques of acting or directing. His conception of theatre was for the most part highly writerly, informed more by his knowledge and practice of verse-form or his ideological positions than by any performative dimension. As a result, his plays have often been branded unperformable and his ideas for the reform of the theatre, expressed principally in his 1968 *Manifesto per un nuovo teatro,* as intellectually stimulating, but incoherent and insensitive to the actual workings of the stage. This view began to change in the years following his death, and in the 1990s, several successful and imaginative stagings of his plays took place, both within and beyond Italy, directed by figures of some significance, such as Luca Ronconi and Stanislas Nordey. Recent critical views, both of Italian theatre and of Pasolini's achievements, have been increasingly warm towards his drama. Here, for example, is Ronconi: 'There is little doubt that Pasolini was no "man of the theatre"; and yet if I had to say . . . what there is of substance in Italian dramatic writing from the end of the war onwards, I would say Pasolini's theatre above all.'[1]

We can usefully divide Pasolini's theatrical work into three distinct phases or areas: (1) his early interest in drama during the 1940s, first as a student and then as a young teacher in Friuli; (2) the intense rush of theatrical creativity in the mid-1960s, when, in a short space of time, he wrote the six verse-tragedies on which his reputation as a dramatist stands or falls; and (3) a miscellany of other activities and work directly or indirectly related to the stage.

1940s

Pasolini was a voracious absorber of intellectual and artistic matter from his earliest school years. Among many other interests, he devoured

Figure 24: Portrait of Pier Paolo Pasolini.

classical drama, Shakespeare and Calderón, at school. He entered a Fascist youth drama competition in 1938 with a patriotic play about the Risorgimento, *La sua gloria*. At university in Bologna, he and his group of friends attended plays and were much taken with foreign contemporaries such as Wilder, O'Neill, Garcia Lorca and Synge, as well as with the classics (a drama on Oedipus, *Edipo all'alba*, dates from 1942). From 1941, first for summers only and then permanently as a result of the war, Pasolini was in Casarsa (his mother's hometown in the Friuli region). There, theatre flourished as a key channel for his cultural activism over a number of years. His poetry in both Friulan dialect and Italian from these years includes a significant number of poetic dialogues. He ran a small school during the war and, after the war, worked in a state school, as well as founding and running local cultural groups which promoted dialect and Friulan cultural identity. In all these arenas he both orchestrated public recitals and created playlets and performances of his own as part of his cultural-pedagogical project. Examples include an elaborate recital evening in July 1944 which included classical music, dramatic monologues, songs and more; a comic single act, *La morteana*, since lost; and a fairy-tale play for young children, called *I fanciulli e gli elfi* (1945, 'The Children and the Elves'). In this ambit, he also wrote two longer pieces, neither of which was performed or published at the time, but which constitute his first sustained pieces of writing for the theatre: *I Turcs tal Friùl* (1944, 'The Turks in Friuli') and *Il cappellano* (1947, 'The Chaplain').

I Turcs tal Friùl is a one-act historical drama in Friulan dialect, set in 1499. It tells of the fearsome Turkish invasion of the region (with obvious parallels with the ongoing German occupation), focusing on a Casarsa family called Colus (Pasolini's mother's maiden name). The youth of the village, led by Meni Colus, against the objections of his more passive brother Pauli, go out to fight the Turks. Although the invaders are repulsed by a providential storm, the young come under ferocious attack and Meni dies. All this action takes place offstage, as classical convention demands, and the dialogue between the brothers, the mother, the choral townsfolk and the priest circles around themes of death, sacrifice and providence, waiting and action, with doses of piety and high rhetoric alongside Meni's cynical contrariness. Pasolini wrote the play using historical archives, as part of his promotion of local cultural identity, and modelled himself in theatrical terms on a mixture of Greek drama, O'Neill (*Mourning Becomes Electra*) and Manzoni's *Adelchi*. It is striking (and prescient in terms of his later work) for its mix of intimate autobiography and the sweep of history, and is uncannily prescient in its portrayal of Meni's death, months before Pasolini's brother Guido was killed whilst fighting in the Resistance (by Yugoslav fellow-partisans).

Six verse-tragedies and a manifesto

Pasolini's theatrical interests seem to have lapsed for a number of years after his move from Friuli to Rome in 1950, under a cloud of sexual scandal. From the mid-1950s he swiftly made a successful name for himself in Rome as a major poet, novelist, committed intellectual and, from 1959 onwards, filmmaker. In 1966 he returned, abruptly and with striking results, to the theatre.

A month-long convalescence from an ulcer, in March–April 1966, resulted in the rapid conception and sketching out of six verse-tragedies, inspired by a rereading of Plato's dialogues, entitled *Orgia* ('Orgy'), *Bestia da stile* ('Style-horse'), *Pilade*, *Affabulazione* ('Affabulation'), *Porcile* ('Pigsty'), *Calderón*.[2] As often in his career, Pasolini created a sort of myth about this epiphanic experience; in reality, the drafting of the plays took at least several months, before and after March 1966, and he went on completing and refining them for a number of years. But there was no doubting the renewed enthusiasm for active involvement in the theatre. At around this time, he became active in the Teatro del Porcospino, a Roman theatre company with strong contacts in the literary world, and in an unrealised project at the Teatro Stabile in Turin to stage classical drama, translated by himself, Alberto Moravia, Francesco Leonetti, Enzo Siciliano, Elsa Morante, Attilio Bertolucci and others. He directed his own play *Orgia* for the same company and produced his theatre manifesto, both in 1968.

This turn to theatre marked (or at least coincided with) a major shift in Pasolini's life and work in many genres and media, opening a final strident phase of his career; one of public protest against, and formal resistance to, the drag of consumerist modernity (fed by, but often in conflict with, the protest movements before, during and after 1968). In poetry, Pasolini's resistance came in the form of rejection of form and prosody and a deliberate descent into near-doggerel. In film, it took the form of silence and primal, mythical mystery. In theatre, by contrast, his assault on bourgeois vanities from within was channelled through the power and rhetoric of the word. He rejected both modern theatrical conventions wholesale: on the one hand, the rounded characters of realist drama or the *pièce bien faite* to the modernist games and nihilist paradoxes of absurdism, all bracketed in his manifesto as *il teatro della Chiacchiera* (theatre of chatter); on the other, the avant-garde *teatro del Gesto o dell'Urlo* (theatre of the gesture or howl). These two branches are simply two sides of the same coin, one bourgeois, the other anti-bourgeois. From the modern canon, there was an element of influence from Brechtian theatre, but only at a remove. Instead, Pasolini's plays use characters as symbols or archetypes, vessels of ideas and impulses, whose voluble confrontations are articulated on stage, overlooked by a form of incantatory chorus or by an introverted, monologising self. They have been described as 'modern

Figure 25: Scene from *Affabulazione* by Pier Paolo Pasolini.

mystery plays',[3] each one intent on staging in turn some of the key ideological and/or sexual fractures of bourgeois modernity and postmodernity ('neo-capitalism', as Pasolini would call it).

Orgia, a piece with overtones of Sartre's *Huis Clos*, charts the destruction of an archetypal bourgeois couple – 'The Man' and 'The Woman' – in a trail of violence, sex and sickness, leading to the drowning of the woman with her children (echoes of *Medea*) and the eventual suicide of the man. *Bestia da stile*, reworked for nearly ten years after initial drafting, is perhaps the most elaborate and self-conscious of all the plays. It is set in Czechoslovakia and follows the poet Jan (a clearly autobiographical figure) in nine increasingly abstract and allegorical episodes (followed by an Appendix of 'fragments'), charting his ambivalent sexual and political progress from a rural idyll during the war to the Russian invasion of Prague in 1968. The final episode is a setpiece struggle for Jan's 'soul' fought between the figures of Capital and Revolution.

Pilade is the only one of the six to return directly to a classical Greek setting, as Pasolini would also do in his famous myth films, *Edipo re* (1967) and *Medea* (1969). The play is set on the cusp between two worlds: the pre-rational world of myth and dark power, and the conformist, bourgeois world of history, reason and order. Pylades is drawn towards the former, and the ensuing conflicts leave him exiled, whilst his companion Orestes pushes through the bourgeois revolution. In *Affabulazione*, the archetypes are now Father and Son, but the Oedipal workings of history are inverted, as the Son is desired by the (bourgeois, authoritarian) figure of the Father, leading to a crisis which will end with the Son's murder.

Porcile is set in post-war, post-Nazi Germany. Two industrialists, Klotz and ex-Nazi Herdhitze – both grotesques – are first rivals, then mutual blackmailers, then partners. The play revolves around Klotz's son Julian, his disaffected love for Ida and his scandalous bestial love for his father's pigs (a symbol of 'difference' and resistance for Pasolini), who in the end devour him bodily. Just as in *Affabulazione* the ghost of Sophocles appears at one point, here Spinoza is given a key role.

Calderón, finally, is the most formally playful of the tragedies, picking up motifs from Calderón de la Barca's *Life is a Dream* and Velazquez' *Las meninas*. The heroine Rosaura wakes up to dreams of three different experiences of Franco's Spain, each of which she rejects: first she is an aristocrat, then a prostitute, then a bourgeois housewife. The complex whole is designed to show the workings of power and the mirrored embeddings of representation and resistance within those workings. The endpoint, or fourth dream, is contended between visions of Nazi concentration camps (a motif of several of the plays) and revolution.

The experience of writing these plays, and of preparing to stage *Orgia* in Turin, led Pasolini to codify his ideas on theatre in the 1968 *Manifesto per un nuovo teatro*. The manifesto posits a new, writerly 'theatre of the word', designed for an élite, bourgeois, intellectual audience of the left, as the only way to overcome the dominance of a bourgeois conformist audience which reduces theatre to empty amusement. (The idea of a workers' theatre is, for Pasolini, hypocritical and unachievable.) 'Theatre of the word' is neither for nor against traditional theatre, but rather ignores it, returning to Athenian models. Action and setting are pared down, to leave language space to initiate an exchange, even an interchangeability, between writer, actors and audience. Pasolini's is, in other words, a theatre of ideas and cultural elaboration, and hardly an act of representation or spectacle at all. At the same time, however, in his plays themselves, the word competes for attention with the fiercely intense presence of the body, the key vessel of idea and ideology throughout Pasolini's work.

Other theatrical work

Besides the two peak periods of theatrical activity in the 1940s and late 1960s, Pasolini maintained eclectic and occasional contact with the theatre throughout his career. Several of these more or less significant activities merit a mention here.

Around the time of his turn to theatre in 1966, his films regularly drew on theatrical models, classical or otherwise. His myth films, *Edipo re* and *Medea*, were in many respects part of the same project as the verse-tragedies, as of course was the film of *Porcile* (1969). *Teorema* (novel and film, both 1968) was first planned as a seventh in the series of verse-tragedies. Despite his hostility to the *teatro del Gesto e dell'Urlo* in his theatre manifesto, it is noteworthy that he cast two of the most radical *avant-garde* actors of the day, Carmelo Bene and Julian Beck of Living Theatre, in *Edipo re*. Also in this period, he planned and made a fascinating preparatory documentary about a film version of Aeschylus' *Oresteia* set in contemporary, decolonising Africa (*Appunti per un'Orestiade africana* (1969, 'Notes for an African *Oresteia*')). At this time also, he was making films with the great comedian, Totò, including the short *Che cosa sono le nuvole* (1968, 'What are Clouds?'), casting Totò and Ninetto Davoli in the roles of puppets of Iago and Othello.

Moving back to the 1950s and early 1960s, we find Pasolini involved as a translator of classical theatre: at the request of the actor Vittorio Gassman, he translated first the *Oresteia* (1960) and then Plautus' comedy *Miles gloriosus* (1963, *Il vantone*, 'The Braggart'). The publication of these translations was accompanied by two of the relatively few essays in theatre criticism Pasolini published. Another worth mentioning is an unpublished piece from 1961, 'Il teatro in Italia', in which he discusses Goldoni, Giovanni Testori and Eduardo De Filippo (whom he admired greatly), drawing the discussion towards his intense interest in dialect, the spoken idiom and the contemporary 'question of the language'.[4]

The same essay also points towards another theatrical interest of Pasolini in these years: cabaret. Principally through his close friendship with the actress Laura Betti, Pasolini wrote several songs and cabaret pieces in the late 1950s and early 1960s (some, such as the unfinished *Vivo e coscienza*, 1963, influenced by Brecht/Weill). Traces of these remain in the torchsong performances in his shocking last film, *Salò o le centoventi giornate di Sodoma* (1975).

Finally, the strongest textual link between the 1940s and the 1960s is the play *Il cappellano*, mentioned above. Written in 1947, it went through several redraftings and different titles in the 1950s and was plundered for other works, before being performed in 1965 under the title *Nel '46!* ('In '46!'). In its various incarnations, the protagonist is a priest or a teacher, troubled by erotic desire for two pupils, a brother and sister. The setting has strong roots in Pasolini's experiences in Friuli, but as the versions develop, the narrative and structure are given increasingly allegorical or surreal form, showing at a textual level the development towards the abstract, ideologising and sexually transgressive plays of the 1960s, which remain Pasolini's most distinctive if difficult contribution to the theatre.

Notes

1 Quoted in Pasolini, *Teatro,* p. xxiii.
2 This is the probable order of conception; see *Ibid.,* pp. cxii–cxiii.
3 J. Gatt-Rutter, 'Pier Paolo Pasolini', p. 154.
4 In Pasolini, *Teatro,* pp. 2358–63.

Bibliography
Scripts
Pasolini, P. P. *Teatro,* ed. W. Siti and S. De Laude, vol. v of *Tutte le opere,* Milan, 2001.

Criticism
Casi, C. *Pasolini. Un'idea di teatro,* Udine, 1990.
Gatt-Rutter, J. 'Pier Paolo Pasolini', in M. Caesar and P. Hainsworth, (eds.), *Writers and Society in Contemporary Italy,* Leamington Spa, 1984, pp. 22–34.
Van Watson, W. *Pier Paolo Pasolini and the Theater of the Word,* Ann Arbor, MI, 1989.
Ward, D. 'Pier Paolo Pasolini and the Events of May 1968: the "Manifesto per un nuovo teatro"', in Z. Baranski (ed.), *Pasolini Old and New. Surveys and Studies,* Dublin, 1999, pp. 321–44.

32 Dario Fo

JOSEPH FARRELL

The style is the man, wrote La Rochefoucauld, but what judgement can be made of a man who is a multiplicity of styles? The very notion would have troubled the French aphorist, but perhaps the most valid and valuable critical approach to the theatre of Dario Fo (1926–) is to recognise and embrace the existence of a multiplicity of masks and styles in the man and the performer. It might be more appropriate to talk of concentric circles making up Fo's theatre, for while he has undoubtedly developed from decade to decade during his stage-life, it would be facile to view his work only as a series of successive phases. His stagecraft, his poetics and his ideology are a swirling legion of contrasting, perhaps even contradictory, currents.

Such assertions are disturbing to the many zealots who have clustered around Fo at every phase of his life, each one claiming that the Fo they identify, or identify with, is the only authentic model. Fo has in the eyes of many a well-established persona as political playwright, so when his *Mistero buffo* ('Comic Mysteries') was first performed in English in Britain in 1990, the sense of shock among critics was palpable. He was already well known to international theatregoers as author of *Non si paga! Non si paga!* ('Can't Pay! Won't Pay!'), and *Morte accidentale di un anarchico* ('Accidental Death of an Anarchist'), and so could be conveniently, if lazily, filed as an *engagé*, Marxist-leaning playwright of a broadly Brechtian tendency, whose subjects were taken from the headlines of the day's papers, whose central concerns were with the forces governing society and for whom performance was a means towards some aim outside theatre. There is some truth in this claim, but *Mistero buffo* gave evidence of a complex poetic, and revealed a creative mind at home in medieval performance techniques and deeply aware of the value of trawling the past for its contemporary relevance. His comrades in the militantly political cooperative for which he had initially performed the play in 1969 had been as disconcerted as British critics. They too expected stage-politics

Figure 26: Portrait of Dario Fo.

to be direct, even rough and ready, and such sophistication as Fo's was distressingly out of place, especially in a writer who claimed allegiance to the popular tradition.

The central task in discussing the theatre of Dario Fo is not to dissect his ideology, which is fairly straightforward, but to establish roots, to locate him in tradition and to identify the complex, occasionally oblique, ways in which his dramaturgy, his poetics and his politics intertwine. Fo is a creature of Italian stage history and is more attached to that tradition than any of his contemporaries. Even although he is a playwright who deals with contemporary issues – Christian Democrat politics, drug-dealing, inflation, the plight of domestic piece-workers, the death in police custody of an (innocent) suspect after the 1969 Piazza Fontana bombing outrage – he is also a performer and writer who could have emerged at any point in Italian history. He could have been the persecuted minstrel in the turbulent Middle Ages, the street jester in the flux of Renaissance court or theatrical debates, the improvising harlequin among *commedia dell'arte* troupes, the Variety performer and even the egocentric 'great actor' in the theatre of Risorgimento Italy. He is simultaneously part of the history of his own time and above history. His intellectual and artistic habitat is tradition, and if, as T. S. Eliot insisted, every creative spirit has to invent his own tradition to which he proclaims allegiance, Fo belongs to a tradition which is specifically Italian.

Primarily, Fo is an actor-author, the representative, central figure of Italian theatre history, but he is also the *giullare,* the medieval jester or popular entertainer who mocked the occupants of palaces both spiritual and temporal, the *fabulatore* or teller of tales who once spun his yarns in villages, the admirer not of avant-garde writers of his own time but of Aristophanes, Molière, Ruzante and Shakespeare, and the one-man performer who moulds scripts to his own needs and tastes as ruthlessly as any 'actor-manager' in the Victorian age. His imagination inhabits a pantheon stocked with works chosen according to the idiosyncratic tastes of the collector, or an Alexandrian library which gives access to techniques, plot structures, performance devices and the whole craft of the writer and actor as practised down the ages. As writer, Fo conducts himself in the manner of a cultured thief, and his knowledge is intended to be applied to his own onstage purposes, that is, to disturb the comfort of holders of power or privilege: Pope John Paul II, Christian Democrat politicians like Giulio Andreotti and Amintore Fanfani and, later, businessman-turned-statesman Silvio Berlusconi have all been objects of his sardonic and pitiless wit. The works, whether the improvised prologues to his stage shows or his scripts themselves, grab attention by their direct appeal, giving the impression of Fo as agit-prop satirist, but underlying all his writing there is a deeply held, intricate philosophy, or poetic, of theatre, populism, politics, performance, entertainment and laughter. In an essay on Totò, the Neapolitan comic actor for whom his admiration was unbounded, he wrote:

Figure 27: Scene from *The Pope and the Witch* by Dario Fo.

A historical, critical analysis of an actor's technique is impossible if the actor does not have a poetic, that is, a code of themes that gives depth and meaning to the actor's personal style. Totò has a poetic that is rich in themes and motifs that weave and dovetail, presenting a whole and complex vision that is always identifiable as being Totò's.[1]

In his later years, after the excitement of the militant Sixties and Seventies, Fo has spent time enunciating and elucidating the philosophy that motivates his work, but he has never become a systematic theorist, so his outlook has to be constructed from scattered speeches, articles, interviews and even prologues to his performances. Chronologically, the first element of the poetics to emerge was the cult of storytelling. Born and brought up on the banks of Lake Maggiore, he came into contact with men skilled as *fabulatori*, men who told extravagant, ironic, fantastic tales as they worked, whether blowing glass or repairing fishing nets. Fo paid homage to their influence on him both in his Nobel-prize speech in Stockholm in 1997 and in his autobiographical *Il paese dei mezarat* (2002, English version *My First Seven Years*), and while Fo is no doubt guilty of myth-making, or tradition-creating, in his treatment of the lakeside *fabulatori,* storytelling has been central to his theatre. It was as a storyteller that he made his debut in the early 1950s with *Poer nano* ('Poor Sod'), a series of monologues, broadcast on radio and subsequently performed on stage. Each tale figures a familiar character, but the tale is given a grotesque and comic twist by being observed through a prism held upside down. Goliath, for example, becomes a cheerful, harmless giant pursued by a conceited upstart called David, while Christopher Columbus, who would make frequent appearances in Fo's theatre, is an eccentric who turns up at the royal court of Spain and smashes over the Queen's dress the egg he was using to explain to the dim royals the nature of the globe.

Fo abandoned the genre of the one-man tale delivered straight to the audience for some years after *Poer nano*, but returned to it in 1969 with *Mistero buffo,* and again in 1977 with *Storia di una tigre* ('Story of a Tiger'), and in 1991 with *Johan Padan a la descoverta de le Americhe.* The storytelling monologue was the format he used in 1993 to pay homage to Ruzante at the Spoleto Festival (*Dario Fo recita Ruzante),* in 1998 to protest against the imprisonment of Adriano Sofri and his companions (*Marino libero! Marino è innocente)* and in 1999 in his play on St Francis of Assisi (*Lu santo Jullare*

Francesco). The list is not exhaustive, and perhaps the Stockholm speech, which opened with a *fabulatore's* story about the sunken village on Lake Maggiore and ended with a reading from a Ruzante play, was as much a storytelling performance as a statement of poetics.

In addition, the monologue provides a platform on which the puckish imaginative power of Fo the writer and the performing abilities of Fo the performer are displayed at the highest. Every creative spirit forges, intentionally or not, the conditions in which his talent will flourish, often in defiance of the creed he proclaims. Even if he established two cooperative companies, Fo is not a naturally cooperative actor. He has never worked with any other major actor in Italy, excepting the special case of Franca Rame, and has blossomed when unchallenged and alone on stage. In the monologue, using the imagination of his audience as the only prop, he fills a stage, wheedling, coaxing or coercing his spectators to see the world as he re-creates it for them, switching from character to character, bringing into existence crowds around the tomb of Lazarus in a sketch in *Mistero buffo*, or ushering them into the sacristy of St Peter's to watch Pope Boniface VIII bully an altar boy. His voice is a flexible instrument which allows him to reproduce the booms of storm at sea, the squawks of imprisoned birds, or the squeals of pain of injured soldiers. The only sound unknown to him is the monotone.

These supposedly medieval tales have a relevance for modern audiences. Although Fo presented *Mistero buffo* as rewritten versions of sketches found in archives, only in very few cases has any source material been found, and even then it is so distant from the original as to make the resultant sketches fresh authorial work, not adaptations or updatings. The *Nascita del giullare* ('Birth of the Jester') is a manifesto for all his work, being the story of a peasant driven from his land but visited, when on the point of suicide, by Jesus, who confers on him the power of storytelling, that is, the power to take the people's rage at injustice and to re-present it in a satirical form which heightens and focuses the inchoate anger. *Tale of a Tiger* was written after his return from China, and while his statement that he had heard it from a storyteller in Shanghai can be disregarded, the tale deals with a soldier wounded on Mao Tse Tung's Long March, and befriended by a tiger with whom he forms a quasi-family unit in a forest cave. The man is cured and runs off, only to be followed by the tiger to townships where it is helpful in chasing off bureaucratic cadres which are harmful to the revolution. Nabokov once wrote that every genuine writer is simultaneously teacher, entertainer and moralist, and while Fo might balk at that description, his stories are never mere *divertissements*.

The storyteller is only one of the concentric circles, but many others are present in his more conventional plays. While still serving his theatrical apprenticeship in the 1950s, Fo met and married the actress Franca Rame. The two have collaborated in life and on stage, and her influence on him has been so all-pervasive as to be invisible. She was born into one of the touring family-companies which had been the backbone of Italian theatre, and had that instinctive sense of theatre, particularly of popular theatre, which he acquired by practice. The popular is another inextricable and indispensable element of Fo's poetics. In newly liberated Milan in the late 1940s, when Fo was a student of architecture, he came into contact with the thought of Antonio Gramsci, whose *Prison Notebooks*, suppressed under Fascism, were made public. Gramsci's distinction between the hegemonic culture of the ruling elite and the subaltern culture of the underlings made a deep impact on Fo, and throughout the vicissitudes and inconsistencies of his career, he unswervingly proclaimed his adherence to notions of popular culture. It was that adherence that made him prefer farce to other genres of theatre, that made him insist in his most political years on the necessity of touring to where people lived and worked, that made him and Pasolini – a fellow Marxist and theorist of theatre but wedded in his 1968 *Manifesto for a New Theatre* to elitist notions of theatre – quarrel with such bitterness, and that explained his distaste for all avant-garde experiments: it was to that style of popular theatre that he returned when the political passions of the sixties and seventies settled. Perhaps Fo was guilty of myth-making on the central point of his philosophical attachment to farce, since genres of drama are imposed by culture, history and tempera-ment as much as by choice: Goldoni's statement that he was 'born under the star of comedy' is equally true of Fo. Be that as it may, it is intriguingly true that the style of popular theatre that Fo arrived at by inclination and study was close to the one practised by the Rame family-company over several generations. They were a family who played for popular audiences and mounted the improvisational theatre known in Italy since *commedia dell'arte*. Fo made his own debut as writer with two programmes of one-act farces, the second of which (1958, *Comica finale*) was based on *canovacci* which had been used by the Rame family on their tours.

The success of these early one-act farces meant that the doors of Italy's major theatres were now open to him, and with *Gli arcangeli non giocano a flipper* (1959, 'Archangels Don't Play Pinball') Fo embarked on what has become known as his 'bourgeois period.' During the period to 1965 (except 1962, when he was involved with a TV show), he produced a play a year, staged in the Odeon in Milan, before going on tour around Italy. The works were comedies rather than farces, but although they were played in the grand 'bourgeois' venues, they contained a vein of acerbic satire against ecclesiastical power, state malgovernment and business corruption that outraged the censors and the establishment of the day. If the target in *Archangels* was the soft subject of bureaucracy, by *Settimo: Ruba un po' meno* (1964, 'Seventh: Thou Shalt Steal a Little Less'), Fo had devised a complex plot structure which allowed him to attack official bribery and the collusion of the church, through the agency of the Christian Democratic party, in the governance of Italy. The setting was a mental institution run by nuns, an evident symbol of the Italy of the time, while the financial-political intrigues are uncovered by the contacts between an ingenuous female gravedigger, played by Franca Rame, and a dead man who reveals to her the collusion between authorities and the speculators. Some audiences were bewitched by the brio of the performance, the zany twists of plot and the carnivalesque exuberance of Fo's inventiveness, leaving Fo himself dismayed, as had been G. B. Shaw before him, to discover that his satirical shafts were blunted by his own humour, and that the audiences he planned to ridicule were delighted by his wit.

In 1968, during the protest movements which marked the 1960s all over Europe and North America, Fo's personal dissatisfaction with his achievements, and his continuing researches into popular culture, led him and Franca Rame to make a very public break with 'bourgeois' theatre and to announce that they would establish a political cooperative, Nuova Scena, to bring politically committed, popular theatre to new audiences in unconventional, or 'alternative' venues. Fo stated that he was tired of providing alka-seltzer to the bourgeoisie, and that he would now become the *giullare* (jester) of the proletariat. Nothing is more typical of the concentric circles in Fo's stagecraft than his adoption of a medieval model to further a socialist cause. Fo reverted to writing farce and the company's first production was a large-scale agit-prop piece, *Grande pantomima con bandiere e pupazzi medi e piccoli* (1968, 'Great Pantomime with Banners and Large and Small Puppets'). The following year, he caused consternation among the comrades with his decision to tour with *Mistero buffo*, a series of sketches and one-man, one-act playlets. The work expressed Fo's own beliefs about the centrality of history for any revolutionary movement, the continuity of popular culture and the presence of political protest in religious (popular) scripts, but not everyone in the cooperative was convinced.

The cooperative collapsed, to be replaced by La Comune, a similar body, whose first work was *Accidental Death of an Anarchist* (1970), conceived as a work of counter-information following the actions of the police in blaming anarchists, not right-wing terrorists, for the bombing of a bank in Milan. An anarchist, Pino Pinelli, was arrested in the immediate aftermath, but died in police custody. Fo's plot involves an investigation by a madman with a genius for disguise, conducted in the very offices where Pinelli fell to his death, making this the blackest of farces. The action concerns contemporary Italian history and most of the characters are based on people involved in the events, but the treatment is rooted in traditional Italian farce, with the madman a modern-day version of the impish, sly, contriving Harlequin of *commedia dell'arte*.

Other works from the same time dealt with contemporary issues, such as the Palestinian conflict (*Fedayn*, 1972), or were written in response to requests from audiences, like the play on domestic work, *Vorrei morire anche stasera se dovessi sapere che non è servito a niente* (1970, 'I Would Like to Die This Evening if I Knew It Was Useless'). This latter work was also critical of the Italian Communist Party, as Fo aligned himself increasingly with the extra-parliamentary left. This cooperative too proved fragile and by 1973 had split. Fo's own views had not changed, and he had another success in 1974 with *Can't Pay! Won't Pay!*. Although it was played around the world as a wild farce, it reflected a moment when inflation was soaring and many Italians decided they were entitled to set their own fare on public transport or to take from supermarkets goods they believed overpriced. However, the energy was draining from the mass political movements as the excesses of terrorism nauseated many who had advocated 'revolution' without enquiring too deeply into what that might involve. This play can be taken as marking the end of the period of Fo's directly political theatre, but he remained a radical thinker, and committed to popular theatre.

The principal cause he adopted in the mid-seventies, under the promptings of Franca Rame, was feminism. Attribution of authorship to individual pieces from this period is delicate: some scripts are credited to Fo alone and others to the couple jointly. Others again, such as *Lo stupro* (1975, 'The Rape'), an autobiographical account of the brutal violation of Rame by neo-Fascists acting with the full connivance of the police, were the work of Rame alone, as was the 1992 double bill *L'eroina* ('Heroin/Heroine') and *Grasso è bello* ('Fat is Beautiful'), but the bulk of scripts from this period, while performed by Rame, were the work of Fo and are written in the comic, grotesque style which he had made his own. The monologues of *Tutto letto, casa e chiesa* (1977, 'All Bed, Home and Church') depict the travails of a modern woman having to cope with the competing demands of factory work and housework. *Il risveglio* ('The Awakening') depicts a woman getting out of bed, leaving her husband asleep while she prepares the baby for nursery and herself for work, only to remember that it is the weekend, the time of rest.

Fo's imagination was as threatening as ever, and in the 1990s he mocked the Pope and later flayed Silvio Berlusconi with the same irony and sardonic wit he had displayed earlier. He took to directing opera, notably Rossini, detecting in him the spirit of the *commedia dell'arte*, although many musical critics were irritated by the onstage flurry of flags and movement which made it difficult to concentrate on the music. The Comédie Française invited him to produce Molière, and he himself produced a work in homage to Ruzante, the Venetian Renaissance playwright whom he regarded as his alter ego. All these activities were in a certain sense an acknowledgement of debts to predecessors and a claim to his own place in a tradition. In 1997, he was awarded the Nobel prize for literature, a decision which caused controversy in Italy but which was accepted calmly worldwide as a recognition of his position as the most performed living playwright of his generation. Fo continued to work with unabated energy, refusing all efforts to consign him safely to the ranks of the grand old men.

Note
1 Dario Fo, *Totò*, p. 9.

Bibliography
Works
Dario Fo, *Commedie*, 13 Vols., Turin, 1966–98.
　Manuale minimo dell'attore, Turin, 1987.
　Totò, manuale dell'attor comico, Turin, 1991.
　Il paese dei mezarat, Milan, 2002.

Translations

Dario Fo (various translators), *Plays,* 3 Vols., London, 1992–8.

(trans. Joseph Farrell), *Tricks of the Trade,* London, 1991.

(trans. Joseph Farrell), *My First Seven Years,* London, 2005.

Criticism

Behan, T. *Dario Fo: Revolutionary Theatre,* London, 2000.

Binni, L. *Attento te! Il teatro politico di Dario Fo,* Verona, 1975.

Dario Fo, Florence, 1977.

Cappa, M. and Nepoti, R. *Dario Fo,* Rome, 1982.

Farrell, J. *Dario Fo & Franca Rame: Harlequins of the Revolution,* London, 2001.

Farrell, J. and Scuderi, A. (eds.), *Dario Fo: Stage, Text, and Tradition,* Carbondale and Edwardsville, IL, 2000.

Hirst, D. *Dario Fo and Franca Rame,* London, 1989.

Jenkins, R. *Dario Fo & Franca Rame: Artful Laughter,* New York, 2001.

Mitchell, T. *Dario Fo: The People's Court Jester,* 2nd edn, London, 1999.

Puppa, P. *Il teatro di Dario Fo: dalla scena alla piazza,* Venice, 1978.

Scuderi, A. *Dario Fo and Popular Performance,* Ottawa, 1998.

Valentini, C. *La storia di Dario Fo,* Milan, 1977.

33 Contemporary women's theatre

SHARON WOOD

In 1954 the American writer and theatre critic Eric Bentley commented that 'Italy, ever as poor in drama as she is rich in theatricality, is finding that a profession of playwrights cannot be legislated into existence even with the help of subsidies.'[1] Within this context it is hardly surprising that contributions to the genre by women have been slow to gather critical mass. A form which requires the cooperation (or establishment) of theatre companies, financial backing and the acknowledgment of female authority in a public cultural sphere was inevitably resistant to incursions by women, whose contribution was decanted into performance rather than authorship. In the late nineteenth and early twentieth centuries, actresses such as Adelaide Ristori, the Grammatica sisters, Giacinta Pezzana, Eleonora Duse and Marta Abba achieved an acclaim never contemplated for or by women writers of the genre.

While women wrote in growing numbers over the course of the twentieth century, becoming increasingly highly regarded as novelists and poets, success on the stage was limited and partial. There had been sporadic attempts to write for the stage, albeit largely by women who made their living from writing in other genres and fields; those who did write for the stage were swiftly sidelined or erased. Anna Maria Mozzoni was a political socialist activist and wrote *Le Masque de fer* in French when she was only eighteen, in 1853; Carmela Baricelli and Gualberta Adelaide Beccari, who founded the journals *L'alleanza* and *La donna* respectively, in the period following unification, wrote for the theatre, and Beccari was particularly attentive to the theatre in her magazine. In 1879 a positive review in *La donna* of a one-act play by Teresa Sormanni nonetheless noted a lamentable 'look of half laughter, half compassion on the lips of the men in the audience', a desire to 'inflict a solemn lesson on the ever increasing daring of women who, having invaded schools, the professions and the universities, are now bursting onto the stage to disturb the blessed glories of the gentlemen'.[2] Paola Lombroso affirmed that 'dramatic writing constitutes a literary form that does not correspond to the intimate nature of woman' who is 'analytic', descriptive and prolix rather than 'synthetic', rapid, intense.[3]

It was hardly surprising, then, that women rarely attempted this genre; when they did they were heavily criticised, damned with faint praise and usually swiftly forgotten. Annie Vivanti, a novelist and known most for her relationship with Giosuè Carducci, wrote some powerful pieces for the Milan stage around the First World War; in *Gli invasori* (1918, 'The Invaders') she describes polemically the plight of women when a hostile army invades, both revealing a decidedly unheroic dimension of war and raising the uncomfortable call in rigidly Catholic Italy for ethically sanctioned abortion. Sibilla Aleramo was a novelist and poet derided by Benedetto Croce for her self-dramatisation in *Una donna*; her staging of *Endimione* in 1923 was deemed largely disastrous,[4] while the melodramas and political satires of the Sicilian Cecilia Stazzone from the 1870s are still largely unknown.[5] The plays of Titina De Filippo, highly successful in the 1930s, were soon forgotten in favour of her brother Eduardo, and were reprinted only in the 1990s. Italy was to wait several more decades before seeing sustained and innovative stagecraft by women writers, when alternative theatrical spaces began to emerge within a political climate of dissent, and when women's social position had shifted sufficiently for their expectations to be considerably raised.

In the 1950s Franca Valeri began to perform her own monologues for radio and television as well as cabaret, and she toured shows such as *Le donne* ('Women'). The prevalence of the monologue in women's theatrical output underlines the difficulties of staging larger-scale performances requiring financial backing and female social authority. Linguistically vibrant and socially satirical, with characters such as *La signorina snob* and *La Sora Cecioni*, Valeri was a forerunner for such as Lella Costa, Valeria Moretti and Franca Rame, taking the pulse of contemporary womanhood in unsentimental, comic and satirical fashion in post-war Italy.[6]

As with male writers, until recently many of the women who have written for the theatre first established their credentials in other genres. Natalia Ginzburg and Dacia Maraini are known more as novelists, while Franca Rame made her name primarily as a performer. Ginzburg worked within the conventions of mainstream theatre, even while she questioned some of its practices. Maraini's more overtly political and politicised theatre takes account both of ideological shifts in the cultural practice of the political left in Italy and of pan-European experiments and developments in dramatic form. Franca Rame incorporates her feminism within a left-wing political stance that meshes with the aesthetic of popular theatre.

Natalia Ginzburg began writing for the theatre in the 1960s. Like many of her contemporaries, she despaired about the state of Italian theatre: the paucity of new material, the stifling predominance of a few, almost exclusively dead, masters, the ease with which even poor productions could be given extensive runs and tours if the right backing – the right political contact – was available. Ginzburg's plays have been strongly criticised by some for having very little about them that is theatrical: indeed, they consist almost entirely of dialogue or rather monologue, a narrative in which the speaker, usually female, recalls past experience. These works are intensely undramatic in the Shavian sense. Ginzburg cannot be placed within the tradition of the well-made play, nor does her work reflect the avant-garde formal experimentalism taking place in much European theatre at the time. To stop speaking is, for her characters, to recognise the fragility of their own position in the world, to admit the abyss within. Language is not an exchange of information, unless it be to convey a sense of the collapsing world outside, or the disintegration of affective relationships. In this sense Ginzburg recalls Chekhov and Beckett. Language figures not communication but non-communication: the difficulty of speaking together is a metonym of the impossibility of living together.

Ginzburg began writing for the theatre relatively late in her career, and she approaches the theatre very much as she does her novels and stories. Writing remains an essentially private act translated into dramatic form. Ginzburg comments particularly on the way in which her female characters are rewritten, re-cast perhaps, in the transition from text to performance, echoing not only the Father in Pirandello's *Six Characters in Search of an Author,* but all writers unaccustomed to relinquishing creative control in the collaborative form of theatre or film:

> I usually imagined my women small, fragile, restless, and untidy. But the theatre plays terrible tricks on you. The people putting on the play didn't care a bit if I said I had imagined these women small, and often they chose tall, well-built actresses. And sometimes I had poor people in mind, but on the stage we got people with beautiful clothes, who looked quite well off. I would protest,

but I couldn't fight them. They would say to you that the theatre
has its laws. Sometimes these laws are absurd and inexplicable,
and they take you miles away from the creature born in your
imagination.[7]

Ginzburg's essentially idealist, writerly approach in her works can be
mapped on to the numerous maternal figures, who must be eluded,
transcended, and who attempt to determine meanings that are inevitably
in flux. The figure of the mother is dominant in her theatre, even if she
frequently does not appear on stage. In *L'inserzione* ('The Advertisement'),
premièred in London in 1965 with Joan Plowright, the lonely and abandoned Teresa and the young student who comes to her flat in response to
her advertisement for a lodger, find in their mothers an immediate topic of
conversation. In *La porta sbagliata* (1970, 'The Wrong Door'), the mothers
of the troubled couple, Angelica and Stefano, are always on the phone, an
invisible but constant presence suggesting a distant hold not yet broken,
like an uncut umbilical cord. In Ginzburg's first real theatrical success,
Ti ho sposato per allegria (1964, 'I Married You for Fun'), Giulia and Pietro
are recently married, an apparently spontaneous and almost unmotivated
decision. Their union, not based on traditional bourgeois grounds of social
compatibility or economic interest, is examined in the light of their parents'
attitudes, in particular their mothers'. Yet the mother, who dominates all
three acts, is finally dismissed as the couple resolve to determine their own
lives: 'At a certain point we have to send them packing, don't you think?
We can love them very much, but we have to send them packing.'

A number of Ginzburg's plays are structured around an absent character, usually male: what happens or is said onstage are ripples, reflections,
the flotsam and jetsam of apparently more significant events being played
out elsewhere. In this sense her theatre has been set alongside that of
Ionesco, Albee and Pinter, similarly defined as 'il teatro delle chiacchiere'
(theatre of chatter), indicating as the critic Pullini puts it 'not so much a
defective lack of dramatic action as a deliberate and intentional filling of
the scene with lines which appear to wander at random and which in fact
are the face of an underlying dramatic substance which barely makes itself
felt'.[8]

The distance between the 'teatro delle chiacchiere' and contemporary
intellectual and political movements of the late sixties and seventies was
underlined by Pier Paolo Pasolini, whose 'manifesto for a new theatre'

called for a 'Theatre of the Word', neither the traditional bourgeois theatre
nor the avant-garde theatre of gesture and scream. Theatre, said Pasolini,
should be a 'debate, an exchange of ideas, literary and political struggle'.[9]
Dacia Maraini similarly sought a new way between traditional theatrical
forms, in which language degenerated into meaningless exchange, and
extreme forms of modern experimentalism, which avoided any engagement
with language at all. For Maraini the refusal to acknowledge the primacy
of the word in theatre indicated the rejection of thought, a narcissistic
pandering to the subconscious:

> Theatre has lost the word. It has become deaf and dumb – an
> angelic, paralysing deafness. A devastating, violent muteness.
> Theatre now expresses itself through more sublime images which
> are abstract and diabolical: more and more suggestive, but less and
> less significant. The sleep of reason generates monsters: white,
> libidinous larvae, cackling birds which rise up out of the darkness
> as in Goya's painting, while man sleeps.[10]

Maraini involved herself in the business of setting up and running
theatre companies, participating in the expansion of alternative theatrical
spaces which could accommodate new work by women, while her theatre
consistently took account of both her feminism and her politics. She began
writing for the stage in the late sixties, alongside Moravia, Gadda and
Siciliano. Her company, La Compagnia Blu, and later Teatroggi, were set
up under the aegis of the PCI (Communist Party) and attempted to settle in
the Roman suburb of Centocelle with the cultural aim of 'decentring',
decanting theatre from established theatrical spaces inhabited only by the
elite. Later she set up the Teatro della Maddalena, run by and for women
writers, including seminars and workshops for a number of women at
the beginning of their writing careers, some of whom are discussed later in
this chapter.

Maraini explores the dialectic of the problematic conundrum of theatre
and politics, the confluence of artistic and political practice, and the
innovatory possibilities of dramatic form. In *I sogni di Clitennestra* (1973,
'The Dreams of Clytemnestra'), a reinterpretation of Aeschylus, Clytemnestra is both the character from Aeschylus and a small-town housewife
whose husband has emigrated in search of work; Aegisthus is a good-
for-nothing who lives off his lover; Orestes is the avenging, tormented son
and a *gastarbeiter* in Germany. Iphigenia is both killed as propitiary sacrifice

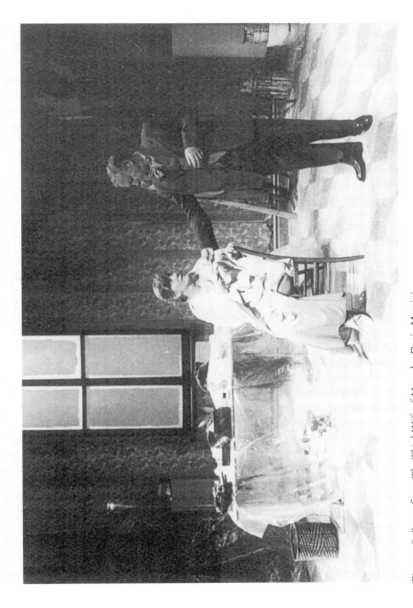

Figure 28: Scene from *The Third Wife of Mayer* by Dacia Maraini.

and married off to settle a debt, subsequently dying in childbirth. The merging of lines from Aeschylus with a modern idiom, the shift between classical myth and the experiences of an ordinary Italian woman in the 1970s, lead to intense and startlingly dramatic juxtapositions. The death of Agamemnon takes place as he lies in bed with his American mistress Cassandra: she believes the murder is only a terrible dream, and sings him a lullaby. In the story's modern aspect, Clytemnestra's belief that she has murdered her faithless man is revealed to be a delusion, as she is threatened with electric-shock treatment in the asylum.

Clytemnestra's 'madness', her unconscious, her dreams, her sexuality which she refuses to suppress during her husband's long absence, undermines the patriarchal order and ushers in an inversion of roles. This is why Clytemnestra must die at the hands of her son, her throat cut at a family dinner while the other characters proceed with their meal. The central clash in the play is between Clytemnestra and her daughter Electra, and constitutes a hard-hitting debate about the allegiances of women which takes the form of a power struggle between matriarchy and patriarchy. Agamemnon states the fundamental Western philosophical claim of patriarchy to Electra, the gendered split of mind and body: 'I gave birth to you with my imagination. Your mother contributed her guts. I gave the truth.' Mother and daughter are as clay within patriarchy, matter to be given form by the male. Clytemnestra makes her own plea for female solidarity:

> You and me, face to face. I'm the same as you. A woman who stinks of onions and the washing. Just like you. But you don't look at me. You don't see me. You think of him, over the sea. Your eyes are heavy with black light. You, my daughter, a woman like me, instead of being on my side you live only for him, you lick the ground he walks on, you keep his bed warm, you are his spy, his guard-dog.[11]

In this play Maraini makes a sustained attack on the family as institution, as purveyor of a hypocritical petit-bourgeois morality and as a fount of erotic perversion. The real polemic of the piece emerges at the end of the play when the Furies – simultaneously the Furies of tradition and three haggard old prostitutes – appear to Clytemnestra in her cell. Matriarchy, the hidden power of femininity and the force of the unconscious, have been tamed and defused: once again, it is women who have lost out:

It is science which has changed us. We have been converted by democratic reasoning . . . we have been tamed for the sake of good relations between men and women. We used to defend women who carried epidemics into the midst of men, now we do penance licking the floor of the house of God . . . We have been tied up, cut into pieces. We have lost our fury like an ancient illness . . . Now we are happy. We are putrid with happiness. Livid with pleasure.[12]

Maraini states repeatedly her refusal to put her politics above her art. This most politicised and consistently feminist of writers acknowledges the supremacy of art over propaganda, of creativity over political rhetoric, the superior power of imagination over ideology.

Franca Rame, longtime partner and colleague of Dario Fo, elides distinctions between politics and drama. While Fo–Rame's manner of elaborating a text, the finalisation of text on the stage rather than the page, makes problematic the attribution to Rame of authorship, even of the feminist monologues, Rame's feminism and her own increasingly recognised creative input had a considerable impact both on the structure and content of their plays. Like Maraini, Fo and Rame sought an alternative circuit, seeking to break with traditional forms and traditional spaces. Rame was not slow to criticise the Communist Party, which she viewed as too rigidly authoritarian and patriarchal, but her persistent attacks on the Right had more serious consequences; in 1973 she was kidnapped and raped by a Fascist gang, acting in collusion with the carabinieri.

Rame shares the radicalism of 1970s Italian feminism: performances of *Tutta casa, letto e chiesa* ('Female Parts')[13] were organised nationally by feminist groups and proceeds went to feminist organisations and women's initiatives. The collection of short monologues, prefaced by the authoritative voice of Rame herself, deals with motherhood, the 'dual role' of women as workers and housewives, sexuality and, perhaps most trenchantly, the failure of the political Left to address women's issues, while the monologue simply entitled *Lo stupro* ('Rape') highlights the continuing violence done to women.

Rame's range as an actress enables her to embody not only the farcical absurdity of much of women's lives, but also its deeper pathos and complex tragedy. Like Maraini she turned to the classics, and in her interpretation of Medea made common cause with Clytemnestra in decrying the equation of femininity with sexual desire: 'Everyone's embarrassed by a woman who's surplus to requirements.' The murder of her children becomes for Medea a conscious act not of revenge but of breaking the patriarchal law which demands women sacrifice themselves to their children and family.

Later plays, written by Rame alone, are equally dark in tone. The main character of *L'eroina* (1991) with its ambiguous title (heroine and heroin), is Mater Tossicorum; having lost one child to Aids and another to an overdose, she deals in drugs, porn videos, dummy phones, all the detritus of modern life, in order to ensure a supply of safe heroin for her remaining daughter. In *La donna grassa* (1992, 'The Fat Woman'), Mattea, 123 kilos, another lonely mother abandoned by her husband, seeks a paradoxical invisibility: 'Besides being decisively closed to all relationships, I'm arid, apolitical, egocentric. I exist neither as a person nor as a woman, despite being obvious.'[14] Mattea's designer-clad daughter, equally unhappy in her failure to find perfect love and marriage, offers little hope that the younger generation have profited significantly from the gains of 1970s feminism and learned to live their freedoms better.

The creation of alternative theatrical female space provided by Maraini's Maddalena Theatre nurtured writers such as Maricla Boggio, Adele Cambria, Sandra Petrignani and Lucia Poli. Cambria's *Nonostante Gramsci* ('In Spite of Gramsci') considers the Communist leader Antonio Gramsci, who died at the hands of the Fascists, from the perspective of his wife Julia and her sisters, and provides both an implicit critique of patriarchal attitudes prevalent in revolutionary politics, clearly reflecting a major dilemma for women in the 1970s, and a meditation on the erasure of women from history.[15] Other works began to explore different aspects of the medium as well as the message. Sandra Petrignani, also involved with the Maddalena Theatre although known primarily as a novelist, wrote *Dopo cena* ('After Dinner'), a radio play which self-consciously continues Katherine Mansfield's short story, 'Bliss'. The final betrayal of Bertha by her husband for the mysterious Pearl Fulton is the starting point for Petrignani's work, in which the husband vacillates egoistically between wife and lover, only to be rejected by both in his turn. The hypocrisies of bourgeois married life and social codes are given a more bitter twist in Pia Fontana's *Bambole* ('Dolls') in which the childhood doll left behind by the little girl of some friends gives rise to transgressive scandal at both a realistic and a metaphorical level. The accusations of sexual molestation of the child levelled at Renato by his lifelong friend prove misplaced; it is his wife who, enraged by the continual parental display of the child ('show us your little red knickers') and her own disillusion, has broken the ultimate taboo; forced to perform fellatio on her husband, she concludes the drama by impersonating the less-than-innocent doll: 'an-cora, gi-rami, an-cora, gi-rami' (Again, turn me over, again, turn me over).[16] Raffaella Battaglini similarly exposes bourgeois pretensions of family harmony. In *Conversazione per passare la notte* ('Conversation to Pass the Night') two aged female narrators, apparently dead, unable to move yet stuck together for eternity in a manner reminiscent of Beckett, while away their empty time by attempting to reconstruct and impose their own versions of memory; the learned but stricken father who may or may not have sexually exploited the maid; the young intruder Lorenzo who may or may not have instigated an affair with both mother and daughter and who may or may not have been murdered by them. The Chekhovian sense of fragile subjective memory and the passage of time is tempered by a modernist disjunction and non-linearity of events, a Sartrean sense of 'l'enfer c'est les autres' and a post-feminist discourse on the abuses of the mother–daughter relationship.

While these later plays exhibit a continuing preoccupation with the role of women, with social and family disintegration, they each refuse to see the woman as passive victim. The expansion of the dramatic possibilities of women's lives, which here have shifted far from the traditional orthodoxies of wife, mother or oppressed female, are paralleled by a formal experimentalism and assurance, linguistic exuberance and not a little desire to shock.

Notes

1 Eric Bentley, *Thinking About the Playwright*, p. 278.
2 Emilia Mariani, 'Donna o angelo? Commedia in un atto della signorina Teresa Sormanni di Milano', quoted in A. Buttafuoco and L. Mariani, 'I volti di Messalina', in S. Ferrone (ed.), *Teatro dell'Italia Unita*, Milan, 1980.
3 Paola Lombroso, *Caratteri*, p. 32.
4 See F. Contorbia, L. Melandri and A. Morino (eds.), *Sibilla Aleramo*.
5 Cecilia Stazzone, *Cinque commedie*.
6 See Franca Valeri, *Tragedie da ridere*.
7 Quoted in Alan Bullock, *Natalia Ginzburg*, p. 65.
8 G. Pullini, *Tra esistenza e coscienza*, p. 274.
9 P. P. Pasolini, 'Manifesto per un nuovo teatro', p. 24.
10 Dacia Maraini, *Fare teatro*, p. 66.
11 Dacia Maraini, *I sogni di Clitennestra*, p. 37.
12 *Ibid.*, p. 41.

13 Dario Fo and Franca Rame, *Tutta casa, letto e chiesa.*
14 Franca Rame, with Dario Fo, *L'eroina* and *La donna grassa* in *Parliamo di donne,* p. 76.
15 For a fuller discussion of this work see Āine O'Healy, 'Theatre and Cinema, 1945–2000', in Letizia Panizza and Sharon Wood (eds.), *A History of Women's Writing in Italy,* pp. 254–66.
16 Pia Fontana, *Bambole,* p. 57.

Bibliography
Scripts

Aleramo, S. *Endimione,* Rome, 1923.
Battaglini, R. *Conversazione per passare la notte,* Milan, 1995.
Cambria, A. *Nonostante Gramsci* in *amore come rivoluzione,* Milan, 1986.
De Filippo, T. *Il teatro,* Naples, 1993.
Fo, D. and Rame, F. *Tutto casa, letto e chiesa,* Verona, 1977.
   Parliamo di donne, Turin, 1992.
Fontana, P. *Bambole,* Milan, 2001.
Ginzburg, N. *Ti ho sposato per allegria e altre commedie,* Turin, 1968.
   Teatro, Turin, 1990.
Maraini, D. *Fare teatro,* Milan, 1974.
   I sogni di Clitennestra e altre commedie, Milan, 1974.
Mozzoni, A. M. *Le Masque de fer,* Paris, 1853.
Petrignani, S. *Dopo cena,* Rome, 1999.
Stazzone, C. *Cinque commedie,* Palermo, 1879.
Valeri, F. *Le donne,* Milan, 1986.
   Tragedie da ridere, ed. Patrizia Zappa Mulas, Milan, 2003.
Vivanti A. *Gli invasori,* Milan, 1917.

Critical works
Bentley, E. *Thinking About the Playwright,* London, 1986.
Bullock, A. *Natalia Ginzburg: Human Relationships in a Changing World,* Oxford, 1990.
Contorbia F., Melandri L. and Morino A. (eds.), *Sibilla Aleramo. Coscienza e scrittura,* Milan, 1986.
Ferrone, S. (ed.) *Teatro dell'Italia unita,* Milan, 1980.
Lombroso, P. *Caratteri della femminilità,* Turin, 1909.
Panizza, L. and Wood S. *A History of Women's Writing in Italy,* Cambridge, 2000.
Pasolini, P. P. 'Manifesto per un nuovo teatro' *Nuovi Argomenti,* 9 (1968), 7–24.
Pullini, G. *Tra esistenza e coscienza: Narrativa e teatro del 900,* Milan, 1986.
Tinterri, A. 'La scena al femminile', in Siro Ferrone (ed.) *Teatro dell'Italia unita,* Milan, 1980, pp. 29–42.

34 The contemporary scene

PAOLO PUPPA

There can be no denying the dearth of creativity in Italian theatre over the past fifty years, a theatre which has been overlooked by the mass media and viewed as marginal by the wider, more advanced sections of cultural opinion. Peter Brook's famous jibe that if theatre went on strike nobody would notice is, in Italy at least, not a joke but the brutal truth.

Several factors have contributed to this condition. In the first place the space for contemporary playwrights in Italy has been much diminished by the rise of the director, and the consequent restructuring and reorganisation of the theatrical hierarchy. Due in part to the resistance offered by the star system among actors and actresses, the director made his entrance some fifty years later in Italy than elsewhere in Europe. The director's revolution brought with it a radical revision of the repertoire, and in addition, as the post-war period wore on, the prejudice against foreign works, especially those written in English, faded away. In *Six Characters in Search of an Author,* the fictional director, interrupted by the arrival of the characters in the middle of the rehearsal for *The Rules of the Game,* declared to his cast, however ironically, that he was reduced to staging works by Italians like Pirandello simply because there were no good works emerging from France at that moment. A visitor to Milan or Rome today would have the impression that British or American works have replaced the French as the standard fare in theatre, and that Italian playwrights struggle to find a place on Italian stages.

It has proved a handicap for an Italian writer to aspire to be a playwright. Italian directors have shown themselves fascinated by foreign or ancient works which they view as prime matter to be remoulded by them: the script is completely subordinate to the director's initiative. Having assumed the role as director-demiurge, solely responsible for the success of the production, the director requires no more than a subplot, a piece of basically inessential material for use as point of departure. This process is not restricted to obscure or mediocre writers or directors. Harold

Pinter was outraged when Luchino Visconti reshaped *Old Times* for its 1973 premiere in Rome, setting the action in a boxing ring in the centre of the stalls, and having Pinter's famous silences punctuated by bells. 'I never heard of or witnessed a production such as this which is so totally indifferent to the intentions of the author,' stated Pinter.[1]

This is not, however, to suggest that theatrical creativity in contemporary Italy is dead, but that it has been directed not towards the script as such but towards the stage production, and indeed it could be said that the most interesting and productive talents of the generation have turned their energies to directing. What emerges could be termed 'derivative dramaturgy', or a 'second power', and in this sense such directors as Luca Ronconi and Massimo Castri can be regarded as genuine authors Italian-style, since they take on the task of restructuring the script, effectively rewriting and reconstructing the play in its entirety. Ronconi first came to public attention with his now legendary *Orlando* (1966), a promenade performance based on Ariosto's epic, with knights on wooden horses careering among the audience and maidens complaining plaintively to passers-by of their abandonment. The same creativity was apparent decades later in his epic adaptation of Karl Kraus's *Last Days of Humanity* (1991), performed in a disused Fiat factory in Turin. Castri made himself almost second author of Pirandello's *Right You Are (If You Think So!)* in the 1979 production, where he reduced the *raisonneur* Laudisi to a wordless, piano-playing bit-part, who giggled nervously any time a search for truth was mentioned. The focus of the production was not on the 'parable' of Pirandello's sub-title but on the neurotic relations inside a dysfunctional family. A metalinguistic approach of this nature cannot fail to be discouraging for new writers. When the curtain rises it is on a revival, a creative one certainly, but still a revival and not an original work. Further, the stage loses its ancient capacity for holding a mirror up to nature, to reality, or to the traumas, big and small, affecting society, a task which has been left to cinema and television.

Another factor, introduced after the riots following Luchino Visconti's 1961 production in Milan of Giovanni Testori's *Arialda,* was the ending of prior censorship, the system which required the submission of playscripts to the classic figure of the commissar for public security. This move, seemingly a matter of only ideological or social significance, became in the event another, and decisive, step towards the autonomy of the stage from a written script which was already subject to the filtering process of directing.

Figure 29: Scene from *L'Arialda* by Giovanni Testori.

Nevertheless, the late seventies witnessed a reconsideration of the scope of directing and doubts over previous styles of director's theatre. In the eighties and nineties, the director lost his central role to become orchestrator, focusing on the supporting cast and leaving greater autonomy to the leading actor. This loss of trust in the director-demiurge coincided with a decline of those forms of the avant-garde known as physical theatre or performance art. However, the most significant developments in Italian theatre at the end of the millennium did not originate as written texts, but were, for example, the productions of Shakespeare by Carlo Cecchi or Leo de Berardinis, or of Kafka by Giorgio Barberio Corsetti, or some striking ensemble performances by unorthodox troupes, above all those of Pippo Delbono or the Societas Raffaello Sanzio. In some, the audience found itself confronted with an aggressive, physical-mental set as well as with a strange and extreme form of dramaturgy where madness and disease – favourite avant-garde subjects – were represented literally. People suffering from autism, Down's syndrome and other disabilities participated uninhibitedly in productions intended deliberately to provoke the audience and combine aesthetic and therapeutic functions. The Delbono group came to the fore in 1997 with *Barboni* ('Tramps'), which included a tragi-comic collection of performers, like the microcephalic deaf-mute Bobò who had spent forty of his sixty-five years in an asylum.[2]

Another interesting phenomenon has been the growing popularity of the one-man show, devised by the performer who may be backed by instrumentalists and who is frequently politically committed. The performer is no longer hidden behind the character created by the playwright, but appears in his own right in a manner reminiscent of the gala evenings organised by the theatrical stars of the nineteenth century. While he may have the allure of a pop star, he seems to have inherited from Dario Fo the need to challenge and provoke the audience.

Such performers often employ both standard Italian and dialect, as does Roberto Benigni (1952–), Oscar winner for his film *La vita è bella*, whose first experience of theatre was gained in fringe theatres, at Communist party festivals or in the popular feasts of his native Tuscany. Benigni's zany comic inventiveness lends itself either to extravaganzas of nonsense or to pointed political or religious satire, and everything from the naïve to the obscene is grist to his mill. His favoured persona is the unashamedly ingenuous little man, at odds with a world beyond his intellectual grasp. Probably the most eccentric and idiosyncratic of these performers is Moni Ovadia (1946–), Bulgarian by birth, who has created his own repertoire of comic, nostalgic but oddly moving and reverential parodies of religious ceremonial, be they Muslim, Jewish or Catholic. The religious aspect of his work is founded on a plea for tolerance and acceptance of all differences, most notable in *Oylem Golem* (1993), a Yiddish cabaret in *klezmer* music. Moni's work is the lament of a people who escaped the Holocaust and gives voice to nostalgia for lost homelands. It also perhaps succeeds in reconciling to the theatre a world, the Jewish world, which had always been suspicious of the figurative anthropocentricism of the stage. He promotes a marriage of Marx and the Marx brothers, telling Jewish jokes of the type studied by Freud, full of humour and compassion, at the expense of Jews themselves.

Marco Paolini (1956–) became famous with *Il racconto del Vajont* ('The Story of Vajont'), a moving monologue on the 1963 Longarone dam disaster, which led him subsequently into an exploration of his own linguistic and cultural origins. His monologue was perhaps the most representative performance of the last decade of the century, and was played in venues all over Italy and abroad. Paolini's version of the tragedy, notwithstanding its easy-going, conversational style, is conveyed in three hours of relentless exposé which leave no prospect of pardon for those responsible. *Milione* (1997) traces events around the airport of Venice and the amusing mishaps of a local commuter, while *Bestiario veneto* (1998, 'The Bestiary of the Veneto'), a collection of extracts from poets of the Veneto, constitutes a tour of the linguistic heritage of the region. The Roman Ascanio Celestini (1972–) is perhaps the most talented member of this group. A fluent raconteur combining syncopated rhythm with a Futurist speed of delivery, he is committed to a theatre which reflects problems of recent Italian history, from work-related sickness to Fascist activity in the ghettos. *Baccalà, il racconto dell'acqua* (1998, 'Stockfish, The Story of the Water') is in the oral tradition of legend and fairy-story, while *Vita, morte e miracoli* (1999, 'Life, Death and Miracles') makes use of material gathered from accounts of peasants' dreams relating to the Second World War but given epic treatment.

The most ascetic of these narrator-performers may be Marco Baliani (1950–) who can hold audiences spellbound with his oral versatility and compelling presence while simply sitting on a chair on an empty stage and narrating historical, moral tales whose function is to keep the audience's civic memory alive. *Kohlhaas* (1989) was adapted from Kleist's *Broken Jug,* while *Corpo di stato* (1998, 'State Body'), on the assassination of Aldo Moro, examined the statesman's last days through flashbacks on his life and that of a whole generation. *Francesco a testa in giù,* (1999, 'Francis Head-Down') concerns aspects of the life of St Francis.

New thinking and new developments have had the effect of liberating not just the lead actor but also the playwright, now free to achieve in himself a unification between playwriting and what could be called 'stage-writing', something achieved by the principal figure of the avant-garde, Carmelo Bene. The result was that from the eighties onwards, a series of tiny cracks began to appear in the rigid structures of theatrical production and distribution. Some distinct, if overlapping, trends can be identified.

The first is a kind of dramatic minimalism, apparent above all in the language used, with a prevalence of different strata of socially determined dialect or slang, after the manner of David Mamet. In opposition to a prevailing and stifling conformity of speech, individual characters express themselves in idioms and codes of reference of their own, but paradoxically this is drama where words seem pitched one against the other, because words themselves are under attack. They had been viewed as false and conventional by Samuel Beckett, Harold Pinter, Arthur Adamov and Eugene Ionesco, playwrights who came to the fore abroad in the early sixties and who thirty years later had attained the status of classics in Italy, where an awareness of the ambiguities of language and the difficulties of communication had always been integral to Pirandello's outlook. The accent falls on the subtext, no longer hidden under the surface script. And yet this very minimalism, which favours silence and is suspicious of words, tends to have the opposite effect, leading to the rediscovery of the necessary riposte. Behind minimalism lies the mirage of the filmscript, since many of these young writers have contacts with film production, and move freely between theatre and cinema where, after the aphasia of the theatrical *avant-garde*, they discover dialogue. Actors too move between the two genres to an extent not seen in Italy since the romantic comedies of the thirties. Interpersonal communication and clear-cut plots, as required by film producers, have made a reappearance among the rubble of the prevailing nihilism and aesthetic experimentalism, but they are often accompanied by a colourless prose which may be an oblique reflection of the minor neuroses, temperamental imbalances and anti-heroic mediocrity of the subjects, and by performances marked by stammering, nervous tics, disjointed gestures and movements, as well as sudden changes of pace, of mood and perspective. The use of professional jargon by the novelist Domenico Starnone (1943–) comes into this category. Starnone was also a schoolteacher, and school is presented as a place now abandoned by the ideologues of 1968, a monotonous and sullen environment peopled by the stereotypes familiar from light comedy or Fascist days. Starnone's *Sottobanco* (1992, 'Under the Bench') appeared first as a novel, *Ex Cattedra,* then as a stage play and finally as a film, directed by Daniele Lucchetti, who had been the guiding spirit of the theatre production.

Umberto Marino (1952–) is another writer who moves between theatre and cinema. *Italia–Germania quattro a tre* ('Italy 4, Germany 3'), staged in 1987 before being made into a film in 1990, focuses on a group who gather on the anniversary of a famous World Cup football match, but whose thoughts go back to their involvement with the left-wing protest movements at the time of the original game. Rock music provides the cue for similar movements in memory in *Volevamo essere gli U2* (1991, 'We Wanted to be the U2'), while *La stazione* (1987, 'The Station'), a contemporary version of the white-knight/black knight contest over the beautiful, defenceless maiden, was also made into a film (1990). School and sport are the favourite subjects of Giuseppe Manfridi (1956 –), some of whose work focuses on the problems of growing up among the lower middle and working classes, as in his *Teppisti!* (1985, 'Hooligans! ') and *Ultrà* ('Fanatics'). The former, written in verse, has a pair of young football fans and a friend caught up in violence outside the stadium, while the latter focuses on a village youth screaming a torrent of abuse over the telephone when he hears on the radio that his football idol has been sent off. Like so many of his European contemporaries, Manfridi was drawn towards poetry, and produced a clever reconstruction of the language of the early nineteenth century in his portrayal of the frenetic last days of the poet Giacomo Leopardi in *Giacomo il prepotente* (1989, 'The Overbearing Giacomo'), which combines blasphemous prose recitatives with arias of delicate verse. His female characters are often neurotic, psychologically unstable or agonisingly vindictive, as for example his angry and aggressive *Electra* (1990), or his *Sposa di Parigi* ('The Paris Spouse'), the story of Camille Claudel, inspired by Rodin, or the morbid *L. Cenci.* Manfridi has become involved in a successful, two-way collaboration with the Irish playwright Colin Teevan, one of whose fruits was *Cuckoos,* directed by Peter Hall in London in 2000, which featured a couple in the delicate situation of being stuck together while attempting anal intercourse.

Edoardo Erba (1954–), who writes for radio, television and cinema, produced in *New York Marathon* (1991) a dialogue reflecting the stops and starts of a couple of joggers in training, but interjected into that process confessions and expressions of resentment, until the metaphysical mode overtakes the physical. His *Venditori* (1999, 'Salesmen') focused on job losses, while *Senza Hitler* (2000, 'Without Hitler') is an ironic fantasy of a Europe where Hitler was never more than a third-rate painter.[3] *Naja* (1987) by Angelo Longoni (1956–) highlights the barrack-life of conscripts, while *Bruciati* (1993, 'Burned') features a couple of clumsy young male prostitutes caught up in a black comedy. All these plays deal with the suffering humanity of provincial Italy, with people on the fringes of society. At the same time Roberto Cavosi (1959–) produced a succession of highly emotional, carefully choreographed, deeply felt pieces based on current political events, as for example his *L'uomo irrisolto* (1990, 'The

Unresolved Man') on a missionary in the Philippines, *Rosanero* (1994) on the mafia as seen by their women, and *Il maresciallo Butterfly* (1996, 'Marshal Butterfly') on the marshal's relationship with an Armenian woman. Perhaps the most remarkable and irreverent of these writers is Fausto Paravidino (1977–), a master of a style of youthful dialogue, whose scripts are collages of disillusioned, insinuating, semi-obscene gags and jokes. *Due fratelli* (1999, 'Two Brothers'), subtitled *A Chamber Comedy in 53 Days*, features an eccentric triangle of two brothers and a girl living in a latter-day version of a 1968 commune. *Malattia della famiglia* (2001, 'Family Illness'), a slice of life involving cannibalistic relations among a group of relatives, was conveyed in the frenzied, comic-strip dialogue he has mastered. He has also produced twin pieces, *Genoa 01* (2001), a brittle documentary commissioned by the Royal Court on the street violence accompanying the G8 summit in Genoa, and *Noccioline* ('Nuts'), on a group of exuberant youngsters who, ten years later, become the victims and perpetrators of police torture.

Others have taken a more overtly literary approach, with no interest in reproducing overheard speech. Rocco D'Onghia (1956–) offers grandiloquent address in places normally judged inimical to such styles, for example, in public toilets. This 'sublime obscenity' acts as a bizarre oxymoron for the precious, prolix recitatives of *Lezioni di cucina di un frequentatore di cessi publici* (1994, 'Cookery Lessons by a Visitor to Public Toilets'), a turgid reflection on a journey from food to its daily death in the body. In *Tango americano* (1994), the butchery exercised by mother and daughter on the domineering father provides the excuse for digressions on the meanings of violence on slaughtered animals. The theatre of the Sicilian Michele Perriera (1937–), director and teacher of generations of actors, has strong symbolic overtones but remains always accessible thanks to the directness of dialogue which has absorbed the influence of the avant-garde but without their downgrading of plot. *Anticamera* (1994, 'Ante-chamber'), probably his finest play, contains a multi-layered, complex range of metaphors for the Palermo of endless lawsuits, a transparency of plot, sophisticated echoes of the detective story and a setting in an abstract space which allows for the initial identification of courtroom and surgery. His vast output, from his early collection *Teatro/2* (1979) to his *Atti del bradipo* (1998, 'Life of the Sloth') is marked by a frequent use of meta-theatrical devices.

One of an interesting group of female dramatists born in the late 1940s and 1950s, the Paduan Raffaella Battaglini (1956–), has written a series of outspoken plays which involve people suffering physical abnormalities and facing incurable diseases and death, but which contain outbursts of extraordinary power and dramatic scenes of total immobility. *Conversazione per passare la notte* ('Conversation to Pass the Night') and *L'ospite d'onore* ('The Guest of Honour', both 1995) are among her more interesting works. Pia Fontana (1949–), who is also a novelist, offers in her theatre a world of untreatable pathologies, of mental delirium expressed in strange turns of phrase or in an immobility of mind and language which explodes in *coups de scène*. In her seductive but disturbing world, characters are surrounded by their own phantasms, engage in pseudo-masochistic games redolent of disgust with themselves and others, as in her *Bambole* (1998, 'Dolls'). Cultural and meta-theatrical allusions were frequent on the stage at that time, as in the vibrant plays of Valeria Moretti (1950–), which combine emotional complexity and searing passion. She is drawn to romantic and libertarian heroines such as the Russian poet Cvetaeva and the painter Artemisia Gentileschi. Moretti has collaborated with cabaret artists such as Luciana Poli in *Le superdonne* (1982, 'Superwomen'), *Dandies* (1987), *Bambine* (1988, 'Girls') and *Sirene* (1991, 'Sirens'). She has also worked with such actresses as Elisabetta Pozzi in *Una tavolozza rosso-sangue* (1995, 'A Blood-Red Palette') or Pamela Villoresi in the prize-winning *Marina e l'altro* (1991, 'Marina and the Other Man'), a success on radio and television in several countries. Her play on Cvetaeva ranks as one of the highlights of post-war women's theatre: in her miserable attic, an equivocal relationship develops between the poet and a thug who has come to rob her. A similar amorous frenzy recurs in *Tavolozza rosso-sangue*, three monologues dedicated to three female painters from different periods: Artemisia Gentileschi, the Renaissance artist who was also a rape-victim, Elisabeth Vigée Le Brun, portrait-painter of Marie Antoinette as she faced the guillotine in Paris and Frida Kahlo, the Mexican painter paralysed after a road-accident. The thread linking the three episodes is the idea of sacrificial blood as a trigger of artistic creativity. *La Viola di Prato* ('The Prato Violet') is inspired by Saint Caterina de' Ricci's vision of the crucified Christ, and is written in the stately language of a sixteenth-century chronicle. Another of this generation of female playwrights, Patrizia Valduga (1953–), who is also a poet, has produced some memorable verse monologues of characters facing death, works which manage to combine a certain irony with emotional, heart-rending power. The rhyming hexameters of *Corpo di dolori* (1991, 'Body of Pain') have overtones of the ghost story as well as obsessions with impending death, not to mention reminiscences of Kantor and Céline. These are apparent too in the subsequent *Corsia degli incurabili* (1998, 'Ward for The Incurable'), a work whose vitality belies its subject matter.[4]

The theatre of this period cannot fail to reflect the varying sense of identity and speech patterns of the constituent regions of Italy, although some playwrights prefer to mix dialects, or to move between standard Italian and dialect. The dialect is scarcely ever naturalistic, but has a poetic function often deliberately adapted to a particular actor's voice. It could be called an expressive, imaginative dialect, often combining different strata of vocabulary within the speech of individual speakers, perhaps to reflect their emotional state and social confidence. It has been said that the difficulty writers have in finding a suitable conversational style once they have jettisoned their own dialect makes the devising of naturalistic dialogue for the stage difficult and unconvincing. The solutions advanced in earlier ages were either to circumscribe the social context of the speakers and rely on a restricted lexicon, or to make the conscious choice of an elevated, abstract diction, an almost self-consciously literary vocabulary. The linguistic exoticism adopted by Giovanni Testori (1923–93) in his trilogy *Ambleto* (1973), *Macbetto* (1974) and *Oedipus* (1977) pointed in that direction, but he combined this choice with a lowering and levelling of the style of the classics. After making his debut as a naturalist with a taste for melodramatic effects, evident in *Arialda* or the almost contemporary, plaintive *Maria Brasca,* his writing changed direction, particularly after the success of a trilogy of works with the actor Franco Parenti, and tended towards apocalyptic, Christian fundamentalism. He himself appeared on stage as reader or even performer, as with *In Exitu* (1988). The stage was made the literal representation of a church nave, as happened for *Conversazione con la morte* (1978, 'Conversation with Death'), *Interrogatorio a Maria* (1979, 'Interrogation of Maria'), or *Factum est* (1981). Theatre was thus brought back to its liturgical roots, healing ancient wounds but still maintaining its own linguistically experimental autonomy. Pier Paolo Pasolini (1922–75) contributed to the debate on language with his *Manifesto for a New Theatre* (1968) where he excludes dialect but stigmatises any attempt at 'purity of pronunciation'.

Various regional repertoires have emerged, as for example the Tuscan group, best represented by the Florentine Ugo Chiti (1943–), now writing for the cinema. His autobiographical trilogy comprises *Paesaggio con figure* ('Landcape with Figures'), set in the early twentieth century and featuring Capataz, desperate for money and possessions, *Allegretto (perbene. . . ma non troppo)* ('Cheerful (Well-Intentioned . . . But Not Unduly)'), targeting the pitiless savagery of Fascism in the region, and *La provincia di Jimmy*, depicting the problems of the incipient post-war economic boom with its shift from party prejudice to Hollywood-dominated mythologising.

In Piedmont and particularly in the hinterland around Turin, Gabriele Vacis (1955–) led the way in exploiting local speech for a series of harrowing, travelling productions for his Laboratorio Teatro Settimo. The emphasis was on storytelling, especially on the retelling of classics, as for example in *Elementi di struttura del sentimento* (1985, 'Elements of the Structure of Feeling'), inspired by Goethe's *Elective Affinities* but told from the viewpoint of some pert servant-girls; or *La storia di Romeo e Giulietta* (1991) based on early twentieth-century tales of the death of young lovers. Alessandro Baricco (1958–), musicologist, novelist, TV presenter, art historian and author of *Novecento* (1997, 'Nineteen-hundred'), one of the most successful Italian stageworks of recent times, is also a native of Piedmont. A one-man narrative piece, *Novecento* tells the life-story of a baby found abandoned on an ocean liner, who grows up on board ship without ever setting foot on dry land and develops into a musician of genius capable of besting Jelly Roll Morton in a piano duel. The tale is told by the protagonist's adoring alter ego, who fails at the end to persuade him to leave the ship when it is about to be scuttled after wartime damage.

In northern Italy, the mixing of dialects has been carried to an extreme by Antonio Tarantino (1935–), a painter who became the leading voice of the new dramaturgy. His language is an assemblage of personalised idiolects and powerful metaphors, giving life to the world of metropolitan tramps, shanty-town residents, beggars fighting among themselves and male prostitutes coming into contact with waves of African immigrants in the hinterland of Lombardy or Piedmont. No other contemporary writer makes such use of religious imagery for secular ends as Tarantino. *Tetralogia delle cure*, a series of monologues by imaginary speakers, depicts a contemporary *via crucis* in a torrent of words not bereft of compassion. *Stabat mater* and *Passione secondo Giovanni*, which he defined a 'Mystery for two voices' and was modelled on the Stations of the Cross, were both premiered in 1994. His *Vespro della Beata Vergine* (1995, 'Vespers of the Virgin Mary') is a fantasy or psychodrama in the style of Genet or Beckett, as is *Lustrini* (1997, 'Shoeshines').

The Veneto too has witnessed a revival of dialect, not least in the later narratives of writers such as Giuliano Scabia, native of Padua (1930–). A director as well as writer, Scabia's stagework includes his evocative *Teatro con bosco e animali* (1987, 'Theatre with Woods and Animals'), his *Fantastica visione* (1988, 'Fantastic Vision') and the essentially theatrical tales of *In capo al mondo* ('At the End of the World', 1990).[5] Sicily too can lay claim to a wealth of innovative writing, often in dialect. Franco Scaldati, poet and actor, was the first playwright to have made a mark outside the region with his mixture of native lyricism and social criticism, conveyed in his lively, disorderly idiom. His *Pozzo dei pazzi* (1974, 'Well of Madmen') is in many senses a manifesto text, thanks to the dualism of two circus-style tramps who toss lines of dialogue back and forward between themselves, but without any principle of differentiation or individuality. Spiro Scimone (1964–) brought together in *Nunzio* (1994) a deft blend of visionary and pathetic elements, while his later one-acts plays, *Bar* and *La Festa* (1999, 'The Feast'), are set in an environment where Mafia violence threatens people whose level of involvement with crime remains tantalisingly ambiguous.[6]

The great Neapolitan tradition still flourishes, with descendants of Eduardo and Peppino De Filippo, and of Eduardo Scarpetta managing theatre companies dedicated both to presenting the work of their illustrious ancestors and to promoting new work. Current writers are as fascinated by the city itself as were their predecessors. Some clever and linguistically polished work has come from Vincenzo Salemme (1957–) who has exploited a well-tried boulevard style to dramatise middle-class concerns, social deprivation and handicaps, and has also made a successful excursion into film with *Premiata Pasticceria Bellavista* (1999). Ruggero Cappuccio's *Shakespea Re di Napoli* (1994), whose title is an untranslatable pun on Shakespeare as King of Naples, is a fanciful, comic fantasy of a visit to Naples by the Bard, written entirely in dialect and free of the passages in standard Italian which writers such as De Filippo inserted to facilitate comprehension for non-Neapolitans. *Ferdinando* (1985) by Annibale Ruccello (1956–86), whose life was cut tragically short by a car accident, has attained the status of modern classic. It features a group of old hags and shady priests expressing nostalgia for the old days and for the Bourbon dynasty. Ruccello had made his debut with *Le cinque rose per Jennifer* (1980, 'Five Roses for Jennifer'), a play on the world of transvestites, a recurring metaphor for the recent Neapolitan school. His delightful *Weekend* (1983) concerns the imaginary adventures of an ageing teacher, an unmarried woman taunted by virile young students and plumbers, who expresses her nervous changes of mood in abrupt switches between Italian and dialect. The first work of Mario Santanelli (1938–), was *Uscita d'emergenza* (1980, 'Emergency Exit'), in which the De Filippo of *Le voci di dentro* ('Inner Voices') is taunted by outsiders who could have emerged from Samuel Beckett. The sense of continuing tradition in such work scarcely needs labouring, but Santanelli went his own way, examining various types of female neurosis and of ideological debate with *Regina madre* (1985, 'Queen Mother') and *Bellavita Carolina* (1987), which features a female undertaker who has a personal reliquary at home, including such items as a bust of Saint Januarius, patron saint of Naples, and blood from her first period.

With Enzo Moscato (1948–) we arrive at the 'night' which Eduardo De Filippo in the famous closing line of *Napoli milionaria!* hoped would pass quickly. Moscato lays bare the dark underbelly of the city and allows it to dominate the scene. 'Life is filth', says a character in *Pièce noire,* and elsewhere in that play man's existential condition is compared to 'a circle in Dante's Hell', or to a 'Babylon'. In *Partitura* ('Musical Score'), even if it is stated that 'the night has passed', Naples is apostrophised as 'Ugly, filthy, lurid sewer of a city'. Moscato treats deviance of all kinds as the norm, or as majority behaviour. The dark side of the family can be regarded as his subject of choice, and his preference is for a melodramatic situation interspersed with popular songs, as in *Festa al celeste e nobile santuario* (1983, 'Feast in the Noble, Celestial Shrine'), *Pièce noire* (1983), *Ragazze sole con qualche esperienza* (1985, 'Single Girls with Experience'), or *Bordello di mare con città* (1987, 'Seaside Brothel and City'). His plays offer a parade of transsexuals and transvestites in ritual clothing, mere celibate automata or bored dolls participating in a romantic, comic vaudeville. With the loss of any residual sexual identity the actor can be male or female and can freely indulge a wide range of moods and expressions. The sacred and profane overlap, so that brothels, for instance, can be blessed by visits from cardinals while still fully operational. The church and the whorehouse, decorated as the Christmas crib, complement one another, and the relationship between the two is a mirror-image for Neapolitan slum-dwellers of the relationship between drawing-room and brothel for the middle classes. *Rasoi* (1992, 'Razors'), part lecture and part performance, part drama and part recital of kitsch song, demonstrates Moscato's preference for the monologue which marked his last productions.

Finally, what might be called the dramaturgy of the stage deserves a mention, that is, work where the script is produced by directors and actors who are themselves playwrights. Luigi Squarzina (1922–) and Mario Prosperi (1940–) can be taken as examples. Squarzina's works include the agonising *Tre quarti di luna* (1953, 'Three-Quarter Moon') on the subject of Italian education at the time of the March on Rome, and the funereal vaudeville *Siamo momentaneamente assenti* (1992, 'We Are Temporarily Absent'). Prosperi's plays include *Il docente furioso* (1989, 'The Furious Professor'), a portrait of the intellectual facing a terrorist threat. Vittorio Franceschi (1936–), actor-author, is an author of considerable versatility who writes by preference for specific companies or actors. In the late sixties, he was a member of the Nuova Scena political-theatrical cooperative along with Dario Fo, and produced committed works like *Un sogno di sinistra* ('A Dream of the Left'), about a bourgeois militant who associates with the Left when it is fashionable but then returns to his class background. After Fo left the company, Franceschi remained as resident writer, but eventually went his own way, producing such works as *Scacco pazzo* (1991, 'Checkmate'), where two brothers are involved in continual idiosyncratic role-play after an incident which drove one to insanity and for which the other assumes reponsibility. *Jack lo sventratore* (1992, 'Jack the Ripper') features a television crew visiting the mother of a modern serial killer to investigate his mindset.

Eppur si muove, as Galileo is reputed to have said when compelled by the church to swear that the earth was still. Italian theatre does not obey the same laws of motion as other Western theatres, but it has been lively and creative at every point in its history, and continues to contribute to the repertoire of world theatre.

Notes

1 Michael Billington, *The Life and Works of Harold Pinter*, p. 237.
2 A. Rossi Ghiglione, *Barboni: Il teatro di Pino Delbono*, Milan, 1999.
3 Edoardo Erba, *Maratona di New York e altri testi*, Milan, 2002.
4 Patrizia Valduga, *Prima Antologia*, Turin, 1999.
5 Silvana Tamiozzo Goldmann, *Giuliano Scabia*, Rome, 1997.
6 Spiro Scimone, *Teatro*, Milan, 2000.

Bibliography

Bernard, E. (ed.), *Autori e drammaturgie: Prima enciclopedia del teatro italiano del dopoguerra,* Rome, 1993.

Billington, M. *The Life and Works of Harold Pinter,* London, 1996.

Pullini, G. *Teatro contemporaneo in Italia,* Florence, 1974.

Puppa, P. *Il teatro dei testi: la drammaturgia italiana nel novecento,* Turin, 2003.
   Teatro e spettacolo nel secondo novecento, 6th edn, Bari and Rome, 2004.

Lepschy, A. L. 'Drama: Realism, Identity and Reality on Stage', in Z. G. Baranski and R. West (eds.), *The Cambridge Companion to Modern Italian Culture,* Cambridge, 2001, pp. 197–213.

Taffon, G. *Maestri drammaturghi nel teatro italiano del 900,* Bari and Rome, 2005.

Tessari, R. *Teatro italiano del novecento: Fenomenologie e strutture (1906–1976),* Florence, 1996.

Index

Betti, Ugo, 252, 347
Bettini, Pompeo, with Ettore Galbini,
    La guèra, 237
Bevilacqua, Giuseppe, 240
Biancolelli, Domenico (Dominique), 4, 118
da Bibbiena, Bernardo Dovizi, 56, 58, 62,
    63, 67
    La Calandra, 42–3, 46, 49, 54, 58
blank verse, 86, 195
Blasetti, Antonio, *BL18*, 344
Bluette, Isa, 236
Bobò, 382
Boccaccio, 58, 67, 77, 91
    Decameron, 43, 52, 53, 54, 77, 78, 79, 86
    Teseide, 19
Boggio, Maricla, 376
Boiardo, Matteo Maria, 19, 77
    Timone, 45
Boito, Arrigo, 226, 232, 325
    with Emilio Praga, *Le madri galanti*, 225
Bologna, Simone da, 107
Bologna, theatre in, 241–2
Bon, Francesco Augusto, *Trilogia del
    Ludro*, 238
Bonarelli, Prospero
    Guidibaldo Filli di Sciro, 99
    Lettere in vari generi, 135
    Solimano, 133, 135
Bonecchi, Paolo, 238
Bonicelli, Giovanni
    Pantalon spetier, 154
    Pantalone bullo, 162
Bonifacio, Baldassare
    Amata, 135
    Lettere poetiche, 135
Bontempelli, Massimo, 279, 287, 344
    La guardia alla luna, 287
    Minnie la candida, 287
    Nostra Dea, 306
    Siepe a nordovest, 310
Borgia, Alfonso, 47
Borgia, Lucrezia, 47
Boscolo, Arnaldo, 240

Bottai, Giuseppe, 343
Boulevard drama, 346
Bovio, Libero, 249
Bracco, Roberto, 262
    Il piccolo santo, 228, 248
Bragaglia, Anton Giulio, 271, 339
Bragaglia, Marinella, 258
Bratti company, 239
Bravure del Capitan Spavento, 111, 114
Brecht, Bertolt, 271, 275, 287, 288, 290,
    352, 357
Bresciani, Caterina, 167
Briccio, Giovanni, 138
Brighenti, Luigi, 241
brillante (comic) role, 233, 294, 299
Brook, Peter, 287, 379
Brunelleschi, Filippo di Ser Brunellesco, 23
Bruni, Domenico (Fulvio), 103, 114
Bruno, Giordano, *Il candelaio*, 81
buffoni, 62, 63, 71, 104
bulesca theatre, 71
Buonarotti the Younger, Michelangelo
    La fiera, 140
    La Tancia, 139–40
del Buono, Luigi, *Stenterello*, 215
Buontalenti, Bernardo, 34
Burbage, James, 33
Il Burchiello (Domenico di Giovanni), 177
burning of theatres, 23

Ca' Arian palace, 69
Ca' Contarini palace, 69
Ca' Foscari palace, 69, 70
Ca' Pesaro palace, 69, 70
Ca' Priuli palace, 69
Ca' Trevisan palace, 69, 70
Caccini, Giulio, 100
Caffariello (*castrato*), 147
Caffè sciantà (*café chantant*), 248
Caldara, Antonio, 188
Calderón de la Barca, Pedro, 183, 210, 350
    Life is a Dream, 354
Calendimaggio (May Day), 139

Dumas père, Alexandre
  Claudio's Wife, 226
  Kean, 220
Duroni, Giovanni, 237
Duse, Eleonora, 207, 222, 225, 226, 227, 230, 232, 323, 325, 328, 368
Duse, Enzo, 240
Duse, Luigi, 238

ecclesiastical drama, 12, 14–15, 20
eclogues, 45, 94
El barchett de Boffalora (Clettro Arrighi), 237
Eleanora of Aragon, 17
Eliot, T. S., 359
Emanuel, Giovanni, 232
entrance by payment, 69
Erba, Edoardo
  New York Marathon, 385
  Senza Hitler, 385
  Venditori, 385
erudite comedy *see commedia erudita*
Este family, 39, 46, 47, 48, 69
d'Este, Ercole, 17, 44
d'Este, Ippolito, 45
d'Este, Isabella, 42
d'Este, Leonello, 45
Euridice, opera, 100
Euripides, 88, 203
  Alcestis, 321

Fabbrichesi, Salvatore, 244
fabula, 45
fabulatore, figure of, 359, 361, 362
farce, 44, 62, 252, 363
Fascism, 286, 287, 300, 309, 310, 339–48, 389
Fatouville, Nolant de, 117
favola, 91
favole boschereccie, 99
Fedeli company, 103, 107
Federici, Camillo, 158
Feet (Synthetic Theatre), 287

female characters, 40, 58, 86, 92, 98, 306, 385
female performers, 31–2, 40–1, 60, 68, 88, 106, 117, 165, 307
  ban on, 130
female writers, 97–8
Ferdinand I, King, 244
Ferrara, theatre in, 44–50
Ferrari, Paolo
  Goldoni e le sue sedici commedie nuove, 225, 226
  La satira e Parini, 225
Ferrari, Severino, 337, 342
Ferravilla, Edoardo, 236, 237, 238
Ferrero, Alfonso, 236
  La regina d'un re, 236
festaiuoli, 17
Fiabe (Carlo Gozzi), 155
Ficino, Marsilio, 67
Fielding, Henry, 155
Filippo (Pippo), son of Baldo, 23
Fiorilli, Tiberio (Scaramouche), 117
Fiorillo, Silvio, 110
five-act structure of plays, 32, 48, 53, 61
Florence, theatre in, 14, 17, 18, 42, 51–7
Fo, Dario, 1, 2, 13, 121, 243, 276, 289, 357–67, 382, 392
  Comica finale, 363
  Dario Fo recita Ruzante, 361
  Fedayn, 365
  Gli arcangeli non giocano a flipper, 363–4
  Grande pantomima con bandiere e pupazzi medi e piccoli, 364
  Il paese dei mezarat, 361
  Johan Padan a la descoverta de le Americhe, 361
  Lu santo jullare Francesco, 361–2
  Marino libero! Marino è innocente, 361
  Mistero buffo, 357, 361, 362, 364
  Morte accidentale di un anarchico, 357, 365
  Nascita del giullare, 362
  Non si paga! Non si paga! 357, 365
  Poer nano, 361

Sannazaro, Jacopo, 67, 91, 94
 Arcadia, 92
Sannazzaro theatre (Naples), 251
Sant' Agnese company, 17, 20
Sant' Angelo theatre (Venice), 151, 154, 155,
 160, 163–5, 166, 180
Santanelli, Mario
 Bellavita Carolina, 391
 Le voci di dentro, 391
 Regina madre, 391
 Uscita d'emergenza, 391
Santo Spirito theatre, 23
Sanudo, Marin, 70
Sarnelli, Pompeo, Posilicheata, 182
Sartre, Jean-Paul, Huis clos, 353
satyr drama, 91
Savinio, Alberto, 287
sbandieratori, 9
Sbodio, Gaetano, 237, 238
Scabia, Giuliano, 288
 Fantastica visione, 390
 In capo al mondo, 390
 Teatro con bosco e animali, 390
Scala, Alessandra, 24
Scala, Flaminio (Silvio), 103
 Il teatro delle favole rappresentative
  ovvero la Ricreazione boscareccia
  e tragica, 111
 Teatro delle favole rappresentative, 100
Scaldati, Franco, Pozzo dei pazzi, 390
Scalognati, 310
Scapigliatura group, 236, 237
Scardeone, B., 69
Scarfoglio, Eduardo, 248, 323
Scarpetta, Eduardo, 244, 245–7, 390
 Don Felice, 246
 La geisha, 250
 Maria, 252
Scarpetta, Vincenzo, 251
 La donna è mobile, 253
Scenario, 114–15, 271, 344, 347
scenery, 35, 36, 93, 120, 127, 151, 175,
 189, 246

Schiller, Friedrich, 150
 Wallenstein, 221
Schlegel, August Wilhelm von, 209
Schmitz, Ettore see Italo Svevo
Schnitzler, Arthur, 271
Scimone, Spiro
 Bar, 390
 La festa, 390
 Nunzio, 390
Scott, Walter, 209
Scribe, Eugène, 219, 314
Scuffiareini (Alfredo Testoni) 241
seating plans of theatres, 34–5
Selvatico, Riccardo
 I recini de festa, 238
 La bozeta de l'ogio, 238
Seneca, 3, 24, 84, 133
 Phaedra, 276
 Thyestes, 88, 275
Serena, Gustavo see under Bertini, Francesco
Serlio, Sebastiano, Secondo libro
  dell'architettura, 35
servant, figure of, 197–8, 252, 319
settenari, 93, 136
Shakespeare, William, 4, 50, 209, 210,
 214, 219, 225, 232, 275, 278, 289,
 290, 350, 359, 381
 A Midsummer Night's Dream, 13, 92, 327
 Hamlet, 275, 277, 290
 King Lear, 276
 Macbeth, 277, 286
 Richard III, 276, 277
 The Tempest, 3
 Twelfth Night, 3
Shaw, George Bernard, 280, 286, 364
Siciliano, Enzo, 352, 372
Sicily, theatre in, 257–65
Siena, theatre in, 14, 42, 58–60
Simoni, Renato, 229, 347
 Carlo Gozzi, 239
 Congedo, 239
 La vedova, 239
 Tramonto, 227, 239